MW00781205

The Everyday Life of Memorials

The Everyday Life
of Memorials

Andrew M. Shanken

ZONE BOOKS · NEW YORK

2022

ZONE BOOKS
633 Vanderbilt Street
Brooklyn, NY 11218

Printed in the United States of America.

Distributed by Princeton University Press,
Princeton, New Jersey, and Woodstock, United Kingdom

Library of Congress Cataloging-in-Publication Data
Names: Shanken, Andrew Michael, 1968– author.
Title: The everyday life of memorials / Andrew M. Shanken.
Description: New York : Zone Books, 2022. | Includes bibliographical references
    and index. | Summary: "This book works with the literature of the everyday,
    memory studies, and non-representational geography to open up a novel
    understanding of memorials not just as everyday objects, but also as funda-
    mental to urban modernity" —Provided by publisher.
Identifiers: LCCN 2021062586 (print) | LCCN 2021062587 (ebook) |
    ISBN 9781942130727 (hardcover) | ISBN 9781942130734 (ebook)
Subjects: LCSH: Memorialization. | Memorials. | Sociology, Urban. |
    Collective memory. | Public spaces — Philosophy.
Classification: LCC D16.9 .S4575 2022 (print) | LCC D16.9 (ebook) |
    DDC 394/.4 — dc23/eng/20220120
LC record available at https://lccn.loc.gov/2021062586
LC ebook record available at https://lccn.loc.gov/2021062587

Contents

Preface

Monuments possess all sorts of qualities.
The most important is somewhat contradictory: what strikes
one most about monuments is that one doesn't notice them.
There is nothing in the world as invisible as monuments.
— Robert Musil, "Monuments," 1927

This book went through multiple incarnations, each with its own working title that offers a peephole into the process of its making. It started in 2006 as *A Cultural Geography of Memorials*.[1] At the time, I was eager to move beyond traditional art-historical methods, which seemed inadequate to the task of clarifying my intuitions about how memorials were behaving in cities and how people, in turn, behaved around them. Recent literature in cultural geography seemed to open up new ways of thinking about memorials, especially in light of the urban and social changes of the modern period that created them, rendered them strange, and often obscured their strangeness. Experimental geographers had begun to explore urban phenomena: the aural, haptic, performative, and otherwise overlooked ways in which people experience the built environment. "Crudely put," Hayden Lorimer writes, "to more traditional signifiers of identity and difference (class, gender, ethnicity, age, sexuality, disability), have been added another order of abstract descriptors: instincts, events, auras, rhythms, cycles, flows and codes."[2] These inquiries have challenged the very nature of what can and cannot be known as they seek out "the

7

provisional, immaterial dimensions of social life."[3] Moving beyond the more material concerns of earlier generations of geographers, beyond iconographical, semiotic, and "textual" analysis popular in the 1980s and 1990s and even beyond the material certainty of the object, these writings in cultural geography were asking how people "and terrain melt into a range of faculties and feelings, emerging amid elemental phenomena."[4] I saw in the ideas of writers such as Lorimer, Nigel Thrift, Trevor Pinch, Bruno Latour, Maria Kaika, and others a way of understanding how people engage with memorials that other fields had not been able to fathom. Put differently, I did not think that Robert Musil's denigration of monuments as being invisible, which serves as the epigraph here and as a point of reference throughout, meant that they were any less present. What better method to "see" monuments anew than one that could venture beyond the visual?

This range of concerns, sometimes assembled under the intimidating term "nonrepresentational theory," would seem to be an enemy of art history and the object.[5] At very least, its interest in nonrepresentational phenomena would push formal analysis to the margins. However, this approach, aptly called "more-than-representational" by Lorimer, plumbs the experience of people and things in space. It need not disregard materialist methods or devalue the visual, although it sometimes does. Instead, it should draw our attention to the nature of the encounter with objects and space as a complicated experience. Just as some scholars have too hastily closed their eyes as a defense against "dictatorial vision," some art historians have plucked the visual out of context. Indeed, formal analysis is a powerful tool, one that bolsters nonrepresentational geography.[6]

This attempt to rescue formal analysis from unnecessary violence was neither reactionary nor *retardataire*. A rapprochement between formal analysis and nonrepresentational theory should not be a paradox. The analysis of form in art, and especially in architecture, implicitly posits a relationship between objects and people. In its most deliberate and politically engaged formulation, form is seen as a form of social reform, a means of enacting social change. This

modernist faith in a kind of material determinism was born of sentiment and faith deeply hidden behind mechanistic and moralizing
language.[7] The house may be a machine for living in, as Le Corbusier
famously said, only after a renunciation of sentiment that is itself a
sentiment of the strongest sort. While "unreconstructed modern-
ists" still walk the earth, architectural historians can now historicize
this arch "position" as a feeling. The urge to historicize the memorial
within similar notions of cultural sentiment while looking closely
at their form, placement, and interaction with people and cities
prompted me to attempt to reconcile formal analysis with cultural
geography's phenomenological turn.

Memorials provide a test case because more than most objects,
they come laden with the invisible elements that enthrall recent nonrepresentational geographers while being complex objects formally.[8]
They are auratic, changeful, seized by the episodic, and blurred by
urban flows. They offer a paradox as well: in response to the same
forces that birthed the new cultural geography, they have increasingly
taken forms that defy formal analysis. In extending formal analysis to
a larger field of observation, a cultural geography of memorials would
look not just at the physical fact of the city, but also to the material
reality animated by use or quieted by disuse. The monument, in other
words, cannot act alone. It cannot shoo away the ubiquitous bird
on its head or banish the traffic snarl that consumes it in honking,
exhaust, road rage, and a melee of signs and commercial gestures.
These interventions of nature and culture may not have been part
of the intention, but they end up being central to the experience of
memorials. In addition to the seemingly incidental and accidental
accumulation of the everyday, memorials often contend with other
memorials that divert, distort, and reorient them, ushering older
memorials into newer scenes. In turn, the additive quality of memorialization, in formal terms and in practice, alters the performance of
the entire space in a dance of people, objects, and places.

Over time, as I encountered thousands of memorials, nonrepresentational geography became less central. I began to see memorials

Figure P.1. An eerie Greek helm on a death mask and hot-blood-red names are now all the stranger since the former cemetery became a verdant park in a housing complex. Napoleonstein, 1836, Kaiserslautern. Courtesy of Kumbalam.

as oddities: curious, comical, at times ridiculous or grotesque, and at their most extreme, freakish. In positive terms, they are a form of *bizzarerie*. As Henri Lefebvre writes: "The bizarre is a mild stimulant for the nerves and the mind." As a stimulant and "tranquilizer," *bizzarerie* is a "risk-free" experience, a "pseudo-renewal, obtained by artificially deforming things so that they become both reassuring and surprising"[9] (figs. P.1 and P.2). A better description of many memorials would be hard to craft, yet it misses something specific about memorials,

Figure P.2. Self-conscious *bizzarerie* in cartoonish baroque. Marten Toonder Monument, Den Artoonisten, designers, 2002, Rotterdam. Photograph by Wikifrits.

which are not always risk-free or tranquilizing. Conventionally, they are made to step outside of their time and place. Frequently, they advance, whether stridently or blithely, with assertive manners and quickly outdated styles. They are fashioned of expensive, permanent materials such as marble, bronze, or granite and plopped down statically in a world hell-bent on change. They are then lifted above the fray, made larger than life, and maintained as strictly noncommercial, even though nearly every other part of Western culture has been monetized. (Some memorials have succumbed, of course.) They are public amid a long slide toward the privatization of everything. Perhaps their most aberrant quality is that they are often intended as mnemonics of loss, death, disaster, and trauma in settings ill-suited for such darkness.

In short, memorials are strange. This led to a second working title: *Why Memorials Are Strange*. At this point, a number of now neglected classics came to the fore. Mircea Eliade helped me understand these oddballs as forms of *hierophany*—his neologism for places where the sacred erupts out of the profane everyday — and to think through the way they play with temporality.[10] Erving Goffman provided an accessible language for understanding what we do at them, including how people create metaphorical roofs over themselves when they gather around memorials. Norbert Elias drew my attention to conventions of behavior and allowed me to look at them in terms of manners and in fact as part of a civilizing process amid waves of unfathomable violence.[11] Classic readings on the everyday bolstered Eliade, Elias, and Goffman's insights. While the literature on the everyday, which is grounded in close empirical observation of the physical or material world, may seem a world away from nonrepresentational theory, in fact, their larger missions dovetail. Both approaches attempt to challenge dominant ways of looking and thinking about the material world, particularly by turning attention to the overlooked and finding novel ways of understanding it. They both study common objects and ground their analysis in thick description that highlights the relationship of those objects to social use.

I sat with this admittedly flippant title for some time, thinking that it was more accessible than the nerdy titles that academics tend to use. But the book does not meditate for long on their strangeness qua strangeness. Instead, it peers through their oddness to think about where we put them, what we do with them, what they do in spite of our intentions, and what they ask of us. In short, it is about *The Work of Memorials*, a third title that riffs on historian Thomas Laqueur's book *The Work of the Dead*, which is a good companion to this volume because both wrestle with the place of the dead.[12] Yet even this title, as succinct and apt as it is, misses the central query: most memorials, most of the time, take their rest in the everyday world. For this reason, *The Everyday Life of Memorials*, a contender for title from the beginning, lingered. It is blessedly direct and dispenses with the seemingly obligatory colon. I have tried to understand how and why memorials and monuments slide between their more rarefied existence and everyday life, how their material properties and the places where they do their work operate in modern cities.

Numerous times I have imagined myself sitting between Erving Goffman and Bruno Latour on a long plane trip, with the other scholars mentioned in this preface butting in from neighboring seats. We land, and I take them all on a jaunt to look at memorials, occasionally stepping into a time machine so that we may take their measure diachronically. We sit in the cafes that line the squares where they throw shadows like sundials, talking about memory, time, history, the everyday, and death as well as observing the way people pause at and pass by them. This book is a kind of nonfiction transcript of that imaginary itinerary, in which, unluckily for you, I'm doing all the talking.

Many interruptions shaped this book. I can only hope for readers who divine (and forgive) the seams they created. I began writing seriously while on a sabbatical in Italy in 2007 but stopped abruptly when I had my first son, Elias. Back in Berkeley with a baby, pursuing a European topic now seemed absurd. I let the manuscript idle and turned my attention to a topic that allowed me to use local archives, which led me to write a book on the 1939 San Francisco World's Fair. A second son, Cy, arrived in 2011, and that made Europe seem even more distant. I continued to hunt down, photograph, and teach memorials, but was stymied by the prospect of writing this book. On a second sabbatical, in Mexico in 2014, I began another book on the visual culture of urban planning and soon found myself with an embarrassment of fragments on two manuscripts. I labored to bring them both along simultaneously. How different could writing two books be from raising two boys!

Very different, it turns out. It defeated me, slowly, painfully, and unconsciously, and I began to drift aimlessly. To break the spell, I did the obvious thing: I started yet another book. The topic doesn't matter as much as the fact that I had slipped into the restless pathology of courting new topics. I contemplated chopping this book into articles. I had been writing shorter-format pieces all along and had many of them in various stages of development. I was a writer of essays, I told myself, not books. But a slow-motion interruption opened up a new chance. My boys matured — and perhaps I did, too. I resolved to stop everything but one project. It was instantly obvious it would be this book. In 2019, I took my whole family to Europe on a memorial death march, driving them forward with the promise of castles and pastries. Bolstered by this research trip and the encouragement of my editor at Zone Books, Ramona Naddaff, the book quickly came into view. I put aside the extensive fragments penned in Bologna and began writing again. Little of what I wrote in the initial burst is left in this text, but much of the spirit remains.

At the same time, waves of iconoclastic rage had begun to sweep across the world, with special ferocity in the United States, interrupting the very narrative of monuments. I worried that a political awakening so tied to monuments would trivialize the topic of this book. George Floyd's murder in May of 2020 intensified the iconoclastic fervor. Dozens of statues came down. Names of buildings have been changed. Former untouchables such as Thomas Jefferson may lose their monuments. The meaning and visibility of many monuments — if not monuments as a cultural form — has been altered, at least for some time. For instance, spectral images of Harriet Tubman and others were projected over the Robert E. Lee statue in Richmond, Virginia. People painted Black Lives Matter slogans on it and held vigils there. Scenes like this could be found throughout the country, especially in the American South, and they filled the news. They cannot be unseen. It seemed as if the everyday life of memorials was being overtaken. Yet the very fact that monuments can be reanimated so dramatically gets right to the core concern of the book. It illustrates how they lay in wait in some other, quieter state. It shows just how unstable they are.

However, this book is explicitly *not* about the ways in which memorials are used as commemorative sites or as symbols of political struggle. There is a small library on these two topics. As excellent as this work is and as much as I have learned from it, it usually gives little thought to their everyday life. The pages that follow attempt to remedy this. This means observing how they slide between heightened moments and the mundane, and it means doing so over a long stretch of modern urban history in order to tease out the conventions that allow memorials to be turned on and off.

The long view also eased my worry. Hot monuments have cooled. Other episodes of intense iconoclasm have faded from memory into dull textbook history. The French Revolution, the historical starting point for this book, caused both real and bronze heads to roll, yet the monuments throughout Europe that were erected in its aftermath are often as alive to the people who pass them every day as streetlights or kiosks. Moreover, violence against memorials is a standard feature of modern urban life. Soviet monuments in the post-Soviet former East Bloc have been routinely savaged and removed. The Arab Spring was channeled in part through monuments, as has been anger over atrocities in Latin America. All around the world, decolonization is visibly demonstrated through the destruction of monuments. It is dangerous for historians to predict the future, but I believe that Americans will look back on the recent destruction of Confederate monuments astonished that they survived into the twenty-first century, rather than seeing this moment as an historical pivot. This is why I have treated this wave of iconoclasm like any other, rather than indulge in American exceptionalism.

In March, 2019, another interruption came like a gut punch. The Covid-19 pandemic closed libraries and archives. Basic books and rare materials were now out of reach. At the time, I had a draft that one might charitably call picturesque; the list of unresolved issues was sublime, the prospect of securing image rights positively grotesque.

My sons were now at home all day, often at loose ends. The whole family rotated through our shared spaces. Sometimes three or four Zooms echoed through the house, when weeks before I had no idea what Zoom was. As California edged its way into a sobering stay-at-home order, I began to make big and decisive editorial decisions. The chapters were then edited largely in very short bursts interspersed with: "Dad . . . can you explain fractions?" "Dad . . . I can't find any information on the Salem Witch Trials." "Dad . . . what is onomatopoeia?" Nonetheless, the writing rounded into shape. But the images and archival gaps still seemed like an insurmountable problem.

After some weeks of fretting, I adjusted, largely because the world had changed since I began the project in 2006. First, many enlightened institutions have given their images over to the public domain. To find them requires a different kind of imagination, one attuned to the logic of the search engine rather than the library and archive. Slowly, I replaced the most unattainable images with more accessible ones, often changing large swathes of text to make it work. Second, out of desperation, I queried my virtual social network. A cousin had a friend in McAllen, Texas, whose thirteen-year-old granddaughter just received a camera for the holidays. Snap! Another cousin visited a memorial in New York City three times to capture the memorial just right. A Russian friend turned me on to Russian Google and supplied the Cyrillic name for an obscure monument in Moscow. Moments later, I had a beautiful public-domain image in my possession. Another friend went to a site in Los Angeles, and as we spoke on the phone, he sent dozens of photographs of the Spirit of Los Angeles monument, which appears in Chapter 10. An acquaintance found images of a statue in Leipzig, and so it went. Many images had to be cut, but surprising new ones appeared and with them new insights. As a result, it is a different book, as it would be if I were to rewrite it in six months or another six years or had I managed to complete it six years ago. To lean on the poet Stanley Kunitz, we are never done with our changes — much like memorials.

Memorials No More

How grudging memory is, and how bitterly
she clutches the raw material of her daily work.
— Lawrence Durrell, *Justine*, 1957

Memorials are typically understood as sacred sites, hallowed ground marked with honorific structures, statues, sculptures, plaques, and other objects that make up an iconography of and setting for mourning, or, more broadly, for commemoration.[1] They are just as commonly seen as political places where groups of citizens battle over the meaning of events.[2] Yet they are also enveloped by the quotidian. Birds leave gifts on soldiers' heads; teens cavort on their steps; rush hour commuters skirt them like any obstacle separating them from their appointments. Frank O'Hara's poem "Music" (1954) bares this reality: "If I rest for a moment near The Equestrian / pausing for a liver sausage sandwich in the Mayflower Shoppe, / that angel seems to be leading the horse into Bergdorf's / and I am naked as a table cloth, my nerves humming" (figs. I.1 and I.2). It is neither the anonymity of the equestrian nor the surging angel that sets the narrator's nerves atwitter. These remain generic, deprived of proper name, in spite of the fame of both subject (General Sherman) and sculptor (Augustus Saint-Gaudens). But the Mayflower Shoppe and Bergdorf's! These O'Hara names. It is the urban scene that grabs him; the memorial is mere foil. It is a scene, moreover, of bathos born of contrast, of solemn high culture brought low, and adoringly so, by commerce, while the narrator eats the most common of fast foods at the feet of an eternal golden

Figure I.1. The proverbial bird on the great man's head. Tom Bachtell, Cartoon of Sherman Monument. Courtesy of Tom Bachtell.

angel. What city dwellers have not, amid the bustle of urban life, taken respite or fortified themselves at a memorial and not bothered to query its identity? Indeed, memorials seem to borrow space from the city, perhaps most conspicuously in those places where market forces create such poignant contrasts. This puts them in constant tension with those same forces.

Most memorials, most of the time, are "turned on" only on special days, such as Memorial Day in the United States, Remembrance Day in the UK, Martyrs' Day in India, or National Day in China. At these moments, they become part of commemorative activity. They are borrowed back from their context, from the everyday, for a higher purpose. The rest of the time they are "turned off." They take their rest as ordinary objects, urban ornament, street furniture.[3] This book is about how memorials are turned on and off, how they move between being moribund and volatile. It explores the way they make way for the daily pulses of urban movement or how commerce and traffic corral them into corners where they can grow old harmlessly. Even the most familiar memorials, ones used repeatedly or ritualistically to cultivate a sense of collective recall, constantly confront the

Figure I.2. By wrapping the pedestal in a generous bench, architect Charles Follen McKim invited people to borrow the memorial for rest, people watching, or waiting to be shipped overseas to fight in a new war in 1942. Augustus Saint-Gaudens, Sherman Monument, 1903, New York City. Photograph by Marjory Collins. Courtesy of the Library of Congress.

everyday, if not also obsolescence. It is more than a matter of curiosity that memorials that were brought into existence at great effort and expense and that serve or once served as sites of heightened social, political, or spiritual importance are simultaneously ordinary, background, banal. Some of them never get turned on again, victims of benign neglect. Others suffer from outright iconoclasm. Empty socles or bases are common sights, especially in Eastern Europe, where erasure is a political art. Memorials whose people have moved on languish unattended. Some memorials disappear entirely and not always as part of political struggle. The Partisans, a Polish Cavalry memorial in Boston Common composed of four exhausted horses bearing beaten soldiers, was removed in 2006. It struck a dissonant note, yet the nearby Ether Monument, with its vaguely medieval Moorish doctor anaesthetizing a patient, remains. Recently, Confederate monuments throughout the United States have been taken down in more assertive political acts or counterinterventions. Time will tell if some of these former Confederate sites become activated, rather than defused, by removal. A missing memorial can be surprisingly potent. It is obvious that memorials are far from familiar, straightforward sites of memory.

In fact, it is their memorial function that makes them peculiar. Memory, whatever the term may mean in this collective, public sense, is the interloper, the foreign substance, in modern cities in modern times. Memory is the uninvited guest as we wolf down fast food, throw ourselves into the flow of work and consumption, or take our keen distance, like O'Hara's narrator, an American descendent of Baudelaire's *flâneur*. Both the monument and the *flâneur* are fixtures of modern public space, but they are opposing sides of the modern Janus. Memory is the strange survivor of an enchanted era of mystery, superstition, and ghosts in an era of secular rationality.[4] Memorials sit in shocking contrast to modern gridirons, streetcars, highways, skyscrapers, electric lines, billboards, T-shirts, knick-knacks, and the human tempest that blows through it all.

If anything, the contrast has become sharper since O'Hara wrote. To take one extreme example, Miami's Holocaust Memorial (1990) manifests how startling this change can be (fig. I.3). If Peace guiding a horse on Fifth Avenue in Manhattan has become an urban non sequitur, what is a colossal fragment of a ghastly arm encrusted with emaciated bodies doing in Miami Beach, just blocks from South Beach?[5] Yes, both are offered context by their plazas and parklike settings, which spirit them away (just barely) from the urban throng. But this requisite spatial gesture only sharpens the

Figure I.3. The Shoa as dark kitsch. Ken Treister, Holocaust Memorial, 1990, Miami Beach, Florida. Photograph by the author.

contrast. Cars whiz down Meridian and Dade Boulevards on their way to the Miami Beach Convention Center, the Chamber of Commerce, Macy's, Walgreens, Chase Bank, and Publix Super Market, all within blocks of — what would O'Hara have called it? — The Arm. One cannot take distance from this Holocaust Memorial. Its histrionics are an attempt to overcome the anonymity to which many memorials succumb, to overcome the Holocaust as an unrepresentable event. The forty-two-foot arm — scaled down from seventy-two feet! — bids never to lapse into urban ornament, to be turned off. It attempts to defy the everyday. But this is as quixotic as resisting time. Should the city overtake it in some unfortunate way or sea levels rise to claim it in what insurance policies call an act of God, might it, like the Polish Cavalry Memorial, be relocated to a less assertive spot? What if the memorial loses its community, or — and I'm being hopeful rather than provocative — the narratives of trauma and victimhood that have been central to Jewish identity atrophy?

The malleability of memorials is surprising only because people create most of them with great expectations for their duration or permanence. Here again they stand in opposition to an age of obsolescence.[6] The tension between the desire for permanence and their actual ephemerality is betrayed everywhere by erosion, physical displacement, acts of iconoclasm, and neglect. To encounter most memorials is to meet this apparent contradiction. They change with the simplest change of intention. They appear one way when people want to see them, and they can disappear when they do not. Or worse, they obstruct the flow of daily life, something to which so many memorials stranded in traffic roundabouts attest. The harried Royal Fusilier spends his days making vain attempts to cross Holborn Road in London (fig. I.4). He stands as a warning to pedestrians who would try the same. Although some patient photographers have made it to the median and waited out the traffic to capture him, this is a most unlikely view (fig. I.5). Most memorials are not prepared for this sort of everyday encounter. They suffer through the mundane, awaiting their moment in the sun when a special day wakes them up

Figure I.4. A Royal Fusilier stuck in traffic forever, nearly camouflaged by the Victorian red brick and terracotta of the former Prudential Insurance Building. Albert Toft, Royal Fusiliers War Memorial, 1922, London. Photograph by the author.

Figure I.5. The Royal Fusilier as seen by a patient photographer. Albert Toft, Royal Fusiliers War Memorial, 1922, London. Photograph by Mike Peel.

or wakes us up to them. Most are calendrically activated, but when calendars drop them, they become marooned, disconnected from the vitalizing energy of commemorative practice. Already many World War I memorials have fallen victim to neglect, even if they were briefly awakened during the recent centennial of the war. One can well imagine a time when the rawest memorials of the present moment go emotionally slack or become politically irrelevant.[7]

To be turned on, memorials such as the Royal Fusiliers memorial or Edwin Lutyens's much more famous but similarly situated Cenotaph in London not only requisition time in the form of Remembrance Day, but sometimes also space by shutting down streets. They rightly appear to be disruptions of the everyday. And this gives the game away. Memorials such as these, perhaps because they must at times be disruptions, find themselves awkwardly stuck in the urban fabric. Is this ensnarement of memorials in the everyday truly inadvertent, or does it serve other functions? How much more interesting if their common life is not coincidental but part of what makes ordinary environments ordinary, or extraordinary interventions extraordinary — part of the creation and maintenance of these otherwise fragile states. Their appearance in a mass society beginning about two hundred and fifty years ago and our diminishing sense of what to do with them as they age or proliferate has intensified this double life.

In spite of claiming a sacred spot for themselves, a place apart, many memorials have been placed at crossroads or junctures, on medians, in plazas, by the roadside, sites where the urban fabric changes its texture. The comical image of memorials trapped in traffic circles has become a transatlantic cliché. The Arc de Triomphe in Paris may be the most famous example, with the French Tomb of the Unknown Soldier added under its vault after World War I. The position of the Soldiers Monument in Mystic, Connecticut, is echoed in memorials in the United States and Europe from the nineteenth century through the present (fig. I.6). The well-intentioned sign on Mystic's railing suggests an ill-fated collision, if not also the

Figure I.6. Another soldier stuck in traffic. Soldiers Monument, 1883, Mystic, Connecticut
Photograph by Jack Delano. Courtesy of the Library of Congress.

unsettled conventions of automobile traffic and signage in 1940. Sherman and the angel, another Civil War monument, began life in a traffic circle when horses were still the most common mode of transportation.

In the history of cities, these are the places that have attracted commerce. The urban historian Robert Lopez linked the crossroads to the quickening of pace that led to the beginnings of urban culture.[8] This overlapping placement of memorials and more quotidian doings could scarcely be accidental. It has something to do with the transactional nature shared by commerce and commemoration. In their most spontaneous manifestations, commerce and commemoration are similar and require similar spaces: a public place for the gathering of people, for a voice to reach the crowd, for exchange to take place, and where impromptu social processes can be given more permanent form. Many of the more sequestered places where memorials can be found, in parks and cemeteries, for instance, respond to similar urban forces.

A Word on the Words

Arthur Danto believes that "we erect monuments so that we shall always remember and build memorials so that we shall never forget."[9] This is too clever to be true. To be sure, monuments have been erected with heroic, aspirational, or celebratory ambitions, while memorials have traditionally been conceived and built to mark death, tragedy, and darker modes of remembrance. Writers have sometimes maintained these distinctions, and with good reason. They often reflect the intentions of the makers, if not the public life of these distinct offerings. Yet the two words are unstable and have been used interchangeably since modern memorials and monuments first appeared. Just like the things they describe, these words blur into one another, as the well-rehearsed etymology makes clear. Monument, from the Latin *monere*, means to remind or remember, while memorial, from the Latin *memoria*, also goes straight to remembrance. *The Oxford English Dictionary* uses "memorial" to define "monument" and vice versa, while both are linked to commemoration. So it is with the physical objects the two words describe. Scratch a monument, find a memorial. Mystic's soldier is called a monument, but it is undeniably a memorial, having been erected to "the brave sons of Mystic who offered their lives to their country in the war of the rebellion, 1861–1865." It doesn't waver so much as act doubly. It is both. In a more cynical frame of mind, Françoise Choay writes that monuments so "pursue . . . a derisory career" that "it has become necessary to add the qualifier 'commemorative'" to them.[10]

The two words are knotted together. Instead of teasing out the monument and memorial strands, my interest is in the knot itself. As James E. Young writes, "the monument itself tends to be replaced by the *memorial*. It is less a monument than site of memory, through which one seeks to keep a memory alive, to maintain it as a living memory and to pass it down."[11] This confusion is native to memorialization. Young continues, "the traditional monument . . . can also be used as a mourning site for lost loved ones, just as memorials have marked past victories. A statue can be a monument to heroism and a memorial to tragic loss; an obelisk can memorialize a nation's birth and monumentalize leaders fallen before their prime."[12] I would go further. Memorials and monuments are shape shifters. They can be disarmingly unsettled. For all of their seemingly stubborn materiality and "land-anchored permanence,"[13] they are surprisingly fickle figures in the landscape. They slide effortlessly between solemnity and anonymity, memory worship and amnesia, arresting monumentality and impediment to traffic. They are all of these things, sometimes by turn, or, depending on one's perspective or needs, all at once. The way "memorial" and "monument" have shifted in what they signify — the way writers slip between the two words — gets right to this restless quality that I believe is central to their meaning.[14] No definition of either will be found in these pages. To stiffen their meaning runs counter to their everyday life.

Their context betrays to what extent memorials, monuments, and statuary blur. A Holocaust memorial, an independence monument,

Figure I.7. Without parental constraints, few children would pass up the chance to climb on Martin Puryear's Slavery Memorial on Front Green, 2014, Brown University, Providence, Rhode Island. Photograph by Carol Highsmith. Courtesy of the Library of Congress.

and a statue of Bismarck follow many of the same conventions of placement, contend with similar urban processes, and are acted upon by people in many of the same ways. This holds true even for the most sober commemorative interventions. The reason that Brown University had to add a sign telling people to refrain from climbing on its Slavery Memorial is obvious: it looks like so many pieces of public art that invite the public to do just that (fig. I.7). As metonymically hackneyed and heavy-handed as the broken chain is, it offers an ideal hand grip for children to test their bodies against the slope. And who could blame them? To a child, it is visually and kinetically like the Half Balls mass marketed by the playground equipment company Goric or the boulders that are frequently placed in playgrounds. It is an invitation to climb.

As early as the revolutionary period, debates over commemoration make clear just how fuzzy these categories have been. Monuments and memorials have often been melted into larger concerns about beautification or drawn into wider urban issues. When Paris erected a statue of the revolutionary Marat in the Parc de Montsouris in 1887, the city argued that if placed in a park, it would not be a monument, but merely a decorative element. Serge Michalski calls this argument "grossly improbable," and given that the monument depicted Marat in the bath that was the scene of his political martyrdom, it is — and yet the city's argument aligns with similar attitudes in other countries.[15] Memorials and statuary of all types have been subjected to the same aesthetic and spatial logic, a mentality that continues to this day. For instance, the Holocaust Memorial boulder in Hyde Park (1983) echoes the nearby standing stone, turning them both into garden shams (fig. I.8). Just five years earlier, another boulder, the Norwegian War Memorial, was installed nearby (fig. I.9). Three decisively different hunks of rock, one setting. And that's just the beginning. In one brisk walk, one can see all three and Wellington in the form of a colossal Achilles, the church-scaled Gothic eye-catcher of the Albert Memorial, St. George Killing the Dragon (the Cavalry Memorial to World War I), and the Diana Fountain. How is

Figure I.8. A standing stone, hiding behind the trees and roadway in the background of this photo, trolls the Richard Seifert and Derek Lovejoy and Partners, Holocaust Memorial, 1983, Hyde Park, London. Photograph by the author.

Figure I.9. False equivalency? Norwegian War Memorial, 1978, Hyde Park, London. Photograph by the author.

anyone to make sense of it all? Nomenclature and formal conventions get us only so far.

Nor will definitions of memory — what a bugbear that term! — appear in this book. Smart scholars have worked the word to exhaustion. Pierre Nora, Kerwin Klein, Paul Ricoeur, Frances A. Yates, and others have shaped my thinking, but memory is one of the marginalia of this book, rather like what a Civil War memorial in a traffic circle is to a driver trying to get out of town.[16] It could be a useful landmark, a directional symbol, or a damnable obstruction, but probably not an occasion for commemoration or political action. *Caveat vector.* The use of memory in the chapter titles, then, is rhetorical. I do not believe, for instance, that people *place* memory in any literal sense or that assemblages of memorials reflect a density of memory in the city. It is true that many memorials provide a place for commemoration, and I do not wish to diminish this vital function. But that is a small part of their role.

Another word that plays a central role in this book, "everyday," is as complicated as "memory," and curiously interwoven with it. Scholars have produced a mountain of literature on the idea of the everyday and its cognates. In architecture alone, the bibliography is formidable.[17] Nearly every aspect of the built environment has been reconsidered through it, typically set against an ill-defined antagonist waggishly called the "not-everyday" by sociologist Norbert Elias.[18] A persistent binary between the vernacular, ordinary, or everyday and the official, extraordinary, or not-everyday is embedded in thinking about the built environment. Chapter 1 attempts to break down the binary, while much of the rest of the book attempts to bring the insights of scholars of the everyday to the study of memorials in the pursuit of a more fluid sense of these terms.

There are, in fact, at least three different, if intermeshed, "everydays" that appear in the book. The first is made up of the objects (hot dogs), settings (streets), and social practices (eating or tourism) that constitute daily life and its material culture or urban dimension. In this usage, "everyday" is roughly analogous to "ordinary," "common,"

"vernacular," and "informal." The second use is loosely a field of
inquiry that studies this first everyday, with distinct manifestations
in architecture, landscape studies, anthropology, geography, American Studies, history, and other disciplines. These first two everydays are expressed most often in opposition to the "not-everyday." A
third way "everyday" appears here refers to the way the everyday and
the not-everyday (note the definite articles) blur in space and time.
This usage resists the opposition of the other everydays because this
everyday sees the quotidian and the frequent eruptions through its
surface as part of an ever-shifting dynamic over time. In fact, this is
the reality of everyday life, where exceptional objects, settings, and
social practices are constantly churned into the humus of the ordinary, reconstituted, and broken down again. Frank O'Hara's poem
observes this everyday in a very particular time and place. It pairs
elements of the first everyday (a sausage) with the not-everyday (a
golden angel) and insists on making them roommates in modern,
urban life. As an artifact of the 1950s, it is no longer experientially
available to us, much like the original meaning of a golden equestrian
statue elevated above the horse and buggies of turn-of-the century
New York City. The everyday is historical.

Memorials are assumed to be not-everyday for obvious reasons.
They are intended as extraordinary and often used for extraordinary events. As expensive objects created by exceptional acts, often
designed by high-profile artists or architects and placed in uncommon settings, they smack of high culture, if not elitism. The forms
they have taken reinforce this reading: obelisks, columns, arches,
and larger-than-life figures drawn from high art, forged in bronze or
cut from granite, engraved with high-minded sentiments, and lifted
above the fray. Henri Lefebvre, one of the pivotal thinkers about the
everyday, calls such monuments "repressive" acts of spatial colonization.[19] There are exceptions. Impromptu memorials and counter-
memorials refuse many of the trappings of traditional memorials.
But most conventional memorials, even the most understated ones,
strive to escape the everyday, while the commemorative practices

that surround them do so explicitly by falling on holidays that check daily routines.

However, I believe that Lefebvre's judgment requires reconsideration. Memorials may be extraordinary interventions erected for formal rituals held on special days, but most of them speak from or to the vulgate of the built environment, as O'Hara's poem reminds us. The fluidity of memorials is often overlooked because of the entrenched binary between the everyday and not-everyday. Pierre Nora, a pivotal figure in memory studies whose ideas will be discussed at length in the next chapter, calls memory "unself-conscious . . . spontaneously actualizing." "Memory is life," he writes. It is a "bond tying us to the eternal present."[20] For Nora and others, memory is habitual, part of folk culture. It just happens. By contrast, the artificiality of modern institutions, including history itself, has eradicated memory. This binary continues in the persistent distinction between official and vernacular memory.[21] As useful as these terms have been, all too often, the reality on the ground is a complicated morass of memorial efforts morphing under the pressure of modern life. Many of the most formal commemorative landscapes were shaped piecemeal through improvisations and compromises over time, sometimes solidifying into an official vernacular.

To be sure, memorials seem to be rooted, permanent, far too premeditated to be everyday. They are quintessentially artificial, constructs of committees, political haggling, or in more dictatorial modes, fiat. From conception to completion, they are anything but rote, habitual, or ordinary, even as they often succumb to tired conventions, hackneyed habits of placement, and everyday use. Yet they often end up as incidental, afterthoughts in the rumblings of urban life. Hence the thousands of memorials in traffic circles and medians, "all too often accept[ing] wildly unsuitable accommodation."[22] It stands to reason that memorials live a double life, the one stubbornly not-everyday, the other on the down low in the everyday. Memory does the same. It is entirely ordinary. People constantly work with memory in the most mundane circumstances of our lives.

The ancients likened memory to a wax tablet, an everyday tool for recording whose underlying banality is brought home by its pliability and evanescence.[23] Yet memory is also extra-ordinary. The art of memory of which Frances Yates writes so vividly reveals how memory is intertwined with practices at once heightened, sacred, mystical, or in any case metaphysical, and at the same time commonplace.[24] The ancients practiced this mighty faculty to improve oratory, the best of them in a way that seemed nearly supernatural. Saint Augustine's "divine memory" borrowed from antiquity's belief that memory is a gift from the muses.[25] Early-modern memory theaters were like *Wunderkammern*, worldly cabinets of curiosity, predecessors to the encyclopedia. In containing all knowledge — all memory — they spoke to a kind of power or control applied on a cultural rather than individual level. This ordering of the past through the social technology of a memory theater presents an awareness of historical time that foreshadowed the stark break of the era of revolutions and the Enlightenment. Such historical consciousness would be institutionalized in museums, archives, and in the work of professional historians across the nineteenth century, but the memory theater's pretensions to organize all of the past into an accessible schema — a memory machine, of sorts — foreshadows how modern cities would march their pantheon of heroes into the public sphere. All of this reinforces the perception that memorials are not-everyday.

As it turns out, both memorials and memory try to have it both ways, or more to the point, people do what they will with them. Even the most strident attempts to exalt memory — the "gigantic generals . . . with impedimenta" — come to exist in multiple realms. People "thoughtlessly strike matches on sandstone portions of eminent divines," quipped the midcentury English architect Hugh Casson.[26] He urged people to pay attention to them "because they are hideous beyond description . . . comical, touching, heart-warming, puzzling, controversial."[27] Casson understood that memorials are props that help people negotiate the ever-shifting relationship between the everyday and the not-everyday. It might be said that this is part of their purpose. Unlike park benches, kiosks, or fire plugs, to name other kinds of urban street furniture, memorials come imbued with contradictory potential. They are by turns invisible and monstrous, pregnant with the past and open to future memory. They landmark death and harbor potential for political action. They are often mistaken for being history incarnate and are destroyed to erase the same. They are tethered to a time line and mythic, outdated and alive to the moment.[28] These are modern contradictions, or at very least contradictions heightened since the political and economic revolutions initiated in the eighteenth century began warping time and space, inventing a new concept of the future, and historicizing the past.

For this reason, the chronology of this book repeatedly returns to this formative moment to situate memorials as characters in the narratives spawned of revolutionary change and the modern reverberations that continue to the present day. For the same reason, the account gravitates geographically to Europe and the United States. These are not just the places I know best, where I have been able to travel, and where I can work with the native languages. They are also where these changes first took hold and found commemorative expression, where convulsive, urban transformation first pressed memorials into this modern narrative role. Many of the conventions of memorialization explored in these pages will resonate with readers from around the world because the urbanization and memorialization of the period are inseparable from the story of colonialism. Memorials in Windhoek, Ho Chi Minh City, Oaxaca, Mumbai, Manilla, and many other former colonial cities land in traffic circles, medians, cemeteries, parks, and squares. All over the world, they are gathered into groups, relocated under distinctly noncommemorative pressures, neglected, abused, and seduced into surprisingly mundane predicaments. This is not to say that an equestrian statue in Windhoek means the same thing as one in Munich. In fact, they may be profoundly different and still reveal something similar about the relationship between everyday life and commemorative practices in modern urban life. For this reason, the geographical and historical boundaries in this account are porous. Memorials across vast geographies over the last quarter millennium have been the public and pliable avatars of a multifarious modernity. I hope that readers better traveled than I will elaborate, confirm, and confound what they discover here. How memorials have been treated over time, where they have been placed, displaced, misplaced, and assembled, goes to the quick of modern consciousness.

CHAPTER ONE

Everyday Memory

Look on my Works, ye Mighty, and despair!
— Percy Shelly, "Ozymandias," 1818

In Pierre Nora's early work in the 1980s in what would become "memory studies," he opposed memory and history in terms hauntingly like the everyday/not-everyday divide. When he glorified memory as ancestral, folkish, sacred, involuntary, part of the enchanted premodern world of "living societies," he echoed the terms then being used to understand the everyday. His rhetoric implied that history is created by dead societies. The distinction recalls the condemnation of traditional memorials as dead and the celebration of practical or functional memorials such as civic buildings, parks, or roads as living memorials.[1] In Nora's reading, history is mediated, deliberate, a duty, never social or encompassing. History, Nora argued, collects traces of memory and removes them from organic practices within communities.[2] In his account, modern archives, museums, history texts — and, one could add, modern memorials — amount to little more than artificial memory.

This is the arbitrary opposition between the everyday and the "not-everyday" that Norbert Elias rejected. Indeed, history is Nora's villain, a position that would put most vernacular historians in a bind. There is a dynamic at work, and it is deadly. These institutions and techniques of organizing the past attempt to freeze modern time and formalize it as history, Nora claims. In the process, they have annihilated the workings of premodern memory.[3] They are part of the "conquest and eradication of memory by history."[4] In case the reader thinks this is just a matter of disinterested social forces, Nora adds that history's "true mission is to suppress and destroy" memory.[5] And, more boldly, "the indiscriminate production of archives" is the "clearest expression of the terrorism of historicized memory."[6] Clear enough: memory good, history bad — really, really bad.

This deeply antimodern provocation nonetheless sketched out a relationship — a dialectic, more than a binary — that sought resolution: the *lieux de mémoire*. This third category, which Nora positioned "between memory and history," is as much a practice as a place or a thing. The only option left to the modern world, he argues, is to collect and cultivate *lieux de mémoire*: places, artifacts, and concepts "where memory crystallizes and secretes itself."[7] These self-conscious sites of memory fashion memory's corpses into a modern compromise where history's assaults on memory have left traces: "If history did not besiege memory, deforming and transforming it, penetrating and petrifying it, there would be no *lieux de mémoire*. Indeed, it is this very push and pull that produces *lieux de mémoire*."[8] The violent clash between memory and history creates what he calls "distance memory," a term that refers to how the acceleration of events in modern times obscures both future and past by distancing us from both.

While Nora's project is marbled with nostalgia, he proposes an out. Historians must refuse to aid and abet the murder of memory and instead rescue the past from becoming merely history or slipping into the ether. Heroically, they are to throw themselves into the rupture of modernity and become *lieux de mémoire* themselves.[9] What seems like an absurd proposition — a person becoming a *lieu de mémoire*! — is more than a mystical personification of memory. It mirrors world heritage practices. UNESCO has increasingly sought living sites of intangible heritage, including people who embody cultural practices such as songs, prayers, and languages that could disappear with their passing. Yet Nora is not clear of the charge of mysticism. All *lieux de mémoire*, he claims, are connected. There is "an unconscious organization of collective memory."[10] He is silent on how this works, but it is the crux of the argument. This self-organizing collective memory salvages for history one of memory's most vital attributes, namely, that it is organic: it simply happens. He declares that it is the historian's responsibility to bring this network to consciousness.[11] This self-organizing collective is effectively an everyday practice, a vernacular form of history pitted against the regimentation of modern institutions.

Nora's interpretation has insinuated itself into memory studies, either as an artifact that requires citation or as part of the hidden assumptions about how memory and history relate. Its mysticism haunts the field.[12] Understanding memorials as part of everyday life is an attempt to dispel this mysticism, free it of conspiratorial instincts, and move beyond it as a redemptive project. Although the everyday is sometimes seen as an antagonist to institutional order, history and the archive, formality, and modernism, in fact it offers a way of seeing memorials as part of lived experience in the context of all of its complicated forms and spaces. "Ozymandias," quoted in the epigraph, tells us as much. Percy Shelley, writing in 1818, in the very era when (in Nora's view) history began to murder memory, imagines a monument without memory. This "lifeless thing," left "boundless and bare" in the metaphorical desert of time, is divorced from history, shorn of all living memory. It is pure fragment. The "vast and trunkless legs of stone," without past or future, could never become a *lieu de mémoire*. As an allegorical figure, Shelley's ruin anticipates distance memory while it plays the traditional role of admonition.

Yet something else is afoot in the poem. While modern memorials warn from their posts at crossroads, public buildings, roundabouts, plazas, parks, and cemeteries, creating an estuary where the not-everyday and everyday flow into one another, Ozymandias speaks from nowhere. It would seem at first that the poet is writing about something that predates Nora's troubles and precedes modern conceptions of the everyday. However, what allowed Shelley to imagine such a timeless and placeless monument in the first place is the same rupture and acceleration of time that Nora believed inaugurated distance memory: the revolutions — political, economic, and intellectual — begun in the eighteenth century. To conjure up such a *thing* is a cultural magic born of the disenchantment and distancing rationality of the Enlightenment. It was not available to poets or artists a century before. In extinguishing the burning bushes of the old regime, reason threatened to render everything knowable, accessible, everyday. Shelley's "colossal wreck" is a secretion neither of the everyday nor of the not-everyday, but rather of a Romantic wrestling with the warping of everyday experience that would eventually lead Nora to posit the *lieux de mémoire*. If anything, then, Shelley lines up Nora in a long lineage of modern mentalities about time, place, and the everyday.

Nora belongs to memory studies, but this chapter teases out how interwoven memory studies is with the study of the everyday. It brings discussions of memory into closer dialogue with scholars of vernacular architecture and everyday urbanism, landscape, and geography, as well as ordinary behavior in daily life.[13] It elaborates on and challenges their work, extending the everyday as a frame of reference and object of study to understand memorials better. Writers on the everyday, whether trained in folklore, geography, history, American Studies, or architecture and landscape architecture, have tended to place ordinary environments, habits, mentalities, and processes in contrast with, if not contest with, extraordinary, exceptional, and special places, days, and activities. I believe that this opposition is largely a fiction, and like most enduring fictions, it has served a purpose: to elevate certain social ideals over others, sanction spatial hierarchies and zoning practices, create academic subfields, reinforce class boundaries, and foster nationalistic sentiment.[14] At its most innocent, the segregation of the everyday is part of a wider attempt to give order to the destabilizing forces of modern life. This organizing role has been seen in universal terms. The keen observer of vernacular landscape, J. B. Jackson, believed that the everyday "landscape represents the last and most grandiose attempt to create an earthly order in harmony with a cosmic order."[15] The way human quirks and habits constantly inflect and interpret that cosmic order makes landscape relative, historical, ideological. With such stakes in place, the binary of everyday and not-everyday, like Nora's opposition of history and memory, cannot be innocent.

The everyday and its supposed antithesis have been ideologues in the world of ideas. When Norbert Elias observed that the everyday arose as a rejection of the assumptions of the "not-everyday," he noted that the latter remained disconcertingly ill defined.[16] For his part, Elias rejected attempts to link his work with scholarship on the everyday, claiming that his classic *The Civilizing Process* was merely mistaken for being a work on the topic.[17] Elias's observations about meals, sleep, bodily functions, and so on were about changes in the "civilizing code" that were "indissolubly bound up with other structural changes in society."[18] In other words, to single out the everyday was to abstract something from the very context that gave it meaning. This is an astounding observation because it rejects the binary between the everyday and its other. In its political mode, the everyday has been a populist, if not also heroic, scholarly realm that attempts to rescue folk culture from erasure by the amnesiac forces of modernity, from a vilified "not-everyday." The not-everyday is curiously akin to Nora's villainous history, and the everyday is like his beloved premodern memory.

Elias created a chart to reveal and poke fun at these assumptions (fig. 1.1). Against the everyday, the chart opposes would-be exceptional events or phenomena, including feast days, the life of elites, great events, public life, the artificial, and self-reflection. To one side sits the mundane, workaday life of the masses, private life and the family, spontaneity and naïveté. To the other sits their supposed antitheses: bourgeois luxury, privilege and power, official life, great events, science, and rationality.[19] Elias's work reveals just how much of a false dichotomy scholars of the everyday have created and maintained. While these familiar divides of scholarship on the everyday

Figure 24.1 Types of Contemporary Concept of the Everyday with the Implied Antitheses

		– A Selection –	
1	Everyday	◄─────►	holiday (feast day)
2	Everyday = routine	◄─────►	extraordinary areas of society not subject to routine
3	Everyday = working day (especially for working class)	◄─────►	bourgeois sphere, i.e. that of people living on profits and in luxury, without really working
4	Everyday = life of the masses	◄─────►	life of the privileged and powerful (kings, princes and princesses, presidents, members of government, party leaders, members of parliament, business leaders)
5	Everyday = sphere of mundane events	◄─────►	everything regarded by traditional political historiography as the only relevant or 'great' event in history, i.e. the centre-stage of history
6	Everyday = private life (family, love, children)	◄─────►	public or occupational life
7	Everyday = sphere of natural, spontaneous, unreflecting, genuine experience and thinking	◄─────►	sphere of reflective, artificial, unspontaneous, especially scientific experience and thinking
8	Everyday (everyday consciousness) = ideological, naïve, superficial and false experience and thinking	◄─────►	correct, genuine, true

Figure 1.1. Chart of the Concept of the Everyday. From *The Norbert Elias Reader: A Biographical Selection* (Malden: Blackwell, 1998), p. 167.

have waned in the last generation, they are still powerfully present, and not just in academia. In architecture, vernacular expressions have been put in contrast to architecture with a capital A, as it is sometimes called: buildings designed by architects within a formal system of patronage and construction. By this account, everyday or ordinary architecture evades or works outside of that system. It is bottom up rather than top down, informal rather than formal, vernacular rather than official.

To what end this cleft? Observers of the ordinary have championed the neglected, routine, and invisible parts of life as a corrective to elite or formal spaces and ways of thinking. Many of the most prominent writers in this mode helped construct the dyad of everyday and not-everyday. For instance, Henry Glassie, the eminent folklorist and one of the early scholars of vernacular architecture, saw modern architecture as a monstrous exaggeration of age-old practices of exploiting nature for human shelter. In pointing to the difference between vernacular and modern architecture, he writes: "When the environment mastered man, and man fought back with plow and axe, the act of struggling against nature with all one's power was courageous. When man sits coddled in a temperature-controlled office, forty stories above the city, the relentless continuation of that ancient struggle seems heartless."[20] While one may well agree with Glassie, the turn to emotion is the tell that he has left the cool realm of rational argument. In his hands, the "plow" and "axe" are heroic tools. The handwork they allow leads to an architecture that "teaches its occupants . . . about their position in the universe" and shows them "the validity of their culture."[21] His story—for that is what it is—elaborates a mythic trajectory from Jean-Jacques Rousseau's noble savage and myths of the primitive hut to ideas about the frontier as a generator of American character and finally to early work on vernacular architecture, with J. B. Jackson as spiritual guide.[22]

With this mythic vision, Glassie emasculates modern "man" for not throwing his body against nature, much as Nora calls on historians to throw themselves into the breech between history and memory. Glassie condemns this effete "organization man" at his desk in his skyscraper for being distant from his object and its inhabitants: "As artificiality spins to extremes, the walls around people come to contain no reminder of the natural origins [of] human endeavor." In turn, "the poetic dimension of technology dissolves. People lose the capacity to connect themselves . . . to the world they inhabit, and so surrender the right to know that they know."[23] His is a nostalgic story of paradise lost, a folktale from an imaginative folklorist about alienation from nature. The stakes for Glassie were nearly boundless. "Vernacular politics are egalitarian," he claims, slipping seamlessly from built form, where the term "vernacular" has a plain meaning, to political form, where its meaning is more obscure. The people whose work we call vernacular, he argues, are held in some interlocking web of "mutual benefit." The idea of an organic society of citizens acting together and creating their world with their bare hands out of nothing once again recalls the frontier myth, while it repeats the wistful longing for organic community advanced by thinkers such as Lewis Mumford, Van Wyck Brooks, and Waldo Frank in the 1920s.[24] This "egalitarian ethic," moreover, is so powerful, it "confines individualistic urges." This makes it blessedly conventional: "the user does not request fantastic shapes or risky operations."[25]

Through this swipe at modern architecture, Glassie mounts a still wider attack. The intimacy of vernacular buildings — that they are shaped by people bound in communal relationships — is unlike the mass, anonymous architecture of modernity. "The egalitarian spirit finds survival hard outside of participatory scenes. New political orders, generous perhaps, even democratic in tone, begin to rise and with them come the evils that breed in ignorance."[26] With the fall of the Garden of Vernacular Eden, evil has been invented, and people wander in the wilderness of modernity: the modern squelches the vernacular and in so doing inhibits community and equality, perhaps even democracy. This vaguely Marxist condemnation of the alienation of workers from what they make and of everyone from the things they own and use looks back to John Ruskin and William Morris, two wide-ranging, nineteenth-century thinkers who leveled scathing critiques of modern society through the glorification of premodern craft. Modern architecture, Glassie concludes, "is no longer vernacular." It comes out of a "political structure . . . of dominance and submission."[27] It is not-everyday, and dangerously so. He could have been discussing monuments.

Putting aside the Cold War fears that may lurk behind this argument, it's true that Glassie came of age as a scholar in a moment when modern buildings and cities were displacing vernacular ones and despoiling vast cultural landscapes at an alarming rate. There was and remains a real enemy. He was already forging these ideas at the time when scholars paid scant attention to ordinary environments while devoting themselves to the tiny fraction of buildings designed by architects, a common lament from champions of the vernacular.[28] By the 1990s, much of the intensity of the battle had subsided. By then, the geographer and historian of ordinary environments Paul Groth could write that vernacular studies had come closer to the "center of architectural history" and that the "ordinary and the official" were now seen "as parts of the same cultural landscape."[29] The wider lens of cultural landscape allowed a rapprochement. Yet however softened, the binary was deeply dyed into the fabric of thought: the everyday was still pitched against the "not-everyday."[30]

This habit of negation is part of the pathology of the field, particularly in architecture. Dell Upton and John Michael Vlach, both leading historians of vernacular architecture, observe as much when they write: "Vernacular architecture is *non*-high style building; it is those structures *not* designed by professionals; it is *not* monumental; it is *un*-sophisticated; it is *mere* building; it is, according to the distinguished architectural historian Nikolaus Pevsner, *not* architecture" (their emphasis).[31] More recently, Upton insightfully writes that the everyday is "an Other of some sort, better defined by what it is not than by what it is."[32] Of course, this is Elias's point in reverse. The "not-everyday" is understood as the ill-defined Other of the contrarian everyday, which was being finely articulated by Jackson, Glassie, Upton, Vlach, Groth, and others. The point is that the vernacular has been defined in the negative, set against official, formal, or high culture and by implication against the monumental. When architects have appropriated the everyday as a recuperative challenge to the status quo of the field, the binary has not relaxed, as one might imagine, but stiffened. This comes out vividly in Stephen Harris's introduction to *Architecture of the Everyday* (1997), where he expresses "distrust of the heroic and the formally fashionable" and "deep suspicion of the architectural object as a marketable commodity" while turning to the everyday as a form of resistance. As he puts it, "there is no How-ard Roark of the everyday."[33] Eliade's retort might be that there is no Howard Roark.

In spite of this spirit of negation, going back at least to the 1960s, "everyday" has been a positive term, but it was forged with its own opposable thumb: the not-everyday. And so have scholars grasped at the subject. Even the most innocuous synonyms arrive with antago-nists. "Ordinary," for instance, not merely emerges in tension with something extraordinary, it also is part of a particular modern atti-tude. In the eighteenth century, "ordinary" took on a double mean-ing. It could refer to "uneducated" or "uninstructed" people, as well as to "sensible" or "regular" people, as distinct from elites.[34] "Ordi-nary," whether dismissive or flattering, indicates something oppo-sitional: "a generalized body of Others," or the masses. As Raymond Williams explains, "it often elicits protest."[35]

"Common" landscapes and places, likewise, assume uncommon ones, and, like "ordinary," "common" is loaded with nettlesome nuances. It means "ordinary" and "nonaristocratic" — alas, another negative! — but also evokes common lands, as in the New England commons, an indigenous, vernacular, and seemingly authentic Amer-ican invention. "Common" resonates socially, as well. Increasingly across the nineteenth century, the word acquired derogatory mean-ing, as in "vulgar, unrefined, and eventually low class."[36] Alongside this "low" common stood an admirable, folksy usage, two strands of the class-based twine of modern Western society. John R. Stilgoe, a historian who studied with J. B. Jackson and another pivotal figure in the field, indulges in the folksy usage when he writes that the land-scape of early America "objectified *common sense*, not the doubtful innovation of professional designers" (his italics).[37] Whether or not the reference to Thomas Paine is intentional, Stilgoe's "common" is charged, but it is also casually hidden behind common usage. When scholars have taken up "common" or "ordinary," they have entered this rhetorical stream, variously positioning these words as other, adopting their pejorative meanings as a badge of honor, or using them to challenge the prevailing scheme. Thus, Michel de Certeau dedicated *The Practice of Everyday Life*, one of the touchstones of scholarship on the everyday, "To the everyday man. To a common hero," and Aaron Copeland composed his 'Fanfare for the Common Man' in 1942, while millions of soldiers fought out the fate of the world under orders from some of the century's most heroic — and dastardly — characters.[38] There are, of course, memorials to both the common soldiers and the "gigantic generals" who sent them into battle.

There is, it seems, no easy, rhetorical way out of the problem. The same spirit pervades wider inquiries into everyday life. "The 'great men' have been replaced by another cliché, that of smart and crafty rebels, who mastered their everyday life with supreme ease and were always ready to play a trick on the powerful."[39] Largely deriving from de Certeau's work, these common tricksters are thought to operate unintentionally, without ulterior motives, as a kind of "wandering" that lays bare the fragility of official power structures, all the more so for being unselfconscious.[40] Art and architecture picked up on this strand of trickster intervention early on. The Situationists, a French group of avant-garde artists and architects that emerged in the 1950s, made subversive wandering part of an improvised itinerary of escape from formality. Before them, but not much before, the surrealists saw in the public monuments of Paris "suitable elements of a dialogue, a dialogue between the *flâneur* and his city," constituting "in André Breton's words, a 'figure of participation' to be questioned and provoked in a free play of rhetorical and poetic associations."[41] Such a mildly subversive way of seeing memorials, like Frank O'Hara's liver-sausage-eating narrator, can now be seen as a tradition, a way of reconciling the complexity of modern life that put memorials, sneakily invisible, at the center.

It is possible to see scholars of the everyday themselves as part of that tradition, as "smart and crafty rebels" playing tricks on dominant and entrenched fields of inquiry in order to pry them open and reveal their shortcomings.[42] In this rendering, the understanding of the everyday as anonymous, timeless, or "objectified common sense" paints it as apolitical, or more aptly, given de Certeau's assumption of naiveté, "prepolitical."[43] This has made the everyday a powerful tool, a purportedly neutral lens through which to dismantle the establishment. But these accounts flirt with what is sometimes called the "political manqué."[44] Just as a working mother's "second shift," when she comes home from her paid job to cook, clean, and care for children, is really part of a political structure of gender inequality hiding behind myths of family, good mothering, and so on, the seemingly unpremeditated "realm of routine," so are eating and bathing, but also handcrafts, shotgun houses, field patterns, signage, and memorials stranded in traffic a political matter hidden behind habits and conventions.[45] It is not that scholars have failed to see ordinary landscapes in political terms, for of course they have, but that the scholarly agenda against the "not-everyday" obscures the politics of the everyday as a mode of inquiry. The "not-everyday" remains cartoonish and obscure, all the better to build a strawman out of it, while the everyday makes hay out of the juxtaposition.

At the urban level, the everyday has served similar purposes. The authors of the influential *Everyday Urbanism* (1999) observe some of the same informal processes within cities that Glassie and others see in vernacular buildings or Nora finds in premodern memory. The book's introduction updates the binary. Here, Margaret Crawford draws attention to the "banal and ordinary routines" and sites and activities of daily life such as sidewalks, shopping, buying, and eating.[46] This is the world of O'Hara's "Music" and of Elias, but it still has an opponent: "Everyday space stands in contrast to the carefully planned, officially designated, and often underused spaces of public use that can be found in most American cities."[47] It is easy to admire the way *Everyday Urbanism* redirects our gaze to the marginal and overlooked parts of cities and finds in quotidian urban experience "the potential for new social arrangements and forms of imagination."[48] Like the best scholarship on ordinary landscapes, the book tries to see "beyond the dominant culture" and reveal the everyday as a realm of "creative resistance," "political contestation," and liberation.[49] It is broadly framed as a fight against the distant abstractions of theory, the top-down impositions of urban planning, and the "authoritarian and absolute."[50]

Again, the stakes are momentous. For the authors of *Everyday Urbanism*, the official processes of city building have created generic, homogenous spaces that erase human differences and "have little to do with real human impulses."[51] Where Glassie turned to preservation as a prophylactic against the anonymity of modern development, *Everyday Urbanism* aims at a radical form of analysis and intervention with redemptive, even revolutionary potential to transform the city through the agency of the common person. It is a "call to action" about social change.[52] Those people pushed to the margins would not only be seen, but also gain a voice and become featured parts of the reconsideration and redesign of cities. Such heroism flirts with Upton's observation about the vernacular as "a discrete, pre-lapsarian arena of social experience," but where Upton believes this realm to be "just beyond our own" and never "directly accessible to us," Crawford opens the door for activist resistance to the totalizing forces of capitalism and urban planning.[53]

If *The Everyday Life of Memorials* demurs at the sometimes combative or ideological streak in the study of the everyday, it is in sympathy with its commitment to seeing wildly varying cultural forms as equally meaningful. I agree with geographer Peirce F. Lewis that "the MacDonald's hamburger stand is just as important as a cultural symbol as the Empire State Building . . . the painted cement jockeyboy on the front lawn in middle-class suburbia is as important a symbol as the Brooklyn Bridge; the Coney Island roller rink is as important as the Washington Monument — no more, no less."[54] Lewis emphasized their importance as part of a struggle to raise the status of ordinary landscapes. His near manifesto of the everyday can now be reframed — and reversed. The Washington Monument is as revealing about American culture as the Coney Island roller rink. It is OK to look at monuments. To do so is not ipso facto to capitulate to top-down elitism. They, too, are also part of the everyday, or at least they are fluid objects brimming with all the possibilities of vernacular and official cultural forms. If anything is fixed, it is these academic categories.

In seeing monuments as malleable, this book attempts to make a friendly amendment to scholarship on the everyday. There is in Lewis's corrective a hint of wishing to cut monuments down to size. In this, he joins a long history. Monuments have been in ill repute almost from their reinvention. John Quincy Adams, for instance, proclaimed that "democracy has no monuments."[55] Such sentiment was transatlantic. Devalued in reaction to nineteenth-century statuemania, monuments were seen as antithetical to modern, Enlightenment society. In a sustained screed against the mania for commemorative statues in England, Thomas Carlyle called them "symptoms of anarchy." "This extraordinary populace of British Statues, which now dominate our market-places, [is] one of the saddest omens that ever was."[56] The twentieth century was equally unkind. A taboo against death made monuments morbid.[57] Fascism made them politically objectionable. Modern art made them embarrassing: "Old-fashioned monumental statuary attracts jokes and pigeons, of course," writes the art critic Peter Schjeldahl. "For generations now, we have lacked the mental means for taking it seriously, even when we notice it."[58] Popular sentiment often concurs. In the midst of a wave of iconoclasm associated with the Black Lives Matter movement in 2020, the comedian Trevor Noah told his audience: "We don't need statues anymore, people. It doesn't matter who they're for, we don't need statues. Statues are like tweets. They might work at the time; the time you make them, they seem cool, but if you leave them up for too long, they're going to become problematic."[59] Here is a kind of iconoclastic urge to sweep away an entire cultural form.

Meanwhile, modern urbanism has stranded monuments as they "weep red rust onto passing cars" or whimper in their roundabouts, which were once part of grand, Beaux-Arts schemes of beautification that by midcentury came to seem hopelessly outdated. Guilt by association.[60] Overlapping with these urban changes, a call for useful memorials such as civic buildings and parks emerged in the nineteenth century and peaked in the mid-twentieth. Its advocates assailed the traditional urge to monumentality as indulgent, vulgar, and dead. The countermonument movement that arose in the 1980s, particularly in Germany, eroded the cultural power of the monument still further.[61] Memorials that disappeared into the ground, projected ghostly images of lost Jewish life onto building façades, and sometimes proposed more dramatic violence to memorials rejected the monumentality of earlier commemorative work with dark and ironic conceptual power. In the same moment, multiculturalism's disregard for "dead white males" did no favors for the legions of heroic bronzes around the world.[62] This canon of "dead" monuments, like literary and architectural canons, began to be questioned at the same time that the everyday blossomed as an object of study: all are part of the same broad movement to reclaim neglected subjects. Where active disdain for monuments can boil over into iconoclasm, passive neglect can be just as damning: "We are well able to look at monuments without seeing them," wrote the architect Hugh Casson.[63] This litany of antimonument(al) attitudes is one reason why so few observers of ordinary landscapes have been interested in monuments; when they do pay attention to them, they do so most often in opposition.[64] It is vital, however, to see monuments again, not as monuments per se, but as changeful elements in the built environment — as revealing as lawn ornaments and perhaps quite like them.

Clearly, I owe a major debt to scholars of the everyday and the wider fields that they represent. I admire their vision and their way of looking. This book would be impossible without their insights. But like Norbert Elias, I remain troubled by the dichotomy between everyday and "not-everyday." O'Hara's liver-sausage sandwich means nothing without Sherman, which is incoherent without Central Park or Bergdorf's or the teaming masses gawking, flirting, littering, and now texting as they move through the scene. They're all part of the total meaning of this urban fragment, which flows into other cultural landscapes that give it meaning. Sherman and his golden angel epitomize the formal. Placed by elites and official committees in a formally landscaped entrance to Central Park, they play the didactic role of keepers of memory, arbiters of culture, reminders of American hierarchies. They are symbols of authority, stand-ins for the powers that placed them there. Yet all of this breaks down in O'Hara's poem, and in real life. The everyday is not just the spaces in between and the neglected buildings, people, and processes in them, but the entire mixed-up scene. It turns out that the formal ain't so formal, and the everyday is constantly under pressure to straighten up and tuck in its shirt. The formal Sherman and its formal setting, planned from above and gilded with high-minded allegory, are part of everyday urbanism. As the geographer Richard Walker has written, largely to prod devotees of the everyday out of their purism: "The city and its monuments are an unending procession of spectacle, high drama, low farce, and play of representations upon the rude stones — fraud on the grandest scale — from classical Athens to Islamic Cairo or from Baron Georges-Eugène Haussmann's Paris to Frank Gehry's Los Angeles."[65]

To be fair, many of the aforementioned scholars would readily accept Walker's reading. Crawford understands it in terms of what Russian literary critic Mikhail Bakhtin called "heteroglossia." Bakhtin held that every word enters an "agitated and tension-filled environment of alien words, value judgments and accents, weaves in and out of complex interrelationships, merges with some, recoils from others," all of which "may leave a trace in all its semantic layers."[66] This way of thinking about words, or what Bakhtin called the "living utterance," offered Crawford a palpable parallel to the built environment.[67] The urban text, so to speak, resounds with many voices at once. This view of everyday urbanism and its complexity guides the readings of memorials in this book, but one significant shift in emphasis gives me pause. "We believe," Crawford writes, "that lived experience should be more important than physical form in defining the city."[68] This corrective is well taken. For generations, architectural and urban historians have obsessed over form at the expense of looking hard at what people are doing in and around buildings and cities. However, this move undermines what I see as the continued potential of everyday urbanism. In drawing attention away from urban form or morphology, it devalues the physical realities of cities.[69]

To valorize lived experience over material reality reconstitutes the binary in a new form. To be sure, people engage in behaviors that can be characterized as high or low, rarefied or ordinary, everyday or special. These categories are used consciously, as when people dress up for religious services or stand for a national anthem, and unconsciously, as when people whisper in museums. However, "lived experience" is constantly in cahoots with physical form. The built and material context that we create expresses, frames, delimits, represents, and makes possible our every act, including acts of protest. After all, the text in heteroglossia is language, and in this sustained analogy to everyday urbanism that "text" is the city itself. What role the monument plays in "lived experience" forms an important part of the everyday life of memorials. As Richard Walker puts it: "Artifacts must be seen in dialectical relation with the ideational side of cultural practices."[70] What people are doing, in other words, cannot be understood without close study of where they are doing it and the objects upon which they act and that act upon them. This is not to introduce a vague or abstract concept of space or place. The material culture of cities in its aggregate forms a setting. This physical setting is not mere context or background; it is instrumental. Lived experience and physical form must not be put in a hierarchy of academic values, but rather studied together. As scholars of the ordinary "denaturalize the everyday" in order to bring it into light, it must also be naturalized with the "not-everyday," as it is in daily life.[71] If the distinction remains, it should be as a thought experiment set up to explore the overall scene.

Glossing Memory

How to dissolve the binary? The first step is to recognize the ambiguity of most memorials as formal interventions intended for sanctified settings that so often become informal objects in changeful settings, then spend their lives flitting back and forth. This fluidity should come to the fore, as Norbert Elias might have insisted. From the beginning, modern memorials came in many forms and played an ambiguous role in an equally ambiguous setting. Many of the "great man" memorials or monuments of the nineteenth century were thrown into the dynamic stream of urbanization that characterized the period. They were used to dignify urban fragments, capacious or meager street corners, or in Europe, to beautify the new boulevards that replaced walls and dilapidated medieval areas. They frequently turned up exactly where the forces of urbanization were most active, where trolleys and modern institutions muscled their way in and created odd bits of space, often public space, and a gradient between new and old.

A telling example was erected in 1887 in Bologna, where the literary figure and restorer of medieval Bologna, Alfonso Rubbiani, coordinated the erection of the tombs of the *glossatori*, those medieval professors named for the "glosses" they put in the margins of legal texts and who are commonly thought to be the founders of Bologna's university.[72] Having found fragments of some tombs in the process of restoring his masterpiece, the church of San Francesco, Rubbiani mounted them on pavilions loosely based on the Mausoleum of Halicarnassus and thrust them to the edge of the new avenue opened up by the destruction of the old wall, just outside the medieval Porta Nova on the western edge of the old city (fig. 1.2). He could have found precedents for raised tombs in the medieval Scaliger tombs in Verona. For the precise source, however, he reasoned that Crusaders on their way back from the Mediterranean might have seen the Mausoleum of Halicarnassus, which was ruined in 1404 and is itself a monument that survives only through hypothetical latter-day reconstructions. The mausoleum had been excavated between 1857 and 1865 — by Alfred Biliotti, an Italian, no less — and would have been on Rubbiani's mind.

Through this topical reference to Halicarnassus, Rubbiani essentially transformed private, forgotten tombs (with a vague provenance) into public monuments, which he did with larger urban-

Figure 1.2. The *glossatori* monuments and the Basilica of San Francesco, Bologna, ca. 1940. The boulevard to the left replaced the old wall, and the old city is just beyond the left frame of this image. Alfonso Rubbiani, restoration architect, 1880s. Postcard from the author's collection.

istic intentions. He placed the tombs precisely where the medieval collided with the modern. As people emerged from the historical core of the city through a *porta* or tower in the medieval wall into the wide, modern avenue, they encountered the stunning but rather antisocial east end of the church. The narrow, meandering medieval streets gave way to the impressively wide boulevard (now taken up with speeding Vespas and cars, but then brandishing its modernity in the form of streetcars) before yielding to the church, set back on its small green. This ensemble of *porta*, newly formed piazza, and expansive boulevard that had displaced the fortified wall demanded a grand gesture, something that could make sense of the changes in scale and speed while unifying the space. Acting in the spirit of the picturesque and the mania for monuments then common in Western cities, Rubbiani made urban monuments of the tombs.[73] He marched them out to meet the novel space, calibrated them to its scale, rather than to the intimate uses of tombs, and used them as a transitional screen for the church. Here, the *glossatori* could narrate the connections between civic life, religion, and learning.

In a city searching for its identity in a recently unified Italy, the *glossatori* provided a comforting image of continuity and an indigenous source around which a myth of greatness could be built. As monuments, they made the founders of the first university into public heroes — a gesture about as historically accurate as using Halicarnassus as a source. In the early 1880s, Rubbiani and his circle dated the university's origin to 1088, a fiction that gave the group several years to plan a momentous eight-hundredth anniversary celebration. The claim is erroneous, although it is still widely believed today. With this, Rubbiani and his cohort hoped to make Bologna the "capitale del mondo studioso."[74] If Bologna could not be the national capital of Italy, or the *caput mundi*, it could lay claim to being an intellectual capital through the *glossatori*. These hiked-up tributes muddy the differences between tombs, memorials, monuments, and mere artistic interventions. They are not so different formally, scenographically, or in their moral and aesthetic purpose than, say, a statue of Garibaldi, but they performed a historical and spatial role that a generic revolutionary hero could not. In pretending to be grand medieval monuments and an eternal part of the church, they smoothed out the everyday fray of this fraught transition. The *glossatori* are a perfect example of heteroglossia, being urban glosses about heroic glossers.

The *glossatori* express this more complicated relationship between everyday and not-everyday with surprising nuance. Whatever the reality behind these masters of marginalia, Rubbiani represented them as extraordinary men of privilege and power, set them up as elites in the institutional and intellectual life of Bologna, situated them conspicuously in a dedicated public place of grand proportion, and tethered them to a great event in the founding of the university and the revival of Roman law. He gave them monumental status.

They were conspicuously "not-everyday." Yet they speak the language of the extraordinary all the more forcefully for being placed in the bustling workaday world, with its pedestrians, shops, and streetcars. This is why Rubbiani edged his monuments away from the church and pressed them up against the sphere of the mundane. The point might be made more forcefully. Rubbiani did not fight the everyday, but he embraced it, threw his monuments into it, and as a man of his day, understood the power of this setting to make the *glossatori* speak. In short, these are everyday memorials.

Many memorials share this with the *glossatori*, even if they pretend otherwise. Part of their function is something similar to feast days. Commemorations, if anything, are extraordinary events, yet they are run through with everyday dynamics and take on their meaning as extraordinary only through association with or by holding back the ordinary, putting it on temporary hiatus and reconciling with its inevitability. With memorials, the lines between everyday and not-everyday are drawn, smeared, redrawn, and smeared again, and not necessarily in some straightforward dialectic. They inhabit a "distinguishable sphere," both marked by the everyday and separate from it, a double life.[75]

Those memorials that transcend the everyday take great pains to do so. Almost any war memorial built before the late twentieth century will make the point (fig. 1.3). Like many memorials, the Soldiers and Sailors Monument in Delphi, Indiana, is set apart from and rises above its setting. The soldier atop, if generic, is larger than life, a heroic figure compared with the mere mortals below. Its materials are exceptional, its workmanship extraordinary. Granite, a hard, igneous rock that is often used for funeral monuments, has been associated with long duration, if not perpetuity. In many memorials like this one, although not at Delphi, marble, a softer stone that can be finely carved, lends statues dignity and refinement. Since fine veins of these two materials are relatively rare, they are often transported from afar, incurring greater cost and giving value to the piece. Bronze, another expensive material that requires great skill to cast, is nearly a metaphor for fixing things in

Figure 1.3. Rudolf Schwarz and Bruno Schmitz, architects, Soldiers and Sailors Monument, 1888, Delphi, Indiana. Photograph by Carol M. Highsmith. Courtesy of the Library of Congress.

time: we bronze personal memorabilia such as baby shoes. My mother owned a bronze shoe set in a small marble base, a minimonument to an evanescent stage of her life, one about which she has no memory. Such materials are "not-everyday." At Delphi, extraordinary materials were used to make the memorial stand out from the red brick and wood that are the standard building materials of the American Midwest. Carroll County held an international competition to find a design, choosing one by Bruno Schmitz, a preeminent German architect responsible for several of the most prominent German monuments of the period. Their lofty ambitions could not have been clearer.

Unlike a building, memorials like this usually have no functional internal space, putting the onus on their external physical form to communicate. Most buildings stand in order to shelter some human need; memorials often stand in order to stand for something. They are what Spiro Kostof calls "mid-space objects" — something meant to be beheld and contemplated, like art objects, with the additional intention that they help people reflect or remember something exemplary.[76] Just as memorials establish a place apart, their related commemorations establish a time apart. This puts an onus on the setting to be a flexible stage for such events. The plantings, street furniture, lighting, and paving scheme — the landscape — are designed to help this double move, allowing people to step in and out of everyday time and space. In this way, a metaphorical "roof" appears and disappears over memorials as they waver in and out of the everyday.[77] What great lengths the sculptor, architect, and landscape architect went to in order to make Delphi's memorial "not-everyday," to create this retractable roof. And what expense the town committed to erect it and set aside a place to remember its dead. The Civil War was undoubtedly an extraordinary event in American history, and many such memorials were built in its aftermath. Each year, towns across the country renew their connection to the Civil War through elaborate ceremonies. So far, this all appears decidedly "not-everyday."

This evidence, however, is counterbalanced by the myriad everyday acts that have diminished, belittled, or undermined memorials.

Figure 1.4. A monument to the Brewer of Ghent unwittingly inspires neo-Nazis. Pieter De Vigne, Jacob Van Artevelde Monument, 1863, Ghent. Photograph by the author.

Figure 1.5. Neo-Nazi graffiti on the sidewalk at the Jacob Van Artevelde Monument, 2008, Ghent. Photograph by the author.

Leaving aside the waves of iconoclasm that go along with revolutions and political turmoil, memorials are constantly glossed, if not threatened, both physically and morally. Postbellum cartoons mocked them alongside the false piety of Decoration Day, the predecessor to Memorial Day initiated after the Civil War. (See fig. 8.5.) The sacred day quickly succumbed to the ordinary. Bicycle races in the nineteenth century (see fig. 8.6) gave way to "horseless carriage races" on Memorial Day. Indianapolis, where Schmitz designed an even larger memorial, hosted its first one in 1911. Memorials themselves suffer indignities more literal and aggressively iconoclastic. In 1957, the Civil War memorial in Lagrange, Ohio (1904), was tarred and feathered.[78] Thieves in England steal memorials and sell them as garden ornaments.[79] The tiniest mark can embroil old memorials in contemporary issues. For instance, neo-Nazis spray-painted their insignia on the paving at the base of the Jacob Van Artevelde Monument in Ghent (figs. 1.4 and 1.5). It is positioned so that one beholds the rampant lion, the great man, and his gesture from the graffiti, which transforms it from a Roman into a Nazi salute. This graffiti is a gesture closer to appropriation than iconoclasm. It doesn't harm the monument, and it can be scrubbed away. But once seen, the monument and its gesture are forever altered. It is a gloss, but the marginalia can eat away at the meaning of a statue.

Figure 1.6. Graffiti of a hanging Jew on the way to the Museum of Martyrdom, Zamość, Poland. Photograph by the author.

Throughout Europe, this sort of graffiti glosses the geography of the European Holocaust with a transitory geography of neo-Nazism. An image of a lynched Jew frowns at people as they walk to the Museum or Mausoleum of Martyrdom, also called the Rotunda, a vast memorial complex in Zamość, Poland (figs. 1.6 and 1.7). In this nineteenth-century fortress, Nazis interrogated, killed, and burned thousands of Jews and Poles. Hundreds of grave sites and memorials to Jews, Poles, and Russians dot the landscape, but the frowning Jew has the first word — and the last, since one must pass it again on the way back into town. Apparently, the tricksters of everyday urbanism and memory are not always heroic. Just as memory studies is often channeled through the Holocaust, a more public or popular experience of memory is channeled through it and inscribed in the same places.[80]

Figure 1.7. One small section of grave markers for Jews murdered at the nearby Rotunda, a nineteenth-century fortress where Nazis interned Jews before sending them to concentration camps. Museum of Martyrdom, Zamość, Poland. Graves for Russians and Poles are marked with Soviet stars and crosses. Photograph by the author.

Figure 1.8. Elaborate railings and lighting once protected Pieter De Vigne's Jacob Van Artevelde Monument, 1863, Ghent. Postcard from the author's collection.

If what memorials ask us to do in the absence of specific commemorative practices and historical knowledge is look backward with a general nod, to acknowledge the past, then not only is history up for grabs, but also memory becomes a labile thing. In other words, memorials begin with only a fragile purchase on the extraordinary events or ideas they mark, and even this can be diminished over time. The monument to van Arteveld, a medieval Flemish brewer and statesman, can be instantly repurposed by neo-Nazis. It is akin to Marcel Duchamp drawing a mustache on the Mona Lisa, bringing down high art with a low gesture, but really it is creating a new piece of art that defies these categories while it preserves them.[81]

Other changes have altered Van Artevelde, as well. Like many monuments of its day, it had an elaborate railing and lighting scheme. It was once its own entity, distinctly separate from the everyday life of the square in which it sits (fig. 1.8). The railing was later removed, presumably melted down in time of war, leaving it "naked" and ushering the monument into the everyday. It is effectively deconsecrated. It now can be "handled," sat upon, more easily glossed. It is a favorite resting spot in the square, a giver of shade, and a meeting place. The initial instinct to rail off monuments was an elitist gesture, a way of protecting them from the unreliable rabble, similar in spirit to the nineteenth-century practice of placing library stacks off-limits to the public. Railings further elevated the status of monuments by separating them from the hoi polloi. In fact, railings were part of the maintenance of the "not-everyday." At the same time, railings betray the fact that monuments, no matter their grandeur or the gravity of their subject, needed to be bolstered against the everyday. Between Van Artevelde's salute and the railing, the latter is arguably the more powerful gesture.

This is brought out more forcefully by Giambologna's equestrian statue of Cosimo I in the Piazza della Signoria in Florence (1594) (fig. 1.9). It is girdled in two layers of railings.[82] This double circuit is the essence of the everyday life of memorials. One was not enough to hold the surge of tourists at bay, and this is to say nothing of how utterly

Figure 1.9. Giambologna, Equestrian statue of Cosimo I, 1594, Florence, Italy, with its rickety double railings. Photograph by the author.

ordinary these railings are. Their skeletal, nearly improvised form suggests a history of failed or pilfered railings in the piazza. Such a history often leaves no archival trace, but the railings tell the tale. Occasionally, terracotta planters are inserted between the railings (fig. 1.10).

Figure 1.10. Giambologna, Equestrian statue of Cosimo I, 1594, Florence, Italy, ashamed of its railings. Photograph by Arnaud Clerget.

They act as bollards and obscure the railings, which acknowledges the metal skeleton as an aesthetic liability. The bollards suggest a change in mood. Not far away, the monument to Giovanni delle Bande Nere in the Piazza San Lorenzo is also encased in another ordinary railing, apparently an ideal place to lock up bicycles. These railings, which date back to the nineteenth century, are clearly expedients, evidence of the violence done to statues by everyday forces. Della Bande Nere is engulfed in the market stalls that sweep in and out of the piazza.

Railings can speak a subtler language. The chain and bollards that surround the Kaiser Friedrich Denkmal in Bremen are a particularly knowing example of how to hold the public at bay with gentle civility (fig. 1.11). Around many memorials like this one, the chain droops nearly to the ground, inviting people to step over it while requiring of them a deliberate act. It creates a threshold, a barrier door. In this image, people stand outside the boundary, showing it in action, so to speak. The bollards, moreover, are of different sizes, indicating where people should penetrate the space. This is a common strategy for creating a retractable roof for memorials.

The removal of railings would seem to be an inadvertent or serendipitous effect of claiming the metal for scrap in time of war. It turns out, however, that wartime salvage drives to remove iron railings from buildings, parks, and memorials, at least in London, were for naught.[83] Little, if any, of the metal was melted down into weapons. Much of it may have been dumped in the Thames. Instead, these drives were "an exercise in creating a sense of solidarity."[84] Put differently, the most ordinary part of the memorial, the very threshold between everyday and "not-everyday," became a means to rally people around an extraordinary event.

Other, more cultural reasons lurked behind this patriotic pretext. By the 1930s, railings were seen as a "disfigurement." The British architectural historian Gavin Stamp espies in the zealousness of their removal the "anti-Victorian prejudice" common in the period. War was but the pretext; aesthetics and changes in taste were the underlying motive. Railings were also seen as "anti-democratic," part of a "folk memory of the 1866 Reform demonstration when the railings of Hyde Park were uprooted by an angry crowd."[85] Many of the squares of the West End were reserved for private use of the householders, keeping the poor and general public out. "What the railing-haters ignored," Stamp argues, "was the simple fact that the things usually had a purpose." Railings maintained gardens, protected monuments, and created a visual barrier that separated them from the everyday urban sphere that surrounded them. In fact, by the end of the war,

Figure 1.11. Louis Tuaillon, railings as a barrier door at the Kaiser Friedrich Denkmal, 1905 Bremen, Germany. Postcard from the author's collection.

most of London's squares "had their gardens enclosed by barriers of chicken wire on crude metal supports, with the low stone plinths, pitted with regular holes or punctuated by sawn-off iron studs, pathetically testifying to the former presence of proper railings."[86] While similar evidence for memorials may be buried in old newspapers, it stands to reason that makeshift railings were not erected quickly. Monuments must suffer greater indignity than human abuse before people intercede to protect them.[87]

Everyday Tactics

While a new wave of memorialmania, as well as iconoclasm, has recently washed over modern urban life, it has been something of a common tactic in recent decades to reject the strategies that traditional memorials have embraced.[88] Stumbling stones, or *Stolpersteine*, jolt people out of their mindless walking, all the more so for being memorials to the Holocaust (fig. 1.12). These slightly raised metal cobbles are inscribed with the names of Jews murdered during the Shoah and laid in front of the places where they once lived. Each one is a vignette, set in motion by the feet of the pedestrian. Each makes a small but enduring claim on the public sphere, despite having no formal commemorative purpose. It is as if the only way to commemorate an event that strains the imagination like the Holocaust is to condense it into its opposite: something inconspicuous, yet palpable, as ordinary as the sidewalk and resolutely nonmonumental. Tens of thousands of them can now be found throughout Europe.

Countermonuments of all sorts play games with scale and permanence or trade in a solemn setting for everyday ones. Common materials and places challenge and check habits of commemoration, if not also everyday encounters. Spontaneous memorials are the most common example, but so is the trash can in Richmond, California that commemorates war veterans[89] (fig. 1.13). For a city with strained finances, such a vernacular improvisation allows the work of commemoration to subvert the glacial processes and expense of formal

Figure 1.12. The slightly raised profile and shiny surface of this *Stolperstein*, or stumbling stone, jolt passersby from their sidewalk routines in Kreuzberg, Berlin. Photograph by Sabine Biedermann, 2020.

Figure 1.13. Unknown artists, memorial trash can, Richmond, California. Photograph by the author.

memorials. At the same time, it puts memory on the street corner, where daily life can encounter it intimately, alongside an equally informal memorial mural. The trash can is a clever way of bringing memory, which is often mysticized and fetishized, back down to earth. Located far from the civic center and major public spaces of the city, the ordinary sidewalk is the public sphere. Few things are more utilitarian than a trash can, and few things less so than a monument to a great man, and this is part of the point. The Richmond memorial breaks down the "dichotomy," a word with a shared root with *temenos* (to cut off): a sacred area around religious sites meant to divide sacred from profane. Memorials have conventionally been divided off from the everyday; contemporary reactions have attempted to challenge this convention.

The gestures that alter the meaning of memorials are readily observed across cultures and time periods. Nonetheless, there are places that limit or inhibit the everyday, but again at great effort. The guards who commonly watch over monuments, especially in totalitarian nations, testify to the threat these memorials face.[90] In national capitals such as Washington, DC, memorials on the Mall enter a sphere that is highly regulated but not immune to everyday inflection. The spontaneous offerings at the Vietnam Veterans War Memorial are part of an everyday-not-everyday dance. Flowers, photographs, teddy bears, even peanut butter and jelly sandwiches are left under the names of veterans, in stunning contrast to the sparseness of the wall and its space. These are whisked away and, when possible, preserved as part of the formal record. Even the least quotidian of memorials and spaces, such as concentration camps, are constantly subject to the everyday. People strike poses as if they were standing in front of a picturesque monument or natural setting (fig. 1.14). At the infamous "Arbeit Macht Frei" gate at Auschwitz, Poland, a sign asks people to refrain from taking photographs out of respect — a warning that they are exiting the everyday world of tourism. Yet this is precisely what people do. Then these photographs enter photo albums or slide shows next to their images of hiking in

Figure 1.14. Tourists taking photographs at the "Arbeit Macht Frei" gate, 2007, Auschwitz, Poland, in defiance of a sign posted beside the gate, as the author did the same. Photograph by the author.

the Carpathian Mountains or partying in Krakow. No strategy can suppress these habits at concentration camps, from the buses that take tourists there and the "museum shops" that commercialize the experience to the social scripts that encourage solemnity and the reflex to frame photographs artfully — or to take them at all.[91]

Auschwitz brings home just how recent the modern phenomenon of memorials is. The gesture of erecting something in built form in honor of a person, deed, or event is, of course, ancient. In fact, it is prehistoric. The first whiff of a modern tradition of memorials arose in the Renaissance, with a few statues of prominent nobles in public squares or spaces modeled after Roman precedents.[92] Many of these were equestrians, and most of them were in Italy, where a class of patrons sought power through art and could do so in public space because the weather permitted it. By contrast, statues of this sort in the wetter, colder climate of Northern Europe can be found predominantly in churches, a wholly different context.[93] The plague columns and wayside crosses that dot the landscape of Europe offer an exception. Yet these are not secular, being tied explicitly in their inscriptions, if not also in their form and placement, to Christianity.

Only with the revolutions of the eighteenth and nineteenth centuries did modern conventions of memorials take shape and find their place. These ruptures gave rise to a new "pantheon" of heroes and martyrs, a secular one to supplant that of the Catholic church and the seemingly stable and eternal order of the ancien régime. These violent churnings cannot be separated from the economic revolutions that brought into being a powerful bourgeoisie and working classes, as well as the urban context in which the violence took place and that was shaped by those revolutions. These new classes looked to public statuary and funerary traditions dating back to Greece and Rome, but also the Christian Middle Ages and the humanist Renaissance. Obelisks, equestrian statues, triumphal arches, columns, Gothic spires, crosses, and great men on plinths appeared across European cities.

Because they quickly became standard, part of the urban furniture of the period, and are now regarded as utterly traditional, we have lost sight of them as stunningly novel interventions in the public sphere. New and old at once, they are of a piece with the invented traditions identified by Eric Hobsbawm and Terence Ranger as a fundamental part of how people wrestled with the ruptures and quickening pace of modernity.[94] Put differently, the modern memorial entered a milieu, the modern city, that was being stripped of firm, long-standing conventions and habits. At the same time, there was no stable everyday but rather a constant assault on conventions, a process in which memorials participated and that they resisted. Modern memorials and the modern everyday are thus intrinsically related.

Such a reading returns to Glassie's understanding of modernity as a rupture. He was among the first scholars to apply this well-worn historical trope to vernacular studies. The twin revolutions, the industrial one emanating out of England and the political one radiating out of France, precipitated a new kind of historical and temporal consciousness.[95] These revolutionary cataclysms accelerated the pace of change and refashioned time as linear.[96] Time's new shape was apparent in the rapid succession of events and institutional changes. Architecture and cities became the material evidence of that change, as well as an armature that shaped and just as often inhibited social form. Physical form is a palpable form of social form, one accessible to the masses and elites alike. Consequently, it offers a vivid way of observing change. Modern memorials arrived in droves in this same moment, as timepieces trying to capture or gloss the quickly moving currents, as markers of change itself, and, through commemoration, as a way of inserting habits of cyclical time into modern time's relentless linearity.[97] Their relationship to modernity and temporal change is still poorly conceptualized. From the start, historical consciousness has been entangled with concerns about how to make cultural memory into something physical and public.

Nora's sites of memory are but one recent attempt to do so. That they come with nostalgic despair, echoing Shelley's Ozymandias, should not be surprising. Everything mighty melts into the everyday, but moderns have felt that sense of loss more keenly because of the dramatic speed of change and the pile of historical debris strewn across the cultural landscape. Memory and its works have resisted, staging their commemorative rebellions in endless recoils. They have disrupted the everyday, even as they have joined it, if not as charged aide-memoires, then as objects that challenge its casual dominion, in a fugue (both in the musical and psychiatric senses) of assertion and capitulation. This movement, sometimes contrapuntal, other times a sloshing storm, makes memorials labile, which is the subject of the next chapter.

CHAPTER TWO

Labile Memory

We should paralyze the hand of oblivion.
— William Godwin, *Essay on Sepulchres*, 1809

As memorials prod at the ever-shifting boundary between the not-everyday and the everyday, they also create porous openings to other realms. The relationship between past, present, and future; the dead and the living; the physical and the metaphysical; the sacred and the profane, can all be espied through the keyholes of memorials. How did memorials come to play this role? As the sacred calendar ebbed and the aristocracy crumbled, memorials increasingly struck their poses right where the emerging secular society would have to reckon with them. Historically, this function dates back to the source of modern memorialization, the French Revolution, with the toppling of royal monuments and the fall of the ancien régime. This image of the execution of Louis XVI tells the tale (fig. 2.1). Monument and machine face off. The base of the former, emptied in a passionate fit of iconoclasm in August 1792 of the equestrian statue of Louis XV — the unpopular father of the just-executed king — is the counterpoint to the guillotine. This stands to reason. The raising of the statue, a masterpiece by Edmé Bouchardon, was a "ritualized expression of the city's submission to the king."[1] In turn, its destruction expressed the city's rejection of kingship, which the decapitation of his son brought to fruition. The scene brings the point home. Charles-Henri Sanson, the figure to the right of the guillotine, holds up the head of

Figure 2.1. The head of Louis XVI is presented to the empty base of the monument to his father. Isidore Stanislas Helman, *Execution of Louis XVI*, engraving by Antoine-Jean Duclos, 1793. Courtesy of the Bibliothèque Nationale de France.

Louis XVI to the crowd. Simultaneously, with a swoosh of his body, he presents the dead king to the dead monument, linking the two, as if to say iconoclasm of the father anticipated decapitation of the son. These are body doubles, made all the more poignant for being bodiless. The royal monument did more than "body forth the absent king": "The real body and the symbolic body, the 'king's two bodies' of French political theory — these the royal monument fused and presented in a tangible, opulent, and public form."[2] Its destruction aimed to sever this bond. The image gives the lie to Robert Musil's line that monuments are invisible, for clearly, they are not.[3] In Paris, even the empty base remained totemically charged. What could be more visible, in fact, than a missing monument?

The rendering of the space abets this reading. The crowd parts for both guillotine and monument, the throng around the first held at bay by a cordon of soldiers some three hundred yards thick, while that around the missing statue is held back mysteriously.[4] Of course, the base would have been an obvious prominence from which to witness the execution, yet no one has scaled it; only a solitary cat, who, sitting like some laughably underscaled sphinx, turns away from the action in a fable about animal wisdom.[5] This aura of space around the twin spectacles is more than a compositional technique. It underscores the fact that the power of the king resided in his physical being, as well as in his effigy. Both had to be destroyed to break the spell of the ancien régime. Iconoclasm was but prequel. The continuous history of iconoclasm speaks to the persistent and uncanny way statues are doppelgangers. What brings this point home most powerfully is the fact that Bouchardon's statue, while acknowledged as an artistic masterpiece, was not carted away to a museum, as many monuments were, but rather was melted into oblivion.[6] As "royal simulacra and bearers of royal memory," statues such as Bouchardon's were too compromised to be seen as mere art. They were "re-presentations of an absent king imposed on the lived space of the city."[7]

A bit of mise en scène in figure 2.1 anchors the king's demise in ancient myth while it opens onto a potential future. In the deep

Figure 2.2. Detail of Pegasus being speared by a bayonet. Isidore Stanislas Helman, *Execution of Louis XVI*, engraving by Antoine-Jean Duclos, 1793. Courtesy of the Bibliothèque Nationale de France.

background, to the right of the forlorn base, a winged horse, a fragment of Mercury Riding Pegasus (Antoine Coysevox, sculptor, 1702), is cut off by the border of the image (fig. 2.2). Pegasus was famously born of the decapitation of Medusa, an obvious parallel to the king. The appearance of Pegasus, a symbol of creativity and purity, suggests that out of the gruesome monstrosity of kingship and the equally monstrous revolution, something pure and beautiful would emerge. Yet the image equivocates: a bayonet inadvertently thrusts at the belly of the horse from beneath. It is a suballegory about the unintended victims of revolution that echoes the destroyed equestrian statue. If these conflicting vignettes were not enough, something intercedes between the point of the bayonet and the Pegasus — a helm perhaps or some bit of military paraphernalia held aloft like a war trophy. Will it be enough to save the Pegasus from being impaled?

This hidden story within the story speaks to the precariousness and complicated reality of the revolution while it draws attention to the nature of bodies, mortal and immortal, monstrous and beautiful, royal and common, dead and alive, all suddenly revealed to be unstable in this moment in which the relationship of bodies to power was in flux — and all told through highly unstable monuments.

In light of the erasure of the royal body and its proxies, the proliferation of monuments to nonroyals in the aftermath of the revolution takes on new meaning. As the German philosopher Karl Jaspers evocatively put it, "the halo round the heads of states had vanished," and new ones took their place.[8] The pantheon of heroes that began to appear in cemeteries — a realm of death — and in parks and public squares replaced the king and other figures of high rank with all sorts of formerly inferior and mortal bodies, from revolutionaries to poets, surrounded with worldly and sometimes mundane attributes, made all the more so by the everyday bodies puddled up around them in daily life. Modern heroes were often represented in modern clothes, some touchingly rumpled and beneath that, as perishable bodies, bodies disengaged from the fixed and God-given inheritance of power. These new statues of exemplary mortals filled up the emerging cities of the nineteenth century. The bronze effigies echoed the royal claims to immortality that the guillotine had cut. To borrow Thomas Laqueur's felicitous phrase, these statues are "not quite dead" — forever.[9] In more positive terms, they cross over into a newly forged intermediate realm between living and dead, a realm formerly occupied by kings and before that by deified emperors, pharaohs, and figures such as Christ and the Virgin. A new afterlife was born, a new immortality invented. In the same period when kings were mortalized, ordinary people were immortalized. Put differently, the rise of the modern memorial accompanied the fall of the old regime and its purportedly enduring royal body. This new pantheon filled up the flaccid space radically emptied by the revolution, the mythic or ideational space between mortal and immortal, the ephemeral and the eternal.[10]

The French Revolution had already attempted to transform these formerly royal spaces and their monuments into celebrations of the event. Their new aspect shows how malleable these symbols and spaces were. Artists such as Jacques-Louis David organized revolutionary rituals, translating religious pageants such as the Passion into secular terms.[11] In the Festival of Châteauvieux in April 1792, David orchestrated "stations" in the manner of Christ's Passion, including the Bastille, now understood explicitly as a monument to the revolution, where he dedicated a statue of "Liberty."[12] At the Place de la Révolution (formerly the Place Louis XV), the statue of Louis XV was blindfolded, four months before it would be sawn off at the legs and removed. To cover the eyes of the former sovereign is a curious move. The gesture mockingly prepared the former eminence for execution while it acknowledged the continued power of his gaze.[13] Such allegorical intervention obscures a deeper level of allegory embodied in the monument itself as a cultural form adopted to smooth over these ruptures with new narratives. As the architectural historian Françoise Choay has argued, the historic monument began as an allegory of patrimony invented to narrate the frightening changes set in motion by the revolution.[14]

It must have been difficult to shake the fear of royal power, much as it was impossible to clear out all of the associations that these spaces continued to foster.[15] With the revolution, people began to think beyond an absolute monarch. A future was summoned and marked with a range of symbols that supplanted the timeless or eternal symbols of royalty. From the start, the new monuments were fundamentally different because they entered a novel temporal stream. The mortal bodies depicted on or implied by them, now severed from divine right, spoke to a different awareness of time, what François Hartog calls a "temporal regime." Louis XV's frozen equestrian statue meshed with a conception of royal time as eternal, unchanging, divine. He lived in a timeline of succession in which past and future were virtually identical. He was melted into a revolutionary timeline that created a radical before — the old regime — and opened into a "not yet," a monumental pivot in time to which these exemplary figures pointed.[16]

The revolutionary festivals recast monuments in space and time. During the festivals, the streets "bore ... the most evident echoes of the past," both of royal and religious processions.[17] Much can be squeezed out of this simple point. The revolutionary pageants and processions were a new conception fitted into the well-worn frameworks and spaces of the old regime. Monuments were tweaked or felled, and new ones were erected. A new pageantry displaced the old ones, but the basic formula of monuments in public space with a choreographed public body remained the same. And why would it be otherwise? Architecture and even more profoundly, cities, are slow to change, while monuments and the temporary costume of festivals are pliable. Modern monuments replaced the vanquished monuments of the old regime, knowing their fate could be the same. As monuments threw darts at the confettilike timeline of modernity, they articulated the chaotic temporal regime that stumbled into existence as the French and Industrial Revolutions altered everyday life.

While the French Revolution was a great historical rupture, it operated as much through emulation of, substitution for, and reference back to the old regime as it did by erasure.[18] To risk a suprahistorical idea, such references to the past were inevitable: people are creatures of habit, both individually and collectively. The past could not be willed away, as some revolutionary thinkers wished: the people could not be taught, as one revolutionary-era writer put it, "to see in a statue only stone and in an image only canvas and colors."[19] In the history of the world, total erasure is rare and usually means genocide. Even the most violent of ruptures—the transatlantic slave trade or the Holocaust—are rife with the sorts of echoes that Richard Sennett sees in the festivals of the revolution, which sought a tabula rasa. Such echoes were all the more powerful after 1789, because the festivals were staged in the same spaces, with many of the same props or types of props as the processions of the dead, saints days, and royal festivals. The transformation from sacred to willfully secular could take place only if monuments were flexible props and if people were still credulous.[20]

When monuments were too slow or costly to build, revolutionary artists such as David turned to imagery (fig. 2.3; see color insert). For instance, David's *Death of Marat* (1793) can be seen as an aborted monument, painted as if the marmoreal Marat had just fallen from his simple temporary pedestal, replete with epitaph, roughly translated as "unable to corrupt me, they assassinated me." In this image

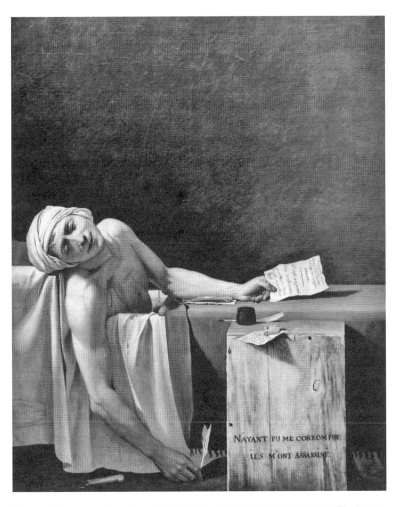

Figure 2.3. A monument manqué. Jacques-Louis David, *Death of Marat*, 1793, The Louvre, Paris.

of assassination cum iconoclasm, monumental tropes abound: the great man with the pen or scroll, the fallen body, the coffinlike bath. These join a variation on the deathbed scene. The white sheet takes the place of painterly drapery, but it can be read doubly as bedsheet and a preemptive unveiling of the monument that never was. Veil becomes shroud. David, moreover, plays with the aesthetics of the ruin or frag-ment, using the bath as a convenient way of decapitating Marat into a morbid bust.

The monumentalization of Marat is an absurdity: a man in a bath — although this would not prevent later artists from trying to do precisely this.[21] What could be more antithetical to the massive equestrian statue to Louis XV masquerading as Peace than a dead, bath-bound revolutionary monumentalized as a fallen monument before it could be erected![22] Before the blood dried. The image is a product of the iconic iconoclasm of the era. Part of its work is to nar-rate the rapid changes.

The monuments that followed the waves of revolution across Europe, especially in the wake of Napoleon's defeat, were thrust into a scene still imbued with Christian and revolutionary mean-ing but also teeming with the commercial and everyday uses that they also sustained.[23] Beyond the rather obvious point that the new monuments were part of the cataclysmic changes in urban form and life of the era, one has to imagine layer upon memorial layer meeting the construction site of the modern city: a Christian and royal foun-dation, the revolutionary subversion, conservative reactions, new national aspirations, local heroes, followed in some places by restora-tions of monarchy and eventually by bourgeois monuments and com-memorative activities all taking their place in the largely commercial milieu of modern urban life. A new secular everyday and a new secu-lar not-everyday — the warp and woof of modern experience — grew out of the revolutionary efforts to subvert the old regime, but many of the same tropes and tricks remained.[24] The age of revolutions was full of burning bushes that spoke and enchanted disenchantments, like the empty base of Louis XV's equestrian statue. That is what these monuments were, even after iconoclasm: burning bushes. It is fair to say that revolutionaries across Europe had monuments on their brain, perhaps because monuments were among the most common, ostentatious, urban gestures of royal power, easy to subvert and iconically potent, both in their subverted state and when replaced. In short, they were labile.

While it is cliché to attribute the foundational mentalities of modernity to the ruptures of the French Revolution, it is cliché for a reason. The story begins here not merely because the old regime crumbled and time began anew, but also because these changes deformed the symbolic order. Monuments would never be the same. To be sure, equestrian statues and the like would continue to be erected in public squares — just look at Washington, DC, or virtually any city with cosmopolitan or political ambitions — but thereafter, they would all have symbolic blindfolds and be one political sea change away from becoming an empty base or nudged to the side. The systematic iconoclasm of the French Revolution sapped the power of the premodern monument and substituted a more pitiful but lovable everyday monument, a historic monument attached no longer to the eternal verities of the old regime, but rather to the secular calendar and the vagaries of modern life and the modern nation, yet still whispering to eternity. At the same time, the link between the real and symbolic body weakened. This is a vital part of the meaning of David's Marat, an eminently mortal body broken before it could be immortalized. An impossible monument. Every monument thereafter would have a little bit of Marat in it.

What the age of revolutions did through outright iconoclasm, urban change achieved through ordinary processes, albeit more subtly. A new kind of monument was coming into being across the nineteenth century, monuments erected in opposition to the monuments of the old regime that nonetheless used many of their formal tropes and placements. At the same time, they entered a greatly transformed, and ever-transforming, urban scene. To borrow Lewis Mumford's useful terms, the "paleotechnic" world gave way to the "neotechnic" cityscape, replete with streetcars and electrical lines, artificial light, a new scale of commercial and industrial architecture, massive infrastructure driven by and built to serve the new technologies, and eventually, automobiles.[25] The old monuments would survive, and of course, not every place in Europe and the United States was on the same schedule, but across the middle decades of the nineteenth century, the erection of public monuments became an artistic, political, and social phenomenon in its own right, linked to the rise of the bourgeois liberal state.[26]

A statuemania swept across European cities, with Paris taking the lead. In the French capital, statues of more or less contemporary figures filled parks, squares, and the remaindered spaces created by Haussmann's urban planning.[27] Paris became an outdoor pantheon of cultural and revolutionary heroes, most of them tied to national events, patriotic sentiment, and culture. Sergiusz Michalski has called this "art in political bondage." But the new memorials were also tied into the vast urban transformations of the period, particularly schemes of beautification or *embellisement* — memory in artistic bondage at an urban scale. In Germany, an analogous *Denkmalkultur* developed, with the heroes of German unification erected throughout the young nation.[28] Hundreds of Bismarck statues still populate German towns, and unlike in France, massive monuments loom over the countryside. Similar stories can be told for most European nations, and because of the rapid colonization of the same period, much of the world.

In the United States, parallel urges guided the memorialization of revolutionary and Civil War heroes, cultural figures, and, increasingly, historical figures sponsored by ethnic communities. The plethora of statues to Columbus, to take one now controversial example, speaks to the way this phenomenon took different forms in different places. So thoroughgoing was this trend that statuemania gave rise to statuephobia, and *Denkmalkultur* was met by *Denkmalskritik*, sometimes leading to iconoclastic acts of destruction.[29] By the end of the nineteenth century, memorials were entangled in artistic battles in a rapidly shifting art world, entwined in urban agendas of improvement, and embroiled in political debates while still being attached to commemoration. They became increasingly complicated objects, both sacred and profane, highly charged and ordinary, and constantly shifting between these states.

The unstable urban scene and political insecurity of the period intensified the malleability of the memorial as a cultural form. The age of revolution begun in the United States and France in the eighteenth century reverberated through the next century across the globe, but particularly in Europe, churning up countless memorials that go straight to just how complicated the emerging commemorative regime was. In Italy, unified as a nation by tumultuous revolution only in 1871, memorials played a prominent role in reinventing local and national identity. An example in Verona is emblematic of the surprisingly complex meaning that seemingly simple monuments can have. In this small city with an abundance of monuments to Romeo and Juliet, a prominent, great-man memorial sits on the Piazza Pradaval, a major square on one of the largest arteries leading into the medieval core of the city (fig. 2.4). When I happened upon it in 2007, it gave up little information. Even the name was missing.[30] It was erected by the society of fine arts and the commune in 1874, just thirteen years after Italy had gained its independence. Whoever this statue commemorated, it had been part of the army of memorials erected in Italy in the aftermath of the Risorgimento, or Italian unification, including the *glossatori* in Bologna. They invoked tradition in an attempt to endow the shallow reality of the new and fragile nation with a deeper history, much in keeping with the range of invented traditions that appeared in this period.[31] Who was this unidentified, long-dead Veronese powerful enough to help narrate the rise of modern Italian identity? Guidebooks revealed nothing. Until recently, Google Maps drew a blank. When I asked a local writer who had written about Verona's history, she confessed ignorance. Some days later, after digging into her library, she came up with a name: Michele Sanmicheli.[32]

Figure 2.4. A monument as clubhouse for teenagers. Giovanni Battista Troiani, Sanmicheli Monument, 1874, Verona, Italy. Photograph by the author.

The name rang a bell. Sanmicheli, the leading Veronese architect of the sixteenth century, was responsible for fortifying the city,
including building the bastion and its monumental gateways, as well
as a number of grand *palazzi*. The placement of the statue was anything but random. It lay at the confluence of streets along the grand
Corso Vittorio Emanuele that began at Sanmicheli's Porto Nuova
(1533–51) and decanted at the Roman arena in the heart of the old
city, where an equestrian statue of the emperor would be erected
in 1883. In drawing attention to Sanmicheli's contribution to the
city's historical infrastructure and Rome, the statue linked a vision
of former greatness with the aspirations of modern Verona, which
hinged on the installation of modern infrastructure. For much of the
sixteenth century, the city had been under the power of the Holy
Roman emperors, who envisioned it as a stronghold in Northern
Italy. Sanmicheli had presided over this period of prosperity. Here
was a local genius and hero, one worth monumentalizing as a symbol
of the greatness of Verona and specifically linked to earlier moments
of infrastructural transformation.

The meaning of Sanmicheli's contributions went beyond mere
civic pride. The modest statue might seem like a world away from
Bouchardon's Louis XV, yet it is part of the aftershock of the French
Revolution and the system of monumental representation unleashed
by it. The speech given at the statue's inauguration threw Sanmicheli
into the "sacred Pantheon" of Italian revolutionaries and cultural
heroes, the ones who would en masse replace the kings (and in this
case, popes) of the old regime and flood the streets of modern cities.[33] The author assembled a mighty roster: Manzoni, Cavour, and
Dante (to whom the city had erected a statue in 1865), improbably
adding Pliny, who was thought to be a native son, as well as nonnatives da Vinci, Correggio, Cimabue, Pisano, and Caracci. A fulsome
tribute to an architect whose statue would lapse into anonymity.
But in the 1870s, the stakes were enormous, rather like France's in
the 1790s. Those nations that forget the great figures of the past, the
inauguration speech asserted, "are not worthy of liberty."[34] Memory

and liberty, the very freedom that dawned with the execution of Louis XVI, were fused and articulated through monuments. By the time Sanmicheli's statue rose in Verona, the narrow sense of the monument as a discrete commemorative intervention had joined a capacious sense of historic monuments of all sorts.[35] History became a tool for tethering past greatness to future possibilities, the "before" and open-ended "not yet" that the revolution had unlocked.[36] That is what the now down-on-his-luck Sanmicheli once meant.

Sanmicheli rose alongside other flirtations with history. Verona, like many European cities in this period, was being transformed by a wave of preservation. Highly selective elements of its past were brought forward, and more recent layers that the early restorers devalued and saw as obstructions were cleared out. About the time that Italy established its independence, "the image of Verona shifted from a Roman city, known for its classical monuments, to a medieval town" whose medieval monuments rapidly underwent restoration.[37] The years surrounding the erection of the statue to Sanmicheli witnessed the restoration of several major churches and the Casa dei Mercanti (1878–84), Loggia di Fra Giocono (1874), Palazzo del Comune (1877), and other buildings that formed the core of medieval Verona.[38] These joined the astounding Scaliger Tombs, a possible inspiration for Rubbiani's *glossatori* tombs in Bologna. This medieval revival opened up a wider appreciation of historic monuments, Sanmicheli's later baroque contributions among them. The new statues of Dante and Vittorio-Emanuele, as well as Aleardo Aleardi (1883), Garibaldi (1887), Veronese (1888), Umberto I (1906), and Cavour (1908) punctuated the city's squares. Sanmicheli's *simulacro*, as the speech called it, was part of this wider retrospective turn and recasting of the city's image. Verona, like Paris — and so many other cities striving for a cosmopolitan image — was becoming an outdoor museum.

Yet his statue tells us none of this, and part of the reason is that statues, historic monuments, and memorials were already being blurred, absorbed into wider urban and historical processes. Statues of this highly conventional type arrived on the scene as pliable forms ready to serve many roles. Their afterlife is vivid. The once-iconic Sanmicheli has become anonymous. Teenagers have adopted the monument, layering the old architect with graffiti (fig. 2.5) — a parallel to the love notes other teenagers deposit in Juliet's fraudulent tomb. What a contrast to the illustration from 1874, which shows the public held at a polite distance by the railing (fig. 2.6).

Across Europe, monuments like this attract groups who valorize their own marginality. In their everyday life, such statues seem to help anchor adolescents as they move from the private, sheltered, and highly controlled world of the home to the public, exposed, and more open-ended world of adulthood.[39] The personal transition thus finds a spatial or formal analogue in the indecisive monument. As teenagers mark it up with the insignias of their emerging individuality, they elevate and individualize the forgotten or ignored memorial. It is not quite a monument to them, but it is their monument. In the process, they have transformed it, rather like blindfolding Louis XV. Like the surrealists who were fascinated with Parisian monuments and played with the vacillating boundary between their iconic and ironic status, the teenagers in Verona seem to intuit some faint residual power in Sanmicheli, a power they put to use as they subvert it with graffiti and wine bottles.

This residual aura makes memorials examples of hierophany, Mircea Eliade's neologism for those moments and places where the sacred erupts through the surface tension of everyday life. The aforementioned burning bush in the Old Testament is one of the most widely known examples. Most monuments are intended to be hierophanic, but nothing can sustain the ecstasy of hierophany at all times or forever.[40] This is why many memorials as spatial interventions are reinforced with the temporal intervention of a sacred day. Such gatherings maintain what Erving Goffman calls "interaction tonus," a focusing and tightening of attention, an "aliveness" to the solemnity of the site and moment.[41] They extend the formality and seriousness of commemoration to an ordinary setting or wake up a slumbering monument.

Figure 2.5. Graffiti on the Sanmicheli Monument, 2007. Photograph by the author.

Figure 2.6. Sanmicheli Monument as one "room" in Verona's outdoor museum, from *Nuova Illustrazione Universale*, year 1, vol. 2, no. 40, August 16, 1874. Author's collection.

Sanmicheli has likely not achieved interaction tonus for decades. He is indefinitely dormant, incapable of meaningful eruption. But his teens are playing with some lingering sense of his solemnity: the knowledge we have in the presence of a formal statue on a plinth that we should be respectful, even if it is turned off. Goffman might have added that the adolescents, who are "ceremonially speaking . . . not complete persons," demonstrate the opposite of interaction tonus, a way of thumbing their noses at the monument's pretense and by extension the rules of adult society.[42] The statue's dim aura offers just enough formality for playful subversion. Here the teens can demonstrate publicly what Goffman calls "situational presence," the call in any given situation for a person to be engrossed. In Verona, their situational presence flouts the situational presence demanded by the larger urban scene.[43] They are in their Sanmicheli bubble, a temporary social cell nearly as coherent as Memorial Day. Ensconced in their own world, they are pointedly oblivious to what surrounds them. This "failure to exhibit 'presence' is a normal, understandable expression of alienation from, and hostility to, the gathering itself," the gathering being the public space in Verona.[44]

Yet the setting is as much a player in this drama as the statue. It turns out that the Piazza Pradaval is a well-known site for drug dealers and homeless people.[45] The memorial, which sits on the piazza's edge, allows teenagers to enter this urban scene tangentially, to dip into it visually, to act out in their own way, using the monument both as a link and as a haven that keeps them separate. The Sanmicheli monument draws these lines in another, subtler way, as well, namely, as a shape shifter. Since many memorials are "on" only at special times, pausing their commemorative duties and resting in the form of civic ornament, their status is changeful. Being neither this nor that, the anonymous Sanmicheli represents something ambiguous, something easily ignored, especially in the rush of everyday life. In this role, it becomes a place for acting out, a place in between for a population in between childhood and adulthood. This liminal status invites graffiti, tagging the memorial as forsaken or neglected ground. In this way, the area around the monument takes on some of the same qualities of the memorial itself.

This betweenness might be seen as awkward, a social problem for adults, making the area a place to be avoided, which adds a repulsiveness to a site originally meant to harbor higher sentiments or to do important cultural work. In turn, the process is part of a course of decadence, which over time has undermined the expectations of the monument as permanent, unchanging, and dignified. However, this betweenness is also an asset, since it shelters (most often harmlessly) a segment of the population without a strong institutional or commercial base in the city. It gives them a boundary with which to play in breaking modest taboos at a public monument and performing their adolescence publicly under the symbolic shadow of a neglected monument. This is to say that the cloak of invisibility that overtakes memorials over time extends to the adolescents who frequent them, so that they behave as if they are almost invisible in its orbit. Paradoxically, at the same time, the mundane memorial takes on an aura; it reacquires the potential for hierophany, or at least enchantment. It becomes once again a place apart, removed from everyday life. The Sanmicheli monument no longer speaks to a resurgent Verona or Italian nationalism, but it has great utility as an everyday object. It provides a place to meet or sit, a bit of shade, and perhaps most importantly, symbolic shelter.

What happens in Verona is part of a much wider European phenomenon. In fact, there is some evidence that the practice goes back a long way. As one midcentury journalist noted, following an Italian court case in 1961: "Adventurous Italian youngsters risk jail every evening to have long kisses of delight in the shadow of walls and monuments."[46] It seems clear that the writer means a broader sense of "monument," including buildings such as the Pantheon and Colosseum, but this hardly ruins the point, since the revolution blurred these categories. The prohibition was handed down by judicial decree: "Public kissing was against the law in Rome" and could "land you in jail."[47] Interdiction, of course, is a potent seducer. One can well imagine the seriousness, and not just the beauty, of these monuments in postwar Italy adding to the thrill. Why lovers sought out monuments and why a law was deemed necessary at that moment is beyond the scope of this book, but it demonstrates just how easily monuments are absorbed into behaviors and contexts that are unmonumental.[48] Although such laws are now defunct, modern conditions have done little to change the practice.[49]

Even the most stolid, stubborn, and stonily permanent monuments can melt into Baudelairean mutability. A simple kiss will do. To construe monuments as threatened by amorousness, graffiti, or loitering—a policy instituted in 2019 in Rome forbids people from sitting on the Spanish Steps—is to imagine rescuing them from the everyday. To reconstitute their not-everydayness serves the agendas of tourism or urban design, which in a city such as Verona are nearly synonymous, and this in turn refashions them as assets.[50] When a monument such as Sanmicheli's slumps into a thoroughly everyday status, it is often seen as blighted and enters a technocratic protocol that aims to restore it to some imagined former glory.[51] It is now common to understand monuments in terms of the aesthetic demands of tourism and consumption. Historic monuments are overtaken by the history concession and lose their specific historical meaning.[52] They are understood as a form of aesthetic and economic infrastructure tied to the fortunes of the city. The Sanmicheli monument is a problem only insofar as it is part of a scene that turns off tourists to the Piazza Pradaval and darkens the mood of the historic, that is, tourist, core of Verona.

Everywhere monuments are treated as infrastructure in a vast system of urban management, and this is part of the volatility of their meaning. For instance, the Florentine monument to the *caduti*, or fallen, of the Battle of Mentana of 1867 (erected in 1902) is now a parking lot for Vespas, formalized by the city's parking authority (fig. 2.7). Here the Italian revolution seems to have lost a battle to the Industrial Revolution in a city meticulously preserved to block out modern scenes so that tourists can suspend disbelief and imagine themselves walking with

Figure 2.7. A soldier battling Vespas and losing at Oreste Calzolari's Monument to the Fallen of the Battle of Mentana, 1902, Florence, Italy. Photograph by the author.

the Medicis. The truth is that both the monument and the Vespas are disturbing anachronisms in Florence, and this site on the edge of the old city marginalizes both just enough to protect the real assets nearby. Throughout Europe, disused monuments serve as parking areas, their sturdy railings used to lock bikes. This is not quite a resocialization of the monument, as in Verona; it is more a concession to reality.

Understood as infrastructure, memorials begin to look and behave differently. In Danville, Illinois, urban change transmogrified Peace into an "unattractive back." A World War I memorial (1921–22) by the prominent sculptor Lorado Taft, it was a late City Beautiful intervention that created an urban vignette in which people were ushered into town on the newly built Victory Bridge and greeted by Peace (fig. 2.8). By the 1940s, when a new wave of memorialization was

UNATTRACTIVE BACK

Figure 2.8. Peace's posterior. Lorado Taft, Peace Monument, 1921–22, Danville, Illinois. From "Unattractive Back," *Architectural Forum* 82 (January 1945), p. 38.

being considered throughout the country, the memorial had come to seem bedraggled and outmoded — not a good thing for Peace in a time of war. This prompted one critic of traditional memorials to quip that it turned "its unattractive back to everyone entering the city. Lorado Taft was the designer but I have seen him blush as he looked at it."[53] Taft had been dead almost a decade, but the point of the apocryphal story is that a civic monument had become an urban eyesore. In Danville, the actual infrastructure — the bridge — forced people entering the town to observe Peace from behind. While the writer's judgment is mockingly prudish, it was part of the rhetorical iconoclasm aimed at traditional memorials in an era that had come to see them as vulgar, indulgent, and moribund. Peace was aging infrastructure, and, as will become clear later, senescence is a great sin for memorials.

That sin amounts to a transgression of assumed boundaries. The corruption of Peace, if not of innumerable statues similar to Sanmicheli's, is perhaps best understood through a more literal analogy to infrastructure failing. When people turn on faucets in their houses, the predictable and dependable flow of water is really a form of nature domesticated. The complex, invisible network of treatment, conveyance, and delivery, as if by magic, brings water into our sinks and showers, toilets and gardens. When this system fails, when sewage backs up in a kitchen sink or bathroom, for example, the home instantly becomes a staging ground for an encounter between culture and reviled nature as the discarded and unwanted seep in and turn the familiar and protected into something monstrous and repulsive. The foul intrusion overturns the domestication of water, including the strict visual, aural, and especially olfactory separation of home from plumbing infrastructure on which it is predicated. The modern understanding of the home as distinct from unruly nature is thrown into doubt. Home is violated, faith in the system that kept it separate is compromised, and the domestication of the human species also is thrown into doubt.[54] This argument hinges on the observation that the *idea* of the home maintains a boundary, holding the domestic sphere apart from unwanted processes or parts of nature itself, even if the house is ultimately dependent on the nature it obscures. The simultaneous "need and denial of the connection of the home to socio-natural processes turns the material manifestations (networks, pipes, etc.) of this connection into the domestic uncanny that surfaces during moments of crisis. In these moments, the continuity of the social and material processes that produce the domestic space is unexpectedly foregrounded, bringing the dweller of the modern home face to face with his/her alienation."[55]

If memorials are seen as commemorative infrastructure or even as the fixtures that emerge out of the commemorative processes of society, they, too, are a form of boundary (as opposed to merely an object) fraught with complexity. Perhaps this is why aging memorials have been dismissed as useless, extravagant, wasteful, a form of urban clutter, and other pejoratives meant to disparage them for the odd, inverted existence they often live out.[56] Revealing Peace's profane nature drew attention to three important elements of the monument's transformation: its ugliness, its impropriety, and

Taft's emotional response. The formal shortcomings of the memorial were tied to disgust, linking its failure to the flow of people into the city. As a failed faucet for commemoration — revealing its rump, instead of some noble quality — it encountered the everyday infrastructure of circulation awkwardly. While this hardly turned Peace into an overflowing toilet, the effect is not so different, rousing shame. Taft's blush stands in for the embarrassment of all citizens. The failure of outdated and ill-placed memorial infrastructure created a new flow of sentiment. Similar jarring emotions seem to leak out of poorly functioning commemorative infrastructure throughout the world.

Peace aged poorly in the twentieth century. But what about memorials to the most haunting traumas served up by modernity? Berlin's Memorial to the Murdered Jews of Europe, a memorial that asks us never to forget one of the most horrific events of human history, is also embroidered with the forgettable trifles of everyday life. People use the large blocks for yoga and parkour, play hide and seek there, and pose for ordinary pictures (fig. 2.9).[57] The memorial immediately settled into its role as tourism infrastructure. It became a popular place for gay men to take selfies to post on online dating services.[58] If a site as solemn and raw as Germany's most high-profile Holocaust memorial can be both casual *and* imbued with high feeling, then all memorials are open-ended affairs.

While this might seem obvious to anyone who has seen old memorials molder or observed the daily tempest that surrounds them, their changefulness is interesting because it seems fundamental to their meaning. This changefulness contradicts the permanence so often sought of them, yet it is part of what brought them into existence in the first place. This is to say that their bid for permanence is so clearly at odds with modernity — what Baudelaire called "the ephemeral, the fugitive, the contingent" — that many memorials draw attention to this very tension.[59] "Never forget" quickly becomes "Meet me for a drink." Berlin is an extreme. Quieter examples can be found all over the world. At Munich's Monument to the Bavarians Who Died

Figure 2.9. Jumping for joy at Peter Eisenman's Memorial to the Murdered Jews of Europe, 2004, Berlin. Photograph by Valentina Rozas-Krause.

in Russia (1833), a woman spends her lunch hour reading in its shade, while a man teaches a boy about its meaning (fig. 2.10).

Traditional memorials such as Munich's obelisk are often maligned for being antiquated, part of tradition, *un*modern. Beneath the most illustrious attempts to discredit monuments as archaic lurks their sneaky mutability and their significance. Robert Musil's quip that there is nothing as invisible as a monument inadvertently gets at this. They are invisible — sometimes. Other times, they come alive: during commemorations, when political tides turn, or simply when they are co-opted for other purposes. In the same register as Musil, Lewis Mumford's denigration of monuments ("if it is a monument, it cannot be modern, and if it is modern, it cannot be a monument") is paradigmatically modernist.[60] From his vantage point in the late

1930s, he could not see just how modern monuments are in their own right, how they pin down an alternative modernity, akin to antimodernism, which itself is an antithesis possible only as part of modernism. In consigning them to a musty premodernity, Mumford seemed content to see modern memorials as indistinct from their ancient ancestors, which is to say that he saw them ahistorically, almost like a reintroduction of dinosaurs. He is easily forgiven; a healthy fear of fascism obscured his view.[61] We now see more clearly that reintroductions, inventions of tradition, even fascist ones, are quintessentially modern.[62] Such historicism is an original strand in the braid of modern culture. If the backward glances of modernity, the revivals and attempts to "breed back," are dismissed as merely escapist, reactionary, or regressive, we risk recapitulating the heroic (and mostly erroneous) stance of modernist autonomy—a stance that would be impossible without historicism. Once seen as springing from antagonistic conceptions of time, modernism and historicism are an inseparable part of the dialectic of modernity.

Part of what makes traditional monuments modern is their contrarianism, their move to hold change at bay or carve out a spot where capital cannot have its way. Even a memorial as relentlessly contemporary in its form as Berlin's Holocaust memorial behaves like many traditional memorials. This *otherwise* posture is physical and urbanistic. Memorials often stand quite literally in the way. The posture is also stylistic. They often look like they come from a different era. Eventually, all of them do. Unlike buildings, they are infrequently renovated or modernized. Consequently, they inject discordant temporal modes into the stream of everyday life. A historical event or a bid for mythic timelessness enters into the rush of commercial time. Monuments would have nothing to oppose if not for the modern habit, and a mentality, of marching forward, despising tradition, devaluing the permanent, valorizing movement and speed. Of course, even as they posture toward permanence, timelessness, and the not-everyday, they change unpredictably, mark time ambiguously, and change lanes, weaving in and out of the everyday. Instead of maintaining

Figure 2.10. Lunch break at Leo Von Klenze's Monument to the Bavarians Who Died in Russia, 1833, Munich. Photograph by the author.

some fictive boundary, memorials demonstrate a profound porosity, an almost infinite gradient of experience that comes out of the frictions between them and their surroundings and, as a later chapter in this book explores, out of how we behave around them.

With Berlin and Munich in mind, Musil and Mumford beg for revision. The 2,711 concrete slabs at Peter Eisenman's memorial in Berlin cannot be invisible to the inhabitants of the scene, but for many of them, they meander in and out of view. For some visitors, the memorial is sacred or didactic, while for others, it is just a photo op, a big thing in a park, an impediment to getting somewhere, a massive piece of tourist infrastructure that requires regular maintenance. It is all of these things and all of them at once. It is an indisputably monumental work in a ferociously modern scene. If an abstract monument such as this can function so dynamically, imagine the mutability of a throwback such as an equestrian statue or an obelisk, with its more complicated way of registering time. This is to say that memorials play with the x and y axes of experience, destabilizing time and place.

This chapter easily could have been broken down into these two realms, but that would have teased out what comes to us already woven. Temporal experience is spatial. Metaphors for time tend to be spatial, and this is not just a linguistic preference. Places shape the possibilities of action, and action is plotted in space. This means that the atomic elements of historical time — events — come into being cogged to their scenes, as well as to the human and nonhuman bodies that are doing things in them: shooting, shouting, suturing, nurturing, remembering. The reverse is axiomatic: spatial experience is temporal.[63] The historical relationship between the two is beyond the scope of this book, but suffice it to say that it, too, is changeful and that this changefulness provides the fissure that memorials have been thrust into as objects that intervene with our sense of time in space.

The meaning of this placement, the establishment and breaking of these boundaries, is the subject of the next four chapters. From one angle, memorial placement is a practical matter of municipal committees and other governing bodies who have to reconcile it with the many considerations of urban management; from another point of view, it is a cultural act of immense consequences. Just beyond the corruptible boundaries of the Holocaust memorial in Berlin or even Danville's Peace lies one of the pivotal boundaries of human experience, that between life and death, a border patrolled by memorials.[64] This is part of the work of memorials, to help the living fathom or obscure their relationship to death. Memorials help the dead speak, and this is intertwined with how people reconstitute time and the everyday, all while these three constituent parts of culture — death, time, and the everyday — have been relentlessly in flux, arguably never more so than in modern times. Where we attempt to paralyze the hand of oblivion, as William Godwin put it in the epigraph to this chapter, is all important, even when the place seems incidental.

CHAPTER THREE

Placing Memory:

Cemeteries and Parks

Memory has a heavy backspin, yet it's still impossible
to land exactly where we took off.
—Colum McCann, *Zoli*, 2006

The way memorials look, their commemorative value, and their
political uses have obscured the equally important issue of where
they land. Their meaning is indivisible from the way they are placed,
displaced, and herded together. At first blush, it sounds trite to
argue that their meaning is geographical, since every thing exists
in a dynamic relationship with its place in the world. Yet things are
not what they seem. From proto-Germanic words like *thingam*,
meaning "assembly," "council," and "discussion," things have their
roots in action, communication, and space. There is no thing without its corresponding behavior, and there is no behavior without
its corresponding place. Just as the etymology of "thing" contains
the hidden spatial and public dimension of the word, the place of
memorials, their *thingam*, reveals concealed meanings. The next five
chapters attempt to restore the older sense of "thing" to memorials.
The account begins by studying conventions of placement alongside their formal conventions as objects in the cultural landscape. To
place is to plot, to initiate a story or even a conspiracy on the ground.
By unpacking two major conventions of memorial placement — the

cemetery and the park—this chapter digs up buried plotlines of modern memorialization. To understand these veiled narratives of memory, we have to begin not with memorials or their place, but rather with death, the thing that so many memorials attempt to reconcile or transmute into another form.

In early modern Europe, about half of all people died before they reached age eight, many dying in their first year of life (fig. 3.1). The other half of the population died more or less evenly across the human life span. In other words, people had even odds of surviving childhood. The "black wall" of death in figure 3.1 was simply a fact of everyday life.[1] Old age had virtually no demographic basis before 1870; in fact, the idea of a life span scarcely existed. This morbid reality powerfully shaped worldviews in early modern Europe. But something changed rapidly and permanently around 1870. If death were charted in the century after 1870, that black wall would move to the other side of the chart. People came to live in a world, our world, where most of their friends follow an expected arc of life and begin to get picked off en masse in a twilight massacre of old age. Most Europeans today needn't fret about war, famine, and disease, the foundation stones of a premodern worldview. They have been born into an age in which death has been revolutionized by mass immunization, superabundant food, and relative peace, war having been exported from the Euro-American theater.

1870 is a pinprick on a time line, too precise to be experienced. But across the nineteenth century, the experience of death and life shifted decisively, ushering in the idea of a life span as part of a horizon of expectation. What did people experience as they paced out that horizon? Regime change. Alongside the political revolutions of the period, land was transformed; trains, telegraphs and telephones, then cars, and finally planes shattered the relationship of space and time. Population grew exponentially, and with that, cities. Monuments appeared everywhere to narrate these changes and celebrate the heroes that made it all happen. As the experience of life and

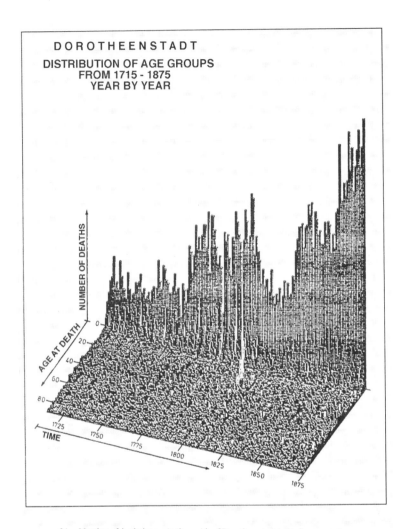

34. Number of deaths by age in the parish of Dorotheenstadt in Berlin, 1715–1875. Total number of deaths: 39,251 (100%). Age 0–1: 12,193 (31.1%); age 1–8; 7,664 (19.5%); age 0–8: 19,857 (50.6%). *Source:* ongoing study using the death registers of the parish of Dorotheenstadt in Berlin, Evangelisches Zentralarchiv, Berlin (West), and the databank in the Friedrich-Meinecke-Institut of the Free University Berlin.

Figure 3.1. Chart of mortality patterns, Berlin parish of Dorotheenstadt, 1715–1875. From Arthur Imhof, *Lost Worlds: How Our European Ancestors Coped with Everyday Life and Why Life is So Hard Today* (Charlottesville: University of Virgina Press, 1996), fig. 34, p. 165. Courtesy of Verlag C. H. Beck.

death in everyday life in Europe was turned upside down, statues of great men, almost all of them dead, many of them martyrs or war dead, arose in cities. Memorials had appeared earlier. Lists of the dead were inscribed on monuments after the Napoleonic wars, but these were men who had been born and died in a world of ubiquitous plague, famine, and war, the deadly trio of grim reapers in the early modern period. In Kaiserslautern, Germany, the red names took their place on a memorial in the city cemetery, one of the new dedicated dormitories for the dead, but a place of death all the same. (See figure p.1.) They and their families were habituated to what for most people today would be untimely death. For them, it was ordinary, however traumatic it may have been. By the Franco-Prussian War, or the Civil War in the United States, such death was becoming uncommon — not-everyday. By World War I, it had become exceptional, perverse, inexplicable . . . unnatural.

This revolution in death was a spike in a gentler, slower change that had been creeping along since at least the 1770s, when Enlightenment rationality had challenged what historian Thomas Laqueur calls the "old regime" of death.[2] Without putting too fine a point on it, as death was being transformed into a clinical, rather than a spiritual matter, as medicine wrested control of the dead body from the priesthood, monuments began to appear in great numbers. As survival into adulthood moved from being a coin toss to a new regime in which a long life was standard and early death an anomaly, as "death lost its role in a cosmic drama," monuments entered the public realm in new and compelling ways.[3] Soon, the old regime, in which a short earthly life was followed by an infinite afterlife, gave way to a new regime with a long earthly life and nothing beyond.[4] The sweet hereafter would slowly shrink into secular oblivion across the late nineteenth and early twentieth centuries. The pantheon of effigies erected roughly from the post-Napoleonic period through the aftermath of World War I absorbed this shift, transferring the onus of a vanishing forever onto great men (and many common ones) and their earthly achievements, rather than on a metaphysical afterlife. Greatness, moral transcendence, and, at the risk of echoing the circularity of some historiography, history itself "created a new enchantment of the dead."[5] This is the metaphysical work of monuments.

No wonder the glorious new monuments were irksome. Statue-mania and statuephobia, the Janus faces of memory in this period, align with this flip in death, with the stirring discomfort of an increasingly secular world. These effigies became both desirable and anathema just as death was spirited out of the public realm and rein-stitutionalized in hospitals and cemeteries. Monuments were being asked, in Laqueur's words, "to patrol the borders between the living and the dead."[6] Of course, not every Lincoln or Bismarck, Balzac or Goethe, is a dead man stalking the living. Committees never sat around tables in some compensatory mood plotting to interject effigies of dead people into the public sphere. The countless statues erected in cities in this period were not first and foremost under-stood as dead bodies. Yet context rallies hard for a deeper reading. Monuments to "great men" first appeared in the new cemeteries of the era, and these monuments derived their forms from familiar funerary traditions. The obelisks, columns, arches, tombs, and other forms erected first as funerary monuments were translated into nonfunerary monuments, often within the context of the cemetery. Soon, the funerary followed the monument out of the cemetery.

In a harbinger of things to come, the French Enlightenment had turned to classicism, often in stripped-down form, abstracting their heroes to express a world of oaths, commitments, idealism, sacrifice, and the transformation of private tragedy into political causes.[7] The French Revolution tethered monuments to death. The king was truly dead and the old regime vanquished only when his statue was totally eradicated. Americans followed similar paths, despite the distinctly different setting in which the Enlightenment unfolded.[8] The intellectual revolution of the Enlightenment drew parallels between natural history and human history and did so explicitly through the idea of monuments. For instance, the Comte de Buffon wrote: "As in civil History written documents are consulted, so in Natural History it is necessary to rummage through the archives of the world, to draw from the bowels of the earth old monuments.["]9 As early naturalists such as Buffon scoured the world, and prominently the "New World," for specimens that would rewrite the earth's history, the leading figures of the Enlightenment in both France and the young United States studied the empirical debris of the classical world, also to measure time or to give measure to their own time vis-à-vis these markers of another age.[10] They did this in a fertile transatlantic dialogue.

Americans overcame an early resistance to commemorative monuments and began to erect them in the beginning of the nineteenth century. Monuments, as a flexible metaphor, were tied to the idea of revolution, simultaneously in human affairs, natural history, time, and, through actual monuments, death. These multiplying links between nature, politics, and culture were reinforced in the emerging built environment of American cities. For instance, most Americans by the mid-nineteenth century would have understood the obelisk of the Washington Monument, then still unfinished, from visiting those cemeteries that marked the new regime of death's transformation of the cultural landscape. The modern regime of death and the modern monument grew up together, whether death was explicit, allegorized, abstracted, or symbolized. By the end of the century, the death masks used as the basis of some statues, including Saint-Gaudens's Sherman — Saint-Gaudens himself visited Sherman's body two days after he died — made the connection explicit. The artist and his world were not yet in the hold of the death taboo that became such a powerful force in the twentieth century. For Saint-Gaudens's generation, death was still a sweet hereafter, and the army of effigies that had begun to populate cities was not yet a zombie apocalypse, least of all martyrs such as Lincoln.

As Europeans and Americans tried to figure out how to handle death in the context of modern life, they placed many of the new monuments in two novel landscapes: the cemetery and the park. The modern cemetery was aesthetically, ideologically, and urbanistically a stark departure from the old burial grounds attached to churches. It leaned on a long tradition of elegy that located death metaphorically in pastoral landscapes. The urban park was surprisingly close in spirit to the new cemetery. It was conceived as an antidote to the city, its natural antithesis. These two eminently modern landscapes rapidly, as quickly as the shift in Imhof's chart, became default places for monuments. There was nothing natural about this placement, as contemporaries noted, but death itself was becoming unnatural. Just as elegy as a cultural form puts the dead in their place as a means of reconciliation with death itself, memorials have been a cultural form useful for reconciling the highly volatile modern experience of death. Where they did this work, and not just their form, is at the root of how they did it.[11]

Churchyards and Cemeteries

The story could begin with any of the innumerable memorials found commonly in cemeteries the world over. So common is this convention that we have lost sight of it as a modern custom, an inflection of a changing cultural landscape. The Confederate memorial erected at Old St. John's Church in Hampton, Virginia, in 1902 reveals both the emergence of the new habit and the changing space it inhabited (fig. 3.2). On the face of it, the old church is a fitting place. The funerary and religious context repatriated the war's dead metaphorically with the dead of their hometown. It linked them with a major institution, the church, that was central to spiritual and social life in the period, tying practices of Civil War commemoration to larger rituals surrounding life and death. Simultaneously, it offered a quasi-public setting without surrendering the memorial to a completely secular site.[12] All the more so at Old St. John's, a colonial congregation founded in 1610 whose present building dates, with much reconstruction, to 1728. The old church had the gravitas to counterbalance the unfathomable cataclysm of the Civil War, which left Hampton in ruin.

Of course, the story is more complicated. Hampton was no ordinary town during the war and Old St. John's no ordinary church. While the town sided with the Confederacy, the Union controlled nearby Fort Monroe. Defending the town was fruitless. In 1861,

Figure 3.2. This Civil War memorial was a novelty when it was erected in Old St. John's Church Cemetery, 1902, Hampton, Virginia. Postcard from the author's collection.

Confederate soldiers chased Union troops away, emptied the town of its white residents — Blacks residents took to the woods nearby or took refuge at Fort Monroe — and in an act of "heroic arson," burned it, including the church, whose walls remained standing as the only recognizable building in town (fig. 3.3).[13] When residents returned in 1865, they found a "shacky, jerry-built" town "reduced to a mass of dreary ruins sprinkled about with squalid lean-tos and squatter camps."[14] The church, moreover, had a messy history before the Civil War. It had been all but abandoned after the War of 1812 and then revived and restored by a different denomination in the 1820s. It was anything but a stable setting. Still, the white residents who returned had little else but its charred ruins. By 1902, when the memorial was erected, cemeteries and churchyards had become standard places for war memorials for Northerners and Southerners alike.[15]

In fact, the convention dates at least to the Napoleonic era in Europe, spread around the world, and has continued into the twenty-first

Figure 3.3. St. John's Church in ruin, 1862, Hampton, Virginia. Photograph by Matthew Brady. Courtesy of the Library of Congress.

century. Yet before the memorial was built in Old St. John's church-yard, only graves and their simple markers graced its bumpy lawn, with a few more ostentatious funeral monuments that came into vogue later in the nineteenth century. What saved the Confederate memorial from being an interloper? It stood amid the graves of 150 Confederate soldiers. It was a novelty addressing a radically new situation thrust into an established setting with which it had an affinity.

Hampton's memorial marks a transition from the old burial ground to the modern cemetery. It shows the emergence of a convention of placing "memory." Into the mid-nineteenth century, most people in the United States and Europe were interred in burial grounds. "Stinking quagmires" and "shunned places of horror," they were often temporary.[16] Graves were personal, private, and familial but just as often anonymous and mass. Hampton's memorial, by contrast, is an entirely different marker: public, civic, national and local, and highly political. In situating Civil War commemoration in a church graveyard, Hampton and other towns passed over more secular, civic landscapes. There is nothing natural about this gesture: it was a choice, one that speaks to emerging attitudes toward death and burial in the period. It may have "suggested martyrdom in the cause of righteousness," as Dell Upton has observed about other Confederate monuments, but the cemetery allowed the extraordinary death of Confederate soldiers to be woven into a continuity of death going back to the colonial period.[17] This continuity masks what was an immensely complicated place.

In cemeteries, memorials entered a landscape layered with centuries of meaning. In the Middle Ages, the cemetery, which was always attached to a church, was the "center of social life," according to Philippe Ariès, having taken the "place of the [Roman] Forum."[18] This stands to reason, since the atrium in front of the medieval church derived from the space adjoining the ancient Roman basilica, which was a civic space. "During the Middle Ages and well into the seventeenth century," Ariès tells us, the cemetery "corresponded as much to the idea of a public square as it did to the notion, now become exclusive, of a space reserved for the dead."[19] It was, in short, "an area of asylum around the church."[20] This function transformed the burial ground, "sometimes into a place of residence, always into a public meeting place, whether or not it continued to be used to bury the dead."[21] The sense of residence was quite literal. People who took refuge there sometimes did so in improvised houses or rooms, some inhabited by the clergy themselves. In this way, informal settlements arose in cemeteries clustered around churches as safe havens, the people being "utterly oblivious to the sights of burials or to the proximity of the large common graves, which were left uncovered until they were full."[22] The cemetery was the "noisiest, busiest, most boisterous, and most commercial place in the rural or urban community" (fig. 3.4).[23]

Figure 3.4. The "noisiest, busiest, most boisterous, and most commercial place." Engraving of Saints Innocents Cemetery, Paris, imagined as it appeared ca. 1550 by Theodor Hoffbauer, late nineteenth century. From E. Champeaux, *Les cimetiéres et le marchés du vieux Dijon* (Dijon: J. Mourry, 1906), p. 6.

The image of the burial ground teeming with everyday life runs so contrary to the contemporary idea of the cemetery as a separate place with a nearly singular function that it requires explanation. Two hundred years of the modern Gothic, from Horace Walpole and Mary Shelley to the horror film, has transmogrified the cemetery. In medieval Europe, cemeteries were often the only public space in town. Before town halls developed, the churchyard served as a place for town meetings, as well as a marketplace and fairground where "merchants enjoyed exemption from taxation and profited from the large numbers of customers drawn by religious, legal, or municipal demonstrations."[24] It was additionally an athletic field and "haven for illicit encounters and dubious professions." Female recluses "chose to confine themselves there," "confined in a *reclusoir* the way women who were found guilty of other misdemeanors were sent to convents or public hospitals, for lack of prisons."[25] They lived in close proximity to "prostitutes and criminals who had been sentenced to be imprisoned there in perpetuity."[26] Not surprisingly, given this criminal element, some judicial proceedings took place in the cemetery, perhaps carrying forward the old role of the basilica as a tribunal, with justice meted out "at the foot of the Cavalry cross," which set a precedent for a monumental figure in the space.[27] The Cavalry cross, in fact, was a place of oratory, sometimes being equipped with a platform for both sermons and secular speeches, a format that would map onto modern commemoration.[28] In short, "the church was the town hall, and the cemetery the public square, in a time when there were no other public places except the street, and no meeting places."[29] This litany of secular and salacious uses of the cemetery suggests that the appropriation of modern cemeteries for leisure activities in the nineteenth century may have been an artifact of centuries of mixed use in this flexible, all-purpose outdoor room.

Established by British colonists, the cemetery at Old St. John's Church originated in the old, premodern burial ground. As a venerable institution, it would have been a meeting place, if not also the secular asylum that Ariès describes as surviving into the seventeenth century. After the war, the church was quickly restored and may well have been pressed into duty to serve many of the functions the old medieval church once did until the town was able to build anew. In fact, in postbellum Hampton, the Episcopal congregation had withered, and the church had come under private ownership. It had become institutionally ambiguous, but the graveyard continued to be a historical site, one that survived into an age of heritage preservation. Whatever its institutional status in 1902, the founding of Old St. John's at the tail end of the long Middle Ages raises the possibility that some of these functions had persisted into the nineteenth century. To be sure, the memorial was placed among the tombstones of the late medieval church graveyard.

Yet memorials such as Hampton's also entered a dynamically changing scene. Under the pressure of modern thought, medicine, and urbanization, mentalities toward death were changing rapidly, and the cemetery itself was being transformed. The very place of death was changing. In the early nineteenth century, the cemetery was gradually detached from the church. It became an institution in its own right, separated from the civic life that it once served. This distinguished and even estranged the activities that took place there from everyday urban life. The new cemetery of the nineteenth century was a place apart, a decidedly new cultural landscape, one that offered nonfuneral monuments a place beyond traffic and the defilements of secular life that apparently troubled the medieval world much less than the zoned soul of the modern one.

Such spatial changes never come about on their own. As the Enlightenment began to rationalize death, the premodern burial ground could no longer be seen through a nostalgic or picturesque lens. This place of rotting corpses heaped in open pits commingling with the other functions of the church and churchyard became a serious problem in the burgeoning cities and towns of the late eighteenth and early nineteenth centuries. The process began as early as the 1760s and 1770s, when hygienic concerns and the need for "functional storage of bodies," in cool Enlightenment fashion, drove a desire to move cemeteries to the fringes of cities.[30] The call for an autonomous cemetery expressed a new attitude. Death shifted from an ecclesiastical matter to an urban problem.[31] As these attitudes took hold across the late eighteenth century, authority over death was gradually removed from the church and reinstitutionalized within the emerging bureaucracies of modern urban governance. Given the central role that the cemetery had played, this was a major rupture, as significant in its own way as the separation of home and work in the same period. Across the nineteenth century, life and death became increasingly separated in Western society, when for most cultures in the roughly two-hundred-thousand-year history of anatomically modern humans, they have been integrated.[32]

The emergence of the cemetery as a distinct institution and space came with vast consequences for processes of cultural memory. At first, the change was visionary, rather than actual. Enlightenment thinkers imagined ideal and separate spheres for death, much in keeping with the rational models that drove utopian visions such as the French architect Claude-Nicholas Ledoux's Ideal City of Chaux, in which every aspect of human experience found its institutional and architectural home.[33] Revolutionary-era visions for cemeteries, now unmoored from churches and the old morbid burial grounds, imagined a parklike setting of funerary monuments and mausoleums, explicitly understood as artful masterpieces suitable as a worthy site to visit, a "museum of tombs," if not a "microcosm of society" where "the nation preserves the memory of great men, as at Westminster Abbey, in England," but transformed into landscape.[34]

In the early to mid-nineteenth century, these visions were put into practice, and the cemetery became a place of wider commemoration. It began to satisfy "those urges that from the Middle Ages to the eighteenth century impelled families to fill the churches with funerary monuments" but now taking on a more public, patriotic role.[35] The new cemeteries were places to visit, where friends and family gathered around the graves of their dead and people strolled in a landscape of national heroes. Père-Lachaise in Paris was the first great model of this vast "cultural domain"[36] (fig. 3.5). Built originally on the outskirts of Paris as an "Elysian Fields" filled with beautiful monuments, it was the culmination of those ideas first proposed in the late eighteenth century. Broken columns, obelisks, neoclassical sculptures, and small temples filled these "beautiful dormitories," which were now more frequently called "cemeteries," from the Greek *koimeterion*, "sleeping place," as opposed to the morbid burial grounds of an earlier age. In fact, almost immediately, war monuments joined civilian graves in the new cemeteries, becoming "routine after the wars of the Revolution and Napoleon."[37]

In turn, as the cemetery became a "museum of fine arts, funerary monuments [took] on a social role." "City folk flocked to these

Figure 3.5. The cemetery as Elysian Fields. Pierre Courvoisier, *View of Père-Lachaise from the Entrance*, 1815. Bibliothèque des Arts décoratifs, Paris.

peaceful, nostalgic gardens to spend the day among the flowers and the trees" and monuments.[38] The war memorials introduced into this setting were but another sculpture in the museum, another lesson, another episode in the leisure itinerary of the bourgeoisie.[39] It is tempting to think of war memorials as parvenus in the cultural landscape of their day, but in fact, the entire cultural landscape of death was novel. Soon, this "statuary pantheon" would be transplanted into the squares and boulevards of cities, following Paris's model.[40] The link between the pantheon of the cemetery and that of urban embellishment speaks to an intricate and underexplored bundle of attitudes toward death, urbanization, and politics in the period.

The appearance of this pantheon in cemeteries in nineteenth-century Europe and the United States reflects the emergence of a "cult of the dead." The shifting attitudes toward death were not just private and familial: they were imbued with national and patriotic, if not also racial meaning. Before the late eighteenth century, officers were buried in churches nearest the battlefield or brought back to the local plot. Ordinary soldiers were buried on the spot of their demise, usually unceremoniously, sometimes in an unmarked grave.[41] In Europe, the age of revolutions marked a sea change: tombs became monuments, and monuments became tombs.[42] Sharp distinctions blurred. Across the nineteenth century, an ambiguity developed between the funerary monuments erected in the new cemeteries of the period and the nonfunerary monuments that arose roughly at the same time as part of the same cultural forces and often placed side by side in cemeteries.

William Godwin's *Essay on Sepulchres* (1809) brings out this change in mentality that powerfully reshaped the built environment. Godwin, the father of Mary Shelley, was a radical English philosopher who wrote his essay in mournful tribute to his wife, Mary Wollstonecraft, who had died in 1797. "Where is Shakespeare? Where is Homer?" he asks. "Can any sensible mind fail to be struck with the deepest regret, when he considers that they are vanished from the face of the earth, and that their place is too probably filled up by some sleepy and lethargic animal, 'dressed in a brief of authority,' pampering his appetites, vapouring his hour, and encumbering the soil which his predecessor adorned?" His solution was to build monuments at the sites where great men had died or taken heroic action: "Let us mark the spot, whenever it can be ascertained, hallowed by the reception of all that was mortal of these glorious beings; let us erect a shrine to their memory; let us visit their tombs; let us indulge all the reality we can now have, of the sort of conference with these men."[43]

To Godwin, the actual place was paramount: "Some spirit shall escape from his ashes, and whisper to me things unfelt before. . . . I wish to live in intercourse with the Illustrious Dead of All Ages. I demand the friendship of Zoroster. Orpheus, and Linus, and Musaeus shall be welcome to me."[44] We might "sensibly mingle with Socrates, and Plato, and the Decii, and the Catos, with Chaucer, and Milton, and Thomas Aquinas, and Thomas à Becket, and all the stars that gild our mortal sphere. They are not dead." "Let them live as my friends, my philosophers, my instructors, and my guides!"[45]

But then Godwin makes a curious move. "Yet to an imaginary person I do not refuse the semblance of a tomb. As has been already observed, poetical scenes affect us in somewhat the same manner as historical: I should be delighted to visit the spot where Cervantes imagined Don Quixote to be buried, or the fabulous tomb of Clarissa Harlowe. I would not therefore refuse in the case of real personages, after all reasonable inquiries had been pursued, to take up with the traditional sepulchre of king Arthur."[46] Here, the game is up. A great forgery to a fictional person was just as vivid as a real tomb in stimulating "intercourse" with the dead. This signals the shift in mentality that let statuemania loose on the world. Figure and tomb could be fictional, and so could the place. This essentially ageographical epiphany would nudge into existence thousands of Joans of Arc, Alfreds, Lincolns, and Bismarcks, figures archaic and contemporary, real, fictional, or historically ambiguous, like Arthur or Rubbiani's *glossatori* in Bologna. Each one, in Godwin's words, was there to "paralyze the hand of oblivion" and to whisper to us "things unfelt before."[47] It is why Juliet's utterly forged tomb in Verona can be a pilgrimage site, alongside a bust of Shakespeare and the phony Capulet house (built in the 1930s), replete with a balcony where young tourists pin love notes with bubble gum and pose with a bronze of Juliet, her breast shined by the groping hands of tourists. It is why monuments are memorials and vice versa and why they can end up almost anywhere, in public squares, streets, parks, and cemeteries. This last thought might be expressed more assertively: it is precisely why they end up everywhere, why greatness is thrown into the mundane, why the oceanic quotidian of modernity is stayed where it flows deepest, and why a modern not-everyday coalesced after the heroes of the ancien régime had lost their heads. Godwin expressed a Romantic yearning for secular reenchantment through commemoration, through monuments.

The wars of the period improved the soil for Godwin's idea. The Franco-Prussian War, according to Ariès, altered the public relationship to war dead in ways that opened up the cemetery to a modern form of commemoration.[48] The bodies of soldiers brought home after the 1870 war "came to be more precisely preserved and the dead venerated." Here, for the first time, the French "drew up honor rolls on stone or metal," posting them in churches or cemeteries. In parallel to Old St. John's, these were the first places to house war memorials in France:

> The church, because the Catholics and the clergy regarded those who had died in such a just war as comparable to martyrs and because the Church considered it her vocation to honor the dead and maintain the cult; the cemetery, because it was the place where the living went to remember and had actually been a kind of competitor of the church since the time the two had been legally separated.[49]

There, the dead were honored both with tombs and with nonsepulchral monuments.

Something comparable was taking place after the slightly earlier American Civil War, albeit inflected by particularly American attitudes. In the United States, the idea of the "Good Death" was "central to mid-nineteenth-century Americans. Dying was an art, following the tradition of *ars moriendi* that had provided rules of conduct for the dying and their attendants since at least the fifteenth century."[50] These rules included comportment at death, how to meet "unbelief, despair, impatience, and worldly attachment," how to emulate Christ's death, and how to pray.[51] Death was patterned into a highly conventionalized act centered on the deathbed, with family and friends gathered around. Even as the art of dying was secularized in both the North and the South, death remained an essentially domestic matter in Victorian America.[52] People died at home in deathbed scenes following well-worn scripts that gave everyone their role and appropriate emotion. "As late as the first decade of the twentieth century, fewer than 15 percent of Americans died away from home."[53] Death was local.

The sudden deaths caused by the Civil War, being displaced from home and occurring on a mass scale, ruptured these conventions.

The change placed a special burden on Civil War memorials to return the soldier metaphorically to his home, or at least to his hometown. Memorials transposed the deathbed scene to a public setting, with mourners gathered around the memorial instead of the bed. The deathbed, moreover, had a didactic function in providing "a critical means through which the deceased could continue to exist in the lives of survivors," not least of all through the moral lesson of their last words. The sermons, music, poetry, and other performances held at postbellum commemorations reenacted the scene of the deathbed, both scenically and rhetorically.[54]

The sudden deaths of modern war implicated the memorial and its placement. Many memorials, even as late as World War II, show soldiers in the act of dying or at peace in death, as a representation of Good Death for the whole community, or nation. These are part of a tradition of idealized death that first took root in cemeteries as part of commemorations. The cemetery was asked to smooth over the rupture of sudden death, of death displaced from home and the rituals of the deathbed. The French model of the cemetery became standard in England and North America, but while Continental cemeteries became jammed with monuments at the expense of green space, the Anglo-American cemetery retained a more open, parklike setting. Many were called parks and served this function.[55] In the United States, the so-called "rural cemetery" "looked less and less like a churchyard and more and more like a garden."[56] Mount Auburn in Cambridge, Massachusetts, founded in 1831 on the model of Père-Lachaise, was among the first and served as an important model for the spread of this cemetery type. It quickly became a site of leisure and tourism in the Boston area.[57] The museum of monuments became a pastoral retreat, which readily accepted nonfunerary monuments and memorials to fallen heroes that joined other statuary to which they were related aesthetically, spatially, morally, and as part of cultural practices such as Decoration Day and its successor, Memorial Day. The Nathaniel Bowditch statue placed in Mount Auburn in 1847 joined obelisks and columns in a picturesque place of contemplation

Figure 3.6. The rural cemetery as a pastoral place of contemplation. Nathanial Bowditch Statue, by Robert Ball Hughes, 1847, Mount Auburn Cemetery, Cambridge, Massachusetts. From William Flagg, *Mount Auburn: Its Scenes, Its Beauties, and Its Lessons* (Boston: J. Munroe and Company, 1861).

and leisure (fig. 3.6).[58] William Godwin's vision was becoming a reality, and not just for cultural elites. A small obelisk called the Harper's Ferry Memorial was erected in 1865 in the Westwood Cemetery in Oberlin, Ohio, to mark the deaths of three "colored citizens" of the town who "gave their lives for the slave." Distant and sudden deaths were brought home and monumentalized. Oberlin's monument is admittedly unusual, but it was part of a common practice in the period.

As nonfunerary, or quasi-funerary more aptly, monuments proliferated in cemeteries across Europe and the United States, so did the range of meanings attached to them. The Confederate Memorial in the Hollywood Forever Cemetery in Los Angeles reveals another aspect of this shifting terrain of the cemetery (fig. 3.7). Like many Confederate monuments, this one was erected to honor the Lost Cause in the

Figure 3.7. The anomalous Confederate Memorial, 1925, Hollywood Forever Cemetery, Los Angeles. Removed in 2017. Photograph courtesy of Atomic Hot Links.

1920s. The granite marker with its bronze shield was placed there by the Long Beach Chapter of the United Daughters of the Confederacy. Its meaning could not have been clearer in a Los Angeles mired in racial tension. Yet unlike Hampton's memorial, it neither celebrated particular soldiers nor adopted the monumentality common to many Southern Confederate monuments. Even the language of its dedication was relatively tame: "In memory of the soldiers of the Confederate States Army who have died or may die on the Pacific Coast." This was not a memorial to the dead, per se, but a monument that marked the continued presence of Confederate ideology on the West Coast. Here Godwin's vision, inviting as it did ageographical and even fictitious monuments, invited a darker, political mood. The Hollywood marker stood in the cemetery for decades before it was desecrated in 2018 amid the nationwide movement to take down monuments to white supremacy. Shortly thereafter, the cemetery removed it.[59] It is unlikely that this strange monument would have been erected in a public park, at a courthouse, or public building in Los Angeles—although these were common sites across the American South. It used the cemetery as cover, making itself inconspicuous in this site of leisure amid the funerary monuments with which it shared a common form and placement. Toward midcentury, as the cemetery shifted from a public space of leisure and mourning into a more private space that sequestered death in an age that avoided it, and, as the "death concession" commercialized these spaces, the Confederate Memorial became a relic of an outmoded habit of placement.[60] More recent events called it out from behind its curtain.

Across the twentieth century, the Anglo-American cemetery changed in ways that would work against cemetery war memorials. Simpler headstones came to be favored over traditional and more ostentatious monuments. In turn, headstones gave way to simple horizontal slabs. "The rural cemetery of the nineteenth century evolved into the lawn cemetery of the twentieth century, a vast expanse of green with small, horizontal funerary plaques that are barely visible."[61] On the English variation on this theme, James

Stephens Curl observed that the generation that came of age after the
First World War rejected the "dark romantic gloom" of the Victori-
ans and "demanded an unmysterious church, a neatly clipped garden
of rest, a bright and shining world."[62] The same fall from grace can be
found in Filippo Marinetti's pithy defamation in the "Futurist Manifesto" of 1909: "Museums, cemeteries!"[63] The changing temper was a
direct spatial manifestation of Geoffrey Gorer's stunning insight that
death became the central taboo in Western society in the twentieth
century.[64] In the years after World War I, the cemetery became a
nearly anti-iconic setting, one anathema to the monuments of earlier
generations and now resistant to nonfunerary monuments such as
war memorials. Now, one way to defuse a controversial memorial
is to move it to a cemetery, as happened to the Soviet World War
II memorial in Tallinn, Estonia, a political lightning rod that was
moved from a park in the city to a military cemetery.[65] It was thus
spirited from the everyday and stored in an obscure, urban corner,
which is what many cemeteries have become, in part because urban
parks have taken their place as public spaces of leisure. Conversely, a
memorial lost in a cemetery is sometimes moved to bring it back to
life. In 1971, Oberlin moved the Harper's Ferry Memorial to the more
central and visible Martin Luther King Jr. Park.[66]

The transformation of the cemetery betrays the new mood that
descended on American culture, if not Western culture more generally especially after World War II, when a reaction against traditional
war memorials set in. This may be why war memorials erected in
cemeteries have come to look awkward, even aberrant. The 442nd
Infantry War Memorial in Evergreen Cemetery in Boyle Heights, Los
Angeles, for instance, pokes out of a horizontal sea of plaques and now
seems like a curiosity (fig. 3.8). In fact, this cemetery tells the story
in full. Originally established in 1877 on the rural cemetery model,
its older sections are built up with towering obelisks and columnar
funerary monuments, while elsewhere, simpler tombstones and even
more recent flat plaques allow verdant lawns to become the dominant note. The memorial, which was dedicated in 1949, honors the

Figure 3.8. The lawn cemetery gives way to tombstones, which crowd around the 442nd Infantry War Memorial, 1949, Evergreen Cemetery, Boyle Heights, Los Angeles, Photograph by the author.

Japanese-American unit that had the highest casualty rate during the war. It is a latecomer to the convention of placing war memorials in cemeteries, so late that it overlaps uncomfortably with the advent of the taboo against death, when the cemetery as a didactic, public space of leisure and contemplation lapsed into disuse. In spite of its visual dissonance in this setting, the memorial makes sense where it is. It reflects the continued need for Japanese Americans in Los Angeles to have a communal place for commemoration after the forced internments of the war displaced their community from Boyle Heights, while many of their ancestors remained buried there. A "home" in the sense of the old funeral "dormitory" remained necessary.

With the reality of Victorian customs of death in mind, war memorials placed anywhere but a church or cemetery start to look like novel interventions — inventions, in fact, that heralded a different sense of what these events meant and where they belonged in the cultural imagination, if not the geography, of the day. In fact, they were seen as artificial in their own day, minus modernity's moral judgment of artifice. Memorials in civic space removed the martyrs from their ancient moorings in church and cemetery and made them part of local memory, urban pride, beautification schemes, or, once linked to days of remembrance, national commemoration. The change in venue is telling. A park, a median, a patch of grass on the grounds of the courthouse, city hall, or capital each came with its own meaning.

Parks, Commons, Greens

When cemeteries came to be called memorial parks, it was more than a death-defying euphemism or a gesture to the pastoral mode of elegy. Cemeteries were serving parklike functions before the urban park became a standard fixture in modern cities. Urbanites took refuge there and found in the early cemeteries an antithesis to the city. The park was, in fact, kin to the cemetery in its intentions, directly related to it historically, and forged out of the same urban conditions.[67] The earliest parks emerged at about the same time that Enlightenment thinkers began to reimagine the cemetery. By the middle of the nineteenth century, they had become important fixtures of European cities. In the United States, urban parks developed a bit later and could look to the new cemetery as a model. The American landscape architect and theorist Andrew Jackson Downing turned directly to modern cemeteries as an inspiration for public parks. For him, parks were places where national character would be formed and taste refined — the civilizing mission turned inward.[68] Alongside the rural cemeteries that he admired, parks were "one of those grand improvements in civilization."[69]

Not surprisingly, memorials found parks almost from their inception. The Civil War memorial in New York City's Central Park, not far from Sherman, sits in a wooded area along a path that was a retreat from the town proper, especially in 1874, when the wall of buildings had not yet formed (fig. 3.9). Such spaces were seen as reliefs from the city, civic spaces with wider cultural ambitions from education and spiritual renewal to citizenship and national unity. Downing called the rousing enthusiasm for urban parks that rose in the wake of Central Park's success "parkomania," echoing the statuemania associated with French society.[70] Parkomania and statuemania were intertwined expressions of modern society.

However, for many nineteenth-century writers, the park, originally understood by its proselytizers as an antidote to the city, was an unnatural place for memorials or statuary of any kind.[71] In the green, leafy spaces that first emerged in London and Paris and a little later in the rest of Europe and the United States, the memorial was situated in a place intended for contemplation, not for commemoration.[72]

Many of Europe's royal reserves, once used as hunting grounds and pleasure gardens, had become public parks beginning in the late eighteenth century. These, alongside the transformation of former bastions, provided a new public realm in European cities. By the 1830s, the greensward of parks in West London offered a model to the world, as did the Parisian parks that Americans frequented on their Grand Tours and later as tourists, especially after the Civil War. In the nineteenth century, Hyde Park Corner was transformed into a site for the cult of Wellington, gradually to become London's primary site for remembrance of war. (Chapter 6 looks at this transformation in depth.) Cities across Europe followed suit, ornamenting their newly formed parks and reserves with monuments and commemorative statues. Americans in the Gilded Age, ever ready to emulate European culture, clamored for their own public parks and rapidly made them into memorial landscapes.

American parks differed mostly because of the greater urgency in the rapidly urbanizing cities of North America, where there were no royal lands or former fortifications to convert to public use.[73] The American park grew out of a number of indigenous prototypes. In

Figure 3.9. War in the park. John Quincy Adams Ward, Seventh Regiment Memorial, unveiled 1874, Central Park, New York City. Photograph by Jim Henderson.

New England, the old commons, with its meetinghouse and town hall, morphed into a more secular public park. Almost by default. the commons had been a multipurpose space. The center of religious and political life, it was also the "temporary courthouse," stage stop, whipping post, and a place of commerce, powder storage, militia training, and education.[74] With its adjoining burial ground, the common took the place of the old medieval cemetery as the public space of the New England town. Once the "monopoly of the Congregational church on town life" had been broken, the "stern Puritan civic center" was liberated to become the town green. It quickly attracted the novelties of Victorian life, including the menagerie of memorials that would be assembled there.[75] To call the emerging landscape a memory zoo would be too cheeky, but not by much. A stroll through Boston Common and the adjacent Public Gardens brings the point home. There, dozens of commemorative sites command some of the best spots. For Memorial Day, the city plants a "Garden of Flags" in front of the Soldiers and Sailors Monument. So vast is this field of thirty-seven thousand flags that red, white, and blue threaten to replace green. A memory park, indeed.

The New England greens "found their counterpart in the courthouse square" that centered the newer towns of the Midwest in the nineteenth century. Many of these were established by New Englanders making their way west. A "leafy oasis," the courthouse square relieved the "treeless tallgrass prairie" of the Midwest. From the beginning, it was called a "park."[76] Courthouse parks were also the sort of multiuse spaces needed by the fledgling towns that took root along rail lines and canals just decades before the public park came into its own. Small businesses and churches gathered round, as did weekly markets and the many other improvised civic functions of the small towns of the Midwest.[77] It is difficult to find one now without a memorial — or a small gathering of them.

The urban park postdated the New England common and courthouse square or park. Spiro Kostof's judgment that it was "anti-city to begin with, both in form and intent" seems a bit harsh, but it was certainly an "invented romantic landscape" that usually broke meaningfully with the city's street pattern. Like the rural cemetery that preceded it, the urban park was a pleasure ground, a release from the tensions of city life and a forge for democracy where "rich and poor could come together as equals."[78] This last aspiration is one reason parks attracted war memorials. It was there that the class divisions so apparent in urban life could be temporarily put aside for a larger national or patriotic concern. Naturally, this logic could be turned around. Parks were also part of the "imposition of moral order" by elites, a cultural means of advancing their values, attitudes, and practices.[79]

From the outset, then, public parks and modern memorials were complicit in creating a symbolic universe that attempted to smooth over class realities and racial inequalities in a landscape that made their root cause invisible.[80] Part of the artfulness of the first parks attempted to counter the corrupt culture of the city with nature as a place ostensibly free of culture. Frederick Law Olmsted, one of the originators of Central Park, is the source of much statuephobia in parks. He plumped for parks entirely free of buildings and memorials. These detracted, he believed, from the pure encounter with nature: "Olmsted was uncompromising on the issue of built structures within his parks. There were to be no monuments, no decorations; the urban square was the proper place for such 'town-like things.'"[81] Olmsted's position was widely adopted, however ineffectively, across the United States. Similar sentiment can be found in Europe. The French painter Edgar Degas proposed walling off "green spaces in order to protect them from new monuments."[82] Degas's impish irony aside, the inescapable paradox is that as memorials invaded parks, they populated an amnesiac landscape, one intended explicitly as an escape from those associations conjured up by memorials, in fact, a space meant to be free of culture.[83] The confusion and consternation over parks and statues reveals just how new this sort of unprogrammed space was.

Olmsted and his followers obviously fought a losing battle. In seeing the urban park as a "middle landscape between raw nature and the unseemly entanglement of the city," they failed to concede to the reality that parks immediately came under immense pressure to serve many purposes.[84] Like the old medieval burial ground, they were beset with demands from all quarters. There were precious few civic spaces to absorb the increasingly complex needs of modern life. Olmsted's insistence on unadulterated landscape met great resistance, not least of all from pragmatic reformers who saw the park as open land that could be put to use as a place of "cultural enlightenment" where they could inculcate values to the masses. Olmsted's purism surrendered to "museums and conservatories, aquariums, observatories, and zoos," and other institutions.[85] Playgrounds and monuments further broadened the urban park's use and meaning.

On the ground, this made parks motley landscapes in small towns and big cities alike. Memorials like the one to World War I in Warren, Ohio, joined civic amenities such as playgrounds, gardens, fountains, bandstands, public stages, and a host of other ornaments and heritage sites, including, for example, the reconstructed log cabin (fig. 3.10).[86] Memory and heritage (which François Hartog calls memory's "alter ego") became cognates in the landscape.[87] Warren has assembled its Civil War and World War I memorials with a new one to World War II in Monument Park. Its pendant, the Every Woman Memorial, stands in Women's Park, the latest addition to what has become a system of parks that flows from the town's courthouse square. She is a counterpoint to the soldiers in form, name, and placement (fig. 3.11). The stark gender division — men in uniform stand at ready, one aiming his gun, while a woman in flowing dress reflects among flowerbeds — may have been what moved one photographer to caption the memorial with a quotation from Virginia Woolf: "As a woman I have no country. As a woman, my country is the whole world."[88] Woolf wrote this resolute rejection of patriotism in 1938 in the context of the rise of fascism, with World War II clearly on the horizon.[89] As the doughboy marches off to war, the woman stands in her outdoor

Figure 3.10. E. M. Visquesney, World War I Memorial with the pioneer cabin behind it, designed in the 1920s and dedicated in 1941, Warren, Ohio. Postcard from the author's collection.

Figure 3.11. The Every Woman Memorial in its domestic "outdoor room," replete with mailbox, 2008, Women's Park, Warren, Ohio. Photograph by Jack Pearce.

room, marked explicitly as a domestic space by the mailbox at the gate. A curious rejoinder to Warren's male figures, it would be a good place to stage a countercommemoration. This is surely not its intention, but it brings home how overencumbered with demands, if not contradictions, American parks can be. Similar configurations can be found around the world.[90]

Lost in this discussion is the reality that this sort of multipurpose park has cosmopolitan roots that date to the "new worldliness" of the American Renaissance.[91] The sober and well-meaning committees that earnestly dedicated memorials were absorbed in larger urban aesthetic debates, particularly about urban beautification. This was especially the case later in the nineteenth century, when the new mood drifted in from Paris with the artists and architects who had trained there. In opposition to Olmsted, the Parisian-trained American architect Richard Morris Hunt pressed for parks with monumental gates and figurative statues following the French Beaux-Arts manner.[92] Hunt's counterproposals for Central Park were rejected, but his vision of the park "as a monumental civic space gained widespread acceptance."[93]

Much of this transatlantic fervor for parks as cultural amenities can be traced through the City Beautiful Movement, which by the turn of the century was firmly situated in American architectural practice and early city planning. Inspired by French urbanism, City Beautiful advocates favored monumental classical ensembles and formally planned axes and promenades, tied together with tightly organized plantings in parterres and along boulevards. This generation added generously to the crowd of statues and monuments in parks and wrangled over their appropriate use and placement. However, the American park has existed in an unresolved tension between Olmsted's pastoral landscape, the formal classicism of the City Beautiful, and the reformist urges of the same period.[94] In the emerging cultural landscape of the park, aesthetics often trumped commemorative intentions: "No public monument has an excuse for existence unless it is primarily and essentially a work of art," wrote one anonymous critic of the rash of new monuments appearing in

New York City parks at the end of the century.[95] Even for more temperate writers, memorials were little more than urban ornament. Mariana Griswold Van Rensselaer, one of the leading architecture critics of the period, all but erased the distinction between memorials and mere statuary. "If a work of art is agreeable to look upon," she wrote, "we may be glad to possess it even if it commemorates a well-meaning nobody."[96] She grouped Saint-Gaudens's Sherman with the American panther in Central Park and, more surprisingly, the monuments at Gettysburg. She considered them together because they were all, in essence, public art.[97] This extended to their sites. What she called "right placing" was a purely aesthetic matter: "a beautiful statue may be shorn of half its effect if badly stationed."[98]

Van Rensselaer made the pretense of memorials transparent. "It should be remembered, first of all, that, as a monument is a palpably artificial thing, the best place for it is where other artificial objects are conspicuous." A monument "should be set at the intersection of roads or paths, on a terrace, near a building, or at the side of a formal avenue."[99] This was little more than a list of emerging habits of placement that staked out a compromise between Olmsted and Hunt. She thus supported the Mall in Central Park as a place for monuments because its formality openly acknowledged its artifice, whereas those parts of the park that pretended to naturalness were unsuitable.[100] While she admired the French in their placement of monuments in formal settings, she deemed them less successful in more "naturalistic" parks. In Parc Monceau, in Paris, where monuments are set away from the road in "wide quiet stretches of lawn," she argued, it disturbs the "repose of the lawn" and their conspicuous artificiality "injures" the "natural character."[101]

Van Rensselaer was among the first to try to articulate concrete rules of thumb for placement. The nature of the statue dictated where it would fit. A seated figure, she believed, looks awkward outdoors and is best placed where "living people sit at rest," where "Seward, poising his pen on the corner of Madison Square, seems sadly out of place," she wrote.[102] Her unease with William Seward's monument seems to have trickled down to the present. Where once the statue of the seated lawmaker sat nakedly on a small grassy berm practically free of plantings, now he is girdled in the pedestrian equivalent of a traffic circle, surrounded with plants and a low iron railing in his sequestered garden office. The word "naked" is not moralizing anachronism. A cartoon of 1895 depicted a "Gaiety Girl" sitting on Seward's lap, trying to "flirt with the famous statesman." Van Rensselaer, the Gaiety Girl, and modern landscapists all saw Seward as out of place. At least landscape architects could take action, and many did, quarantining statues to the corners of parks and obscuring them with plantings. John McLaren, who served as the superintendent for Golden Gate Park in San Francisco for over fifty years, famously marginalized statues. To this day, many of them can be seen fighting with foliage.

As McLaren's work in Golden Gate Park suggests, conventions of placement were improvised in a maelstrom of conflicting agendas and aesthetic visions. They would be hardened by practice and through major writings in the early years of landscape architecture as a profession. One early canonical text in the field, Henry Vincent Hubbard and Theodora Kimball's *An Introduction to the Study of Landscape Design* (1917), carried Van Rensselaer's basic formulation to several generations of landscape architects. Writing just before American parks would be pressed into accommodating World War I memorials, they used nearly zoological logic to categorize placement by specimen:

> One might expect to find the figure of a warrior or of Victory as a monument in a battle-field. Almost as surely should one expect that a statue in an orchard should be of Pomona or some of her mythologic kin; a statue in a grove, a dryad; a statue in a flower garden might well represent Flora or Vertumnus; and we are not surprised to find Peter Pan playing his pipes in Kensington Gardens.[103]

This was more than an argument for statuary being in cahoots with the spirit of the place. In an argument by omission, they frowned upon placing war memorials outside of battlefields.

Other memorials were pushed to the edge by facing them either to the street or toward the park, "becoming thereby a part of the

Figure 3.12. World War I infantry charge out of the trees of Central Park. Karl Morningstar Illava, 107th United States Infantry Memorial, 1927, New York City. Photograph by Jonathan Etkin.

screen or framing of the park and not in themselves ever dominating the motive."[104] The Sherman statue is a quintessential example, and it set a pattern. The 107th United States Infantry memorial at Central Park (1927) was likewise pushed to the park's edge (fig. 3.12). Here, the ensemble of World War I soldiers advance from the wooded thicket bordering Central Park, as if mounting a charge. The vignette is acutely cut off by Fifth Avenue. Three traffic lights and multiple lanes of traffic thwart their charge down 67th Street. Behind them lies a playground, its slides, rocks, and water elements all obscured from the memorial by the low wall of Central Park and the green wall of trees. From the beginning, Olmsted and his partner, architect Calvert Vaux, "saw the necessity of interposing natural objects between the observer and the urban wall beyond the park."[105] Landscape architects carried on the concern for protecting parks as natural

settings from the incursion of statues. The attitude was international
in scope. As the prominent British architect Reginald Blomfield put
it: "bronze figures are too trenchant, too strong, if you like, to take
their place among the gentler beauties of the garden" because "they
do not grow in with nature."[106] Almost any view of the 107th Infantry
statue drives this point home.

Yet something more than aesthetics was at work. Architecture, and
even more so monuments, posed a threat to landscape architecture.
Landscape architect George Burnap reviled memorials in part because
they intruded on his work, on landscape as an art. They challenged
the purity of landscape architecture as an independent pursuit. But
Burnap's trouble went deeper than professional jealousies. He wanted
to supplant the "plethora of petrified generals" with replicas of Greek
statuary such as the *Discus Thrower*, which would provide "healthier
inspiration value."[107] This suggests something was at work well beyond
Olmsted's attempt to preserve a direct encounter with nature. "The
usual effigy should be banned from park precincts," Burnap wrote,
proposing that the "G.A.R.'s and the D.A.R.'s and the S.A.R.'s ... apo-
theosise [sic] their forebears" with fountains rather than statues.[108]
"Who is responsible for leaving these monstrosities exposed?" he continued. "Why are they not put in the Salon des Indépendents as at Paris,
or in the Hall of Horrors as in the Washington Capitol, or decently
interned as at the Campo Santo at Genoa," the main cemetery of that
city. One can well imagine that Burnap, writing in 1916, feared a horde
of new memorials would descend on American parks after the war.
He was updating a Victorian attitude. In 1885, *Puck* lampooned the
"hideous monuments" going up in American cities, proposing instead,
just as Burnap did years later, fountains and benches (fig. 3.13; see color
insert). Seward sits lower left.

Burnap's revulsion ties the statuephobia of the nineteenth century
to the death taboo of the twentieth. As symbols of death, memorials
were not just to be removed from parks, but "interned" in cemeteries. His word choice was anything but innocent. Death was to be
zoned, spirited away like prisoners of war. Burnap complained that

Figure 3.13. "No More of Those Hideous Monuments!" *Puck*, August 19, 1855, centerfold by Bernhard Gillam. Courtesy of the Library of Congress. The title seems to say it all, but the leafy background makes clear that the monuments are not the only issue. The insert not only replaces the monument with a fountain, but also places the latter in an urban scene.

new parks are often designed in anticipation of the "future occupant," "like preparing the tomb against the inevitable day."[109] His hang-up was not just the monument as a mnemonic of death, but also that parks had begun to telegraph these morbid intentions in their very design. The attitude recalls the reaction against funeral monuments in cemeteries in the same period and provokes the question of whether such monuments, then already falling out of fashion, came to be associated with the similar monuments then being erected in parks. Were commemorative works in 1916 contaminated with the same deathly aura that had come to spook moderns later in the century?

Statuephobia and the death taboo collaborated in the devaluation of monuments of all sorts, particularly after World War I. One way out of this dilemma, of course, was to make the entire park a memorial, the ubiquitous memorial park, and to do away with the monument or reduce it to words on a plaque.[110] In fact, memorial parks began to dot the American landscape after World War I. With tidy efficiency, the memorial park dispensed with many of the objections to conventional memorials, although, not surprisingly, statues have often crept back into these parks. The parallel to the emergence of the lawn cemetery — as noted, also sometimes called a memorial park — is almost too obvious to mention.[111] Without a figurative statue or an expensive monument, morbid symbols could be avoided along with the artistic dilemma of representing modern soldiers and the problems of placement. Less obviously, memorial parks could also handle obsolescence. When memorials no longer have active commemorative communities, they often become derelict, while parks continue to be useful. In some sense, the memorial park performs an Olmstedian end run.

Parks helped work out other modern problems, as well. They sopped up the leisure hours that were an emerging phenomenon, and later social problem, in modern society and helped people negotiate the quickening pace of change. Memorials worked in tandem with parks as places to pause the clock. They countered the relentlessly linear shape of modern time with cycles of commemoration in parks that posed as timeless natural environments.[112] Where commemorations bring people back in circular fashion to a moment in the past, the modern city has been stubbornly contemporary, an engine of progress and forward motion. The park, as a place apart, has been a site for shaping an alternative time. As first conceived by Olmsted and his followers, the park was a place outside of the city's quotidian time, a place of "passive reflection."[113] While memorials were viewed as an intrusion on nature's ability to afford this reflection, they could bolster the park as a refuge from modern time and by extension from culture itself. These terms could be reversed. A parklike setting could smooth over uncomfortable memory. As late as 1984, the competition for a memorial at the Gestapo Headquarters in Berlin during World War II insisted that the site incorporate a park and a children's playground.[114]

These moves are not without paradox. Memorials are symbols of decisive events, often of a traumatic and cataclysmic nature, that are keyed to what Mircea Eliade eloquently called the irreversibility of modern time,[115] while parks pretend to suspend this sort of acculturated time. This paradox has been complicated in recent decades by the rise of self-consciously created memorial parks dedicated to just such events. These can be found all around the world and take many forms, from the dark Parque de la Memoria in Buenos Aires that memorializes the crimes of the dictatorship to a park in Taoyuan in Taiwan, where an outdoor gallery of relocated statues of Chiang Kaishek has been formed.[116] The most famous example is the Memento Park outside of Budapest, where monuments to former Communist luminaries have been assembled. By contrast, Moscow's Victory Park (see Chapter 7) is the triumphalist variation on the phenomenon. Consequently, it is fair to see parks and memorials as collaborating in creating a place of resistance to modern time.

At least since the historian Frances Yates's often-cited book *The Art of Memory*, scholars have emphasized the importance of place to the workings of memory, assuming variously a quasi-scientific or mystical connection between the two.[117] To this way of thinking, physical surroundings act as a spur for personal and collective memory. To recall an event, it would seem, we need merely summon up the place where it happened, and its place in the mind will be revealed. American myths play into this idea, as when people recall where they were when John F. Kennedy was shot. Popular culture often assumes the link between memory and location comes down to instinct; some of the best scholarship does the same. Perhaps only neuroscientists can settle this question, but it is evident from the examples in this chapter that where we place those mnemonic devices we call memorials is often arbitrary or pragmatic. It is at the whim of urban change, shifts in mentality or taste, and the most mundane processes of daily life. Conventions of placement emerge from a complicated web.

The form of memorials so often derives from funerary traditions that it should not be surprising to find conventions of placing them doing the same, forming an arc or common tradition in the West that may be traceable back to ancient practices, both in the built environment and in elegy, which placed death in a pastoral setting. Cemeteries and parks brought the pastoral into the mean city, which had been figured as the opposite of pastoral. Contrary to Olmsted's purism, these pastoral retreats were already steeped in culture, elegiac, and seen through the lens of loss and death. It would be a mistake, or even a modernist point of view, to see this in the pejorative. Even a park free of memorials could be resonant with death. "The poetic world to which the pastoral elegist 'escapes,' this imaginary world, is not — as it is sometimes said to be — *less* substantial than the world he actually inhabits. On the contrary, it is in important ways made to seem *more* substantial (*more* concrete, *more* comprehensible) than the 'real' world."[118] As with poetic laments, so with landscapes of mourning.

In the cemetery and the park, the memorial found changeful and liminal spaces where moderns could reconcile themselves to death in the decades that death itself was being transformed. In a world in which "all that is solid melts into the air, all that is holy is profaned," the cemetery and park were counterworlds where the immaterial, the aesthetic, and the invisible could be solid, where people could, to recall Godwin's plea, "sensibly mingle" with the dead and "paralyze the hand of oblivion," in contrast to the relentless melt of urban life.[119] Here, the everyday could be enchanted. As death was transmogrified from a tangible and eternal afterlife, richly imagined in word and image for centuries by the Christian church, into secular nothingness — a nowhere — cemeteries and parks gave substance and place to the disappearing imaginary of death. They did this, moreover, as death was ushered out of everyday life, medicalized, bureaucratized, and placed in special institutions. In turn, these new spaces provided a new everyday setting for death. The park and cemetery were not alone in this. As the next chapter explores, a host of other urban spaces were reenvisioned to accommodate memorials.

Figure 4.1. Glupov, or "Stupid Town," with its monument to a vainglorious and anonymous military hero who lords over the route into town on his obviously unplanned and unpaved plot of dirt, with a pathetic bench placed to give a picturesque view of his backside. The undated illustration appeared on the cover of the satirical *The History of a Town* by M. Saltykov-Shchedrin, 1979 [1870]. From the collection of the Russian State Library, Moscow. KukryNikSy, artists. Photograph courtesy of HIP/Art Resource, NY.

CHAPTER FOUR

Misplacing Memory: Memorials in

Circles, Squares, and Medians

Monuments, poor things . . . all too often accept
wildly unsuitable accommodation.
— Hugh Casson, *Monuments*, 1965

As the last chapter made clear, where memorials have landed is as
invented as modern memorials themselves (fig. 4.1; see color insert).
In addition to cemeteries and parks, they are commonly erected in
front of civic buildings and appear where street patterns leave spare
spaces. This stands to reason: these are the principal public spaces in
towns and cities. They are also spaces where institutions border on and
push back against the market, or, just as frequently, where capitalism's
claims are weaker, those places of noncommercial transaction, the
urban leftovers that improvers of cities sought to beautify. Such habits
of placement are curious because these sites of commemoration col-
lide with landscapes that serve some other purpose or no official purpose at all. When memorials have no intrinsic relationship to their site,
it changes their meaning and frees them to interact with their context
differently. This could be insidious, as when towns in the American
South placed Confederate monuments in front of courthouses to bolster racist ideology with the false authority of the law. The sculpted
soldier on his high plinth, sometimes with gun in hand, standing in
front of hall of judgment, planted a grave warning in places pushing

Figure 4.2. The Iron Chancellor stands in a fountain in a roundabout enmeshed in electrical wires that power streetcars. Ludwig Habich, Bismarck Monument, 1906, Darmstadt. Photograph by the author.

to roll back the freedoms of Black people in the South. Even when the place of memorials is more innocent or expedient, it is still saturated with significance.

Most commemorative interventions are geographically arbitrary. Their place in the world is as bound by convention as their form. The Maos, Bismarcks, Stalins, Husseins, and other eminences, as well as allegories of Peace and Independence and many war memorials erected by zealous committees, or autocrats, often have an ulterior relationship to their place (fig. 4.2). Yet as the last chapter explored, even the most modest war memorials placed in cemeteries and churchyards or on village greens were novel interventions. They introduced mnemonics in places that rarely had served as sites of public commemoration. Much like parks and cemeteries, these sites were the spatial equivalents of neologisms — *neotopisms* — in their own right and undergoing rapid change under the pressures of urbanization. To place memorials required new rationales. New conventions needed to be established on the fly. As much as memory in popular lore is rooted in place, many memorials are curiously ageographical. People have had to find a place for them in the context of these changes.

The "great men" on their pedestals are not the only monuments that seem out of place. An extreme example sets the edge of the inquiry, links up with the tradition of memorials in parks, and leads to the less charted urban fragments that are the subject of this chapter. The Holocaust Memorial in Miami Beach, like all American Holocaust memorials, cannot mark a site of the Holocaust in any literal way (fig. 4.3). Although it marks the tragic diaspora of the Shoah, it is ageographical. For such a sober subject, the setting is all-important, but it is also incongruous. It lies beside the Miami Beach Convention Center and its massive parking lot, adjacent to the Miami Beach Golf Club and the city's Garden Club, in a largely commercial area with busy, multilane streets fronting two sides of the site. This unusually large parcel was converted into a parklike setting designed especially for the statue. Yet to call it a park is misleading. Unlike the sort of urban parks discussed in the last chapter, the Holocaust

Figure 4.3. A giant arm amid the palms in a park. Ken Treister, Holocaust Memorial, 1990, Miami Beach, Florida. Photograph by the author.

Memorial takes over the entire space, making it a Holocaust park, an absurd proposition.

Such a placement, such a concept, requires a justification, an argument. That argument is the Holocaust itself. The reasons in Miami Beach are not obscure. When Jewish survivors in Miami met in 1984 to discuss building a memorial, Miami Beach was seen as a fitting location because it had such a high number of survivors, some twenty to twenty-five thousand at the time. Nonetheless, considerable opposition arose and converged on issues of place.[1] Miami Beach was "a place of sun and fun," one Garden Club member, Florence Shubim, proclaimed: "Gloom is doom! Don't turn one of the city's few bright spots into a cemetery." Little did she know her comment condensed a century of debate about the place of memorials in American culture, with many parallels to similar debates around the world. The memorial was to take up a city-owned plot that the neighboring Garden Club had eyed for expansion. Advocates for the memorial prevailed, but not before they observed a more mystical justification for the site: the physical address was 1933–1945 Meridian Avenue, the numbers corresponding to the years of the Third Reich, leading "many to believe that the Memorial was *bashert*," or fate, which also swayed city legislators.[2]

The memorial's location required an argument, because aside from the numerological happenstance of the address, it lacked an intrinsic relationship to its site. The "park" was necessary to make a clear separation from the ordinary urban tissue that surrounded it, but it also created a jarring juxtaposition with the memorial itself. The landscape lulls one into the contemplative, leisurely, escapist — and, yes, elegiac — mood that modern parks are meant to evoke, made all the more so by the noncommemorative garden it abuts. This is what made parks likely places to deposit memorials in the first place. They were antidotes to the workaday world of the city. Force of habit has made this convention seem natural. But the monumental bronze limb in Miami Beach is so clearly not natural that it lays bare the forced convention.

Memorials in churchyards, cemeteries, and parks at least found a dignified public place and could tap into religious or civic traditions, however recent or changeful. By contrast, many memorials have found their way onto what Mariana Griswold Van Rensselaer called the "little squares and open corners where, alone or in combination with trees and shrubs, monuments of one sort or another are eminently appropriate."[3] Van Rensselaer's writing on the subject, which at times could sound like an etiquette guide for statues, was really about the beautification of these "left-over or cut-off pieces of land often found at street convergings."[4] These urban crumbs posed nettlesome problems for cities. Such remnants often came under the jurisdiction of the park authorities that came into existence beginning in the late nineteenth century. This was a bit of municipal wishful thinking. Most of the locations were anything but pastoral, but their aspirational assignment as parks confesses a desire to recast the city, in whatever morsels could be found, into something more parklike. *Rus in urbe.* Toward the end of the century, major cities began forming art commissions to handle the contentious business of placing memorials.[5] These new municipal authorities, in turn, had to work with one of the most crucial, if mundane, problems cities faced: traffic. Memorials began to appear in medians, traffic circles and roundabouts, or along great boulevards and in prominent squares. These habits surely derived from France, or Europe more broadly, the source of so many American conventions, but they also learned from the wider elegiac tradition that had been central to the reconciliation of death through its propitious placement.[6]

Many conventions of placement are easy to understand, at least superficially. Place transforms memorials, which acquire meaning through context, adjacency, and commemorative practices. Cemeteries at least are places of death; churches have long hosted graveyards and are places of piety (as well as sites for the reenactment of the central death of Christianity); and parks are places of reflection. Even traffic circles are nodes of heightened attention, as can be piazzas and civic buildings, when they offer public space for official commemorations. The "entrances" to towns offer a prominent site for monuments to do their most traditional work of moral admonition or exemplification. They are all eminently practical sites, as well, being public, available, and usually free of the need to use eminent domain to purchase the land. Yet each of these sites is also far more complicated. Each changed in order to become a realm of memory. In turn, modern memorials acquired their meaning in relationship to these various places.

At their worst, public monuments appear to have been thrown to the cars. The Royal Fusiliers Memorial on High Holborn in London (1922) is the urban equivalent of sticking something in the attic (see figure 1.4). It is difficult to fathom an artful reason for its placement. Without shutting down the street, it affords no place for commemorations and offers no good purchase from near or far for pedestrians to take it in. To encounter it up close, to read its inscription or gaze at the statue atop, would have been a hazard even in 1922. The obvious prototype in terms of placement, Edwin Lutyens's Cenotaph, built in London just two years earlier, had several distinct advantages: it was beautifully designed by a major architect, and it was sited on Whitehall, a generous boulevard that served as the major parade route for Remembrance Day in Britain.[7] From the end of World War I, when a temporary cenotaph by Lutyens was erected there, the street was closed to traffic for these commemorations.[8] The Royal Fusiliers Memorial, by contrast, is undistinguished, its site unforgiving. The most that one can say by way of a sympathetic reading is that there was a long history in Europe of erecting crosses and other quasi-commemorative monuments at major crossroads and byways, where their very location was meant to disrupt, to redirect the mind from the mundane to the spiritual realm. Throughout Europe, statues of religious figures punctuate urban pivots, as does the Virgin lamenting her railings in Carcassonne, France (fig. 4.4), built in the era of statuemania (1861). In fact, it appeared just after the castle was restored, turning the site into a major tourist attraction. The Virgin was erected at the foot of the bridge between the town

Figure 4.4. Our Lady of the Guardrails. Statue of the Virgin, 1861, Carcassonne, France, Photograph by the author.

and the castle, where she greeted this new secular stream of traffic. Although she was set discreetly next to a religious institution, she is now so conspicuously misplaced that the permanent railings proved inadequate, and a ghastly tangle of guardrails was added to fence her off. The inscription reads: "Notre-dame de Consolation priez pour nous" (Our Lady of Consolation prays for you). Just don't get too close. The Royal Fusiliers Memorial may have been placed with similar intentions and to induce a similar interaction, only to be engulfed by a faster and more relentless urbanism than could not have been foreseen in 1922.

The Virgin looks increasingly out of place in a secular world, but there is one perspective from which the London memorial works remarkably well: the best way to get close, it turns out, is in a bus stuck in traffic, preferably a British double-decker bus.[9] Here, in its most quotidian moment, blocked by a big red bus, the memorial gives an intimate audience to its elevated passersby paused there by the pulse of traffic. At 16.5 feet high, the pedestal lifts the bronze soldier, who is another 8.5 feet tall, just above bus eye level, where he still stands heroically. The uppermost inscription, however, is what our imagined commuter would see when she looks up from her *Daily Mail* or *Guardian*: "To the glorious memory of the 22,000 Royal Fusiliers who fell in the Great War." The new breed of memorial that celebrated the everyday soldier was often tossed into the most ordinary of places, and the unintended result is an extraordinary encounter.[10]

Since every city has its urban fragments, this is an international phenomenon. A more complicated example, the Mexican-American All Wars Memorial (1949) in Boyle Heights, Los Angeles, inhabits a "leftover" in the Mexican-American neighborhood of Cinco Puntos (fig. 4.5). Here, two grids converge, and five roads cross, leaving two triangles on which a series of related memorials have been installed. The site is quintessentially ordinary. A well-known Mexican restaurant sits astride the site, a Mexican supermarket across the street. Residential neighborhoods spread out to the north and south, and the impermeable wall of Evergreen Cemetery (discussed in the previous

Figure 4.5. A classic memorial on a traffic island. Mexican-American All Wars Memorial, 1949, Boyle Heights, Los Angeles. Photograph by the author.

chapter) abuts the site, as well. Cesar Chavez Avenue, the historic core of the Mexican-American community, cuts through the site; in fact, the memorial interventions spill across the intersection onto the second island. Even the memorial landscape is cut by a street! The site reflects the community's desire to commemorate the overlooked military contributions of Mexican-Americans, but it also demonstrates just how little public space and power they had at their disposal.

Its quasi-official status — it is maintained primarily by local businesses, high school groups, and veterans associations — is exacerbated by the fact that the intersection divides two distinct planning authorities.[11] Neither the Los Angeles Department of City Planning, which oversees Boyle Heights, nor the Los Angeles County Department of Regional Planning, which oversees unincorporated East Los Angeles, claims responsibility for the site. In fifty years of urban plans for Boyle Heights, nothing about Cinco Puntos has changed on official maps, which don't even show the memorial.[12] Community initiatives in the 1970s with far greater sensitivity to local heritage also neglected the memorial and its site.[13] While plans were drawn up by the Los Angeles Department of Transportation in 2014 to place the memorial in a traffic circle — where else! — in order to highlight it better, the area clearly has low priority.[14]

Placing the obelisk here was a matter of local pride, but it landed here as much by default as by design. Unlike the Japanese-American community that had been in the area for generations, in 1949, the Mexican-American community did not have a long history in the adjacent Evergreen Cemetery. There were precious few parks or civic spaces in the area. What is now a liability — Cinco Puntos's ambiguous jurisdiction — was an asset after the war because it allowed the community to work around official channels. The site also enables the memorial to be easily turned on and off. In anticipation of Veterans Day each year, locals clean up the memorial and stage the area with chairs and other temporary structures. Veterans stand for a twenty-four-hour vigil, keeping the memorial turned on.[15] The rest of the year, it provides a sliver of shade and a resting spot for locals (fig. 4.6). The entire affair is a vernacular memorial with official ambitions. As Boyle Heights faces gentrification, Cinco Puntos will likely be absorbed into L.A.'s formal planning schemes, and if the Mexican-American community is displaced, the memorial could become a more generic landmark — or be moved.

The desire to formalize the Cinco Puntos memorial with a traffic circle is now a reflex, a habit in urban planning with a history that goes back nearly to premodern Europe. Traffic circles quickly became a standard way of creating order and reconciling cars and public monuments at the turn of the century, both in modest intersections in small towns and in grand urban planning and beautification schemes in the world's largest cities. In 1904, William Phelps Eno, an American pioneer in traffic design, planned the circular flow of traffic around New York's Columbus Monument (erected in 1892) and its pendant on the east corner of the park, where the angel first led Sherman in a traffic circle. In Paris, Eugène Hénard girdled the much earlier Arc de Triomphe in the Place d'Étoile in 1907.

Early photographs of Columbus Circle show the space chock-a-block with streetcars, automobiles, and pedestrians. In one image, a woman pushes a baby carriage across tracks while streetcars come and go and automobiles jockey with pedestrians for right of way.[16] It is nothing like the present circle, with its careful segregation of pedestrians and cars synchronized by traffic lights. Such circles had roots in the *rond-points* of early modern landscape design, where multiple *allées* or paths converged in a park. Hénard and American planners knew the many *rond-points* of the Parisian parks well. In fact, in the mid-nineteenth century, Olmsted and Vaux imagined a kind of *rond-point* at the Merchants' Gate in the southwest corner of Central Park, where Columbus Circle would eventually land.[17] This circle softened the corner of the park, tied together the paths and roads that met there, and helped along the transition between park and city. The traffic circles, then, were an extension of the park system into the city, and the monuments placed in them were similar in spirit to

Figure 4.6. A man sits in a spire of shade at the Mexican-American All Wars Memorial, 1949, Boyle Heights, Los Angeles. Photograph by the author.

those placed at entrances of parks. These techniques of park design beat back the hard-edged urbanism of the period. In New York City, the parks commissioner controlled the placement of monuments in these remaindered spaces.[18]

While Eno's and Hénard's circles are often seen as the first ones, distant precedents in New Orleans and Indianapolis dimly reflect baroque traditions. In 1877, New Orleans dedicated Lee Place within Tivoli Circle, an older circus that linked uptown and downtown New Orleans. The word "circle" links back to "circus"—as in Piccadilly Circus—a word that came into use for urban settings in the early eighteenth century.[19] In New Orleans, a column with a bronze of Robert E. Lee atop was erected in 1884, and the area became known informally as Lee Circle. The still grander Monument Circle in Indianapolis is anchored by the Soldiers and Sailors Monument, a massive Civil War memorial finished in 1902.[20] As in New Orleans, the circle predated the monument. It had been set aside as Governor's Circle in the original speculative plan of Indianapolis of 1821. In keeping with the Midwestern habit, the green became the main public space of the city and was renamed Circle Park in 1867. A statue of Indiana Governor Oliver P. Morton went up in 1884, soon to be displaced by the Civil War monument, planning for which began in the 1880s.[21]

The circles in New Orleans and Indianapolis were important civic spaces transformed by their memorials. In Indianapolis, in particular, a complex public space came to be dominated by the memorial and by traffic, as if these were the twin poles of modern civic experience. Both circles have served as icons for their respective cities, appearing in guidebooks and on postcards. Both have been major sites of commemoration. Fifteen thousand people attended the dedication in Indianapolis, and thousands of people have commemorated the Lost Cause in Lee Circle.[22] In the wave of protest against anti-Black racism that swept through American cities in 2017, New Orleans removed Lee and plans to replace him with a fountain. George Burnap is grinning in his grave. (See Chapter 3.) While many Confederate monuments will be disarmed in museums or

Figure 4.7. Monument to monumental urbanism. Antonio Rivas Mercado, Angel of Independence, 1910, Paseo de la Reforma, Mexico City. Postcard from the author's collection.

Figure 4.8. The median's revenge. Ignacio Asúnsolo, sculptor, Jesus Aguirre, architect, Monument to Cuitláhuac, 1964, Paseo de la Reforma, Mexico City. Only one of the supertowers remains today. Postcárd from the author's collection.

"disappeared" into warehouses, "Lee Circle" will surely survive in local parlance for generations. Circles resist iconoclasm better than statues; words can be even more durable.

It did not take long for the monument in the circle to become formalized, with monuments conceived as integrated parts of larger urban schemes. A series of them punctuate the colossal axis of the Paseo de la Reforma in Mexico City. Conceived at the turn of the century, they are staged chronologically as a narrative of the history of Mexico (figs. 4.7 and 4.8). Inspired by Haussmann's Paris, this is the "grand manner" at its most ambitious, cosmopolitan, and imperial in scale. Some of the monuments sit on agoraphobia-inducing public spaces. Others, such as the much later Monument to Cuitláhuac, are wedged in supermedians between busy streets, accessible only by hard-edged pedestrian bridges. This string of monuments has been seen as a form of conquest, a "path of power" and a "representation of the course of the nation towards supreme order and progress."²³ The monuments speak to the desire of the state to shape the world, or at least to shape consciousness. But they are also locked into the mundane, if also aggressively monumental, infrastructure of everyday life.

The monument in the traffic circle is a quintessential part of French, Iberian, and Hispano-American urbanism from Lisbon to Buenos Aires, but examples can be found around the world, from Awassa in Ethiopia, Bangkok, Barbados, and Berlin to Bucharest, Cairo, Calabar in Nigeria, and Leningrad. They are common in former European colonies and are favorites of dictators, who use them to thrust conspicuous symbols into the most visible spaces in the name of progress or nation or "the people." Democracies use them, as well, building on the persistent confusion between the classical tradition and democratic institutions. Just after the turn of the century, the commissions that revised Pierre Charles L'Enfant's original design for Washington, DC, placed monuments in the traffic circles that linked the major arterials in the plan. Nearly every node in the city ushers traffic into a commemorative circle. Versailles is the most commonly cited source, but this reference obscures more contemporary influences. The same instincts that transformed the cemetery into a national legion of honor is writ large on the American capital, giving a historical anchor to the throw-away line that Washington is a necropolis.

Smaller towns have turned to this cosmopolitan gesture in their attempts to modernize streets. As baldly historical moves introduced into the stream of modern life, they are a material expression of modernity's struggle to reconcile the new with the old. In Mystic, Connecticut, the Civil War Memorial of 1909 was not placed in the center of town but rather in an intersection of rutted, dirt roads, with walking paths nearby (fig. 4.9). There, it ornamented the transition from town to a leafy, residential area. A streetcar soon carved an arc through the intersection, followed by automobiles. Soon, the memorial was absorbed into a commercial scene. The once pastoral memorial became part of a traffic circle and at some point, the "Slow

Figure 4.9. Soldiers Memorial with trolley tracks and mud, in 1915, Mystic, Connecticut. Photograph courtesy of the Mystic Seaport Museum.

Go Right" sign appeared, now replaced by one that reads "Keep Right." (See figure 1.6.)

Traffic almost always trumps memory, as does urban development. Once the car became king, the pedestrian became a hazard. Mystic's memorial, now dangled in its traffic circle, is surrounded by businesses and their parking lots, including a bank, a liquor store, a pharmacy, and a boutique. A postoperative rehabilitation facility housed in a building constructed in 1930 offers the best position for viewing the memorial today. Tourists wore out the grass there in pursuit of the best vantage point for photographs. At some point, an ungainly barrier was erected to protect the grass, and then a compromise was struck: the city installed a granite commemorative bench suitable for contemplating the statue. The barrier remains to corral visitors. It is a classic negotiation between the everyday and not-everyday. These interventions maintain a fragile détente between urban realities and the memory industry.

Admonishing Monuments

Hundreds of English and French villages sport similar statues where roads converge or roundabouts bring traffic into town. Angels and crosses at crossroads and circles are so common, they form a type of placement, both opportunistic in its use of available fragments and historical because it echoes the traditional place of the small-town plague column or wayside cross going back to the Middle Ages. Wayside crosses became direct sources for many World War I memorials. (See figure 8.2.) The cross not only likened the sacrifice of the soldier to the inaugural sacrifice of Christianity, it also repurposed the funerary monument from the cemetery, having fallen into disuse under the death taboo, for civic purposes.

A monument so placed plays an additional role of warning, recalling the etymological source of the word, from the Latin *monere*, to admonish. As such, monuments such as these are allegorical. As narrative devices, they let us into a story midstream.[24] Monuments appeared in abundance with the ruptures and transformations of the public realm of modernity, where they helped narrate these changes. The spaces where they've been erected let them wag their fingers most emphatically, urgently, and publicly.

This warning function of modern memorials originated with a shift in mood. Beginning in the early 1700s, Greco-Roman literature supplied a range of heroes who were absorbed into art as didactic figures.[25] Writers and artists scoured the past "for lessons in virtue that were ultimately to permit an extraordinarily close identification of the historical past with the changing political goals" of the present.[26] From the mid-eighteenth century on, "the *exemplum virtutis* — the work of art that was intended to teach a lesson in virtue — began to dominate iconographical choices with particular relish for events culled from Greek and Roman history."[27] Historical figures and their classical precedents in art were used as social figures to extol the abstract virtues of the day, from stoicism to Rousseauan simplicity, honor, and loyalty. With the revolutions that followed, modern heroes joined this dramatis personae. This is William Godwin's world of "glorious beings," real, legendary, and fictional. The statuemania of the nineteenth century thrust these exemplars from the past, now including the recent past, into nearly every public space in European and American cities.[28]

The "moralizing current" of the revolutions forged a new "realm of emotional experience" embodied in the treasure trove of imagery that sculptors turned to for the new cemeteries, statues of national and local heroes, and memorials.[29] Heroes and allegorical figures rose on columns and plinths, a pantheon that shaped the course of sculpture so thoroughly that "the logic of sculpture" became "inseparable from the logic of the monument." As Rosalind Krauss has argued, traditional "sculpture is a commemorative representation."[30] This is as true for the Duke of Wellington as Achilles in Hyde Park, London (1822) as it is for Independence alighting in Mexico City. For every monumental installation, however, there were hundreds of more modest efforts that are equally revealing. For instance, the form of the column at Torfou (1827, fig. 4.10), a figure manqué erected in honor of a battle in the French Revolution, recalls the stark classicism of Jacques-Louis David's *Oath of the Horatii* (1785). As Robert Rosenblum remarked about a similar column, the "severity of . . . style, like the severity of the oath, creates, as it were, a *tabula rasa* of a new epoch."[31] The column now seems like such a stolid, unthinking choice that we forget that it, too, had to be invented — or reinvented and conventionalized — as a type. Torfou's column was once as fresh as the *Oath of the Horatii*. In keeping with David's enthusiasm for "archaeological realism," the creators of Torfou's column would have been aware that the Greeks saw "any man or woman on whom he or she depended" as a column "and could not look at a column without experiencing this vital assimilation."[32] The lone column, reduced to near primal simplicity as it is in Torfou, is a witness to the chastening moral foundations of the French Revolution. It is simultaneously figurative, allegorical, metonymic, and abstract.

Placement also had to be settled and conventionalized. To accomplish this, people looked to the past, as well. Whereas the Horatii took their oath on David's radically simplified pictorial stage, the column

Figure 4.10. The column as moralizing force. Colonne, 1827, Torfou, France. Postcard from the author's collection.

at Torfou sits at a crossroads (now a roundabout) near where actual fighting had taken place. The difference is instructive. David painted realistic bodies in an abstract setting; Torfou is an abstraction in a real setting. This kind of veracity could be extended generally to the land of the nation as a form of patrimony, a word used to describe cultural inheritance tethered to national identity. The inversion of abstraction and realism suggests a relationship between these new commemorative forms, the political art of the period, and landscape itself. How powerful it must have been to externalize the painterly world of David and the revolution in real places, just as the French awoke to the idea of national patrimony.[33] With such memorials, the *exemplum virtutis* found its place in daily life, not just in salons, private collections, and museums.[34] The *exemplum virtutis* provided a flexible, socially available language for commemorative statues. Form could be secondary, especially in the twentieth century, when the stylistic wars of the previous century had cooled. When heroes gave way to simple soldiers on bases or generic doughboys or *poilu* in France, the inscriptions carried on the noble sentiment, remaking everyman into a virtuous example of the ideal citizen and, importantly, *placing* him in everyman's land.[35]

The legacy of the revolutionary-era *exemplum virtutis* has been a continuous part of modern urban experience. These "great men" have cast their shadows for centuries.[36] In some cases, mythic founders were exhumed from obscurity in an age that zealously invented traditions. The ancient Gallic Vercingetorix rose on plinths around France.[37] The one in Gien (erected in 1887) stands guard at an intersection along the main road that leads into the center of town from the train station. Bologna's *glossatori* monuments belong to this tradition. Their legend was plucked from the archives, they were disinterred from the Basilica of San Francesco, and the monuments to these formerly invisible legal scholars were erected in a public place where they could have a moral impact in a city then asserting its independence. (See figure 1.2.) A little later, the town of Winchester resurrected the ninth-century King Alfred. (See figures 9.4 and 9.5.) He stands with raised sword in symbolic defense of a median with parked cars near a roundabout on the way into town, just in case some Vikings speed into town. He has suffered from urban change, especially the advent of heritage tourism. By the 1960s, the "huge cloaked bronze figure" had became "quite daunting to any spectator trivially musing on burnt griddlecakes."[38]

Such grandiose gestures would seem to be an artifact of a bygone age, but Alfred as a type continues to resonate. Danylo in Lviv, Ukraine, was erected in Halytska Square in 2001 as a post-Soviet intervention and as part of the city's transformation into a mecca for Western tourism (fig. 4.11).[39] Danylo Galitsky (1201–1264) is a complicated historical figure. He ruled over parts of the Ukraine and Poland (Galicia) and was part of a dynasty that held western Russia. This made him an apt symbol for Soviet unity and gave the original impetus in the late 1940s for his monument. But Danylo was also exiled as a child. He heroically returned in 1221, united Galicia again, founded Lviv,

Figure 4.11. "The great man" monument reprised. Vasyl Yarych and Roman Romanovych, sculptors and Yarema Churylyk, architect, King Danylo Monument, 2001, Lviv, Ukraine. Photograph courtesy of Валерий Дед.

expanded his domain, and repelled the Mongol invasions in the 1240s. This made him an equally appropriate symbol of local sovereignty against a powerful invader. For a city that has been passed from one outside ruler to another, Danylo's resurgence is a potent symbol. Alas, these metaphors of independence meet inconvenient historical facts. Danylo was eventually forced to submit to Mongol rule and served out his years as a vassal of the khan. But Danylo's return in equestrian form never leads to such pedantic and inconvenient details. Here, he commands his eponymous square, refortifying the city he founded, precisely where the city's bastions once stood. It was in these spaces that many European cities built the more spacious boulevards of the nineteenth century and found room for the nationalistic statues that ornamented them. It was also here that cities could create public squares at the scale of the burgeoning modern city and ornament the transition from old to new. Former East Bloc nations toppled their Stalins while they erected Danilos as sneaky counterpoints in urban sites spiffed up for modern tourism. As the next chapter demonstrates, heritage consumption has been playing similar games with monuments at least since the Second World War cleaned the urban slate.

The *glossatori*, Alfred, and Danylo all dredge up and invent traditions. Like the Sherman statue, they now seem like old-fashioned attempts to bring the past to bear on present political circumstances. At best, they are quaint or picturesque, melting into the wider interest in heritage. Tourist maps number them alongside other historical "attractions"; preservation committees catalog them; monument hunters photograph and pin them to Pinterest. Whatever the *glossatori* or Alfred's statue meant when they were erected, they have become more generic historical monuments — heritage — while the more recent Danylo leans on the same conventions of form and placement to try to achieve instant status as a monument.

What they have become should not obscure the original intent to warn, which was highly particular to their local and national politics and to their placement. Yet their situation could work against this specificity. By dint of their placement, they also aired a more general admonition about modernity itself. Stationed at the hem between old and new, they stitched together disparate fabrics that were not just physical, but also temporal. They slowed down movement and invited retrospection right where modern urban processes threatened or disturbed what had seemed like a timeless situation. They were part of the larger strategy to which early preservation belongs, but as deployable props, they offered geographical flexibility. These sorts of monuments can go anywhere — or nowhere. They were placed where they could best stretch out the present, as if it were enduring, rather than fleeting. In a moment when the rise of history as a professional practice created a dynamic and expansive sense of the past and the revolutions had bequeathed an equally dynamic sense of the future, the present was pinched, reduced, devalued. Such monuments, while seeming to belong to the past, were often positioned where they could hold these processes at bay and best harmonize past, present, and future. By the mid-twentieth century, their warnings would become illegible, obscured by a range of factors explored in the next chapter.

Figure 5.1. A pop-up playground, 2009. Plague column, 1690, Alter Platz, Klagenfurt. Photograph by the author.

CHAPTER FIVE

Displacing Memory

Memory is imagined; it is not real.
Don't be ashamed of its need to create.
— Nick Cave, *The Sick Bag Song*, 2014

Every memorial that has been placed or misplaced can also be displaced to accommodate shifts in values or taste, the heritage industry and tourism, and paradigms of urban planning, among other urban changes. Memorials are frequently deconsecrated or dehistoricized and put into new assemblages that suppress their discomfiting ability to mark time and death. For example, a seventeenth-century plague column, or Pestsäule, sits at the center of a pedestrian zone, lodged within a larger network of memorials and statues in Klagenfurt, Austria (fig. 5.1). It was moved there in 1965, three years after planners pedestrianized the area, the first such effort in Austria — one small part of the larger reinvention of the town, especially its historical center, in the postwar period. For over two centuries, the column had stood on a church square that lies at the edge of the pedestrian area. It now marks the town's medieval core, the crossroads of the Alter Platz. In its new role, it satisfies the multiple formal and social demands of such a space. As a monument, it anchors the rather amorphous funnel of the street and lends gravitas to an area that otherwise can read as denuded, an effect of the overly vigorous scrub of postwar reconstruction, restoration, and gentrification. The city was bombed forty-seven times. Seventy percent of the buildings were destroyed. What you see

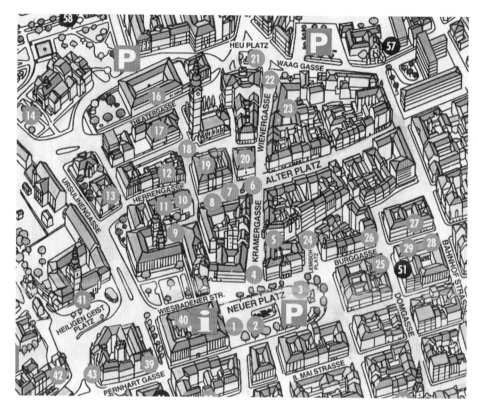

Figure 5.2. Map from Klagenfurt's historic zone. From *A Walk through the Old Town*, © Tourism Region Klagenfurt am Wörthersee GmbH, 2017.

in Klagenfurt is as much artful reconstruction as it is fastidious preservation. As an eye-catcher, the plague column draws tourists into the flow of the center. It is a pictorial device, an urban form of *repoussoir*, the painterly technique that plants a formal element, often a building or tree, in the foreground of an image in order to frame and give measure to the middle and background. The compositional strategy leads the eye into a scene. From the crossroads of the Alter Platz, the column gives a spatial gauge to the "new old" area — whether or not Klagenfurt's urban planners were aware of such pictorial techniques. As a historical marker (number 6 on the map; see figure 5.2), it offers a station on the tourist itinerary, which can be traced on a map from the tourist office with blurbs about Klagenfurt's major historic sites.[1]

Plucked from its former position in front of the Heiligengeist-kirche on Heiligengeistplatz (number 41 in figure 5.2), the plague column, whose first incarnation, in wood, goes back to 1680, is no longer in dialogue with the church that gave it its sacred meaning (fig. 5.3). The column embodies a specific change in urbanism, one entangled with the postwar vogue for pedestrian zones. Planners moved it to the Alter Platz in order to convert the Heiligengeistplatz into the bus depot — so much for the Holy Ghost! At the same time, pedestrianization disencumbered the Alter Platz, which became a space for leisure, shopping, and tourism. Tourists arrive by the bus-load and shuffle through the older city without having to encounter cars.[2] Along the way, they can play connect the dots with the major monuments and historic sites. Meanwhile, the column, with its representation of the Trinity, no longer resonates with the statue of

Figure 5.3. Klagenfurt's plague column in its original location next to the Heiligengeist church. This square is now the bus depot. Engraving from Siegfried Hartwagner, *Klagenfurt, Stadt: Ihre Kunstwerke, historischen Lebens-un Siedlungformen* (Salzburg: Verlag St. Peter, 1980), p. 116. Courtesy of Verlag St. Peter.

Christ affixed to the front of the Heiligengeist church (figs. 5.4 and 5.5). For centuries, these features faced one another on the square. In fact, without the help of an additional plaque, tourists and locals would need special knowledge to deduce its original intent.

It is just one of many changes for the column, which received its half moon and cross in 1683 to mark the Austrian victory over the Ottomans in battle, a second plague from which the town was spared. In its new place, instead of invoking God for sparing the town from these plagues, it evokes a generic sense of history, an aesthetic of age that puts it in dialogue with the square it pins down. Tourists (and locals), after all, don't want to shop and take coffee amid reminders of plague — and the Pestsäule in its new position poses no such threat. It can take its rest as a beautiful, vertical ornament imported as scenery, a formal device that would help people negotiate the city. Klagenfurt's column was thus part of reestablishing a mental image for a city nearly erased by the war.

What makes this urban gesture even starker is that plague columns proliferated in premodern Europe when people were under constant threat from plague, famine, and war, a world before secular memorials.[3] As a prayer given permanent form, it was one of the many ways that people attempted to create stability in precarious times, or as the Swiss historian Arthur E. Imhof might have put it, how they "relieved themselves of the psychological strain" of the uncertainty of life. Through everyday habits of marriage, land tenure, baptism, and burial, they transformed despair "into the certainty of salvation," which "in turn contributed to psychological stability."[4] Klagenfurt's plague column somehow survived into the modern period to stand in a highly ordered, tourism-based European city in which plague and famine are distant historical facts and war has been scuttled into far-off lands, at least for the time being.[5] What to do with these columnar religious pilgrims that have wandered unwarily from the foreign country of the past into the deconsecrated public sphere of the present but to turn them into urbanistic *spolia*? Whereas in the Middle Ages *spolia*, or fragments of older buildings

Figure 5.4. Figure of Christ on the plague column. Photograph by the author.

Figure 5.5. The Crucifixion on the Heiligengeistkirche, once in dialogue with the plague column. Photograph by the author.

from pagan Rome, was inserted into new buildings to ward off evil spirits, Klagenfurt's repurposed column does just the opposite: it renders such superstitions archaic by transforming a former symbol of precariousness into a picturesque landmark, or worse, mere history. For what is less enchanted, as Pierre Nora suggests, than history? Particularly history curated for tourists.

The plague column was but one part of a larger urban strategy in Klagenfurt that reveals just how unfixed memorials are and how cities displace their aides-mémoire for purposes alien to remembering. Since the 1950s, nearly every memorial in the town has been moved, altered, or reoriented in the reconstruction of the pedestrian zone after World War II. Postwar planners inherited a north-south axis already marked with two monuments: at the top, the Floriani Monument of 1781, erected in memory of a disastrous fire, which sits in the Heuplatz on the northern entrance to the pedestrian zone (number

Figure 5.6. Hercules protecting Maria Theresa from the Lindwurm on the Neuer Platz, Klagenfurt, 1593. Franz Pönninger, Maria Theresa Monument, 1873. Photograph by the author.

21 in figure 5.2), and the Lindwurm (built originally in 1593), a dragon that serves as the mythical symbol of Klagenfurt's founding, which closes off the south side of this axis on the Renaissance Neuer Platz (number 3 in figure 5.2) (fig. 5.6).[6] The statue of Hercules was added in 1636. Improbably, this massive monument was reoriented to face south in 1972. Hercules can now better protect Maria Theresa from the dragon. This shuffling adjusted for another change. The first incarnation of the Maria Theresa Monument of 1765 sat on the other side of the square (fig. 5.7). Had they not flipped her in the 1970s, she would have trained her royal gaze on the dragon's posterior. The move to this more dignified position put her in dialogue with another monument, this one to the medieval founder of Klagenfurt, Bernhard von Spanheim (number 24 in figure 5.2) (fig. 5.8).[7]

Yet like the plague column and Maria Theresa's statue, Spanheim's neo-Romanesque monument began life elsewhere and in a different form. He was originally erected in the Alter Platz in 1932, at the core

Figure 5.7. Original statue of Maria Theresa, 1765, Klagenfurt. From Siegfried Hartwagner, *Klagenfurt, Stadt: ihre Kunstwerke, historischen Lebens-un Siedlungformen* (Salzburg: Verlag St. Peter, 1980), p. 166. Courtesy of Verlag St. Peter.

of the town he founded (fig. 5.9). The first Spanheim, who was made of metal, was melted down in 1940 for obvious reasons, only to be rebuilt in stone in 1954 on the same site. Pedestrianization displaced Spanheim eight years later, when the Pestsäule was erected just feet from where the medieval knight had stood. He didn't find his present home facing Maria Theresa until 1981. Spanheim looks longingly at the empress from his fountain in Lemisch Platz, where he anchors this important midblock entry into the pedestrian zone from the Neuer Platz (fig. 5.10).

One more twist further brings out just how much these monuments have become pawns of urban design. Spanheim replaced a statue to Franz-Joseph, Maria Theresa's great-great grandson, the Habsburg emperor who created the Ringstrasse in Vienna and oversaw the modernization of Austria just as the statue to Maria Theresa was being rebuilt in Klagenfurt. Placed so, the two figures once created a dialogue about the greatness of the Habsburg Empire in its

Figure 5.8. Bernhard of Spanheim Monument, 1954, as rebuilt by Arnulf Pichler, Lemisch Platz, Klagenfurt. Photograph by the author.

Figure 5.9. Josef Valentin Kassin, the first Spanheim Monument, 1932, in its original location on the Alter Platz. Postcard from the author's collection.

Figure 5.10. The 1954 Spanheim Monument gazing at the second Maria Theresa statue, 1873. Photograph by the author.

waning years as he stood guard at the edge of his eponymous square.

Marching the medieval Spanheim into the Alter Platz placed the local hero at a site of major urban change. His late date links him more to the reactionary politics of the 1930s than to contemporary attempts to stabilize modernity through themed environments in the United States — Disneyland opened a year after Spanheim was reerected. But this misses the larger point. The strategy provided a way to recall founder myths at the precise moment and place that modernization and urbanization transformed historic cores. Tradition and history were symbolically thrust into the fray. Spanheim is similar to the *glossatori* in Bologna and some of the famous founders and patriots in American cities: "great men" and nation builders whose revival spoke to long-enduring memory amid disorienting change. To recommit to this practice in 1954, as happened in Klagenfurt, aligns the city's immediate postwar planning with the sort of eerily faithful reconstruction that took place in cities such as Nuremberg after the war.[8] In displacing the statue of Franz-Joseph, a distant and nearly mythic past erased a more recent past that could not be blurred by the mists of time. Franz-Joseph has disappeared. The medieval replaced the modern.

Without putting too fine a point on it, a mnemonic of medieval Klagenfurt displaced a mnemonic of nation at the juncture of the medieval core, while Spanheim, in gazing at Maria Theresa, directs *our* gaze from the local founding back to a symbol of empire long before it eroded. Monuments hold Klagenfurt's pedestrian zone in a web of local, royal, national, and mythic gestures of founding and survival, but none too vivid to upset the tourist. Just in case these sober statues ruin the mood, the *Wörthersee Mandl* (1962) bubbles up in the jog between Spanheim and the plague column (fig. 5.11). As the legend goes, the dwarflike man with his arm around a beer keg warned the heedless revelers who lived in the area of their impending doom should they not stop their bacchanalia. They ignored him, and he opened the tap, which created a great lake and wiped out the village. This folktale told in bronze and marble, just like the serious

Figure 5.11. A Grimm warning and an open beer keg in the pedestrian zone, Klagenfurt. Spanheim stands just around the corner. Heinz Goll, sculptor, 1965. Photograph by Denise Wenig.

monuments, winks at them like some impish dwarf from the Brothers Grimm. *Mandl* lampoons the monument as warning. He tells us not to take Klagenfurt's more serious monuments too seriously.[9] Empress, knight, dragon, dwarf: the entire Altstadt becomes a fable of time and space distorted. Here, history is the loser, and memory is an afterthought. Neither matters a whit. In place of both, visual delight in the guise of heritage is molded in the service of pleasure and consumption. When the Pestsäule rose three years *after* the *Wörthersee Mandl* in 1965 in the Alter Platz, at the center of this web, it began the process of locking the historic core into place with memorials as vague heritage posts.

The point of detailing the pattern of this web is to see the displacement of memorials, monuments, and even some public art as vivid parts of postwar schemes in conservation planning and the deliberate construction of heritage cores that cater to tourism. Similar efforts can be found around the world. Like deconsecrated churches, Klagenfurt's monuments speak less to specific memories or even to precise historical events — even if they can still be asked to do just that — than they nod generically to history. In fact, relieved of the burden of specific commemorative practices, they are free to adorn, mark space, or, as an ensemble, demarcate and ennoble the old city; in effect, to affirm its historicity in another pivotal moment of transformation. Klagenfurt is but an example in extremis of what happened in many European cities — and some American ones — across the twentieth century. Its example points out the convergence of monuments, tourism, and urban planning within the project of heritage conservation. As cities used their historical assets in order to reinvent themselves in terms of tourism, monuments became the visual, spatial, and symbolic pieces they used to create their larger effects.[10]

What made Klagenfurt, or any city, susceptible to this sort of reshaping? Like most European cities, it was transformed by the geopolitical and technological dislocations of the past two hundred years. As towns modernized in the nineteenth century, their old cores were often left to molder. The physical fact of their premodern urban morphology made them resistant to cars and other forms of modern transportation, as well as to the modern infrastructures of comfort and communication. Electricity, heating and air conditioning, plumbing, garages, and other amenities were easier to build into new developments than to retrofit into medieval or Renaissance towns.[11] An openly hostile attitude set in, and municipal administrators began to eviscerate the historic fabric of cities in the name of modernization. Georges Haussmann's assault on medieval Paris is the best-known example of what became endemic to European urbanism after the mid-nineteenth century.[12] Space here precludes a detailed history of Klagenfurt's transformation, but it followed the general pattern of many European towns. World War II marked a major inflection point, especially in war-torn cities. In the postwar decades, commercial and residential patterns of land use changed dramatically, creating "a functional vacuum" into which cities plugged "a mixture of leisure-shopping functions," including craft shops, boutiques and antique stores, cafés and restaurants, most closing outside of shopping hours.[13] Broadly speaking, there were two ways to respond to these changes. One was the "brave new world" approach to modernization, as seen in Rotterdam's archetypal modern pedestrian zone, the Lijnbaan, where an entirely new commercial and residential zone was created atop the ruins of the war, with no attempt to preserve, reconstruct, or even gesture toward what had been there. To the other extreme, cities fossilized their historic centers as "large open-air museums" in an effort to create what has been called, appropriately if inelegantly, the tourist-historic city.[14] What saved historic cores from the deadening effects of modernization during the same period was their historical value and the concentration of population near them. The past could be manipulated, but only if planners could take control of the historical material as if it were a plastic medium.[15]

Historical assets were treated with wider urban intentions, because preservation was grafted onto a more expansive mission.

Throughout the nineteenth century, and especially in the twentieth, official government bodies slowly absorbed the apparatus of historic preservation, more commonly called "conservation" in Europe, in the form of commissions on art and monuments, which began listing buildings and creating a theoretical basis for conceptualizing, and manipulating, historical assets. In the postwar era, when attitudes toward government's role in heritage conservation changed significantly, urban planning absorbed conservation. Reconstruction and urban development were reconciled with the historic parts of cities that had survived the two world wars or were painstakingly rebuilt.[16] Conservation, long the bailiwick of "private initiatives and local, civic, rather than national, concern," became part of public planning.[17] At the same time, the purview of conservation widened to include neighborhoods or districts, and a form of conservation zoning emerged, formalized in the idea of the *zone protégé*, or protected zone, a term coined in 1962, the same year that Klagenfurt pedestrianized its historic area.[18] Klagenfurt's planners, who seemed hopelessly backward in 1954 with the Spanheim monument, were in step with the vanguard by the early 1960s. Or more likely, they moved in two directions at once.

This emphasis on historical townscape in place of the monument "brought the town planner to centre stage in place of the architect and art historian."[19] Conservation planning thus assimilated the grand, utopian planning of twentieth-century modernism, taking on its moral prerogatives, visions of totality, and the role of government in the process. Under cover of preservation, heritage, or patrimony, planners were able to channel some of the ideas birthed in the more radical context of the rise of the Modern Movement in architecture; Le Corbusier's radical vision to create a city of skyscrapers on top of Paris is the most widely cited example.[20] The same areas that modern architects and planners had proposed to raze and rebuild were now under their control to be planned comprehensively in terms of preservation. It became standard across Europe, and to a lesser extent in the United States, to place large urban tracts under designation, submitting them to "a new permanent and general form of urban management."[21] While historians of preservation understand these vast institutional and socioeconomic shifts, less attention has been paid to the subtler sleight of hand that treated historic monuments as moveable historical assets, nudging them into useful places in order to construct, not reconstruct, a meaningful urban diagram — a diagram that is fundamentally modernist in its clarity and consumerist in its intentions.

As modernist as this diagram is, it also looks backward to Camillo Sitte, the late nineteenth-century Viennese pioneer of urban design whose work was still a presence in planning education and practice in the postwar period; a Viennese publishing house reprinted the third edition of his *City Planning according to Artistic Principles* in 1965, just as Klagenfurt refashioned its historic core.[22] Sitte was also a seminal figure in redeeming medieval urbanism and forging a counterargument against the more common destruction of the surviving medieval fabric.[23] What would Sitte have thought of Klagenfurt's playful use of monuments? While he may have frowned upon displacing the column so casually, he would have recognized the "artistic principles" that his fellow countryman put into practice. Sitte derided the "modern folly" of centering "every little statue" in a magnificent public space. The ancients, he counseled, "placed their monuments around the plazas and against walls."[24] He considered it a *principle* — that high-minded word nineteenth-century ideologues wielded with near biblical fervor — to keep the centers of plazas open and he devoted the entire second chapter of his book to the topic. The plague column in Klagenfurt is Sittean in this regard. It is "set aside from the central axis," where it makes no pretense to magnificence and disencumbers the space visually and functionally.[25] It also recognizes the irregularity of the space, where multiple streets decant into the lozenge-shaped plaza. Many of the other statues in Klagenfurt are placed more formally, befitting their more formal plazas, and thus are un-Sittean.

The artful use of monuments in Klagenfurt could have had mid-century sources, as well. The Townscape Movement, led by Gordon

Cullen, urged the "reading" of cities through a picturesque, even cinematic, lens that celebrated architectural heritage on formal and aesthetic grounds. In *Townscape* (1961), Cullen invented the concept of "serial vision," a method for parsing the formal qualities of a town and its spaces while encountering it on foot (fig. 5.12). Cullen's drawings take the reader through a "sequence of revelations" provoked by "sudden contrasts" of shadow and light, open and enclosed space, building and nature, and so on. An anonymous column draws the walker into a space, creates a human-scaled encounter with the base in space, and guides the walker around it to further *mysteries* (his word). As his language suggests, behind these formal observations lay something deeper: a kind of "illumination," "like nudging a man who is going to sleep in church."[26] This kind of revelation lies somewhere between Lefebvre's *bizarrerie* and Eliade's hierophany. To be sure, Cullen was shepherding the reader to a secular revelation about the everyday built environment, in particular, about how vernacular urban forms, especially those drawn from the past, could create aesthetic dramas. While *Townscape* is often seen as regressive, nostalgic, or sentimental, all crimes against modernity, it is also a strand of modernism, pitched against the tabula rasa makers such as Le Corbusier. In trying to reconcile the historical parts of European cities with modern realities, Cullen introduced monuments as aesthetic propositions, props, in fact, for urban design, a field just then emerging. Cullen's monument, even more than Klagenfurt's plague column, is entirely ahistorical.

Cullen's abstract monument recalls how Kevin Lynch's *Image of the City* (1960) gave planners license to treat memorials as aesthetic devices. Along with paths, nodes, edges, and districts, landmarks were one of the five formal elements that Lynch believed structure the experience of the city. Lynch, who was among the most influential planners of the period, presented his system as a universal syntax, virtually ahistorical and vernacular, and foundational to how people construct mental maps.[27] Such a system must have resonated for a city such as Klagenfurt that had been obliterated by the war. Lynch generalized landmarks so thoroughly that virtually any memorable

To walk from one end of the plan to another, at a uniform pace, will provide a sequence of revelations which are suggested in the serial drawings opposite, reading from left to right. Each arrow on the plan represents a drawing. The even progress of travel is illuminated by a series of sudden contrasts and so an impact is made on the eye, bringing the plan to life (like nudging a man who is going to sleep in church). My drawings bear no relation to the place itself; I chose it because it seemed an evocative plan. Note that the slightest deviation in alignment and quite small variations in projections or setbacks on plan have a disproportionally powerful effect in the third dimension.

Figure 5.12. The monument as pure urban scenography. From Gordon Cullen, *Concise Townscape* (New York: Van Nostrand Reinhold, 1961), p. 17. Reproduced by permission of Taylor and Francis Group.

feature in the landscape would do. They simply had to be singular in form and memorable in context. Towers, domes, whole buildings, weathervanes, trees, and signs all could play the part. He saw how potent monuments could be as placemakers. His sketch of a square anchored by a simple obelisk-like form reduces the idea to its basic elements (fig. 5.13). Alongside this sketch, he wrote that a node can be all the "more remarkable if provided with one or two objects which are foci of attention."[28] This "classic" arrangement for outdoor spaces could be complicated with "transparences, overlappings, light modulation, perspective, surface gradients, closure, articulation patterns of motion and sound."[29] This sometimes maddening abstraction collapsed all manner of landmarks into one category. While Lynch himself was a sensitive urbanist who was highly attentive to local differences, his work could give license to planners to treat memorials as generic landmarks, as abstractions.

Whether or not Klagenfurt's planners looked directly at Sitte or learned from Cullen or Lynch, their way of thinking about the relationship of public spaces, buildings, and monuments persists to this day in urban design, the Sittean influence being especially strong in Austria and Central Europe. But Sitte could not have anticipated what happened in Klagenfurt, where the town's memorials have been used to frame its protected zone. After all, Sitte wrote about cities before

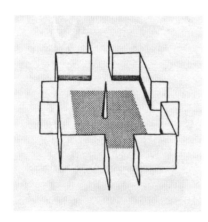

Figure 5.13. The monument as purely formal gesture. From Kevin Lynch, *Image of the City* (Cambridge, MA: MIT Press, 1960), p. 102.

the automobile—and two world wars—had changed the game. It should be no surprise, with all of this movement and change, that the historical integrity of Klagenfurt's old city was thrown into doubt. The absence of memorials to World War II, or even to World War I, within this aesthetic diagram brings home most vividly the disengagement of these memorials from their historical roots. There are numerous memorials to the two world wars in Klagenfurt, but they are either obscured or sit well away from the old city. An antifascist monument, *1938*, is a gruesome affair: a vertical rectangular block with the upper three-quarters of its length crushing the spindly bodies caught under its weight. Impossibly skinny legs jut out (fig. 5.14). It sits prominently on a green at the university, a forty-five-minute walk from the old city, far from where it could disturb the vague historical aura. Elsewhere, a mural depicting a crumpled soldier, along with the words "Wir sind für euch gefallen" (We fell for you), and plaques with names cover an outdoor wall of Saint Rupert Church (fig. 5.15). Devotional candles are still in active use there, but the church is far from the tourist itinerary. Anything that could break the illusion of Klagenfurt as a picturesque old European town is beyond the pedestrian zone. The Artillery Memorial for both World Wars comes closest. The massive metal lion sits on a green strip between one of the main arterials and a parking garage. But even this was moved—twice. The war, the very event that led to the destruction and eventual reconstruction of the old city, is virtually edited out of the built environment. World War II still haunts Austria; it lives on at the margins of Klagenfurt.[30]

Put differently, Klagenfurt essentially deallegorized its memorials. Allegory is literally a "speaking about" something in another guise. Moving the memorials has severed this connection or veiled their original allegorical potential.[31] The plague column, which once spoke to God's whims and the Turkish threat to the Christian West, is now allegorically blank; Spanheim, a medieval *exemplum virtutis*, has lost his moral aura. This sort of shuffling of memorials amounts to a kind of iconoclasm, that most violent disruptor of imagery, which at base removes the allegorical potential of a monument. When people

Figure 5.14. Fascism zoned out of the tourist area. Rudolf Peyker, *1938*, 1988, University of Klagenfurt. Photograph by the author.

Figure 5.15. All hints of "the fallen" remain safely away from the historic zone. World War II Memorial, St. Rupert's Church, Klagenfurt. Photograph by Johann Jaritz.

melt down the kings, lasso down the Stalins, or dismount the Confederate generals who stood as figures of a powerful elite upholding their system of dominance, they are attempting to silence them as allegory, as monuments.

This set of maneuvers — moving, reframing, or destroying memorials — has been a common strategy during a long period in which allegory itself was in seemingly fatal decline. By World War II, allegory appeared to be all but moribund. As the architect Joseph Hudnut wrote during World War II: "Do not ask the monument what is hidden. The monument does not remember."[32] To Hudnut, memorials were mute, drained of memory, allegorically empty. Part of this issued from a modernist desire to quash traditional sculpture, to render artistic allegories defunct. The parallel development of abstraction in modern art and architecture contained an iconoclastic urge to expunge style and figuration. Curiously, however, iconoclasm also flatters allegory. If Klagenfurt's old monuments were truly bereft of memory, the city's more recent memorials would not need to be so thoroughly kept from the center. If anything, *1938* is a powerful allegory about the "little guy" and the horrors of the *Anschluss* and war. It is as if the crucified Christ from the plague column has been taken down, turned into "everyman" and "everywoman", and crushed beneath the very monument itself, now turned upside down as an allegory about the abuses of fascism. It is also an allegory about the totalitarian meaning of the column as a memorial type. But its placement is the point here: it sits where it can do no serious harm to Klagenfurt's tourist economy. Another memorial to victims of Nazi euthanasia also lies on the periphery, on the grounds of the mental hospital where these murders took place — appropriate, but peripheral. The city has effectively zoned its allegorical warnings, carefully placing the ones that could still speak beyond the sanitized area of the Alstadt. At this historical distance, plagues are harmless, World War II is not — not yet, anyway. One day, the statute of limitations on the disasters of the twentieth century will also expire. One day, memorials to our present-day traumas will also seem charming, and we will take coffee, or some futuristic drink, in the shadow of Covid-19 memorials.

Klagenfurt as Informational City

While the creation of the tourist-historic city predates the work of sociologist Manuel Castells on what he calls the "information society," pedestrianization has rendered these cores highly open to the developments that he details. At first, these rebuilt towns were centers for leisure and recreational shopping, but they would soon find economic texture with the array of dispersed businesses that arose from the globalization of the economy under the forces of information technology. What Castells calls the rise of "information-based production" made these old cities viable again, but in a very particular way.[33] He writes, beginning in the 1970s, the service economy organized itself "around the dynamics of information-generating units, while connecting their different functions to disparate spaces."[34] In an information-based economy, the traditional links between production and place are broken, and the location of the control of knowledge is scattered "across undifferentiated locations and secretive spaces," which "denies the specific productive meaning of any place outside its position in a network whose shape changes relentlessly in response to the messages of unseen signals and unknown codes."[35] This ushered in the unraveling of "place-based societies."[36] The same set of changes to an information-based economy encouraged processes already at work in the historical cores of European cities. It helped the neglected historical cores of European cities reinvent themselves, now as centers of pleasure, tourism, shopping, and service, while allowing them to insulate themselves from some of the aspects of the place-based economy that are most troubling, especially industry. Relatively free of cars and industrial sites as visual and polluting reminders of the old economy, they became pristine service centers, in some cases more isolated and purer than malls, which arose at the same time to serve the service economy — and, ironically, which were based on some of the features that these old urban cores once had. This cleansing is not just the socioeconomic context for Klagenfurt's staging of its old city: it is the aesthetic underpinning. What happened to Klagenfurt's memorials and memorials throughout Europe and the United States mirrored the economic displacements of the period. And why would it be otherwise? They were simply absorbed into the tourist economy that is a vital part of the turn away from place-based societies.

One of the consequences of the fashion to pedestrianize the historical centers of Europe, Klagenfurt's included, was the creation of an urban body language that simultaneously embodied and obscured the emerging economic order. It is now difficult to see the vibrant, functional historic cores in Europe as invented and even harder to see them as postmodern or what Freud would have called *Unheimliche* (roughly, uncanny), but this is exactly what they became in the postwar decades. The pedestrianized zones have become themed environments of a sort, but the theme (genuine history lovingly preserved, continuity, tradition) hides the telematic backroom of wires and the credit system that brought it to life as a new kind of place. This is not to condemn the frankly heroic work of preservation and reconstruction in Europe's historical cores (casualties of war and time), but rather to acknowledge how strange these spaces must have been at first when they were reinvented and to draw attention to their continued peculiarity. It is not merely the eerie simulacrum of reconstruction in cities like Klagenfurt that are painstakingly rebuilt — I'm tempted to say resurrected — to hide all traces of its destruction but rather the creation of an urban other that at first appears disturbingly like the original.

While so much critical writing has fingered Southern California and in particular Disneyland as the archetype of the simulacrum, in fact, it is in these subtler reconstructions of European medieval cores that we find the simulacrum in its most devastating form. Embedded with virtuosity into a real medieval fabric, supported on real Renaissance columns, resurfaced with stone from the same quarries on which the vaults of these towns depended, the *centro historico, vieille ville,* or *Altstadt* phenomenon in Europe creates a modern doppelgänger of its vanished self. These reconstructed historic cores are uncomfortably close in spirit to Disneyland, a contemporary intervention produced by many of the same economic forces. Jean Baudrillard's idea of the simulacrum can be a guide.[37] So many European towns seized on their original cores — sacked by time, ruined by war, or quartered by modernity and its technology — and carefully brought them back to a state that, in fact, never existed. Using a combination of mimesis, suggestion, and information technology, they conjured an illusion of historical authenticity. Even with the careful markings of self-conscious preservation or the blank stare of plate glass on modern storefronts that have forced their way into premodern facades, these areas only grudgingly betray their falsehood. Some might argue that they have enough of the original DNA to count as real, and this may be so, if one wishes to continue the false dichotomy of real and fake. They are simply the next recombination of Europe. Some of the early attempts at preservation, going back to the mid-nineteenth century, started historical cores on this course.[38]

Discovering what has been invented is not always obvious. Since the car is a relative newcomer to Europe's medieval cores, these areas were never pedestrianized in the modern sense. Originally, horses and carts, animals and hawkers, filled them, joining the debris, sounds, and smells that these forces throw into the street. Most historic cores grew out of the heterogeneous mix of commerce, religious institutions, preindustrial production, and residential life born of the protocapitalism of the Middle Ages before being partly abandoned by modern technology and its spatial needs. And now they are one of the homogeneous, staid, and staged fronts of the informational city, which is nowhere in particular, but emerges to create places wherever it can attract people to its products.

Klagenfurt's pedestrianization dovetails with the beginnings of this process. Its newly paved streets in the 1960s were a form of modernization dressed in nostalgic clothing, but preservation and the quarries of paving stones that covered the two historical cross streets of the medieval town could not alone create a sense of place out of the essentially cold placelessness of the economics behind its emergence. The creative use of memorials, which are more malleable and moveable than buildings, gave it the trappings of a traditional place. The plague monument, in particular, marks the key axis in this process and draws people forward, offering a gesture toward civic space, a place to gather.

Why are these gestures important? Why can't the informational city simply invent a new built environment to conduct its business? Because, as Castells cryptically wrote, "people live in places, power rules in flows."[39] One way to understand this is literal: people cannot dematerialize into cyberspace. But while some people might choose to enter the slipstream of information and abandon their bodies, as foreseen by William Gibson and other science fiction writers, habits of the body persist, and for good reason. Conventions of gesture, movement, and interaction in space do not immediately adjust to economic or geopolitical changes, nor should they. Globalization does not make a body global, and in fact, it may encourage some bodies to act locally, to embrace modes of encounter or behavior in space that offer succor in the face of change. The displaced monuments of Klagenfurt provide props for an otherwise potentially alienating space in which people can carry on long-standing spatial practices.

At the same time that Klagenfurt pedestrianized its historical core and was transformed into a tourism-based economy, a kind of architectural theme park called Minimundus was founded (fig. 5.16). Here, two parallel and interrelated processes worked together: the creation of a historic center and the establishment of a pseudohistorical theme park, albeit in miniature, both of which arose out of an emerging attention to heritage or patrimony and an attempt to use it to generate tourism. While Minimundus displays models of architecture from around the world, it is heavily skewed toward Austria, with the expected spate of castles and modern Austrian buildings and infrastructure sharing space with the chestnuts of the architectural canon.

As a highly selective romp through the history of architecture,

Figure 5.16. Austrian Gothic and Italian baroque face off at Minimundus, Klagenfurt, which opened in 1958. Photograph by the author.

Minimundus supplies what Klagenfurt's reconstructed center cannot: a worldly and expansive experience, from ancient Egypt to the contemporary moment, as told through the monuments of the world. The Parthenon and the Palazzo Vecchio join the Sydney Opera House and the Eiffel Tower. Minimundus makes a sincere attempt to show major monuments from around the world, including the Osaka Fortress, El Castillo at Chichen Itza, and the Temple at Borobudur. All but one of these buildings is demountable and taken under cover in the winter. This makes the arrangement at Minimundus malleable — not unlike the way Klagenfurt has treated the monuments of its old city, as moveable props. The combination of the close archaeological reconstruction of the monuments in miniature alongside the extraordinarily liberal grouping suggests that Minimundus and Klagenfurt's historical core share a similar ethos. In both cases, the high fidelity of detail obscures the quiet deceit of the ensemble.

Two other similarities deserve mention. Minimundus's larger monuments are roughly the same scale as the memorials that define Klagenfurt's pedestrian zone; both are pedestrian zones, the one verdant, the other urban. The early theme parks such as Disneyland and Minimundus emerged at the same time as postwar pedestrianization. They were self-consciously created as places of refuge from the car: Suspension of disbelief required such a break. At Minimundus, the view of the street and parking area is totally obscured, but the palpable memory of them makes the bodily experience of the encounter with the monument all the more poignant. The same relationship of the monument to the body of a walker and the memory of the car or bus occurs in the old city.

The two ventures, pedestrianization of the historic core and Minimundus, are spatially related as well since Klagenfurt is a staging ground for lake tourism, and Minimundus lies on the axis between the town and Lake Wörthersee, creating a triad of related attractions: old city, historical theme park, and a resort based on the natural resources of the lake and mountains, all of which are part of the heritage of the area. As an ensemble, these three layers of tourism provide a variety of complementary attractions in different seasons. Minimundus offers the otherwise provincial Klagenfurt, which lacks major individual architectural monuments, an encounter expressly through major monuments, and many exotic ones, at that. This is a theme park that understands how to abstract a monument from its place for the benefit of a larger aesthetic and quasi-historical experience. It could have offered the same lesson to historic Klagenfurt.

Minimundus, founded in 1958, just four years before the pedestrianization of Klagenfurt's historic core, provides the context for the restaging of the plague column. After all, the plague column is nearly as artificial as the models of Minimundus, but their juxtaposition produces the opposite reading. Minimundus makes the Alter Platz seem authentic and enduring after it had undergone such radical change that it no longer behaved like its former self. This distinguishes it from Jean Baudrillard's famous reading of Disneyland as a simulacrum. Instead of a perfect copy of something that never existed, Klagenfurt simply staged a graceful setting for tourism using its historical assets. Its indifference to historical precision is in fact modernist. In spirit, it lies somewhere between Sitte and Le Corbusier. The not-everyday has been choreographed in the service of the everyday. This assemblage of memorials as historical assets as part of a larger program of urban planning is the subject of the next two chapters.[40]

CHAPTER SIX

Mustering Memory

The city, however, does not tell its past,
but contains it like the lines of a hand.
— Italo Calvino, *Invisible Cities*, 1972

Stroll through Hyde Park Corner in London, that verdant hinge between Hyde Park and the jumble of parks that flow from it, and you enter a war zone: a park given over almost entirely to the memory of war, from the French Revolution to yesterday. It is possible that no city has created such a concentrated site of war memorials since ancient Rome. Beginning with the Wellington Arch in the early nineteenth century, this ill-defined plot of land, formerly on the edge of London, slowly took shape as a highly defined *temenos*, a sacred precinct cut off from the everyday in the center of the city. This was done neither by forethought nor according to some master plan, although plenty of architects and planners have had a go at the site. Londoners muddled and muscled it into existence, and this stands to reason. Seldom have cities stepped back to consider what presence the memory of war (and with it, sacrifice, victory, death, and mourning) should play in everyday life. War unfolded too chaotically across the last twenty decades to fashion a deliberate commemorative landscape, and so have cities, whose inherent messiness is matched by the precariousness of urban planning and the creative destruction of capitalism. Where to put the complicated bundle of facts and feelings, debts and tributes? The reality of modern war, and of modern cities, begot a novel and largely improvised cultural landscape of remembrance.

Much modern planning assumes a tabula rasa, an idealized ground utterly free of historical artifacts. But most cities, even those leveled by war, are more complicated. An endless run of modern cataclysms has left piles of memorial debris at the feet of planners and preservationists, some of whom, like the philosopher Walter Benjamin's angel of history, sought to "make whole what has been smashed" by reconciling it with their plans.[1] As in Klagenfurt, when memorial objects and spaces are assembled, their meaning changes. They become a collective and operate in concert. At Hyde Park Corner, in Benjamin's prophetic words, they seem to speak to "one single catastrophe."[2] Befitting a phenomenon that snuck up on modernity, no word exists for groupings of memorials. The Greek *temenos* gets at some of what is at work in modern urban memorial agglomerations, that is, the reservation of a special place for memory or more cynically, the effort to get the memorials the hell out of the way. But *temenos* by definition misses the everydayness of these spaces. Such accumulations behave differently by dint of being in a group, rather like groups of animals do. In English, most collective nouns for animals are evocative: a "sloth" of bears, a "cackle" of hyenas, a "murder" of crows, a "parliament" of owls. To this might be added a "muster" of memorials. From the Latin, *monstrare*, the word literally means to display or reveal and calls forth ideas of proof, inspection, and illustration. These ideas survive in the English word "demonstrate." After 1400, the word came to refer to the gathering of troops, as in "passing muster." "Muster" thus combines a military meaning appropriate to many memorials with that of assembly and manifestation (for example, a "muster" of peacocks) fitting for commemoration.

Intriguingly, the same root also leads to "monster," linking back to the role of monuments as warnings (*monere*). In this sense, memorials are monstrous, and not only as reminders of horrific events, but also as physical manifestations. The earliest monuments, it has been proposed, were trophies composed of shields and weapons erected on ancient battlefields. These gruesome monuments were placed where the tide of battle turned, hence "trophy," from the same root as "trope." In effect, the enemy's deaths were "turned, or troped, from murders into sacrifices" in order to appease the gods.[3] Roman triumphal arches were frequently bedecked with sculpted arms of the defeated. The persistent appearance of dead bodies and weapons or vignettes of combat and ascension found on modern memorials suggests the continued resonance of this archaic gesture.

The waves of memorials that arose alongside modern war muster up something different than ancient trophies or premodern monuments. They smooth over a shift in modern war; one might venture that they were created to do so. In early modern war, soldiers were mercenaries or conscripts, frequently unwilling participants in battles fought between kings and nobles over land or insults that only remotely affected the common person. Only with the revolutionary period did a more voluntary soldier-citizen emerge, alongside the noble cause of sacrifice for the nation.[4] Many modern memorials attempt to turn the horrific mass murder of a nation's young in war into a sacrifice in the name of patriotism. At Hyde Park Corner, Charles Jagger's massive Royal Artillery Memorial does so grimly, while the memorial to the Royal Machine Gun Corps thinly veils the mechanical horror behind Michelangelo's lithe David. (See figures 6.6 and 6.7 below.) The death of the citizen-soldier had to be euphemized, justified, or sublimated in war memorials. It had to be troped, that is, made into a trophy that turned the loss into something dignified. Mustering tropes performs a similar transformation—the singularity of each war is melted into a larger collective of nation, patriotism, heritage, local identity, and in recent decades, multicultural representation.

To photograph Hyde Park Corner's memorials is to despair. It is impossible to capture even one of them without tourists photobombing or locals strolling about. The very prospect of a pure photograph is absurd, of course. Still, for many people, it is hard to shake off the urge to eradicate (other) tourists from photographs, all the more so for an architectural historian such as me. It is nearly a reflex to wait out the bodies and the shadows of clouds, the cars and the birds, and capture the would-be unadulterated form in order to make buildings the protagonists of my stories. In London, I found myself seeking the *etymon*, the true and actual thing itself, despite knowing that such a thing is a modern fable of authenticity. Buildings — and memorials — are complicated by everyday life and their histories. This is their natural state, and to make it otherwise is like breeding back, the strange effort to revive an extinct species. Pathetically, breeding back only creates a pseudobreed, one with phenotypic resemblance to a lost animal but with its own genetic character. It is a sham, a form of unnatural selection. The obvious parallel to preservation is disturbing. I was doing the same thing with my camera, to capture a nonexistent original monument (or moment). The memorial assemblage at Hyde Park Corner, in all its messy history and teeming with tourists, is the thing itself. It is also archetypal, an example in extremis of what happens when memorials are mustered.

Hyde Park Corner has changed so dramatically over the centuries, and our eyes along with it, that it is nearly impossible to reconstruct, to breed it back. Yet even the attempt to construct a basic time line of change is troubling. The drive to assemble the history of the place is part of the same attitudes that forged it. Paradoxically, the memorial assemblage becomes a form of erasure, obscuring historical events, meant in historian Reinhart Koselleck's sense of those essential pivots "that irreversibly define and launch pent-up processes."[5] The memorials were all built to mark historical events, moments saturated with meaning. Yet all of these pivots have been collected into something with a radically different time signature. They are one, regardless of their moment in time, a menagerie, like the assemblage of animals in a zoo. Zoos collapse the disparate geographies, habitats, and evolutionary lineages of the animal kingdom into one improbable place. Memorial mustering collapses historical pivots no less improbably: Wellington and the Royal Machine Gun Corps are about as closely related as a bear and a lion. The memorial menagerie doesn't completely nullify the pivot, of course. It is still legible if one works at it, but the assemblage highlights the whole: here is *British war*. Too little attention has been paid to where we place reminders of our most meaningful temporal pivots, where we make space for time.[6] At Hyde Park Corner, the pivot has been part of a complex negotiation between high sentiment and everyday processes.

By the time it received its first monument, Hyde Park Corner was already thick with meaning. The area sits on a gentle prominence between Green Park and Hyde Park, at the juncture of six major streets that for centuries has been a traffic snarl. In the eighteenth century, it lay on the edge of the city, where proximity to the royal palaces of St. James's and Kensington and "the mansions of Piccadilly and the wealthy residences of Mayfair, created an atmosphere of distinction . . . where the Great West Road decanted its endless flow of travelers into the metropolis."[7] An ordinary toll gate was set up for controlling the flow of goods and people, but it was seen as "the ideal site for a magnificent formal entry into London, marking the termination of the Great West Road" and as the royal route between the palaces and parks.[8]

Some of the leading architects of the day tried their hand at monumental gateways, each with its own quasi-commemorative meaning. In the mid-eighteenth century, Robert Adam designed a series of elaborate triumphal arches to replace the toll gate and provide a suitable formal entrance for London, which was now the largest city in the world and an imperial capital that lacked the architectural embellishments of Paris or Rome.[9] Adam's plans and others from the same period lost their luster after Britain lost the American colonies. In the aftermath of the War of Independence, an expensive triumphal arch would have been ridiculous.[10] Toward the end of the century, John Soane produced a number of extraordinary designs for triumphal gateways for the site, which would have linked the increasingly developed area with a newly enlarged Buckingham Palace through Constitution Hill. Political tangles and the revolution on the continent quashed these plans. The defeat of Napoleon in 1815 revived the idea, now in the context of British victory and the first wave of modern war memorials that swept through Europe.[11] A triumphal arch was now fitting.

Soane continued to work on the project, imagining Hyde Park Corner as part of a royal triumphal route into the city.[12] After much political wrangling, the project fell to Decimus Burton, a leading architect who had trained under Soane. In the mid-1820s, Burton designed a monumental ensemble of screen and arch. This replaced the old toll gates, now an embarrassment, and linked the parks with the royal approach to Buckingham Palace.[13] The screen, visible in the upper left corner of figure 6.1, still serves as an entrance into Hyde Park itself. Ringed with bas reliefs of cavalry and charioteers inspired by the Elgin Marbles, it sounds the first triumphal and martial notes. The screen faced Burton's triumphal arch, a memorial to British

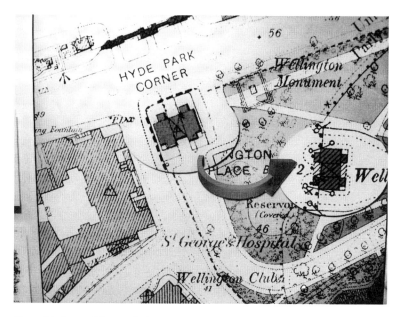

Figure 6.1. Proposal from a display at the Wellington Arch, 2006, map showing where the Wellington Arch would be moved. Photograph by the author.

Figure 6.2. Sir Richard Westmacott, Wellington as Achilles, 1822, Hyde Park. The statue's posterior caused a stir in early nineteenth-century London. Photograph by the author.

victories in the Napoleonic Wars, and gave much-needed shape and pomp to the confluence where Piccadilly and Knightsbridge Streets meet Grosvenor Place (fig. 6.1). The ambitious plan for a monumental entrance to the city gave way to a grand entrance to Green Park that doubled as a war memorial.

The arch was part of the burgeoning cult of Lord Wellington and immediately became part of an early assemblage. In 1822, a colossal bronze of Wellington as Achilles had been erected in Hyde Park, about two hundred yards from Burton's arch with which it was

clearly in dialogue (fig. 6.2). As early precedents for placing memorials in parks, the arch and statue were novelties, as unusual as the
public parks taking shape around them. The colossal Achilles was
the first nude statue erected in England since Roman times, and the
arch and monumental gate were extremely rare interventions in English cities.[14] That the area would become a site for the celebration of
Lord Wellington was anything but happenstance. Wellington lived
at Apsley House on the northern edge of Hyde Park Corner. Daily, he
could observe his Achillean avatar, forged of cannons captured from
the French, or stroll through the arch that marked his victory over
Napoleon at Waterloo. In the 1830s, a movement arose to top the arch
with a statue of Wellington, and in 1846, the largest equestrian statue
in the world was installed there. It was now officially Wellington
Arch. The outsized statue was the object of withering ridicule, as was
the bare posterior of Achilles, but so long as Wellington lived across
the street, they remained untouchable.

In spite of these Greco-Roman monuments, by the 1880s, the everyday had overtaken them. Traffic overwhelmed Hyde Park Corner, and
two major changes to the road system decisively altered how it functioned, both as an intersection and as a place of remembrance. Until
1883, the corner was continuous with Green Park, which flowed into
the grounds of Buckingham Palace.[15] It stood where royal parkland
met the civic realm. That year, Duke of Wellington Place, a multilane
roadway, formally cut off Hyde Park Corner from Green Park, creating an amorphous traffic circle that functioned like a small discrete
park within the larger string of parks in West London. A few years
later, a new roadway cut the corner between Piccadilly and Grosvenor
Place, where the arch sat.[16] It now abutted the edge of a roadway.

As so often happens, the ordinary required extraordinary action.
With Wellington now long dead, along with most of the people
who had agitated for the equestrian statue, the arch was vulner-
able. A hole was opened in the arch's top, and the massive statue
was dropped through it and placed in Green Park to await its fate.[17]
The entire arch was then moved to the center of Hyde Park Corner

Figure 6.3. J.E. Boehm, Wellington equestrian statue, 1888, which appeared after the maligned statue atop the Wellington Arch (behind) was removed, Hyde Park Corner, London. Photograph courtesy of CrisNYCa.

as the visual terminus of Constitution Hill, but now oddly isolated, sitting more like a "park ornament than the grand urban entrance" it was intended to be (fig. 6.3).[18] The equestrian statue escaped being melted down and was soon removed to Aldershot, where the British Army was headquartered. A more modest statue of Wellington on horseback was erected facing Apsley Place.[19] By the late 1880s, the improvisations of Victorian traffic engineering had cleaved off two smaller traffic islands from the western side of Hyde Park Corner.[20] At the same time, with its three memorials to Wellington, the area continued to be a major site of remembrance. The Quadriga — a chariot drawn by four horses — carrying Peace (Adrian Jones, sculptor) effectively replaced Wellington in 1912. It was an inauspicious time to celebrate peace. Britain entered World War I in August of 1914, and a new wave of memorials altered the site in the 1920s.

Meanwhile, the advent of the automobile intensified traffic problems. By the 1920s, when Londoners contemplated where to place memorials to World War I, Hyde Park Corner was one of the busiest intersections in London. It was also firmly entrenched as a site of memory and fit all of the clichés of memorial placement — and displacement. Wellington gave it gravitas, the parks provided a suitable setting, and traffic planning had left over a series of disused fragments that were readily available for "improvement" or "beautification," two of the sincere euphemisms of urban planning in the period. The Office of the Works contemplated building a monument to the Great War there so massive that it would have filled up Hyde Park Corner and dwarfed the arch.[21] Instead, more modest additions arrived. In 1925, after much haggling and many false starts, two memorials took their place on these islands, one to the Royal Artillery, the other to the Machine Gun Corps of World War I (figs. 6.4, 6.5, and 6.6). Not incidentally, the new memorials lined up with the centenary of the Wellington Arch. At this point, the creation of a thoughtful memorial ensemble was out of the question. The two memorials landed roughly on axis with the screen and within the orbit of the arch and the Wellington equestrian statue, which stood on a third, larger island, all without any comprehensive plan.

An air of inevitability surrounded the placement of these memorials, yet the site elicited concern. Lionel Earle, who as the secretary of the Office of the Works had authority over the placement of statuary, warned: "One has to be careful to avoid a nest of memorials at one spot clashing and vying with each other."[22] For the Royal Artillery Memorial, the Committee on Sites for Monuments in the London Area settled on the larger of the two small islands, overcoming objections that it would be disharmonious with the Wellington statue and

Figure 6.4. Hyde Park memorials on their islands, with Burton's screen at the top and the arch abutting the road to the right. The Royal Artillery Memorial sits on an island across from the arch, and the Machine Gun Corps Memorial sits below that. The Wellington equestrian statue is on the largest of the islands. Photograph courtesy of English Heritage.

Figure 6.5. Derwent Wood, Machine Gun Corps Memorial, 1925, on the now consolidated island of Hyde Park Corner, London. Photograph by the author.

Figure 6.6. Charles Sargeant Jagger, Royal Artillery Memorial, 1925, closing off one side of Hyde Park Corner, flanked by the Wellington Arch and Wellington equestrian statue. Photograph by the author.

Quadriga.[23] At least the sandstone howitzer aims its nozzle away from Peace. Sensitivity to the ensemble, such as it was, is evident in the committee's deliberations. It rejected an obelisk proposed by Edwin Lutyens for the Royal Artillery monument on the grounds that it was higher than the Wellington Arch, which by placement, if not import, had to be the dominant note.[24] Charles Jagger's design, while enormous, won the day because its horizontal massing fit the site better.[25] Unsurprisingly, the pressures of traffic impinged mightily on these aesthetic issues.[26] The Standing Art Commission worried that Jagger's memorial would "preclude alteration in the line and direction of this cross-traffic area."[27] Evidently, the memory of moving the Wellington Arch persisted. The Machine Gun Corps Memorial faced similar issues before finding its place on the smallest island.

What comes out emphatically in these exchanges is that no one knew where to put memorials or even who had jurisdiction over the land.[28] It turns out that since the Crown owned much of the parkland, the two islands were available largely because they were not royal parks and, as rather forlorn fragments, they were free of commercial pressure.[29] So perfunctory were these placements that a speed limit sign obscured the view of the Machine Gun Corps Memorial from Grosvenor Place. The artist, Derwent Wood, paid out of his own pocket to have it removed.[30] This gives the lie to the winning argument that it was "a quiet spot not surrounded with traffic."[31]

Just the opposite was true. The two memorials sat amid a whorl of activity, including the arch. In fact, traffic choked Hyde Park Corner long before the automobile arrived (fig. 6.7). In 1949, the museum curator Dorothy Stroud wrote, "traffic grinds its way round three large islands with their sculptured memorials, and a host of smaller pedestrian refuges marooned in a sea of noise and movement. It is the sorry outcome of nearly two centuries of lost opportunities, of hopes half realized or mutilated."[32] Various plans were hatched to reconcile memorials and traffic, the best known being Edwin Lutyens's in the late 1930s. Lutyens, whose fame rested in part on his Cenotaph and the battlefield memorials he designed in Europe, imagined formalizing

Figure 6.7. Traffic jam at Hyde Park Corner, 1880s. Postcard from the author's collection.

Hyde Park Corner as a terraced rectangular traffic island with its memorials moved to be completely subservient to the overall design.[33] Classicism and traffic, rather than commemoration, were his ruling considerations. Lutyens wanted to nudge the arch considerably farther down Constitution Hill and make the Machine Gun Corps Memorial disappear. In his design, three equestrian statues appear as generic placeholders, rather like Klagenfurt's plague column. Lutyens's plan met staunch resistance — one critic ridiculed it as "uglification."[34] War mercifully interrupted the debate. In 1951, the London County Council's proposal for a giant roundabout, with an underpass to link Knightsbridge and Piccadilly, was accepted and finally built in the early 1960s. While far less formal than Lutyens's scheme, it functioned much the same way by creating a single island for all of the memorials. The new plan claimed the smallest island for roadway, displacing David to the north edge of the newly formed Hyde Park Corner. Traffic so thoroughly trumped these memorials that in the late 1950s, both the Ministry of Works and the London County Council proposed moving the Royal Artillery Memorial as well.[35]

Jagger's behemoth remained. Nonetheless, a single, discrete island now existed, where the chaotic corner had become a muster of memorials, a self-reflective landscape in which memorials were their own context. This memory island at once confirms the belief that World War I unleashed an obsession with memory and reflects the extent to which utilitarian concerns could dominate — or perhaps quarantine is a more apt description — this obsession.[36] The site also seems to embody the common narrative among historians of art, literature, and culture that World War I was a dramatic break.[37] David may be a biblical figure interpreted through Michelangelo, but he was stranded in traffic and then moved like a park bench, forced to moon the traffic on Piccadilly Street and thrust Goliath's sword at the arch. Although it is now tempting to see his mighty sword as ironic, aligning it with the literature produced in the aftermath of the Great War, in fact, David is in earnest, as is the entire assemblage. It all speaks to an attempt after World War II to put the entire business under strict curation.

This stands to reason. As much as World War I was a historical pivot, World War II changed the commemorative mood dramatically. As Paul Fussell observed, while World War I produced a veritable library on the war experience, World War II was characteristically quiet. On the silence of the later war, Fussell wrote: "If loquacity was one of the signs of the Great War — think of all those trench poets and memoirists — something close to silence was the byproduct of experience in the Second War."[38] Literary reticence was matched by a reluctance to erect major memorials after World War II, a parallel way of remaining quiet about the war. Hyde Park Corner embodies this reticence materially and spatially. For decades, there were scant signs of World War II there.

World War II did appear, albeit unobtrusively, in the form of plaques. In 1949, the names of the 29,924 soldiers from the Royal Artillery who died in World War II were added on bronze plaques laid on a horizontal stone platform built alongside the Royal Artillery Memorial.[39] As people contemplated Jagger's memorial to the World War I artillery corps, they could gaze down at plaques with the names of their World War II counterparts. Elsewhere, World War II made quiet appearances. An inscription on the Royal Air Force Memorial on the nearby Victoria Embankment was added for those who died in World War II. The Guards Division Memorial, which was damaged by shrapnel in World War II, was emended to commemorate members of the Household Division who died in World War II. Of course, these addenda speak to the state of postwar England. London lay in ruin. Signs of war were everywhere and would remain so for years, alongside rationing. Memorials were a relatively low priority, compared with the larger reconstruction effort.[40]

While traffic engineers and urban planners had their way with Hyde Park Corner in the decades after World War II, the memorials would remain virtually static until another change in mood in the 1990s, when a series of new memorials to World War II began to appear, now in the context of the fiftieth anniversary of the war.[41] The Australian War Memorial to World War II was unveiled on Remembrance Day, 2003, at the corner of Grosvenor and Duke of Wellington Places (fig. 6.8). It understands its role in the now self-conscious mustering. Built along the lines of Maya Lin's Vietnam War Veterans Memorial in Washington, DC, its curved wall gently descends into the ground. This buffers it against traffic, further encloses the island, and gestures to the other memorials.

Diagonally across the island, the New Zealand War Memorial to the war dead of both world wars is a pendant to its antipodal neighbor (fig. 6.9) — a field of sixteen cross-shaped bronze girders thrust diagonally out of the ground at different heights. Instead of resolutely setting the edge, as so many memorials do in parklike settings, this one wanders across the path, forcing interaction with passersby while also refusing to behave like a typical sculptural mass. The berm on which it ascends cuts off the park from the street so that the memorial does not have to do so. In turn, from the berm, one gains a purchase from which to see the entire assemblage. For over a century, Hyde Park Corner has functioned increasingly as a place apart dedicated to remembrance. With these last memorials, it

Figure 6.8. Tonkin Zulaikha Greer, architects, and Janet Laurence, artist, wall of the Australian War Memorial, 2003, which sets one edge of Hyde Park Corner and hides a pedestrian underpass. Photograph by the author.

Figure 6.9. A mustering of memorials. John Hardwick Smith, architect, and Paul Dibble, sculptor, New Zealand War Memorial, 2006, Hyde Park Corner, being photobombed by David, right middle ground, the Wellington equestrian statue, and the Royal Artillery Memorial in the background to the left. Burton's screen can be seen to the right rear. Photograph by the author.

is now known in official language as a "saturation zone," a site where new memorials can be erected only as exceptions granted by the Department of Culture, Media and Sport (DCMS). How memorials came under this jurisdiction is another story, where the administrative structure tells its own tale. Municipal policy aims to prevent the area from becoming a "graveyard of memorials" that would diminish the parks as a public amenity.[42] Memorials and parks remain at odds, and the death taboo is still alive and well in England, or perhaps this fear merely recognizes the everyday as vital to civic life. Either way, it is now difficult to imagine any more memorials landing here.

Suffice it to say that the mustering of memorials at Hyde Park Corner has been a complicated affair. As in Klagenfurt, the history concession has recast the entire area in terms of heritage. The island makes a tidy stop for tourists, who can take in two hundred years of British military history in one place. It is part of a war itinerary that has shifted in meaning as the United Kingdom has confronted its declining status as a world power. English Heritage's pamphlet, *Remembrance*, provides a map and pithy descriptions of the memorials (fig. 6.10). The map marks thirteen memorials between Hyde Park Corner and the Victoria Embankment Gardens in that nearly continuous strip of park west of the bend in the Thames that gives this part of London its character. The brochure was disseminated from a small office in the Wellington Arch owned by English Heritage since 1999, yet the various Wellington memorials make no appearance, as if they belonged to a wholly distinct cultural phenomenon. Thus was remembrance segregated from the longer tradition with which it has been entangled, both culturally and geographically at Hyde Park Corner. A more recent publication with an excellent historical account reversed course and massaged Wellington back into this malleable mustering.[43]

The temporary elision of Wellington, or the Napoleonic moment, from *Remembrance* may reflect the shift from a cult of hero worship to the common soldier. These two modes of memorialization often share the same space without the same commemorative practices.

In other words, the original spatial dynamics surrounding the Wellington statue and arch — royal routes and the review of troops on the way to Aldershot — have waned, and the area was brought into line with the emerging commemorative (and tourist) practices of the late twentieth century. As the nineteenth-century instinct to place memorials as notes in picturesque settings gave way to the convenience of assembling memorials in one place for Remembrance Day, Wellington came to be increasingly out of place. The spatial conception of the English landscape garden tradition yielded to that of institutionalized mass gatherings on official days. These changes rendered the Wellington Arch an antiquated relic, a commemorative non sequitur in a memorial landscape. Its restoration in the guidebook in 2015 shows how heritage musters assets more promiscuously than remembrance.

The memorials at Hyde Park Corner, like so many memorials, have had to reconcile the economics of land, traffic, and crowd control with the changing demands of commemorative practice, all while being assembled into a cultural landscape of remembrance, tourism, and heritage. They are an extreme example of a convention that has taken shape with the accumulation of commemorative sites across a particularly violent and memory-obsessed century. The convention lays bare just how much memorials are at the mercy of everyday realities. By the time a World War II plaque lands on a World War I memorial, the forces that battle over land use, appropriateness, and cost, at least in a democracy, have already had their melee, licked their wounds, and moved on to other contests.

Utility is among the greatest factors in the evolution of the additive tradition, which relates only vaguely to those art traditions in the West that have hewn so closely to Romantic ideals of individual genius and originality. It is not merely art or sanctity but profane expediency, pattern, and precedent that fix many memorials in their place and later displace them. The result is an official vernacular, a muddle of informal moves, measures, and improvisations that over

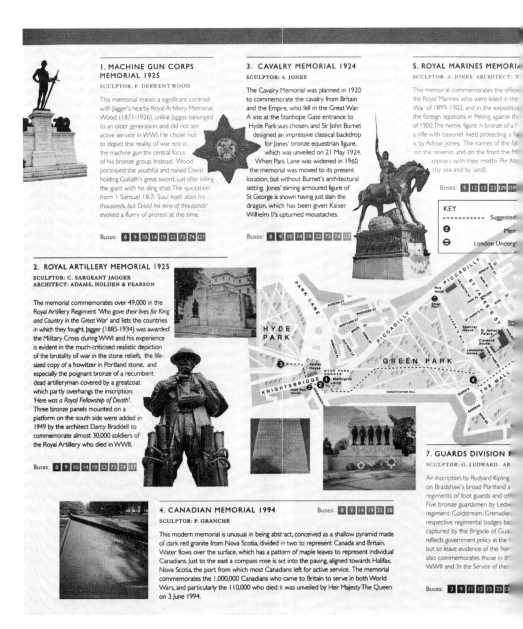

Figure 6.10. English Heritage map of memorials near Hyde Park Corner. From *Remembrance*, English Heritage Pamphlet, undated. Courtesy of Historic England.

6. ROYAL ARTILLERY MEMORIAL 1910
SCULPTOR: W. ROBERT COLTON
ARCHITECT: SIR ASTON WEBB

In 1905 members of the Royal Artillery set up a committee to organise a memorial to the 1,000 of their comrades killed in the South African War of 1899-1902. Webb, architect of the nearby Admiralty Arch, was appointed as architect, and Robert Colton ARA as the sculptor. The figure of Peace restraining a great horse is typical of the allegorical manner of much Edwardian sculpture. A note of greater realism is introduced by the bronze panels to either side, depicting garrison and mountain artillery, and by the panels listing the names of the fallen.

Buses: 9 12 15 23 139 159

9. IMPERIAL CAMEL CORPS MEMORIAL 1920
SCULPTOR: C. BROWN

The Imperial Camel Corps was formed from British, Australian, New Zealand and Indian troops to serve in Egypt and the Middle East against the Ottoman Empire. Brown's figure of a soldier riding a camel set on a tall plinth is smaller in scale than the other memorials described here. The names of the fallen are listed on the pedestal.

Buses: 9 11 15 23

13. CENOTAPH 1920
ARCHITECT: SIR E. LUTYENS

This is the national memorial to those from the British Empire and Commonwealth and their Allies who lost their lives during both World Wars and subsequent conflicts. Lutyens (1869-1944) produced a design within hours in June 1919 for a temporary structure in Whitehall as part of the nation's Peace celebrations the following month. It was replaced by the permanent Portland stone structure modelled by F Derwent Wood which was unveiled on 11 November 1920 as part of the burial ceremony of the Unknown Warrior in Westminster Abbey. There are no straight lines - every surface is subtly curved - and the raking verticals would meet at an imaginary point one thousand feet above the ground. The power of the monument lies in its apparent simplicity and brevity of inscription: 'The Glorious Dead'.

Buses: 3 11 12 159

12. CHINDIT FORCES MEMORIAL 1990
SCULPTOR: F. FOSTER
ARCHITECT: D. PRICE

This unusual memorial is dedicated to all the men who fought in the Chindit forces, formed, trained and led by Major General Orde Wingate to carry out operations behind Japanese lines in Burma in 1943 and 1944. The Chindits were recruited from the armed forces of the United Kingdom, Burma, Hong Kong, India, Nepal, West Africa and the United States. They were named after the chinthe, a mythical lion-like beast, the guardian of Burmese temples, which appeared on their badge. A bronze figure of a chinthe by Frank Foster appears on top of the memorial. The reverse of the memorial commemorates Wingate himself, who was killed in 1944.

Buses: 3 11 12 159

10. BELGIAN NATIONAL MONUMENT 1919
SCULPTOR: V. ROUSSEAU
ARCHITECT: SIR R. BLOMFIELD

In the autumn of 1918, even before the Great War had ended, an official committee was set up under two princesses of the Belgian royal family to erect a memorial in London as *testimony of Belgium's deep gratitude towards Great Britain for the aid so generously bestowed upon Her during the war*. Sir Reginald Blomfield's setting, a semi-elliptical recess of Portland stone, frames Rousseau's bronze group, a woman representing Belgium accompanied by two children bearing garlands and wreaths. To either side are low-relief sculptures of Justice and Honour; and above are carved the shields of the provinces of Belgium.

Buses: 9 11 15 23

11. ROYAL AIR FORCE MEMORIAL 1923
SCULPTOR: SIR W. REID DICK
ARCHITECT: SIR R. BLOMFIELD

Blomfield also designed this tall, obelisk-like memorial of Portland stone on the Embankment, dedicated *'in memory of all ranks of the Royal Naval Air Service, Royal Flying Corps, Royal Air Force and those air forces from every part of the British Empire'*, killed in the Great War; the RAF had in fact been founded by the merging of the first two organisations in 1918. A later inscription adds a dedication to those who lost their lives in WWII.

Buses: 3 11 12 159

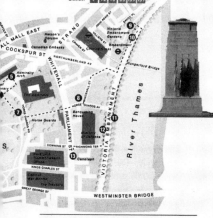

8. THE GURKHA REGIMENTS MEMORIAL 1997
SCULPTOR: P. JACKSON

This is the newest of the memorials described here, commemorating all the Nepalese soldiers to have served in the 16 successive Gurkha regiments since their foundation in 1816. The regiments are listed on the back of the pedestal, and the many theatres of war in which the Gurkhas have served on the left side, ending in Bosnia, 1996. Philip Jackson's bronze figure, traditional in form and heroic in scale, demonstrates the continuing vitality of memorial sculpture.

Buses: 3 9 11 12 15 23 139 159

time become sedimented into a form that comes to appear wholly formal — formality arrived at through informal means. As a result, memorials have often been the stepchildren of public space, pawned off onto those civic buildings and spaces that had extra room or placed on the odd swath of grass. The easiest way to do this was to drop a statue on a green or urban fragment and landscape the area around it. Once a site such as this is fixed, it sets a precedent for all subsequent memorials, establishing the grounds for the next case, if not drawing other memorials to the purported sanctity of the spot.[44]

Yet the forces that have shaped the modern city are only part of the story. Mustered memorials and the commemorations that many of them anchor show to what extent the succession of modern wars have all blurred into one phenomenon. In effect, assembling memorials to different wars on a single site concedes something about the reality of modern war as a continuous engagement. They become a single deposit. As the historian George L. Mosse has shown, this melting of wars into a larger nationalist sentiment is part of the legerdemain of the modern state. It serves the nation by rousing the citizen, historically the male citizen, through an appeal to ideals or myths that often have little or nothing to do with the singular war itself — virtue, national spirit, masculinity, emancipation from the quotidian, adventure, Christianity. With war justified in these terms, death in war was reconstituted, as well; as Christian sacrifice secularized in terms of nation, as a noble spending of virility, as brave defense of the homeland, or as an example of virtue for future generations. This "cult of the fallen soldier," as Mosse calls it, is an instrument of forging a collective.[45] Collecting memorials is one way this collective has been mustered, given a concrete place, and reinforced by commemorative practices.

As much as repurposing World War I memorials for World War II made practical sense, the strategy had to overcome some sticky dilemmas. The backward gaze typical of memorials to the Great War — the way they embrace a "traditional vocabulary of mourning derived from classical, romantic, or religious forms" — anchored the startlingly new experience of the war in the age-old verities of Christianity, the ancients, and other enduring expressions of Western civilization. This posture toward the past recalls Walter Benjamin's angel of history, who flies into the future with her gaze fixed firmly on the past.[46] By the Second World War, the game was up. The crosses and columns, angels and dragon-slaying St. Georges, even the simple bronze soldiers on plinths, had become hopelessly outdated and unconvincing, having slipped into an unusable past, the detritus piling up at the feet of the angel. This was not just the doing of radical changes in art, but also of the Holocaust and the larger memorial exhaustion that set in after World War II. The angel of history had not so much turned her back on the past as temporarily closed her eyes in weariness. Yet so many of these memorials were conscripted into serving the memory of World War II, if not also later wars, or mustered into assemblages where their meaning would be transformed.

Some of the nationalistic sentiment that this collective expresses issues from the serendipitous overlap of conflicts and commemorative cycles. In the United States, for instance, Civil War memorials established precedents of placement and commemorative practice to which future memorials often had to respond. While the Civil War, the Spanish-American War, and World War I seem like distant conflicts with distinct commemorative communities separated by generations, in fact, Civil War memorials appeared in great numbers only in the late nineteenth and early twentieth centuries. They frequently postdate the Spanish-American War, and many of them were still new when the Great War began. To put this in the context of commemorative cycles, the fiftieth anniversary of the end of the Civil War overlapped with World War I. This was a fertile intersection, since by a quinquagenary, those who fought in a war are nearing the end of their lives, lending urgency to memorialization. In the American South, many Confederate monuments were erected in the aftermath of World War I in the context of a white supremacist agenda, but the solemn aura of the recent war must have helped them into being as well.[47] A similar situation existed between the Franco-Prussian

War and World War I in Europe, if not also during the unfolding centenary of the Napoleonic Wars, which bumped up against the Great War. Such overlaps have led to the layering of commemorative practices and sites with regional inflections that Americans and Europeans are only now trying to reconcile. Even the widespread instinct to modify Confederate monuments with plaques, historical explanations, and countermonuments is a form of mustering.

It turns out that these monstrous monuments to a racist ideology are difficult to defeat. While memorials have been routinely kicked to the curb, melted down, reoriented for practical or aesthetic reasons, or simply crowded out of relevance, Confederate monuments have taken on new meaning, renewed by the resurgence of white supremacy and racial tension in the United States. But it is also an old meaning: their original meaning as monsters, as witnesses to barbarity that translate the wickedness of war into an appeal to noble sacrifice for nation, is labile and easily co-opted for new purposes. These monsters still serve a purpose, if a complicated one, both for those who wish to celebrate the Lost Cause and those who desire to vanquish this ideology and its symbols.

This acknowledges the repulsiveness that so many critics since the nineteenth century have found in conventional monuments, those statues, obelisks, arches, and more elaborate confections thrown into public spaces since the age of revolutions. Their devaluation, especially in the twentieth century, while clearly part of a shift in taste, hides the problem of how to handle the horrible realities of sacrifice and death in an increasingly secular world. When people believed in totems and when idols were vessels for communion with the supernatural, such objects were enchanted and charged with meaning both terrible and beautiful. Barbarity was rooted in the inscrutability of gods and demons, in a sphere beyond human power and comprehension. The object — the bone of a martyr gilded and bejeweled in a reliquary — served as a metonymic intermediary to that sphere. While Christian symbolism has been ubiquitous in memorials, the rapidly secularizing mood of the twentieth century has had a more ambivalent relationship to such religious traditions. The descent into savagery of modern war had no easy explanation, no obvious outlet or place in the public sphere. Hierophany has no prescribed place in the secular world. As the ever-insightful Philip Johnson noted at the end of World War II, much of this premodern meaning had been quashed by the Protestant Reformation, but with curious results: "Though we are no longer religious we still have some of Cromwell's iconoclasm in our blood. When we see monuments of marble and bronze, we see Veblen's 'conspicuous waste.' We consider monumental statuary semi-idolatrous and remembering our eighteenth century New England fear of the bogey of Popery, we frown upon any ceremonial ritual that is likely to arouse our emotions."[48] These were the words of a crafty modernist using religion to argue against traditional memorials. But the issue went well beyond the differences between branches of Christianity or aesthetic movements.

One way out of this dilemma was to favor useful memorials such as civic buildings and memorial parks and highways. Another was to muster the memorials, to zone the monsters. The latter was a double move. On the one hand, it created strength in numbers and a focal point for commemoration while it also girded them against the city, all the better to make them hierophanic while erecting a firewall around the burning bush. On the other hand, stranding memorials and moving them here and there at the whim of traffic engineering or the cultivation of the leisure realm is tantamount to urban planning as iconoclasm. In other words, mustering memorials can make them disappear as readily as does melting them into the everyday. Whereas individual memorials face destruction with changes in regime, traffic, or taste, groups of memorials are more stubborn. Part of the reason is simply practical. Iconoclasm is a violent, disruptive act, but it is quick, cheap, and difficult to resist. Recently, some Confederate monuments have been taken down under cover of darkness, with little recourse once the deed was done. By contrast, the destruction of an entire site cultivated as a memorial precinct requires an act of urbanism, an expensive and time-consuming foray into city planning that operates somewhere between human and geological time.

Menageries of memorials of all types sit among other markers of heritage and history. In many American towns, convenient civic spaces have been shaped as outdoor museums or, less charitably, as open-air storage units for memorials. Public spaces around the world herd memorials for reasons that range from the eminently practical to the stridently political. For every sober memorial dedicated by an earnest committee, another one is foisted into a public space where its placement — if not its entire reason for being — is perplexing. One default has been to corral them together. These assemblages are often encountered as part of everyday life, as people stroll through the civic realm, go to and from work, or take moments of leisure in the open settings in which such memorial groups take shape. This complicated, layered landscape is governmental and commemorative, informal and secular all at once. It can have the mien of a museum and the pace of a park. Often it appears as a fait accompli, as at Hyde Park Corner, with all of the authority of an official landscape, but it is in fact the work of many hands laboring piecemeal over long periods of time, the way vernacular landscapes take shape.

This way of zoning memory is also part of a managerial mood, a technical approach to city planning that first emerged in late nineteenth-century Germany as rapidly expanding cities wrestled with how best to bring order to the forces of urbanization. It is no coincidence that zoning emerged in urban planning just as the era of statuemania dawned, as committees contemplated where and how to build memorials and cities used monuments to steady their new boulevards, streetcar systems, and infrastructure — to steady the upheaval of modernity with national heroes and martyrs. In the aftermath of the Franco-Prussian War in Europe and the Civil War in the United States, monuments became an increasingly common part of everyday urban experience, part of the marbling of beautification, urbanization, and patrimony, often tinged with nostalgia and tinctured with patriotism.

A similar spirit prompted early attempts to set aside historic districts, with its origins in projects such as the turn-of-the-century Skansen — this time on an actual island and not a traffic island — in Stockholm. This collection of vernacular buildings rescued from defunct villages and farms set a precedent in the zoning of historical artifacts in cities.[49] Attempts to "red velvet" historic zones, tellingly called *zone protégés* in French, gained momentum across the twentieth century, finding their way into codes and laws increasingly since the 1960s. Zoning became folded into preservation law across the world from Mexico to Macau and marked in every European language by terms such as *Altstadt, vieille ville,* and *centro storico.*[50] Assembling historic properties was a prophylactic against the incursions of modern urbanism. It is modernity's other, an inoculation of memory against modern amnesia. The next chapter explores the consequences of subtler acts of assembling memory.

Figure 7.1. Plague column, 1924, Soboth, Austria, turned memorial to the two world wars. Photograph by the author.

CHAPTER SEVEN

Assembling Memory

Memory is imagination in reverse.
— Stephen Evans, *The Marriage of True Minds*, 2008

Memorial musters are acts of bricolage assembled in the service of a larger synthesis. Like stew, they transform their ingredients into a different substance. Unlike a recipe, most memorial groupings are improvised over time. By World War I, it became common in the West to add names, plaques, and other addenda to preexisting memorials. A few early examples suggest a *longue durée* for this additive tradition, a particular kind of mustering that extends back to early modern Europe. Klagenfurt added the half moon to its plague column in 1683, making it double as a monument to the Austrian triumph over the Ottoman Empire. (See figure 5.1.) This set up a potent parallel between the Ottomans and the plague. In the nearby village of Soboth, another plague column became the town's World War I memorial in 1924 and later came to mark World War II dead (fig. 7.1). These two plague columns, both pairing dissimilar events, recall Henri Lefebvre's concept of *bizarrerie*.[1] They jolt or pique passersby, introduce strange forms, changes in scale and materials, and interject strikingly not-everyday ideas such as plague and war into the everyday. Lefebvre believed that "the bizarre is a mild stimulant for the nerves and the mind." As a stimulant and "tranquilizer," it is "risk-free," a "pseudo-renewal, obtained by artificially deforming things so that they become both reassuring and surprising."[2] A better description of many late nineteenth-century or early twentieth-century memorials would be hard to find. These sorts of contrasts are intrinsic to everyday life, part of how people reconcile the monstrous with the mundane. In Soboth, a giant wooden sculpture of a boot — a humorous emblem of alpine hiking — sits next to the memorial like a piece of American roadside architecture plopped down in the Austrian mountains (fig. 7.2). The memorial and boot, it turns out, are the starting point for an itinerary of *bizarrerie* composed of local legends, history, and aesthetic pauses.[3] In Soboth, the additive tradition extends into something bigger and more complicated. Here, as elsewhere, memorials conspire with heritage, tourism, and in some cases folklore to form nearly boundless cultural landscapes of assemblage. It is a tasty stew for an ironic tourist.

Like the mustering in Hyde Park Corner, assemblage is usually a double convention, one part being material and anchored in place, the other social and rooted in commemorative practices. This doubling is largely overlooked because conventions themselves have been anathema to modernity, understood as a mentality that celebrates novelty, innovation, and the exceptional. Yet noticing and parsing conventions is vital to understanding everyday life. From the Latin *convenire*, the word convention literally translates as "coming together," with a dual meaning that is social and geographical. A convention might be understood as an agreement done in place. While modernity busied itself quashing conventions, old conventions persisted, often invisibly or in new forms, while new ones sprang up alongside modernity's novelties. Memorials constantly straddle the line between old and new conventions, between the surprising and the soothing, between *bizarrerie* and cliché. The additive tradition taps into the double "coming together," usually with a light touch.

Plaques and other additions can appear with little notice. As cheap and quick amendments, they rarely draw attention or require the hard labor that James E. Young calls "memory work."[4] While they may alter where people stand, wearing rough patches into the grass, their effect can be trickier to judge. The difference between

Figure 7.2. Giant hiking boot with memorial, Soboth, Austria. Photograph by the author.

a free-standing memorial and a plaque can be extreme. As mid-space objects, free-standing memorials usually encourage frontality, gathering, or encirclement — the creation of a metaphorical roof.[5] They shatter space, make place, or embrace a crowd. By contrast, most additive plaques deflate, reduce, and stand aside. They are like memorials with all the juice squeezed out of them.

Whereas many memorials assert, declare, or declaim, plaques demur and defer. They allow the thing to which they cling to take pride of place. They privilege words over form, personal exchange over public forum. They are easier to ignore or miss entirely. And because they're relatively inexpensive and easier to install, they're more likely to disappear. This modesty often implies a memorial of secondary importance or a desire to make memory speak more softly. At their least commemorative, they become informational, little more than historical explanations, like history dressed up in the garment of memory or an indecisive blur of the two. In short, their claim on space, if not on posterity, is more reserved. Instead of devaluing plaques and other additions as lesser, banal, flat, disembodied, or "easy outs," these characteristics are part of how they harness and inflect memorial conventions.

It almost goes without saying that additive memorials mean different things in different places, yet it is a pervasive, international phenomenon that can be found both in world capitals such as London and Paris and in provincial villages. The examples in this chapter give a sense of what happens to memorials under duress of the palimpsest of modern tragedy and reveal the peculiar inflection additive memorials have in each place. In Austria, for instance, where a full reckoning of the nation's role in World War II awaits, the doubling of memorials to the two world wars remains unquestioned.[6] In Soboth, commentary is hidden in the tiniest gesture: someone has flipped the donation box. The iron cross remains unchanged, but the word *Danke* is now upside down, a subtle jab at the status quo (fig. 7.3).

In France, a more complex situation has evolved. Plaques commemorating World War II have been added to World War I

Figure 7.3. Upside-down donation box on memorial, Soboth, Austria. Photograph by the author.

memorials almost as a reflex, not just signaling but in fact reinforcing the continuity between the two world wars. Much of the rhetoric
and bellicosity of war, if not also the politics and cultural sentiment,
was internalized and carried into domestic life between the wars.[7]
No wonder the two wars have been glued together. A more recent,
postcolonial reckoning has asked many French memorials to pan
backward to wars that were long unacknowledged and to accommodate subsequent wars. Plaques to every French military conflict,
including the colonial wars in Indochina and Algeria, now can be
found affixed to memorials throughout France. The one in Cannes
shows a typical example of this settled convention (figs. 7.4 and 7.5).

The initial impetus to put the two wars together at French memorials is easy to understand. As George L. Mosse has argued, World
War I was a watershed in how the fallen were treated, both in their
presence, significance, and symbolism and in the utter scale of death.
Commemoration of the Great War dwarfed memorialization of all

Figure 7.4. Albert Cheuret, Monument to the Dead clad with plaques, 1918, Cannes, France. Photograph by the author.

Figure 7.5. Detail of additive plaques on the Monument to the Dead. Photograph by the author.

previous wars. Just as the First World War has been understood as closing the long nineteenth century, as a cleanser that banished the "old world" and ushered in modernity, its memorialization might be seen, at least in Europe, as doing something similar to the memory of previous wars. With World War I, memorials became ubiquitous in everyday experience, and commemorations became increasingly formalized throughout the West. They set the pattern for memorialization for decades. It is thus no surprise that memorials to the Great War would become burdened with memorializing later and earlier wars. They mark a pivot in modern life and memory while establishing the place of memory in towns and cities. All the more so in France, where the entire nation mobilized, and few families escaped personal loss.[8] Yet the issue is gravely complicated by the difference between the two wars in France. While the French commemorated the so-called Great War as part of a patriotic cult of the dead, during the Second World War, France was invaded, Paris occupied, and the nation divided, with whole sections of the country collaborating with the Nazis. How could this older patriotic cult of the dead, which had centered on monuments such as the one in Cannes, continue blithely after the disaster of the later world war and into the period of decolonization?[9]

In Germany, where interwar politics was particularly brutal, the additive approach is still more complicated.[10] Resentment about the Treaty of Versailles and the terms of peace after World War I played no small part in spurring World War II. In Germany, memorials became a bridge between the two wars. Adolf Hitler made a practice of visiting World War I memorials. Many of them remain unchanged, even today, with the mere addition of plaques to the Second World War. In some cases, the additive impulse goes back further. In the Bavarian town of Velden, a grotto honors soldiers from the Franco-Prussian War. Plaques were added after each world war, drawing a continuity between grievances that predate Germany as a unified nation and the world wars. New memorials were still being erected in the 1930s as the National Socialists took power. In fact, the Third Reich erected World War I memorials to stimulate nationalist fervor and remilitarization, replete with typically heroic figures and Nazi symbols. The Nazi eagle remains on the memorial in Webenheim, a small town near the French border. Such reuse of memorials for World War II was part of a more ominous continuity than similar repurposing in Allied nations. This dim view can be balanced against a more sympathetic one. Many German memorials to the First World War were *Kriegerdenkmalen*, memorials to the soldiers, not to the war, per se.[11] Nearly every German town has one, often with the names of the fallen, where people could go to have an intimate encounter with their lost loved ones. Such familial practices continued after World War II; fresh wax can still be found on the sconces where people burn candles.

The pathos of these memorials lives alongside the darker meaning they acquire through addition. The mural painted on a building on the Schlossplatz in Berchtesgaden — Hitler's favorite vacation spot — brings this out vividly (fig. 7.6; see color insert). Joseph Hengge, who created the original one in 1929, painted a crucifixion flanked by scenes of modern war and how it touched Bavarian life, all

Figure 7.6. Hitler and Freud both vacationed in Berchtesgaden, Germany, and would have known this mural well. By Joseph Hengge, 1929; repainted 1952. Photograph by the author.

medievalized by shields, Gothic script, and the setting itself. These were typical European themes in memorials — Christianity, medievalism, folkish gestures — especially in Germany, where symbols of resurrection redirected sentiment away from the shame of defeat toward a heroic ideal of sacrifice for a higher cause.[12] When the Allies took the town during World War II, they had the mural painted over. After a moratorium on new memorials imposed by the Allies expired in 1952, Hengge returned to repaint it, changing only the dates, text, and the vignette on the far right side. In place of a battle scene, the artist painted a more morbid death scene, with a priest praying over a body before haggard men carry him away. In keeping with general sentiment in Germany, he tempered the nationalistic text from "They fell for freedom and the honor of the Fatherland" to "They gave their lives. Their sacrifice is our reminder." Otherwise, it remains creepily unchanged: the experience of Nazism is given asylum by the same metaphors of sacrifice, crucifixion, and national rebirth, all warmed by Bavarian imagery, as if no new thinking had to go into the memory of the Second World War. Beneath the vaults, the memorial continues with a ghoulish bronze soldier's head, stuck to the wall like a taxidermic specimen, and plaques to the two world wars (figs. 7.7, see color insert; and 7.8). People continue to use the ledge as a commemorative site; in 2019, a votive candle to "Lisa" sat next to another one to the Virgin (fig. 7.9). And so it went, and goes, in many German towns.

The additive tradition is also common throughout the Anglo-American world and the former British colonies, including in Canada, Australia, and New Zealand. The phenomenon in these Allied nations comes with its own troubles. Additive memorials place multiple wars in one frame of reference. Such slippage is evident in period discussions about memorialization. In 1947, Lord Chatfield, who was admiral of the fleet and president of the War Memorials Advisory Council in England, argued that "though to us the two wars are twenty-five years apart, time will close the gap until they are looked back on as one great struggle against evil."[13] This attitude is in part the work of days of remembrance.[14] In commemorative practice, if not in

Figure 7.7. Memorial plaques in the arcade beneath the mural in Berchtesgaden. Photograph by the author.

Figure 7.8. Death mask on the wall beneath the arcades at the war memorial, Berchtesgaden. Photograph by the author.

Figure 7.9. Votive candles placed at the war memorial, Berchtesgaden. Photograph by the author.

consciousness, wars have run together. The congestion of wars has made assemblage practical, whether as groupings of memorials or by means of additive plaques. Perhaps this is the most appropriate way to acknowledge more than a century of continuous warfare.

If only such madness lay behind the method. The improvised reality comes out painfully in the memorial to the Royal Fusiliers, discussed in earlier chapters. Instead of erecting a second memorial to the Royal Fusiliers who died in World War II, Londoners carved an additional tribute into the World War I memorial on the Strand in London. To avoid the same problem recurring in the future, they cut out some stone and added a dedication to "those fusiliers killed in subsequent campaigns" (figs. 7.10 and 7.11). No one will ever have to propose or reject another Royal Fusiliers memorial again. This is the additive tradition at its most perfunctory.

Such additive plaques or inscriptions rarely mean anything as works of art, but as examples of the place of memorials, they become wonderfully expressive. They make sense of the rapid succession of wars, which are treated like one phenomenon, as Lord Chatfield presciently anticipated. The plaques speak to an understandable

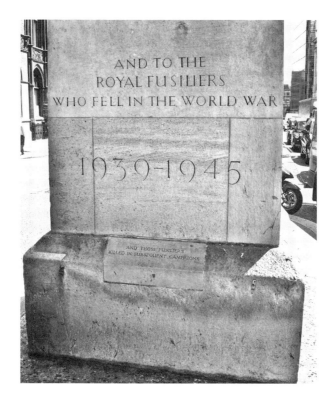

Figure 7.10. Additions to the Royal Fusiliers Memorial, London, after World War II. Photograph by the author.

Figure 7.11. The end of all plaques? Its sloppy insertion speaks to the perfunctory nature of this addition. Royal Fusiliers Memorial, date unknown. Photograph by the author.

memorial exhaustion after World War II, to be discussed in the last chapter, while they gesture to continuity. Even the naming of the wars is additive. The generic "World War II" lent its name retrospectively to the Great War whose business it finished. It is no wonder that conventions of memorialization followed. The generation that had fought World War I, that memorialized it, and that then led the charge into World War II had little energy left for fresh memorials. In fact, many war memorials from the Great War had scarcely been finished when the Second World War began. That same generation then immediately entered the Cold War, again a continuation in many ways of World War II, but fought out through proxy wars in Korea, Vietnam, and elsewhere. The dead from all of these engagements are often named on one monument.[15] From this angle, the additive war memorial is the most telling monument of our times, a confession of the violent pathology of modernity and the nearly comical but in fact tragic, inability to face it in a mature manner. It is a confession that these Allied nations have not started what the Germans have been doing for well over a generation. There is no word in English for *Vergangenheitsbewältigung*, the German term for working through the past, particularly humanity's most vile deeds.[16]

"All Wars" Memorials

This damning judgment does not come lightly. Yet it has been scripted into memorials for a surprisingly long time, particularly in the development of an additive memorial type: the "all wars" memorial. Thousands of them dot American towns and cities, but they can be found in Europe, as well. The All Wars Memorial in Oberlin, Ohio, is both unusual and representative of the larger phenomenon (fig. 7.12). It dates to 1943, an odd moment to erect a war memorial. It reconstitutes *spolia* from a much earlier Civil War memorial (fig. 7.13). The original memorial of 1871 took the form of a sandstone Gothic spire with marble tablets engraved with the names of fallen soldiers. It stood at a prominent intersection in the small college town, across from the main public square, where both town and gown could

Figure 7.12. Plaques from the destroyed Soldiers Monument inserted into the brick wall of the All Wars Memorial, 1943, Oberlin, Ohio, Photograph by the author.

Figure 7.13. Soldiers Monument on its public corner, 1871, Oberlin, Ohio. Photograph courtesy of the Oberlin College Archives.

247

encounter it. By the 1930s, it had lapsed into near ruin — locals called it the "sunken church" — and it soon succumbed to neglect and anti-war sentiment common in the interwar period. It was dismantled in 1935, but the placards were saved, and even before Pearl Harbor, a new memorial was planned for a verdant setting more removed from both commerce and college. The new memorial, a simple, but digni-fied brick wall created to receive the old tablets, with ample room for future names, reflects the substantial changes in taste that took place between the 1870s and 1940s.[17] Stone became brick; an assertive vertical monument became a horizontal surface; a Christian symbol became a pedestrian wall of names. It anticipated Maya Lin's wall, but in the vernacular material of the riverine towns of the Midwest.

The more remarkable change has to do with the new conception of a memorial to all wars. By the 1940s, Memorial Day practices in the United States were becoming increasingly institutionalized, largely under the purview of veterans' groups such as the Veterans of Foreign Wars and the American Legion, whose numbers swelled after World War I.[18] Dating back to Decoration Day, the predecessor to Memo-rial Day in the United States, commemorations frequently included parades and the movement of people from prominent civic spaces to memorials that afforded enough space for crowds to gather and a focal point where speakers could read poems, eulogies, and roll calls. They had to accommodate music and offer a place where veterans, widows, and gold-star mothers could be made a visible part of the pageant. After World War II, the old morbid cemetery and urban roundabouts and medians became troublesome places for these ceremonies. As wars piled up, survivors of one war overlapped with those of the next, and it became vital that these commemorations could be held at a sin-gle site where multiple generations could be accommodated. Hence the establishment of the "all wars" memorial as a type. These are open-ended memorials. They leave room to stitch future casualties into an unfolding history. Names continue to be added to Oberlin's memorial. The most recent addition died in Kandahar, Afghanistan.[19]

The concentration of commemoration called for a different kind of space, well illustrated in Oberlin. The terraced wall created a natural stage for commemorations, a raised background for a ceremony in which veterans could be elevated, mourners foregrounded, and a more amorphous crowd puddled in the glade. Where the Gothic spire had once centered an urban gathering in the round for an intimate group of Civil War veterans and mourners who could be elevated on its base, the All Wars Memorial displaced a complex body of veterans, survivors, and patriots from the commercial and civic center to a parklike setting. It gave commemoration of all wars its own place. This picks up on the theme of zoning memory; it disengaged commemoration from commerce.

Memorials to all wars flourished under other more specific conditions, as well. The 442nd Infantry War Memorial in Boyle Heights, Los Angeles, discussed in Chapter 3, was erected in 1949 "in memory of American soldiers of Japanese ancestry who fought, suffered, and died in World War II." (See figure 3.8.) It served the local Japanese-American community, which had used Evergreen Cemetery for generations because it was one of the few cemeteries that buried people of Japanese descent. Over the years, plaques have been added to the sides and back of the monument for Japanese Americans who died in the wars in Korea, Vietnam, and Iraq. While its name has not changed, it is effectively an "all wars" memorial for the Japanese-American community, which continues to hold annual Memorial Day ceremonies there. The long history of Japanese Americans in Boyle Heights and in Evergreen Cemetery lend the site its gravitas, making a virtue of the cemetery as a site. Nearby, the Mexican-American All Wars Memorial has a similar story. (See figure 4.5.) It was erected after World War II and has grown into the commemorative center for the Mexican-American community. It now commemorates the three hundred and fifty thousand Mexican Americans who have died in military service since the Civil War. The two Boyle Heights memorials are ethnomemorials. For all of their importance for assembling their respective communities together, they also divide them from larger Memorial Day commemorations. As they muster, they also

Figure 7.14. An early example of a memorial conceived as a tribute to soldiers of all wars. J. Otto Schweizer, artist, All Wars Memorial to Colored Soldiers and Sailors, 1934, Philadelphia. Photograph by Kevin Block.

splinter. But this reflects the geographical divisions of Los Angeles, if not the reality of race and ethnicity in the United States.

A precedent for such ethnomemorials to all wars is the All Wars Memorial to Colored Soldiers and Sailors in Philadelphia, built in 1934 (fig. 7.14). Possibly the earliest to be conceived as an "all wars" memorial, its promoters wanted to place it on the Benjamin Franklin Parkway, Philadelphia's Champs Élysées. On this grand boulevard with museums, sculptures, and public spaces, the memorial would have joined other prominent monuments, including the new Civil War Soldiers and Sailors Memorial (1927) and the massive monument to George Washington that sits in a traffic circle in front of the Philadelphia Art Museum. In an era of acute racism, the city's Art Jury blocked this prominent placement, while the Black community rejected the alternative, Fitler Square, which was seen as run-down and undignified. Instead, it was shunted to an isolated part of the sprawling Fairmount Park, where it could do no harm. In the 1990s, with a different political culture holding sway, it finally found its place on Benjamin Franklin Parkway, where it rejoined this larger memorial and cultural context.[20] It now sits on a small plot in front of the Franklin Institute, a science museum founded in the nineteenth century, where it taps into the didactic and political role that urban memorials have played since the era of statuemania.

An even older "all wars" memorial reveals the sometimes banal surface of this convention. The obelisk in Oakdale, California, erected in 1929 by the Ladies Improvement Society, commemorates the American Revolution, Civil War, Spanish-American War, and World War I, even though Oakdale did not exist until 1871 (fig. 7.15). No later wars have been added, probably because commemorations in Oakdale still take place in the cemetery rather than at the memorial. It thus was defunct as a memorial from its inception. Visible from one of the main routes into town, it was but a pretext for beautification: war in a park, sponsored in the name of municipal beauty by women activists. Here, war is nearly an abstraction, without name, place, or deed. To put a sharper edge on Oakdale's intervention, in

Figure 7.15. War memorial as garden sham, 1929, Oakdale, California. Photograph by the author.

Figure 7.16. Every memorial strategy combined into a vast commemorative landscape at the War Memorial Park, McAllen, Texas. Photograph by Ellie Villareal.

the country's most isolationist moment, a monument to war — to all wars — seemed like the right note to interject into a small-town park. Apparently, isolationism did not preclude Americans from celebrating war or preparing its youngest citizens for it.

The recent Veterans War Memorial of Texas in McAllen shatters Oakdale's abstraction in a bid for the most literal and forceful call to arms. It exposes the work that "all wars" memorials can do (fig. 7.16). McAllen has created much more than a memorial. It is a cultural landscape of war honoring "all those who have served in America's wars of the 20th and 21st century," although it was later extended retrospectively to the American Revolution despite the fact that McAllen was incorporated in 1911.[21] Sponsored by the local chapter of the Daughters of the American Revolution, it was conceived in

Figure 7.17. George Washington and palm tree on the Texas plain, War Memorial Park, McAllen, Texas. Photograph by Ellie Villareal.

much broader terms than most memorials as "an educational, cultural, and historic facility to assist future generations."[22] On a vast plot adjacent to the town's convention center, a series of polished granite walls serve as text panels to tell the story of American war and patriotism, honoring the flag, the Constitution, the Declaration of Independence, and the "Founding Fathers." Other walls extol abstract virtues such as valor and courage and, like many memorial walls, list names. The panels are arrayed around a 105-foot black

Figure 7.18. Army WAC and Navy WAVE, War Memorial Park, McAllen, Texas. Photograph by Fontaine Dearth.

granite centerpiece called the American Spire of Honor, with statues here and there to George Washington, the Navy WAVEs and Army WACs, and individual Texas soldiers (figs. 7.17 and 7.18). More statues are planned. This is a memorial with mission creep, but that very fact illustrates what it means to assemble memory.

Memorials to all wars like the one in McAllen may still function strictly as memorials on certain days, but many of them host a dense thicket of assumptions, political ideologies, and civic ideals, as well as being part of a larger emotional geography with war at the center. McAllen's memorial was fashioned ex nihilo to be a cultural landscape unto itself where people can wander into this thicket. Its autonomy as a place speaks to the desire to separate out this constellation of functions, ideals, and motives, to set it apart from the everyday more emphatically than memorials in parks, squares, and roundabouts typically have been. Of course, some of this goes to the horizontality of cities in the western United States, where land on the fringe is cheap, and the automobile changes the dynamics of where people drive memory into the ground. In this sense, nothing could be more ordinary. In McAllen, people get in the car to have this encounter, just as they do to go to the mall or supermarket.[23] Of course, it makes all the difference that McAllen is a border town that aims its patriotic spectacle at a perceived enemy in an era of acute xenophobia. Seen from a Mexican perspective, it is an aggressive gesture.

It would be wrong to assume "all wars" memorials are an American pathology or a peculiarity of land use. The Monument to the Defenders of the Russian Land in Moscow (1995) lifts three bronzes representing ancient, Tsarist, and modern Russian soldiers on a rough-hewn stone plinth (fig. 7.19; see color insert). It sits in the vast memorial assemblage of Victory Park, but it is keyed to Defenders of the Fatherland Day, which itself has a complicated history that helps make sense of the memorial. This Soviet version of Remembrance Day began in 1919 to commemorate the creation of the Red Army. The day predictably expanded in scope after World War II, becoming Soviet Army and Navy Day, and changed again after the Soviet Union collapsed.[24] In 2002, Vladimir Putin "Russianized" it and gave it its present name as part of a much broader propaganda effort to stimulate militarized patriotism in Russian society.[25] Not surprisingly, it has come to mirror Putin's masculinist rhetoric and self-display, doubling as Men's Day.[26] This explains why the Monument to the Defenders of the Russian Land, while sitting amid memorials to nearly every military conflict in Russian history, does not duplicate them. Its charge is different. The three soldiers tower over flowers

Figure 7.19. Selective memory at Bichukov Anatoly's Monument to the Defenders of the Russian Land, 1995, Moscow. Photograph courtesy of Тара-Амингу/Tara Amingu.

that spell out the word "Rus," forging a line of connection between the medieval Rus, Tsarist Russia, and the "Great Patriotic War," the Russian name for World War II. In leaving out the Russian Revolution, the monument conspicuously elides the Soviet moment.

The entire setting speaks to the shifting politics that the monument represents. Victory Park was conceived in the 1950s under Khrushchev, with its first monuments installed under Brezhnev, largely as part of the Soviet cult of World War II. The park languished under Gorbachev, when revisionist accounts of the Soviet role in World War II undermined the cult. Work resumed with special vigor in the 1993 as part of a post-Soviet project to glorify Russian national identity. The park opened and Defenders was unveiled in 1995 for the fiftieth anniversary of World War II.[27] Like its American counterpart in McAllen, the Monument to the Defenders of the Russian Land is part of a post–Cold War realignment. Both are only nominally memorials, although, as the final three chapters of this book argue, what exactly memorials are, how they function, and what we do at them is anything but settled.

Figure 8.1. Thomas Hudson Jones, artist, and Lorimer Rich, architect, Tomb of the Unknown Soldier, 1929, Arlington, Virginia. American Forces Information Service, Department of Defense. Photograph courtesy of the National Archives.

CHAPTER EIGHT

What We Do at Memorials

While memory still holds a seat in this distracted globe.
— Shakespeare, *Hamlet*, act 1, scene 5.

At the Tomb of the Unknown Soldier in Arlington, Virginia, when
the soldiers on duty observe visitors behaving in ways they deem
inappropriate, they bark: "It is requested that all visitors maintain
an atmosphere of silence and respect at all times!" Or more simply:
"Behind the chains and rail!"[1] (fig. 8.1). At times, they reposition their
guns while they yell. Right away we have to pause for a moment to
imagine how the social script for this astonishing scene was written.
The tomb was built in the 1920s to honor the unidentified soldiers
who died in World War I. Over the years, it has become one of the
most venerated sites of commemoration in the United States. But it
didn't start that way. In the beginning, people did decidedly ordinary
things there. They shrugged off the sepulchral form and the unidentified body parts hidden within it — they ignored the larger setting of
Arlington National Cemetery and its acres of graves — to picnic and
play on and around the tomb. They posed for photographs in ways
that troubled veterans.[2]

Over the years, veterans groups began to organize surveillance
and formalize conventions of behavior. In 1937, soldiers were stationed
there around the clock to combat the misbehavior. This response is
curious in a number of ways. First, it demonstrates that no clear conventions governed etiquette there. In fact, what people were supposed

to do at the memorial was not just an afterthought, it played no deliberate role in the design of the site.[3] This stands to reason. It was an entirely new kind of memorial, albeit in a common enough setting, a cemetery. Even the public's informality is not surprising. It is a residue of Victorian habits of taking leisure at cemeteries. The soldiers were part of an improvisation, a correction, a way of figuring out what people should and should not do there (the word "should" being etymologically related to the German *schuld*, meaning variously guilt, debt, or obligation). The obligation that a memorial shoulders — the *should* that it conveys to us — is frequently unfixed. In fact, such obligations have undergone constant change since the French Revolution.

A second curiosity is that the mischief at the tomb in Arlington spurred another common enough response to the site's ambiguous demands: soldiers, armed and in uniform, preside over monuments around the world.[4] As soldiers, they draw a living connection to the dead ones buried in the tomb. They are a reminder, in the absence of clear conventions, of the gravitas of the monument. Their living bodies also take the place of the sculpted bodies commonly found in front of memorials.[5] Their uniforms and weapons, if not their very bodies, are deterrents. When these fail as visual symbols, and people cross some imaginary line of behavior, this is when the soldiers bark. These verbal gestures, both in form and content, enforce what Erving Goffman calls "interaction tonus."[6] The term refers to the unwritten conventions of behavior, particularly bodily comportment, that hover around social interactions. The soldiers' stiffness tells us to stiffen our own bodies. In maintaining this tone in perpetuity with round-the-clock surveillance, their taut bodies guard against other bodies doing loose things. *Their* obligation becomes *ours*, or at least that's the idea.

Their act of endurance and commitment raises a third curiosity. The presence of their bodies prevents the monument from lapsing into ordinary time, extending the duration of obligation to eternity. Because of them, the tomb is always turned on, and here a paradox appears: debt is paid by making it never-ending. The soldiers' vigilance speaks to the power of the everyday, to the immense effort required

to hold it at bay. Without them, the tomb would have become pictur-
esquely derelict, like the ancient Roman tombs fantastically engraved
by Piranesi; in fact, it was on its way to Piranesian ruin in the 1930s.

The tomb itself is nearly inert. A simple marble box sculpted
with pilasters and wreathes and fitted into a rise in the grand stair,
this stripped-down Roman sarcophagus does not come with user
instructions. What do we do here? Circumambulate? With difficulty.
Kneel, say a prayer, place a wreathe, eat a cookie? Not likely, at least
not anymore. For years, chains and rail have cordoned off the area.
These nonhuman actors, as Bruno Latour would call them, conspire
with the guards. If anything, the tomb is a station on an itinerary,
a place for official commemorations or a pause on the way to the
amphitheater at the top of the hill where official military ceremonies
take place. Most of the time, it is a station on the tourist itinerary, an
American Buckingham Palace, where people can observe the soldiers
maintaining that odd cousin of interaction tonus, noninteraction
tonus, as they strain to enchant the place with solemnity, to induce
hierophany. Here the ever-present push and pull of the everyday life
of memorials is at high pitch.

This round-the-clock surveillance shines new light on commemoration, which can be understood as a temporary institution with
an authority structure, hierarchy, and roles, all brought together for
the event and then dispersed. There are, to be sure, more permanent
institutions that arrange, perpetuate, and prop up commemorations,
but organizations such as the Veterans of Foreign Wars, the American Legion, and similar ones around the world usually serve other
functions as well. Memorials routinely lack dedicated and constant
institutional tending, and this is part of why they weave in and out
of the everyday, why they blink on and off. Without the temporary
institution of commemoration (or the vigilance of soldiers) guarding
over a memorial, people have little idea what to do in front of it.

To understand what goes on at and around commemorative
infrastructure, we would do well to commit to the sort of dedicated
observation that happens at the Tomb of the Unknown Soldier. We

would do well to sit for hours in front of memorials, to see them the way ethnographers have observed buskers, markets, and street performers, and to sort out the spontaneous and organized ways people act at them. Being neither an anthropologist nor trained in ethnographic observation, I have turned to visual and material evidence and inflected it with insights from ethnographic studies of distinctly different sites that have surprising affinities with memorials.

Temporary Roofs

The transformations that memorials undergo during commemorations can be understood as pop-ups, moments when people erect temporary roofs over themselves, using the monument as mast.[7] Such a roof is evident in Stanley Spencer's painting *Unveiling Cookham War Memorial* (fig. 8.2; see color insert), but visit almost any memorial on its special day, and a clutch of people will have erected a similar invisible shelter. One of the first things that people do at commemorations is sort out social distinctions or hierarchies. In Cookham, the crowd bushes around the scene, but Spencer poignantly caught the peculiar drama of the many flavors of obligation. Around an inner circle of young widows in white who hug the memorial cross, Spencer crushed an earthy and ragtag mass of young men, hats in hand — one of them has placed the memorial program in his mouth! The crackling energy in the meager space between the line of men and women seduces a young widow to twist around. She meets the gaze of one of the young men, a suitor, perhaps, as others lock their eyes not on the cross, but on the woman, whose leg daringly opens up into the space. To make her status absolutely clear, Spencer has her clutching yellow flowers, rather than red poppies, which were already the symbol of Remembrance Day. By contrast, the most committed woman to her right holds a black vase as she seemingly kisses the base of the cross, her hand overlapping meaningfully with the British flag. Is this an unveiling or a mating ritual? Tragically, it is both, something that Spencer, who had fought in the war and lost a brother, whose name was inscribed on this very memorial, captured with admirable sympathy.

Figure 8.2. A drama of loss, love, and distraction. Stanley Spencer, *Unveiling Cookham War Memorial*, 1922. Private collection. Photography courtesy of Bridgeman Images.

Figure 8.3. Too hot for decorum, Memorial Day, 1942, Greenbelt, Maryland. Photograph by Marjory Collins. Courtesy of the Library of Congress.

Understood from this angle, the painting is all about obligation. The whole crowd seems to lean in, revealing the invisible force of the ceremony. But at the frayed edges, the less committed turn this way and that. They lounge, snooze, chat, and dreamily take in the sun as innumerable minor and unknowable dramas draw their attention here and there. A handful of people turn fully away from the cross, including a clergyman, who stares at the sky. What keeps some of them in the game and what lets others wander? Put in more academic terms, what is the social and material logic of the Cookham gathering?

Some answers come from photographs of similar commemo-

Figure 8.4. Aerial view of Memorial Day, 1942, Greenbelt, Maryland. Photograph by Marjory Collins. Courtesy of the Library of Congress.

rations. At the Memorial Day event in Greenbelt, Maryland in 1942, with the war raging, civilians, veterans, soldiers, and children took respite from the heat and tedium on the grass (fig. 8.3). One man crouches as he smokes a pipe, while the boy in the foreground goes shirtless. This is the look of begrudging obligation. The photograph opens a window onto the moment when interaction tonus has crumbled. In a bird's-eye view of the event, a number of shirtless children stand or sit at the edges, while most of the people hang their heads in what must have been a prayer or a moment of silence — enforced nonmovement (fig. 8.4). These stragglers tie the commemorative group into the background, where a snack bar gives way to beach umbrellas and a vast pool teeming with swimmers. Kids line up to take their leap off of the high dive, and we see the collision of a late-May heatwave and Memorial Day, where the thermometer hit ninety-two degrees in the late afternoon that day. Many people at the event would have wanted Goffman's roof to be more than metahorical.

The heat is enough to explain this everyday scene, but there is more: the pool was opened on Memorial Day in 1939 and nearly every Memorial Day thereafter, including in 1942 when fifteen hundred people "cooled themselves at the pool."[8] Fifteen hundred people! About half the population of the town. From its inauguration, Greenbelt's Memorial Day was linked to recreation at this very spot. Commemorative and recreational cycles were synched. Under these conditions, the adults in Greenbelt could barely maintain their obligations, while the children were freer to break frame, to relax under the sacred roof.

Remarkably, the crowd has drifted away from the temporary stage and the memorial flag pole to stand in the shadow of a building that sits outside of the photograph's frame. Did they stray there step by step over the course of a long ceremony, clinging to the shadow, rather than to the memorial, as in Spencer's painting? The nearly complete loss of interaction tonus in figure 8.3 suggests as much. In Greenbelt, the heat and recreation broke the sense of obligation and undercut the material and social logic of the temporary institution. The literal commemorative stage, which was arranged physically for both visual and acoustic effect and metaphorically to create a tight assembly, as in Cookham, has become absurdly isolated. The image bares the vital role of improvisation in such commemorative performances: the arrangement of people, the program, music, readings, lists of names, and gun salutes all create hierarchies of scale, height, sound, divisions of people, and shifts in attention that give order to the event — until they don't. All the more so in Greenbelt, a new town founded in the 1930s. The program not only syncopates the event. It is a social technique that lets people know when to stiffen and relax and how long they have to stand at attention, all of it ushered in materially or acoustically through the transfer of things and sound, flowers, wreathes, recitations, readings. These guide commemorators through the experience and divide the audience from those leading the performance, but they also dissolve this separation at strategic moments, as when widows are brought to the "stage."

Playing at Memory

The history of Memorial Day goes right to the ambiguity of obligation, or what we do at memorials. Nearly since its origins in Decoration Day, Memorial Day has been given over to leisure activities. While Decoration Day began as a reverential holiday, the turn to leisure on this day of remembrance happened much earlier than might be assumed.[9] The decoration of graves dates from the 1860s, both as a spontaneous form of commemoration and officially, by order of the Grand Army of the Republic. By the 1880s, "parades replaced processions" and "commemoration gave way to celebration."[10] Baseball games, horse races, and other public amusements became standard fare.

Its perceived decadence is evident in a *Puck* illustration from 1883, which uses the corruption of Decoration Day as a pun to expose the political corruption of the moment (fig. 8.5; see color insert). Here is a Shakespearean scene about false debts, replete with men in drag playing absurd and disingenuous roles. A giant crocodile tear drips from the eye of Ulysses S. Grant. A little girl in finery is about to lay a wreath, but she turns out to be a miniature Thomas C. Platt, the political boss of the Republican Party in New York. This is about making fun of the entire prospect of remembrance when so much is ignominious and failed in American politics. Note that there is no spatial structure, no social order, as in Spencer's painting. The central focus, ostensibly on the damaged "empire" monument, is broken by the rabble of dignitaries each doing his own thing. Here, the carnivalesque subverts the high seriousness of the day. The demographic chaos reveals just how fragile the temporary institution of commemoration is, how easy it is for our debts to be overtaken by other cultural forces.

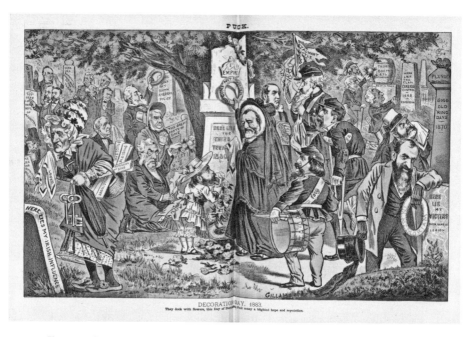

Figure 8.5. Decoration Day as Shakespearian farce, *Puck*, May 30, 1883. Bernhard Gillam, illustrator. Courtesy of the Library of Congress.

The transformation of Decoration Day into a day of leisure is vividly narrated on a cover of *Bearings*, a cycling magazine from the late nineteenth century (fig. 8.6; see color insert). The first Decoration Day bicycle race took place in 1881 in Boston, replete with a bicycle parade, solemn ceremonies, and a competition. The bicycle replaced the horse in the parade. Horseless carriage races soon followed. In fact, the Indianapolis 500 was keyed to Decoration Day from its beginnings in 1911. Such races are easily lampooned. They seem frivolous, substituting mere leisure for commemoration. But this substitution was meaningful, as the image makes clear. Healthy, virile bodies in taut action replaced soldiers and the compromised or dead bodies typical of the Victorian visit to the cemetery on Decoration Day. Color replaced war uniforms or the monochrome headstones of the cemetery. Memorial Day races also ushered in a temporal shift when a new phenomenon — the bicycle and later the automobile — displaced a traumatic

Figure 8.6. From memory to leisure in one image. Charles A. Cox, cover, *Bearings*, ca. 1890–1900. Courtesy of the Library of Congress.

event from the past. Speed, in some cases going in circles around a racetrack, took the place of the procession, dirge, or commemorative puddle. Competition replaced contemplation, spectatorship replaced participation, and the ornament of mass spectacle replaced the more intimate decoration of graves with flowers. The sartorial conventions of commemoration — uniforms, black suits, and white dresses — were swept aside for leisure clothes or the uniforms of the competitors. The bicycle, moreover, was a symbol of liberation, a way of throwing off social restrictions and conventions.[11] The car even more so. As symbols of modernity and free movement, they must have been blatant counterpoints to the static and increasingly old-fashioned memorials that had been the focus of days of remembrance. Yet behind this shift to leisure, it is not difficult to imagine a profound change in how people fathomed their debt to those who had died.

The whole bespeaks a substitution that sublimated reminders of war, death, loss, mourning, national tragedy, and so on. The races counterposed commemoration or the memorial as a historical deposit with an event that defied calcification and dispersed focus. It is nearly a cliché that commemoration was transmuted into leisure, but what a remarkable shift! I don't mean to suggest that the races obliterated or worked against remembrance, although that has been argued.[12] To be fair, commemorations persist to this day, and many leisure events on Memorial Day continue to incorporate sober elements. But the races and other leisure activities such as barbecues slid an alternative range of images, bodily practices, and settings into view on the same day that had been reserved for remembrance, and most of those images and practices were not mnemonic or intrinsically commemorative in nature. They were also resolutely ordinary, or at very least eroded the official sense of obligation that had been established a generation earlier. This dramatically recast commemoration in the United States.

This interjection of leisure into a day of remembrance could be innocent, a simple matter of taking advantage of leisure time in an era before the weekend had solidified as a cultural phenomenon.[13] Or it might reveal a deeper pathology, a way to displace the emotional realities of mourning and the traumas of war. This possibility invites a more psychoanalytical reading of these races and similar events as a kind of transference. In Freudian terms, a "compulsion to repeat" replaced "the impulsion to remember."[14] The *Bearings* cover performs this Freudian "working through" almost too well. The marching soldiers, some markedly in black, make way for the colorful racers, while a line of wizened veterans with canes at the bottom come to watch the race. The way the eye is invited to read the page brings home the meaning. From the top, the image asks us to zig-zag our way down, reading from left to right, as is standard in English. "Bearings," the title, gives way to the soldiers, who march against the grain of reading, from right to left, while their bayonets do an about-face. The cyclists then thrust powerfully against the text, while the bicycle frames reverse course. In turn, the line of veterans gently guides the reader right to left, to the text at the bottom, before exiting the page bottom right. The change in font conspires in the temporal shift that is the central motif of the image, from the old-fashioned typeface atop to modern sans serif at the bottom. The whole creates a back-and-forth of soldiers, bayonets, bikes, vets, and text that takes the reader from the Civil War to its modern substitution via repetitive leisure.

Freud proposed his method as a way to guide the patient back from repetitions that obscured trauma toward remembering by creating "an intermediate region between illness and real life through which the transition from the one to the other is made." Freud called this region a "playground."[15] This extended reading brings up the possibility that some memorials, and the days that we reserve for commemoration, function like playgrounds, intermediate zones between grief and the everyday. Rather than pure escapes, perhaps these playgrounds are one way that people settle debts that are hard to face. If this is so, it would help explain why so many memorials are situated in everyday places, plopped into sites of leisure and the workaday world, where we *work* through them.

Still another layer complicates the *Bearings* image. Decoration Day, like any remembrance day, took an ordinary day out of circulation, giving it a special status akin to feast days in the Catholic calendar. It delivered a hitherto anonymous Monday to the not-everyday. In theory, this reserved the day for not-everyday activities, for commemoration. But in a secular context in which conventions of commemoration were improvised on the fly, expectations remained fuzzy. Even the most cursory examination of such commemorations in Europe and the United States in the period shows a wide variety of activities that underwent dramatic change in short order. In other words, the date was fixed, and sometimes the place, but the conventions of behavior were not. This ambiguity provided an opening that allowed events such as bicycle and horse races, baseball games, and other forms of leisure to come to the fore. For some people, a sacred day became a three-day weekend, nothing more.[16]

Busking Memory

The Freudian interpretation of working through fails to account for how a commercial workday was taken out of the stream of productive economic behavior and then returned to it almost immediately. Races and baseball games are immensely productive capitalist events. They redistribute wealth, often from the masses to economic elites, and in the case of some races, they interpose the economy of gambling, with all of its seductions. The temporary economy of a race is like a limited-time offer. The analogy is not totally whimsical: commemorations compress remembrance, or social debt, temporally into a single day, much as special sales compress opportunities to buy. The formal similarity is anything but arbitrary; it is echoed in the very flexibility of the word "debt."

From the inception of Decoration Day, businesses capitalized on the cultural need to express memorial debts. Beginning in the nineteenth century, clothing stores used Decoration Day as a pretext to boost sales to a public habituated to dressing up in public. The summer vacation season began on Decoration Day weekend, especially after World War II. Even the more house-bound forms of celebration, such as those centered around the barbecue, are bound up in consumption. Beginning as early as the 1940s, the late-May issues of magazines were flooded with advertisements of people at leisure, eating and drinking around a barbecue. Money quickly migrated back into commemoration, and with this, the multitudes were drawn away from the cemeteries and war memorials and brought instead to the commercial realm. Memorial Day sales became a fixture of the day and remain so today. Put differently, at first Decoration Day behaved like Sunday, like a true Sabbath, when most stores were closed. Over time, it morphed into a special day of consumption.[17]

These changes may seem stark, but they may have felt gradual. After all, Memorial Day processions and later parades often marched through the main commercial artery of a town to the cemetery or memorial site, self-consciously connecting the civic and commercial realm to spaces of commemoration and, originally, death. From the start, business opportunities abounded, for flower sellers, hawkers of memorabilia and refreshments, and local store owners. Victorian photographers drummed up business from "parties desirous of having their grave lots photographed."[18] In some measure, commemoration has always comingled with commerce. It might be said that this is the point of such an event in the United States: to muddy the civic, commercial, and commemorative, to show the deep and abiding relationship between freedom in everyday life and the sacrifice of war that protected that freedom. A darker reading lurks beneath this one. This mingling normalizes war and prepares the young for it. In fact, children appear frequently in Decoration Day images, often dressed as miniature soldiers. Their innocence relieves the tension and speaks to the didactic function of these events while it forecasts a future embodied in the assemblage of memorials and melting of wars into *war*.[19]

To be sure, no memorial inscription ever read: "They fought so that people could watch bicycle races." The shift speaks to a form of release in which leisure and the everyday are doing powerful work, especially in the United States, where wars have become increasingly distant, invisible, and conducted through proxy and where death has been increasingly spirited out of public view. The same might describe the diminished presence of war on Memorial Day in the United States today. To be fair, veterans groups continue to take it very seriously, but this stands in contrast to the overall culture. The *Bearings* cover captures a transitional moment of this transformation. This is all to say that what we do at memorials, even on those days when they are most turned on, has changed dramatically and has been put under pressure by this turn toward leisure on special days. Of course, what we do at memorials conspires, or at least contends, with where they have been placed, displaced, mustered, and assembled. The park and cemetery invited leisure, while the modern boulevard and traffic circle, as symbols of modernity and movement, called people to the very places where the everyday could be momentarily but manifestly disrupted, and in turn, where its banal repetitions could worry memory's sharp edges away.

Inside the Chains and Rails

A still finer grain can be found in the analogy between commercial transactions and commemorations. Returning to Spencer's painting, the minor transgressions are alluring because of the assumption of obligation, expressed through engrossment and linked to "the inner spirit of the engrossed person."[20] As Goffman observes, we take for granted the extraordinary amount of "limb discipline" required of every social situation, all the more so in formal settings. For a crowd at a commemoration, staying composed, remaining alive to the situation, gauging the realm of acceptable gesture, these are no small feat, as observing children at such gatherings makes plain.[21] Most places offer an escape from such engrossment, a bathroom with a lock in a restaurant or party, for example, where people take refuge from the demands of the situation.[22] Most commemorations, by contrast, are unforgiving; they are spatially naked, without shelter. Hence the importance of the ragged edge, where people let their limbs relax, their faces sag, their inner spirits leak out to some unknown beyond, like the minister in Cookham. As at the back of a class, so at the back of a crowd. Here, the bodies can go flaccid with impunity.[23]

Such obligations are tolerable only because they are temporary. While memorials make a bid for permanence, commemorations, like bicycle races and sales, are resolutely limited-time offers. This is their reason for being, that is, to turn memorials on (and off). Limited duration is their essence. Scheduled ephemerality establishes welcome constraints on commitment. It circumscribes how long people must stand at attention or even give attention, wear their face of mourning or remain in the garment of grief. The onerousness of the burden is obvious from how often people lapse even while under this roof, as almost any honest image of a commemoration shows.

In this regard, the commemorative program is a revealing text in both content and structure.[24] As an itinerary of obligations, it offers a way for people to know the claims on their "inner spirit" and thus on their bodies. Second, it is a clock, a way for people to gauge the length of these obligations and to tick them off, one by one. The program punctuates the event with a series of intermezzos, brief pauses when interaction tonus is suspended. Entire crowds can be seen pulsing with this rhythm of bodily regulation. Third, the program is like a magazine in the doctor's office: it is a "secondary involvement," a momentary respite from engrossment. Under the pretense of being engaged, one can mindlessly peruse the program and secretly earn release from the scene.[25] But mostly, programs help people track their way through the muddle of modern remembrance, converting eternal debt into a bounded event. They are the temporal chains and rails.

Like limited-time offers in sales, commemorations create artificial scarcity by constraining time. Remembrance Day and its kin create the equivalent of scarcity, a rarefication of time, for a memorial. Such days squeeze commemorative action into a bottleneck, thereby giving special impetus to participants to buy into the performance.

While the "roof" circumscribes the space of obligation, the special day or program narrows the terms of obligation. Commemorative days turn on commemorative sites; they temporarily cog time to space and then release them and us. Commemorations requisition space temporarily in order to allow people to choose their level of commitment. Passersby know to skirt the area, while the deeply committed can venture deeply into the crowd. Standing in the group obliges participants and effectively puts them in the performance. Participants go from offstage to front stage in some sort of gradient as they move closer to the focal point, but this theatrical metaphor fails to get at the transition from the everyday to the not-everyday or how people are brought into a solemn mode. Techniques to pull the crowd in, such as the laying of wreaths or artifacts, song, and the calling of names, can be likened to sales pitches, where participatory gestures, call and response, and personalization all work to intensify commitment and draw the crowd in, or in the language of street hawkers, "twirl the edge."[26] The busker first tries to muster a crowd and then works to dissolve the line between being part of the audience and part of the performance. Commemorations do something stunningly similar.

Studies of commemoration seldom consider these sorts of questions or acknowledge the materiality of the event and its space; the way sound, bodies, voice, curbs, paving, shade, permanent and temporary structures, lights, and codes, written or unwritten (all those elements within the metaphorical roof) shape behavior. So much of the relationship between the material environment and behavior is tacit, absent as much from the process of design as it is from the informal ways people appropriate and adapt spaces of commemoration. As in sales pitches, the more commemorations ask participants to engage physically, to work with what could be called its liturgy, the more committed they become to the event. It is how events lay claim to the inner spirit. Part of the point of commemoration is about showing these obligations socially, about the paying of respects in the right time and place and with the right tone.

What to make of the messy and unresolved nature of commemoration in a pluralistic society, one distanced from traditional rituals of mourning? Where people come to events without a clear sense of how to act, form and space arguably carry greater burdens. The renewed interest in innovation in memorial design in recent years and, paradoxically, the reappearance of conventional forms — forms that suggest deliberate and predictable social scripts — speak to a simultaneous desire for new modes of commemorative obligation and the comfort of conventions.

The intention here has not been to explore in anthropological or ethnographic detail how people behave when they gather at memorials, when they voluntarily enter the commemorative orbit, although thick descriptions of such events would be welcome.[27] We might learn more, for instance, from scholarship on auctions, street performances, buskers, and funerals. An ethnography of commemorations would enrich the logocentric work of historians and the object-based approach of art historians. Memorials are settings for behaviors, yet we know little about what roles people play or how conventions of behavior have been established and how they have changed over time. How do people know their role? How much is improvised? How are hierarchies of obligation sorted out? For instance, the way street hawkers "build the edge" through voice and gesture and draw people in, knowing that spatial proximity intensifies obligation — this is an anthropological dynamic with immense promise for understanding what people do at memorials.[28]

This is not to demean commemoration as a memory pitch but rather to learn from studies of analogous social gatherings. The all-important presentation of goods, the "dem" (for demonstration), is eerily similar to commemoration. Sellers use voice and gesture to escalate the sense of obligation incrementally, lowering the price, adding in extras, giving away "freebies," staging limited-time offers, or handing out empty bags to prompt people to fill them up. At commemorations, the material components act in similar ways. People pass out or sell small flags and pins, flowers, and other symbols of identification and obligation. Rather like a name tag at a conference that one has forgotten to remove after leaving, suddenly revealing an affiliation that becomes embarrassing, these objects of identification tie people to the gathering. Anthropologists who study such pitches have shown how the revelation of personal identity and moral interaction is vital to commercial transaction.[29] It turns out that economic transactions follow personal obligations that defy rational economic behavior. The parallel to commemorations is all too obvious.

Much of this discussion points to the stark disjunction between memorials and commemorations, on the one hand, and the events they mark, on the other. War, for instance, is bloody, chaotic, transgressive, mass in scale, and among the most complicated events humans organize. It might be said to be the opposite of organization, in spite of the hyperorganization of the military that tries to control the chaos. Memorials, by contrast, are usually clean, static, rulebound, physically bounded, and limited in scope. They are not events at all, even if they invite them in the form of commemorations or political gatherings. While some memorials mirror the things they memorialize, many of them are curiously unlike the events, people, or ideas they honor.

This dissimilarity extends to what we do at memorials. When people gather together at memorials for official commemorations, the events, unlike war, are more predictable, conventionalized, scripted, and controlled — the opposite of modern war or almost any event that gets memorialized. Not that memorials should emulate their events, approximate them metaphorically, or gesture to them *pars pro toto*. Most memorials either abstract or allegorize an event, ideal, idea, or hero and do so for good reasons: they distance the memorial from its subject as they bring people to it. And how valuable is this double action, this push and pull! It might be considered the fundamental work of the memorial. The gap lets people look again at something raw or troubling while it provides enough moral, social, or emotional distance to let them weave in and out of their obligations to the dead, to their grief and the grief of others, and to society. This social and emotional distance is negotiated materially, experienced bodily, and bounded by a setting requisitioned temporarily by a social group, mourners, veterans, and so forth. The role of the memorial itself in this constellation is the subject of the next chapter.

Figure 9.1. The grim docent at Charles Sargeant Jagger, Royal Artillery Memorial, 1925, Hyde Park Corner, London. Photograph by the author.

CHAPTER NINE

What Memorials Do at Memorials

In the Land of Memory the time is always Now.

In the Kingdom of Ago, the clocks tick . . . but their hands never move.

There is an Unfound Door (O lost) and memory is the key which opens it.

— Stephen King, *Song of Susannah*, 2004

At the Tomb of the Unknown Soldier in Arlington, where the last chapter began, the soldiers bark in an attempt to extend the temporary institution of commemoration indefinitely. Living bodies perform the work that dead ones no longer do: they "patrol the boundary between the living and the dead," amplifying the memorial's own attempts at the same.[1] As this collaboration between dead and living suggests, what people do at memorials blurs with what memorials do at memorials. For instance, the bronze bodies at the Royal Artillery Memorial, discussed in Chapter 6, perform a number of duties for their monument (fig. 9.1). The central figure at the rear stands guard, rather as the living soldiers do in Arlington. When the memorial was first built on its now-vanished island, it had a less distinct sense of frontality, and commemorations puddled all around it. This soldier doesn't bark, but he too patrols, solemnly. The memorial's designer, Charles Sargeant Jagger, made him larger than life, but not overwhelmingly so. He raised him on a double plinth, which stands atop three easily scaled mortal-sized steps. His remarkable gesture tells us more. He stands contrapposto, his right foot jutting just beyond the bronze base, while he seems to lean lightly on the monument and open his poncho. Far from the great-man statues of an earlier era, this somber debt collector invites people to approach, to mourn, to express their obligations.[2]

His fallen comrade, a recumbent figure to one side, hearkens to medieval tombs (fig. 9.2). The English public would have known the type well from nearby Westminster Abbey. This body does more than the typical requisite flanking figure. The text that runs beneath him reads "a royal fellowship of death." The words wrap around the corner of the plinth and walk the reader to his head, where, gazing through his feet, the Wellington Arch is perfectly framed, echoing, in fact, the form of his helmet. A stitch has been sewn and a new picture has been made: World War I, which started nearly on the centenary of Wellington's heroic exploits against Napoleon, is threaded into the British experience of the Napoleonic Wars, where the common soldier is likened to the great man, and Jagger's massive block fills up the vacancy of the triumphal arch. This combination of sculptural and urban gestures meld sacrifice, loss, heroism, and victory across time.

Figure 9.2. A recumbent soldier links the fallen of World War I to Wellington and to medieval tombs. Charles Sargeant Jagger, 1925, Royal Artillery Memorial, with Wellington Arch behind. Photograph by the author.

The link provides a reminder that the Royal Artillery Memorial caps a triumphal way through Hyde Park Corner that now includes a host of other war memorials. As the connection to older wars grows more tenuous, these assemblages of memorials consolidate our debts. The figures on Jagger's complicated pile conspire with the living to create a choreography of informal commemoration in the absence of set conventions. This is all the more poignant for the fact that it originally stood alone on a traffic island, where people had to work to get there. The entire affair is about mustering the everyday encounter into something dignified.

On the surface, memorials such as Jagger's are about memory. Yet they do their commemorative work intermittently, ambiguously, and sometimes not at all. At times, they work against recall or redirect attention to entirely different concerns. Memorials are also undependable keepers of history, even if people expect this of them.[3] They wiggle around too much to be sober historians. In many cases, their commemorative purposes veil deeper issues. They help people fathom the fluctuations of time as culturally contingent rather than terrestrial or biological. Memorials play a role in marking and stabilizing these fluctuations amid the agitations of the modern world. As memorials respond materially to modern temporality, they also help people negotiate changing attitudes toward death. Time and death, moreover, have been interwoven throughout time. The Greek philosopher Epicurus held that death ends time, just as birth begins it.[4] Almost universally, death has been cogged to time, marking new eras, making culture of generic time. The ancient world was so rife with epochs marked by the deaths of emperors that such new time counts are literally uncountable.[5] It turns out that much of the shepherding of people from life into death and death into the past is about working through consciousness of time. In turn, memorials have been one of the cultural inventions people use to explore this consciousness. Time and death, abstractions seemingly a world away from the everyday, have also been interwoven with everyday life throughout history.

Being collective and public, memorials watch over mortality differently than a burial plot or tomb. As Thomas Laqueur has argued, what people have done with mortal remains is paradigmatically what ushers nature into culture. Through their treatment of dead bodies, people across cultures through the millennia have invited the dead to speak.[6] Even as the relative suppression of dead bodies in the more recent past signals a shift in consciousness about what dead bodies do in culture, it still illuminates modern difficulties with aging bodies, death, and time: absence is still a profoundly important way of dividing nature and culture. The presence of dead bodies, moreover, may be less important than their intimation. While Laqueur argues that the presence of mortal remains is essential, William Godwin's ruminations (discussed in Chapter 3) make it clear that representation is often sufficient. A bronze of a fallen soldier or one being lifted to the heavens will do as symbolic stand-ins for the dead. In fact, effigies need not be morbid in aspect; they can be simulacra of a long dead figure or a lone column. As the eminent art historian Rosalind Krauss reminds us, in its traditional role, "sculpture is a commemorative representation."[7] We scarcely need a dead body under a hunk of stone to go straight to death. Any statue of Lincoln evokes his martyrdom. Nor is tragic death like Lincoln's necessary. In fact, the vigorous gestures of many great-man memorials draw out through implied contrast the work they continue to do in death by modeling an exemplary life or deed. That this is a cliché of memorials does not diminish its resonance. This chapter examines the work of memorials as time keepers and as metaphorical undertakers, the way they have complicated time and negotiated the realm between life and death.

In focusing on these two roles, I do not mean to suggest that this is all that memorials do at memorials. Close observation of almost any memorial will show how busy they are herding and organizing people, elevating some participants while puddling the rest on the mortal plane, reinforcing social hierarchies, and trying to tell us what to feel.[8] Of course, I don't mean this literally. In these roles, memorials are docents, not dictators, yet we might think of the gross motor moves of memorials as deeply influential. Color, girth, texture, height, the richness of materials, paving, water, and railings are all gestures. These formal qualities ask something of us: to slow down, look up, walk with care, choose to go in or stay out, or simply to make way. It would seem that memorials that embrace "fields" — where landscape, instead of an assertive figure, comes to the fore — disperse this gestural potential and are thus less commanding. But landscapes such as Peter Eisenman's Holocaust Memorial in Berlin gesture through a double action of immersion and dispersal. Their request is no less assertive. In Berlin, people report feeling disoriented, anxious, lost, overwhelmed. Do we have any more self-determination in Eisenman's field of forms than we do when dwarfed by a space-shattering Stalin? Here, the distinction between memorials that are turned on and off begins to blur because many of these observations work both when commemorations attempt to spark hierophany and when memorials lapse into the ordinary.

Time

Martijn Wallage, a present-day philosopher, writes of walking to his office at the University of Leipzig and coming across the statue of an "old dean," bronze book in hand, flowing robes frozen in the busy plaza, and he is moved to quote Goethe's Faust: "There is no past or future in an hour like this, the present alone is our bliss"[9] (fig. 9.3). Statues do seem frozen in time, resisting what goes on around them. As Wallage puts it, they seem to exist in "a *nunc-stans*," an eternal present, "a standing or remaining in the now."[10] This is Frank O'Hara's experience of Sherman; it gets right to the quick of the everyday experience of memorials. At the same time, memorials are constantly raising a temporal ruckus. They exist in many times at once, condensing — or as the historian Reinhart Koselleck would put it, sedimenting — moments in one spot.[11] The encounter with the old dean tethers two obvious moments in time, the present of the author and the period of the "old dean." Even to name him so is to peg him in time, a different time, while the very manner of

Figure 9.3. "The old dean," anonymous as those who sit on his steps. Ernst Rietschel, 1850, Albrecht Thaer Monument, Leipzig. Photograph by Frank Vincentz.

the statue's execution betrays still a different era. Statues — in fact, all memorials — reflect the biases and fashions of their moment of creation in the choice of subject and form of representation. Would anyone now choose to make a statue of the old dean, whomever he is?[12] If somehow his reputation survived or was revived enough to warrant a new statue today, it would turn out very differently. In any case, the bid to eternity is constantly upset by the wear and tear of everyday life. Memorials bear the scars of use, abuse, and neglect, which are timepieces of another sort. All of these temporal remind- ers are condensed and brought into the present when we encounter them. What is more, no special effort is needed to observe such clues. They come to us. The Leipzig statue need not be dated to be the "old dean." He wears his date.

On the face of it, dates on memorials are trivial, an obligatory component so common that we tend to pass quickly over them. Dates are fixed. They are arguably the most rote and least interpretable part of a memorial. Yet they are also paradoxically in tension with the memorial. Dates bracket a life, pointing to the finite, an Epicurean birth and death of time. Memorials unbracket that life, gesturing to the eternal. Dates recall mortality; memorials make a pitch for immortality. Dates pin a life to the modern time line, to history unfolding rationally; memorials, as argued in earlier chapters, muddy time. This is why a memorial without dates is perplexing, perhaps as much as one without a name.

The temporality of memorials is intrinsically complicated. Almost any example in this book speaks to this point. Most memorials are neither strictly linear nor rigorously cyclical in how they register time. Rather, they tend to be temporally oversaturated. For instance, the statue of King Alfred in Winchester (twice dated, with the years of his life and the erection of the statue on the thousandth anniver- sary of his death in 1901) ties the time of the great medieval king to turn-of-the-century issues (figs. 9.4 and 9.5). A millennium collided with a momentous turn of time. Preposterously, one writer lionized Alfred as the inventor of the modern workday, claiming he counseled

Figure 9.4. Hamo Thornycroft, King Alfred Monument, 1901, Winchester, England. Postcard from the author's collection.

Figure 9.5. Hamo Thornycroft, King Alfred Monument, 1901, Winchester, England. Photograph by the author.

setting aside eight hours each for work, sleep, and recreation and study. The idea originated in utopian socialist thought in the early nineteenth century but had been gaining traction in Britain and the United States in the 1890s.[13] By no coincidence, the British Labour Party was created in 1899. The statue's two dates laminate Alfred's time onto the era of pan-European statuemania, when people sought enduring heroes from the murky past to narrate the issues of their day, foremost among them the quickening pace of change itself.

Alfred's gesture and style tell us more. The bronze Alfred stands on a menhir-like plinth and holds his sword high. While a recent resurgence of monumental sculpture like this can be found around the world — in fact, a bronze of Alfred with shield was erected at Alfred University in 1990 — this manner of representation is now, to put it in polite, and telling, terms, outdated. This is to say that its very style marks a time fundamentally different from our own and from that of Alfred the man, who for many tourists in Winchester is about as illustrious as the old dean. His placement draws attention to the statue's complicated time signature. He poses on his island at the head of a parking strip, dividing one of the main routes into town. When he first raised his sword in 1901, he lorded over pedestrians and horses, but quickly entered the realm of cars. Transformers pop up at one of the corners of his base, and tufts of grass grow out of small concrete drums, a remainder of some postwar paving scheme gone wrong. It is a palimpsest of time, with layer scribbled upon layer. Our charge upon seeing the Alfreds of the world may not be to exfoliate these leaves of time, but we take them in, not as some kind of *nunc-stans* drained of time, but rather a *tempus-imbricatis*, or a multiaxial temporal hinge. Statues like this are drunk with time.

Time seeps in still again with the jarring problem of anonymity. We all pass statues of notables who have slipped out of consciousness: old deans likely outnumber the Lincolns, Gandhis, and Maos, those figures who stubbornly resist being forgotten. An anonymous monument is a paradox, a mnemonic that we have forgotten something, and this in turn goes to time's passage. A memorial may lull us into a *nunc-stans*, but it is an eternal present flooded with melted time. What to make of this time puddle in which memorials sit? Walter Benjamin wrestled indirectly with the idea through his idea of the *Jetztzeit*, when "what has been comes together in a flash with the now to form a new constellation."[14] The *Jetztzeit* need not be passive. Hannah Arendt likened it to a pearl diver plucking a pearl from the depths and bringing it to the surface. For Benjamin, this active search for pearls was part of changing the present.[15] Hence memorials that attempt to bring to the surface a moment of the past, to bring it back persistently, with a clear intention to preserve it for the future, often with words such as "Never forget." However "old" they may seem, they are also like Arendt's pearls, working over the present, if not altering the future. Such memorial pearls, if you will, are one way that these two defiantly abstract parts of human consciousness — time and its accomplice, memory — find their material trace in the built environment, all the more so in an age of tumultuous transformation.

Why use statues to tell time? Memorials have proliferated across a period of vast temporal warping, from the time scrape of the French Revolution through the accelerations of the Industrial Revolution and the rationalization of time beginning with the railroad in the late nineteenth century. They flourish at Epicurean pivots, violent transitions when time seems to end and begin anew. In the aftermath of the Russian Revolution, Lenin proposed a series of plaster monuments, temporary tributes to revolutionaries that would be made permanent if their legacy endured.[16] The move allowed instant commemoration on the cheap while turning each monument into a flexible commemorative clock, leaving it to the people to extend or blot out its horizon of expectations. There would be no old deans in Lenin's scheme. They would be fake pearls tossed back into the depths of the past.

As precise clock time came to dominate modern life, memorials offered a counterpoint, a third hand if you will, that pointed much less rationally, but no less willfully, to an alternative count. Moderns fabricated and continue to live in a world that insists on time's rationality, but this is a state of affairs created and maintained through the powerful technology of clocks, schedules, and calendars. These social and literal technologies maintain time as concrete in the face of its much more elusive reality. "Our imaginations are essentially atemporal," writes Verlyn Klinkenborg. "To human minds, time isn't transparent. It's invisible."[17] Just like Musil's description of memorials![18] Hence the compulsion to materialize it, to blow metallic dust over its invisible form as it slithers past, to speed-draw metaphorical rooms to contain it, to periodize, capsulize, obsess over origins and endings, dawns and apocalypses, to drive its definitive pivots into copper plates, and to preserve the records of these efforts in bronze, stone, concrete, and acid-free paper in air-conditioned archives. Forget them all. If deep time, or even our time, is our quarry, these strategies are all folly.

Indeed, our most adjustable tool, language, stammers at the task. Few words exist for describing time without resorting to metaphors that are anything but temporal.[19] Time marches, flies, flows, runs or drags on; we can steal a moment, which is a modern usage, since the irreversibility of secular time makes it impossible to go back to pick up something we left in the past. In fact, the conceptual framework for understanding time is often directional or, more broadly, spatial.[20] Susan Sontag's "time's relentless melt" is a glacial version of Heraclitus's river, into which we never can step twice because it is ever-changing.[21] At least memorials offer a way around the metaphorical limits of language. To be sure, many specific memorials mark a point in time that is plotted on the calendar and through commemoration interject into the modern time line a circular return more commonly associated with premodern cultures. But memorials also play games that defy horological time. They try to impose forever onto, say, June 6, 1944 (D-Day) — an eternally precious past projected into the future in perpetuity through commemoration. A pearl. This temporal work is also historically grounded: memorials began this labor as modernity denaturalized time and abstracted it from natural cycles into artificial counts, such as the workday.

Yet memorials defy both rational and natural modes of telling time. The old dean can never retire — and poor Alfred's arm! It must ache so. These express a superficial *nunc-stans*, a broken clock face if you will, behind which the more complicated works continue to spin. Perhaps the reason that memorials can play with time in ways that seem patently absurd is that they are already spatial. In being placed, no matter if the context is some grim traffic circle, they can get at time, or bring us to it, in ways that language cannot. Their rise as a modern form depends on their ability to countenance time in their own peculiar way, to put on one face in the present while keeping more complicated rhythms for those who seek them. Put in the terms laid out in Chapter 2, they are temporally labile. Whereas Mircea Eliade, the great scholar of religion, drew a sharp split between premodern, cyclical modes of time and modern, linear ones, memorials show that in reality, the difference is not so clear.

To Eliade, modernity eradicated circular time, and the loss was dire. Cyclical time had once allowed people to understand disasters in terms of archaic events — the great flood or battle — that took place in a far-off and hazy golden age, one distant enough to elude historical certainty. Over time, the new trauma would be absorbed into the archaic one. This "revolt against concrete, historical time" takes the form of a "periodical return to the mythical time of the beginning of things, to a 'Great Time.'"[22] Such myths explain the world, and in so doing, they reassure people that nothing is arbitrary. A natural disaster rapidly becomes "the Flood," a loss in battle turns into a new incarnation of an archaic battle fought time out of mind. People then followed well-worn cultural scripts in order to calm the gods and themselves. As new wars and singular events become manifestations of eternal events, they lose their uniqueness as singular events. They lose, in other words, their potential to knock time out of its orbit. Such myths prepare cultures for misfortune. They give people collective conventions of behavior, modes of release from anxiety, and the means to begin anew.

In Eliade's view, when linear time replaced cyclical time, it rendered arbitrary the very events that constitute time's passage. It deprived them of their external logic. Modern history explains individual events, but it provides no cosmic or transcendent order into which they fit, much less conventions for dealing with the aftermath of cataclysm. It denies the chance of mythic renewal. Modernity dammed the great floods and channeled them into Chaplinesque time factories that disciplined people's bodies in work, sleep, consumption, and leisure, the same discipline ascribed to King Alfred. Eliade was writing in the aftermath of the Holocaust and the bombing of Hiroshima and Nagasaki, events often seen as unprecedented and thus as historical ruptures. Understandably, he saw rational, historical time as an existential crisis because it deprived people of conventions for dealing with horrific events individually or collectively. Eliade's text is nothing short of a warning about modern, secular society's incapacity to manage catastrophe: "How can man tolerate the catastrophes and horrors of history — from collective deportations and massacres to atomic bombings — if beyond them he can glimpse no sign of transhistorical meaning; if they are only the blind play of economic, social, or political forces, or, even worse, only the result of 'liberties' that a minority takes and exercises daily on the stage of universal history?"[23]

Monuments would seem to be ineffectual in the face of such existential crises. Yet events such as the Holocaust are like the rest of modernity, but even more so.[24] (Although, as an aside, it is easy to see how the Holocaust is used as the great cataclysm). The creation of linear time and the rejection of circular time, because it was seen as mythic and irrational, provoked a return of the repressed time metaphors of premodern life. Here monuments had a role to play.

Monuments can be understood as part of this return of the repressed. They create permanent fixtures around which new archetypes might be founded, while commemorations spin cyclical practices around linear events. They bend time's arrow. Just as modern time attempted to pull premodern, cyclical time taut and banish the possibility of eternal return, people stuffed this lost time into monuments, not just in cycles of commemoration, but also by creating artifactual time posts. Eliade himself proposed a number of ways in which modernity invited cycles back into modern experience, citing in particular Friedrich Nietzsche and Oswald Spengler, T. S. Eliot and James Joyce.[25] But he was surely too reserved on the issue. Modern time does more than allow cyclical time to sneak back occasionally. Without recurrence and repetitive processes, "singular events . . . could not even occur."[26] They are mutually dependent. As temporal devices, memorials point us to earlier layers of sediment, to various surprises or pivots, irreversible events, and singular people. They thus contain multiple temporalities and serve as pivots that mark a before and after or suggest a "not yet." Alfred is a once and future king, a rebuttal to Epicurus and to modern linear time. Memorials foster cycles of commemoration that gesture back in perpetuity to a point in time and tap into recurrent abstractions and sentiments we wish to make permanent. Some of these seem to float free of time: honor, freedom, gratitude, sacrifice. All of this hides a surprise. The historical pivot, the event, and commemorative recurrence can merge and become one and the same, since what was once a pivot (the Franco-Prussian War, Sanmicheli's moment, or an eminence who changed the world such as "the old dean") inevitably ages out of relevance. People no longer use it to tell time. As it slips into deep time, which even Eliade thought takes only decades rather than centuries, its place on the rational time line gets fuzzy. And with this, its narrative potential shifts. It is absorbed into something vaguer or bigger that blurs its singularity, as when memorials to many wars are assembled. Singular wars, once vivid and hot in our collective imagination, become part of a phenomenon of war — glory, nation, sacrifice — or of a cyclical action, such as the commemoration of all wars. Time's arrow is shot in circles.

Occasionally, the opposite happens, and circles become arrows, as when white nationalists "turned on" the Confederate monument in Charlottesville, Virginia, on August 12, 2018, at the Unite the Right

Rally. The violence of that evening attached the monument to a new irreversible historical event, which could be given greater meaning if it comes to be commemorated cyclically. This process gets ever more complex because memorials are often built much later than the events or people they commemorate. Confederate monuments built in the 1920s refer superficially to the Civil War, an irreversible historical pivot, *and* they refer more assertively to the Lost Cause, the racist regime of white supremacy meant to subjugate Blacks Americans in the South and elsewhere. The Confederate monument transforms the singular pivot, which is mere pretext, into something of boundless duration. It comes to represent a mentality with an entirely different temporal nature. In this way, a memorial to an event can stand in for something un*event*ful, a deeper structure, a persistent attitude, in this case, a dark wish for permanent racial domination or a fantasy to return to a golden age before the pivot. This is one of the traditional roles of monuments as warnings, in this case, standing permanent guard over a fragile and changeful racial order. Such monuments shout out "Eternity!" in the face of cultural evanescence. Champions of the Lost Cause used monuments to turn a singular event trapped in linear time, a settled matter, into a circle. After 2016, white nationalists used this circle to create a new pivot: a backward ideological mentality brought back a singular event that had been dormant. An ugly, misbegotten pearl. The wave of iconoclasm that followed is an attempt to throw it back into the sea, to block it from the *Jetztzeit*. When activists took over the Robert E. Lee Monument in Richmond in the wake of the murder of George Floyd in 2020, they did more than appropriate it for the Black Lives Matter movement. By projecting an image of George Floyd onto the equestrian statue, they countered the timeless Lost Cause with a new historical pivot.[27] Images of Martin Luther King, Jr., Frederick Douglass, Harriet Tubman, and others joined Floyd, making a plea to replace Lee with these pearls — a timeless Black pantheon — as part of the *Jetztzeit*.

This commentary on the political co-option of memorials would seem to creep beyond the core concerns of this book, but in setting the edge of what memorials do temporally, it gets at the everyday experience of time. What happened at Charlottesville and Richmond is an extreme and vivid version of what happens at memorials every day. Monuments, which exist in a fitful and sometimes openly hostile relationship to linear time, arose significantly and in numbers alongside the accelerating changes of modernity. It does not overstate the case to say that it is their purpose, however flawed or ineffective, to challenge rational, linear time. The issue can be historicized, although it is not the intention here to trace out a full history of the changing relationship between monuments and attitudes toward time. Such a history would be messy, selective, and possibly as intangible as time itself. Suffice it to say, the French Revolution made awareness of time's acceleration acute. One compelling response to this acceleration was to reach for permanent material objects. "There is no festival without a monument," writes the historian Mona Ozouf of the French Revolution, "for only the monument gives eternity."[28] More broadly, "Europe's most momentous crisis of time" gave rise to memory and patrimony as "signs and symptoms of our relation to time: as different ways of translating, refracting, obeying, or obstructing the order of time."[29] We could do worse than to turn back to William Godwin, a voice from that past, who called for monuments to be erected "to resist the inevitable erosion of time" and to respond, in Laqueur's words, "to the sense of cataclysmic temporal rupture experienced by the post-revolutionary generation."[30]

Such responses have gone well beyond cerebral hero worship. They were felt. After visiting Alexandre Lenoir's Museum of French Monuments, where monuments threatened by the revolution were salvaged and assembled, the French historian Jules Michelet (1798–1874) wrote: "In fancy I filled those tombs — I felt the dead, as it were, through the marble; and it was not without some terror that I visited the vaults, where slept Dagobert, Chilperic, and Fredegona."[31] The public monuments that Europeans and Americans subsequently thrust into the streets and public spaces of their cities — and into those of their colonies! — brought these timepieces and an array of emotions into everyday life. Godwin and Michelet get to the crux of the matter: representations of dead people were meant to stabilize time at the very moment when the old temporal regime was under assault. After the temporal pivot of the French Revolution, through which Godwin lived, monuments summoned an exemplary past and hitched it to a future that supplanted the timeless or eternal symbols of royalty and the church. From the start, then, the new monuments, as well as those saved by people such as Lenoir, entered a novel temporal stream. They moved beyond a despised "before"—the old regime and its monuments—and expressed an aspirational "not yet" to which these exemplary figures and events pointed.[32] Monuments were used to unfurl or plot modern time.

Eventually, the before and after acquired radically different values. By the twentieth century, references to the past rapidly became anathema. The new attitude was most virulently expressed by the Futurists. Filippo Marinetti wrote of the "gangrene of professors, archaeologists, tourist guides and antiquarians," which he wanted to cut away.[33] This attitude has been seen as a quintessential part of a shift toward a regime of futurism, which initiated a confrontation between two attitudes about time and the past, the new one driving ruthlessly forward, displacing an older, retrospective mentality that gave us museums, heritage sites, and monuments. Whereas Marinetti discredited heritage and monuments and longed to create a constantly churning temporal tabula rasa through violent destruction, traditional monuments have to be seen not merely as inert specimens of historicism, but as attempts to resist a quickening world, to manage the Marinettis of modernity. The terms might even be reversed. Instead of seeing historicism as the status quo and modernity as the heroic protagonist rising up to jolt the laggard heel draggers forward, historicism may be seen as a cultural invention aimed to thwart or slow futurism, which appeared as a set of attitudes long before Marinetti. The statuephobia of the nineteenth century anticipated Marinetti's attitude, a mentality that continues in the disparagement of "dead white males," which in turn has been a steady refrain in efforts to discredit the "old deans," among more obviously objectionable characters, of the world.[34]

We might well condemn monuments to white supremacy, sympathize with the desire to diversify who gets monumentalized, or even find monuments ridiculous or outdated as a cultural form and still probe the rhetorical strategy of the phrase "dead white males." Seen from François Hartog's point of view, rather than a rearguard position, the phrase resonates with another change in mentality about the past. The glut of monuments to long-dead men that Godwin once thought would "paralyze the hand of oblivion" and steady the ship of modernity have come to be seen as emblems of patriarchy, ethnocentrism, racism, authoritarianism, colonialism, and, echoing Marinetti, the fusty past itself, unmistakably smeared by the word "dead." The past has been under assault for generations. In fact, by the early twentieth century, the past was so reviled that "historians who wanted to challenge the accusations of the 'bankruptcy of history' (which became blatant with the First World War), had first to prove that the past was not synonymous with death and a desire to stifle life."[35] Every American high school student forced to take a class in history has felt the deadliness of the past. "Dead white males" plays with this now largely assumed synonym. The power of the phrase is in its enjambment, almost like a rhetorical counterpunch to the process of assembling memorials. It builds this discrediting of the past into a larger edifice of race and gender. While these latter categories have been extensively examined, "dead" flies under the radar.

Put another way, there are widely available ways of thinking critically about whiteness and maleness, but the dead have eluded such thought. The dead are often dismissed with impunity, and when they are, it reprises and updates the ancient attitude of Diogenes, who counseled his followers to dump his body over the walls of Athens once he died.[36] Monuments disapprove of this attitude toward death as the end of time. They seek to retrieve the dead in perpetuity and insist on their power to speak to the present and future. What would it mean to care for or about the bodies of dead white men, if only in effigy? That this question was difficult to type and was erased and rewritten several times demonstrates the discomfort I feel in posing it. It is not my intention to champion dead white males or their statues. Yet it is obvious that dead white males are not dead, or not quite dead. If they were actually dead, we wouldn't need this dismissive triad. We would not need to kill them a second time with the aspersion of death, to equate them with nothingness. Whiteness and maleness defy such existential cancellation, but deadness in modern culture is defined in exactly this way.[37]

Diogenes illuminates the stakes of this rhetoric. When applied to a statue, "dead white males" turns the monument into a metonym for something that should be dumped over the walls of the city, so to speak. It transforms the *exemplum virtutis* into an example of vice or viciousness and prepares the cultural ground for Marinetti-like cleansing. This stands to reason, since the phrase gained traction as part of the canon-busting mood of the 1980s. The "great men" who once played a prominent part in the moralizing currents of the eighteenth and nineteenth centuries were being metaphorically assembled and lassoed down from their canonical pedestals. In Godwin's time, dead "great men" were synonymous with cultural greatness. Michelet felt their presence! Their celebration was tethered in the nineteenth century to emerging conventions of high and low and mapped, however imperfectly, onto parallel structures of the everyday and not-everyday. The discrediting of their monuments is surely kin to the anti-Victorian sentiment that arose in the early twentieth century, in the same moment that reviled the past itself and instituted the taboo on death. "Dead white males," then, does something that "white males" alone could not have done. "Dead" makes all the difference.

Monuments could be dismissed as "dead white males" — note that they are not likened to them but in many instances called them directly — because statues and death have been paired for centuries, if not millennia. Going back to the archaic period in Greece, columns were erected at burial sites in explicit reference to the dead buried within.[38] The tradition persisted or was revived repeatedly straight into the twentieth century.[39] In this family of forms, the memorial oscillates between presence and absence, in Ozouf's felicitous phrase.[40] The broken column of *1938* in Klagenfurt takes up this formal tradition darkly in response to the crisis of fascism, subverting the reserve of the stolid column by melodramatically thrusting dead bodies back into its fractured form. (See figure 5.14.) Seemingly forever, the memorial has been the dead body manqué, balancing presence and absence. "Dead white males" picks up on this tradition, but alters it again in response to a pointedly different crisis. Its iconoclastic urge is epochal, a paradigm shift. It ventures well beyond the statuephobia of the nineteenth century and Marinetti's derogation of the past, which was masculinist to the core. It steps beyond the living memorial movement's zealous dismissal of traditional memorials as "dead" in the context of the taboo against death, and it leaps beyond the countermonument movement of the late twentieth century, which was still dialectically bound to the monument as a cultural form. Clearing away the "dead white males" is a kind of *damnatio memoriae*, multiculturalism's metaphorical regime change, an attempt to reset time by shepherding one of the cultural markers of a previous time out of view.

Yet to understand it as iconoclasm, as a political act of erasure, misses something. By disappearing the dead bodies of that regime, "dead white males" breaks up the *tempus imbricatis*, the way people have used memorials to read the crazy clock of modernity. To be clear, I'm not advocating shedding tears over it all. Every commemorative statue has its statute of limitations, and most of the toppled monuments deserve their fate. Roman emperors regularly cleared away the monuments of their predecessors. Americans will be just fine without the towering Lee. The long view is unemotional for the same reason that time is invisible. It is easy to imagine that many of the "dead white males" will eventually disappear or some future Lenoir will assemble them in museums, and perhaps someone in some future fit of memorialmania will propose a memorial to the disappeared "dead white males." Putting aside the absurdist nature of the proposal — there are plenty of absurd proposals for memorials! — we can readily see that such a memorial would be an elegy to an epoch. A death knell. All of this hand-wringing about time and death makes clear just how intertwined monuments have been with conceptions of time and death.

Death

First an excursion, a scenic detour, because sometimes we cannot see the landscape for the memory. In one of his widely read pieces, Bruno Latour demonstrates what a potent thing a door is. One would have to smash a wall, walk through it, and then rebuild the wall in order to accomplish the same work that the door does. Doors "maintain the wall hole in a reversible state."[41] Imagine the number of times each day we use doors to breach and restore walls for privacy, safety, or climate control, and it is obvious that the door saves us countless hours and energy, not to mention aggravation. Latour is being cheeky, of course, but he draws attention to several important realities. First, the simple hinged door is an invention, a technology. Second, it performs an immense amount of work that goes unnoticed. Third, in doing so, it is the door — a thing — to which we "delegate" much of the work of opening and closing a wall. To Latour, it is a character, as in a story, with whom we interact. Finally, the door, like all tools or technology, imposes upon us; it alters our behavior or prescribes in some way, however small, ways of moving, acting, and interacting. Technologies can even discriminate. Think of the small hands of a toddler or someone with arthritis fumbling with a door handle.[42]

If a hinged door can be so complicated while seeming so simple, what of memorials, which, if less utilitarian, also perform invisibly? Like a door, physical memorials perform work in commemorations and in everyday life. What work does a memorial help people do? Or, put differently, what do people delegate to it? And in what ways might a memorial alter our behavior or discriminate? Of course, the answers to these questions depend on the memorial, its culture, and its place in space and time; the answers, in other words, would fill this book and many others. The account here will therefore be severely restricted and merely point to the possibilities. It might prove useful to begin with the least material and possibly the oldest of memorials to show how even the elegy, a verbal memorial, does something analogous to holding a wall hole in a reversible state. The elegy has traditionally made the invisible — typically, a dead person — visible, if only in word or through metonymy, abstraction, or some other form of representation.

Many of the oldest known memorials were oral or literary tributes, laments performed in song.[43] Literary memorials allow the body and material representations of it to disappear. They tilt the scale of absence and presence strongly toward the former by substituting words for the body or the body manqué. To be sure, laments often took place alongside dead bodies or at tombs, but they also can transcend place and materiality. They can be immaterial and performed anywhere. The advantage of literary memorials is obvious. Dead bodies are full of troubles. They are often seen as polluted and are laden with social taboos, some of which stem from their actual corruption over time. Dead bodies present limitations on time and physical space that memorials of all sorts can overcome. Just look to traditions of handling dead bodies going back to ancient Egypt to see what a complicated and expensive business dead bodies can be. Modern bodies came with other complications, most notably, social taboos linked to miasma theory and the increasing alienation from death.[44] Literary memorials dispense with these dilemmas by decoupling the body from physical and geographical realities.

It is not so much that an elegy is a pyramid manqué, but it performs some of the same work, if in a profoundly different way. Modern elegies, written in an era of expanding literacy, performed a similar vanishing act on the body. For a cultural form that marks the loss of someone loved or revered, bodily absence in the elegy is striking, all the more so because physical memorials often recall the lost body by representing, abstracting, allegorizing, or implying it. The absence of the war dead in the nineteenth century came as a trauma that elegies and physical memorials, which have been seen as materialized elegies, attempted to smooth over.[45] Much as a door is a wall hole held in a reversible state, a memorial can be a dead body or bodies in a transformed state that stages a particular relationship between the dead, mourners, and the place in which they perform their lament. Literary memorials undertake, reduce, or translate that body into a radically different form.

In his elegy "In Memory of Y. B. Yeats" (October 7, 1939), W. H. Auden grappled intuitively with these relationships. The poem is emblematic, if in the extreme, of modern elegy's exploration of dead bodies, time, memory, and place.[46] "He disappeared in the dead of winter," it begins. With this seemingly innocuous opening salvo, Auden "disappears" the body and replaces it with a landscape, not a literal one, of course, but an elegiac landscape in which time collapses.[47] Yeats did die in January, but that only partly explains why "the brooks were frozen, the airports almost deserted," frustrating both natural and relentlessly scheduled time. Another time, that of "public statues," is veiled by snow dropped by the dead winter in which Yeats disappeared. The poet's body and the statues become enmeshed in an absence that stubbornly insists on bodily presence. As Auden was writing, death was ubiquitous. Just weeks before, Germany had annexed western Poland, and Europe was descending rapidly into the Second World War. In fact, in "In Memory of Sigmund Freud," also written in 1939, Auden asks, "When there are so many we shall have to mourn / . . . of whom shall we speak?" Yeats's death, however, is the death not just of an exceptional person, but also of a certain Europe. Auden's Yeats is a modern *exemplum virtutis*. To Auden, he deserved an instant monument, like Marat, and, like David's painting of the revolutionary writer, the poet proposed an impossible monument as a way of saving the world from utter despair. Repeatedly Auden refers to the absent Yeats by way of physical place, in fact, vast cultural geographies and built environments: "The provinces of his body revolted / The squares of his mind were empty / Silence invaded the suburbs." Then, like some Egyptian priest preparing a corpse, with nods to the medieval reliquary and William Godwin's call for monuments to great men, Auden guides Yeats's body to another state: the body of "the Irish vessel" "is scattered among a hundred cities."

Here the elegy turns in on itself, for this is a poem about poetry, even if "poetry makes nothing happen," it is itself "A way of happening, a mouth." At this moment, a moment of cultural collapse, Auden reveals the hinge of elegy's Latourian door via transfiguration: "The words of a dead man / Are modified in the guts of the living." Poetry is the transfiguring wafer, ingested by reading or recitation. Flesh is spirited away into words, as Yeats body was disappeared, and then reembodied in the reader. This is what the elegiac memorial can do, dematerialize the body and give it a visceral afterlife — a mouth indeed. Auden ushers Yeats to the "bottom of the night," where with his "unconstrained voice" he can "still persuade us to rejoice" as darkness descends on the world. In this way, the dead are made to speak through memorials. Turning this around, we can ask, "What do memorials do at memorials?" In their most stripped-down form, to bring Latour and Laqueur together, they hold the door between life and death ajar, forestalling an Epicurean end of time so that we may converse with the dead indefinitely.

In Auden's elegy, as words disappear the body, they simultaneously reconstitute it by reference to statues. By laying him in state rhetorically, Auden holds Yeats's memory in a pliable state. Imagine the work we would have to do without the elegy, how we would have to goad the dead to speak, preserve and prepare the body, advertise and stage commemorative encounters in the "hundred cities," and then reverse the process, only to have to repeat it anytime we needed Yeats's example. Auden's elegy maintains Yeats as "almost dead."[48] Like physical memorials, elegies do more than patrol the border between life and death; they rumble into existence a strip of limbo and cultivate it, and they do so economically. This is not to say that poetry is cheap, but it doesn't require committees, design competitions and reviews, funding (not as much as a monument, at any rate), a municipal budget for maintenance, and public space. The last item in this list may be the most important, since a statue, like the body of the dead, inhabits only one place. People must go to it. Even the hundred cities would have to choose one spot each — would it be a cemetery, a park, or a busy roundabout? An elegy can go anywhere people read, and as per Auden, it ends up in our guts. Its relationship to space and time are radically different than a fixed memorial.[49]

Yet the elegy is also a limited technique. The physical memorial, rooted in place, more or less, and constantly referring us to its many temporal moments, is a different technology, vital for bringing people together. Parallel to the dispersed community of readers of an elegy such as Auden's, who may not know one another, a physical memorial has the potential to assemble a community of people who wish to turn it on for a moment. It can make something happen.

The hundred cities never received their statues of Yeats.[50] Even if the poet had been multiplied across the land, his memorials would have behaved differently from Auden's lament. While monuments have been seen as a form of elegy "in its most reified format, transferred from the printed page to the eternal fixity of stone or bronze," literary and built memorials are decidedly different, as are elegiac images.[51] Yet we might learn a great deal about material memorials from elegies. "A lament for a king will not sound just like a lament for a fellow poet; but both king and poet can be brought into the pastoral world; both can be mourned here." While this landscape varies, it "remains a concrete, palpable world, a world in which the elegist can place diffuse, intangible feelings of grief and thereby win his release from suffering."[52] The analogy to physical memorials need not be belabored. Prominent people long dead look down from the heights of their pedestals. Angels lead heroes such as Sherman, and us, to better worlds, while the anonymous fallen lie suspended between life and death, like modern *transi*, those sculpted effigies of moldering bodies one finds on medieval tombs. Just like elegies, memorials of various types work the hinge between life and death, but in placing death so often in a pastoral setting — a park, a cemetery, a green patch that aspires to more — they summon an interstitial realm already laden with meaning.

The dramatic transformations in the natural and built environment in the modern period destabilized the place of death. The pastoral, the age-old place of death, was itself dying. More pointedly, it was being murdered in slow motion by modernity itself. This turned elegy into "an elegizing of the very self attempting to stand its ground in a world gone awry."[53] Modern elegies continued to place death in the pastoral, but "the pastoral is now also the very subject of mourning, not just its context."[54] The theme dates back to the early nineteenth century, when pastoral paintings began to broach the destruction of the landscape under pressure of modern industry and the displacements, poverty, and ecological destruction it caused. Did the memorial placed in an urban park merely situate one form of loss within a landscape implicitly about another kind of loss, a place whose purpose was intended to hold the destruction of nature in abeyance? It is tempting to think that such pairings have attempted to widen the boundary between life and death, to keep the door open in the very moment that nature was being despoiled and death disenchanted. In dramatic terms — for what is more dramatic than death, especially the death of nature? — the memorial in a pastoral setting begins to look like a deathbed scene of sorts, ever linked to the pastoral cemetery (etymologically a dormitory), which allowed the public to sit at the bedside of nature's demise. Behind the nineteenth-century urban park lies a lament. No wonder many park advocates resisted memorials and statues, which named and vividly advanced this morbid undercurrent.

The problem of placing modern death was complicated by other changes. Modern memorials arose in numbers after the French Revolution, particularly after the Napoleonic Wars, in a rapidly secularizing age in which Christian elegy was losing its universal currency.

A Europe that confiscated and decommissioned churches, treated death as a miasmic public hazard, and displaced the graveyard to the municipal cemetery on the urban fringe had to craft a new relationship to the dead, at least in part because traditional places of lamentation were tainted or disappearing.[55] The modern cemetery and the modern park, both imagined as pastoral landscapes, were born already imbued with elegiac pathos. They were born dead, meant in the best possible sense, as sweet escapes. "Death is indeed no stranger to Arcadia," writes literary scholar Ellen Zetzel Lambert. "We might, I think, go so far as to maintain that the presence of death enhances the pastoral version of felicity. . . . The pastoral landscape pleases us not, like the vanished groves of Eden, because it *excludes* pain, but because of the way it includes it."[56] Modern memorials frequently followed this logic of place, much to Olmsted's chagrin.

When the postrevolutionary generation began to erect memorials to their heroes in cemeteries and parks, placing death in a conspicuously pastoral setting, they were following long-standing literary and painterly traditions, which is to say, habits of mind that linked death to certain landscapes. As Chapter 3 explored in detail, both cemetery and park were antidotes to the modern city, if not explicitly antiurban.[57] The simultaneous distaste for memorials in parks suggests a repression of the elegiac tradition, a repositioning of conventions of the setting for death, a kind of zoning that quarantined it away from everyday life and cities, a way of closing the door between life and death. The death taboo, in its earliest incarnation, was not just a modern mentality, but also a material and geographical impulse. Auden keenly knew this. He puts Yeats everywhere, throwing his words to the winds so that poetry itself might play the former role of Christianity as the agent of transformation.

Richard Bentley's frontispiece to Thomas Gray's "Elegy Written in a Country Church Yard" (1753) plays out many of these associations and bridges the elegy to the built memorial as two techniques for working the door between life and death (fig. 9.6). Published first in 1751, Gray's poem predates the convulsive shocks of industrialization,

Figure 9.6. Lichgate as the border between life and death. Thomas Gray, "Elegy Written in a Country Church Yard," 1753, frontispiece.

but as the most widely read elegy of the era, it influenced several generations of elegiac poetry that wrestled with these changes, all the more so for being set in a landscape that would soon be under threat, the old churchyard. In the image, a Gothic arch lies half in ruin, a stale cornucopia piled to one side, while two old men stand at a grave in a bumpy churchyard. The arch is more than a visual frame for the image; it serves as a lichgate to the church, placing the reader in the processional route along which the dead body, the lich, was carried on the way to burial. Corpses were sometimes placed under the lichgate, awaiting the service, the first part of which sometimes took place under the lichgate itself.

The decrepit arch is both passage and an object unto itself, one deserving close study. Bentley carefully detailed the moldings and ornament on its left side, but on the right side, a tree trunk has replaced the colonettes that receive the load of the arch, and foliage has overgrown the exact place where the arch would land. Here, at the border between life and death, at the moment when the living usher a corpse into the beyond, we find a cultural intervention, the pointed arch, spanning the boundary between culture and nature, and the right side of the arch itself springs from a tree. A symbol of Christianity, the pointed arch was at that very moment central to the birth of the Gothic Revival, a movement that was one of the enduring bridges between the literary and architectural imaginations in this period. Bentley, a friend of Horace Walpole, was a significant figure in the new fashion. As the Gothic arose as a literary genre and the Gothic Revival took root across Europe, Gothic spires became a common memorial type. Karl Friedrich Schinkel's National Monument to the Liberation Wars in Berlin (1821) is an early prototype. Oberlin's Civil War memorial is a more modest example (see figure 7.13). Such spires came laden with religious and, in Europe, nationalist associations, but they also echoed actual Gothic monuments that had survived, such as the Banbury Cross or the Butter Cross in Winchester, whose very name speaks to a long history of the everyday overtaking the sacred (fig. 9.7). Its steps sheltered a small market in butter, milk, and eggs. The type was flexible, allowing Christian architecture, sculpted bodies, and inscriptions to be experienced in the round. The spire form allowed one or more effigies to be placed in arched niches, much as the arch in Bentley's frontispiece frames the implied body in the graveyard.[58]

Figure 9.7. Butter Cross, so named because of the butter sold on its steps, fourteenth century, restored in the nineteenth century, Winchester, England. Photograph by the author.

The form persisted through World War I at the war memorial at York, England, in which soldiers in their modern garb stand in the niches. Such neo-Gothic spires were a common monumental form for nineteenth-century tombs, showing the free flow between funerary monuments in cemeteries, public monuments to "great men," and memorials.

Bentley's frontispiece draws a direct line between written elegy, pictorial elegy, and physical memorials. For all of their differences, the literary elegy and the material memorial have shared common ground and worked together to help people imagine what to do with the dead, where to put them literally and metaphorically, and where to put ourselves. Perhaps this is why some form of elegy remains nearly obligatory at commemorations, as if the words are summoned to compensate for the rhetorical limitations of stone and bronze. It is true that some of the most chilling memorials reduce the elegiac and material near to zero. On Israel's Yom HaShoa, its Holocaust and Heroism Remembrance Day, alarms sound at 10:00 A.M. and the entire nation — Jews, in any case — stop whatever they are doing for two minutes to observe a collective moment of silence. The lack of words painfully conjures the absent dead as it points to the inability of words to compass the tragedy. The absence of a material memorial transforms the entire nation into a Holocaust memorial site. Such a stripped-down memorial is possible only because the Holocaust is stitched obsessively into the culture in words and material traces, taught in schools, remembered in synagogues, and bolstered by rituals and events, much of it rooted in specific memorial sites. Even the silence has its compensatory other: Jews around the world read the names of people murdered during the Holocaust. In these two minutes, elegy is ubiquitous.

This all points to the distinct properties of these different forms of memorial. A paper lament, so to speak, reduces flesh to the thinnest of objects and comes with special abilities. It can be stored much more conveniently than a body, copied, disseminated, archived. In some measure, these processes guard against destruction and perform the work of longevity, if in a different way than, say, a granite monument does, while enabling different modes of destruction. Formless and with the capacity to be placeless, elegy can also be absorbed into performance differently than a tomb or grave, stripping down the lament or ritual to a minimum. It offers up a body manqué and presents it in ageographical form. This was vital for the early Christian world, which inherited ancient elegiac traditions and accommodated them to the extreme conditions of the diasporic outlaw religion. Perhaps under the extreme conditions of war, Auden picked up on this dispersed potential of elegy, a quality that seems to draw it closer to the properties of memory itself. Yet the poet instinctively hedged and sought to sediment the word in something solid.

Indeed, physical memorials seem intent on defying the properties of memory. At their most literal, they strong-arm people into commemorative compliance. The starkest contrast to Israel's moment of silence is the cadaverous arm in Miami Beach (see figure 1.3). *Pars pro toto*, it morbidly represents the dead and the mass burials of the Holocaust. Composed of writhing bodies, it wears death on its sleeve, as its sleeve. It is adorned in death.[59] Its embrace of monumentality sets it against elegy, as well. Yet the scabrous arm goes a step further, asserting itself monumentally as a fragment. A part for the whole that can never be whole, it is difficult to avoid reading it cinematically as a still from a horror film fashioned into a public monument.

None of this tells us much about the Arm as a technique. If we steel ourselves to look beyond the unbearable cliché of the hand emerging from the grave or rising to the heavens, something interesting emerges. Jews who perished in Europe reemerge in the United States. Just as a door is a wall hole held in a reversible state and a literary memorial is an incorporeal monument, the Arm is part of an elegiac tradition that transforms and transports, in this case, the millions of European Jewish bodies to an urban oasis in commercial Miami Beach, in a park, no less. In this way, it becomes an apt symbol of the Jewish diaspora and the diasporic quality of the Holocaust as a figure in Jewish culture.

Yet the Miami Beach Holocaust Memorial is not just an arm, just as Latour's door is not just a door, but also an array of interlocked technologies: the handle, the hinge, the automatic sensor and opener, and timed closer. All conspire to alter dramatically the experience of walking through a wall. In Miami, the arm's setting is too complex to unpack completely, but in brief, it delivers us to the Arm as the culmination of a highly choreographed sequence. The curved pergola, leisurely and parklike, lulls one into the promenade, a pleasant relief from the Florida heat (fig. 9.8). To one side, the Arm looms in one's peripheral vision. To the other stretches a granite wall, that memorial cliché. It has become a reflex to cover the shiny slabs at monuments with "history": data, images, maps, facsimiles of actual documents, an archive uncovered and eaten into stone. The opposite of elegy's dematerialization! The contrast to Maya Lin's reserved wall at the Vietnam Veterans Memorial in Washington, DC, could not be starker. In Miami, "Never forget" means cutting this archive into the granite, a quarry of facts. The gallery is a history lesson, a time line of horrors: a map of Europe with the numbers of Jews killed in each country; a photograph of Berlin's synagogue burning on *Kristallnacht*; a photograph of Nazis "having fun cutting off the beards of religious Jews"; a document from the Wannsee Conference showing numbers of European Jews to be exterminated; a photograph of naked women about to be executed; Jews being deported; prisoners peering out of a cattle car; Auschwitz; emaciated, mangled victims of Mengele; cannisters of Zyklon B ("*Giftgas*"); piles of bodies; a prisoner feeding a body into an oven; and liberation. In the world of Holocaust denial, this unflinching documentation is what dates the Miami memorial most emphatically. It is a prophylactic against revisionist history. Behind every image one sees oneself hazily reflected in the granite and behind that, occasional sightings of the Arm (fig. 9.9).

After the assault of documentation — an appeal to the heart through brutal facts — the memorial moves to other strategies. The pergola and its dark granite give way to a passage of Jerusalem stone, and here, the memorial pivots physically and metaphysically

Figure 9.8. Granite storyboards under pergola. Ken Treister, Holocaust Memorial, 1990, Miami Beach, Florida. Photograph by the author.

Figure 9.9. Visitors see themselves and palm trees superimposed over an image of Zyklon B cannisters. Ken Treister, Holocaust Memorial, 1990, Miami Beach, Florida. Photograph by the author.

(figs. 9.10 and 9.11). We leave the historical realm of the Holocaust and enter the spiritual realm of Judaism. Now under open sky, we glimpse the Arm in its sanctum sanctorum. How to get there remains a mystery. The walls continue to talk. An eternal flame in a sconce evokes the lamp in *the* Temple, the one snuffed out by King Antiochus and the source of the Chanukah story. Facing the sconce, two large menorahs in the shape of trees of life, with bases of skulls, sit oddly on the ground, forcing the flow of traffic into the central arch of the domed pavilion. A Jewish star in the dome's oculus gives off a mystical light, projecting the blurred and inverted word *Jude* in Hebraicized German across its vault. The word Nazis forced Jews to wear on their sleeves is charted against the heavenly firmaments of the dome. We've entered the eternal Jerusalem, and references to Rome, ancient Syria, Judea, the Old Testament, and the sun usher us into a downward slop-ing hall that leads to the inner courtyard with its arm, now visible. Irregular cuts in the wall and ceiling let light in and pay homage to Daniel Libeskind's Holocaust Museum in Berlin. Each cut opens onto a fragmented view of the inner circle, and as we collect these anticipa-tions, we descend, now below grade and below the water line, for the entire courtyard rests below the massive pool that isolates the Arm from the city. A few more steps, and we are there. Behold, the Arm!

Bronzes of dead and writhing bodies lie in the courtyard; a few stand at the base of the great appendage. A mother with a baby. Incon-solable metallic children. A man plaintively reaching for a lost loved one who is being spirited up the shaft. So many figures. All enclosed by another curving granite wall, this one with names. Could there really be six million! Histrionic death. There is no room for the death taboo when it comes to the Holocaust, but representation seems inapt to the task. Few memorials labor as mightily as this one does against the everyday. Yet the commonplace appears. In the orange pylon under the lamp or the trash can encased in Jerusalem stone. At the sign with its beautiful patina: "Begin," with an arrow, because the route is not intuitive. If the everyday had its way, people would rarely follow the memorial's prescribed route. They'd go straight to the Arm and miss

Figure 9.10. Eternal lamp and a small quarry of Jerusalem stone. Ken Treister, Holocaust Memorial, 1990, Miami Beach, Florida. Photograph by the author.

Figure 9.11. Dome and descent to the Arm. Ken Treister, Holocaust Memorial, 1990, Miami Beach, Florida. Photograph by the author.

Figure 9.12. The Arm from viewing platform. Ken Treister, Holocaust Memorial, 1990, Miami Beach, Florida. Photograph by the author.

all of the "documentation." Finally, the denouement. Beyond the wall of facts, the path of spirituality, and the horrific courtyard of names and bodies, the route leads to a platform that juts into the pool and perfectly frames the site as seen through a viewfinder (fig. 9.12). The memorial culminates in a photo op! The Holocaust and eternity fuse with our time, collapsed in the personal archive of our iPhones. We can now refresh ourselves with a sip of water from the Jerusalem-stone-cladded water fountain and return to the "Holocaust Memorial Parking" lot, with its broken, standard-issue, concrete park bench. Indeed, this is one memorial that is hard to forget.

In the end, however, we are left wondering exactly what this massive intervention in Miami is. Monumental, commemorative, sober, but also kitschy. (In this, it is not alone among Holocaust Memorials.) It is not so far from roadside architecture, dark Pop Art for an urban scene of cars, conventioneers, bikinis, botanical gardens, and Art Basel Miami, which takes place at the Convention Center next door. The elaborate grounds are an elaborate hinge that works a door between all of these things and the Holocaust. To walk through this door is to confront time and death in dimensions rarely experienced in the everyday world on the other side of the "wall." It is also to confront a confounding intervention, one that speaks to the profound strangeness of memorials as a cultural form — and that is the subject of the final chapter.

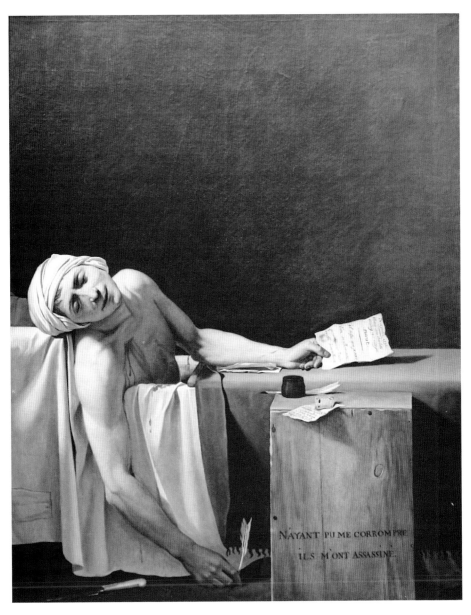

Within the painting, the box bears the inscription:

NAYANT PU ME CORROMPRE
ILS M'ONT ASSASSINÉ.

Figure 2.3. A monument manqué. Jacques-Louis David, *Death of Marat*, 1793, The Louvre, Paris.

Figure 3.13. "No More of Those Hideous Monuments," *Puck*, August 19, 1855, centerfold by Bernhard Gillam. Courtesy of the Library of Congress. The title seems to say it all, but the leafy background makes clear that the monuments are not the only issue. The insert not only replaces the monument with a fountain, but also places the latter in an urban scene.

Figure 4.1. Glupov, or "Stupid Town," with its monument to a vainglorious and anonymous military hero who lords over the route into town on his obviously unplanned and unpaved plot of dirt, with a pathetic bench placed to give a picturesque view of his backside. The undated illustration appeared on the cover of the satirical *The History of a Town* by M. Saltykov-Shchedrin, 1979 [1870]. From the collection of the Russian State Library, Moscow. KukryNikSy, artists. Photograph courtesy of HIP/Art Resource, NY.

Figure 7.19. Selective memory at Bichukov Anatoly's Monument to the Defenders of the Russian Land in Moscow, 1995. Photograph courtesy of Тара-Амингу/Tara Amingu.

Figure 7.6. Hitler and Freud both vacationed in Berchtesgaden, Germany, and would have known this mural well. By Joseph Hengge, 1929; repainted 1952. Photograph by the author.

Figure 7.7. Memorial plaques in the arcade beneath the mural in Berchtesgaden. Photograph by the author.

Figure 8.2. A drama of loss, love, and distraction. Stanley Spencer, *Unveiling Cookham War Memorial*, 1922. Private collection. Courtesy of Bridgeman Images.

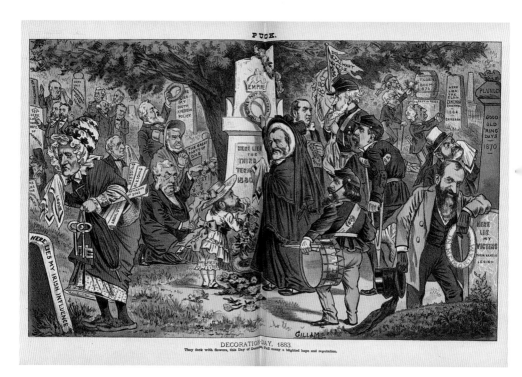

Figure 8.5. Decoration Day as Shakespearian farce, *Puck*, May 30, 1883. Bernhard Gillam, illustrator. Courtesy of the Library of Congress.

Figure 8.6. From memory to leisure in one image. Charles A. Cox, cover, *Bearings*, ca. 1890–1900. Courtesy of the Library of Congress.

Figure C.1. A monumental pile of non sequiturs. Saul Steinberg, *The Pursuit of Happiness (Prosperity)*, cover of *The New Yorker*, January 17, 1959. © The Saul Steinberg Foundation/Artists Rights Society (ARS), New York. Reprinted with permission of *The New Yorker* magazine.

What Is This?

Memory is like plaster: peel it back and you
just might find a completely different picture.
— Jodi Picoult, *Handle with Care*

In 1959, Saul Steinberg drew a mock monument with all the bells and
whistles, a pile of the countless confusions of the nineteenth-century
monument: great men wear outdated clothing, anonymous figures
clog space, and obscure or absurd allegories jam an undistinguished
base (fig. C.1). Steinberg stacked them all on a birthday cake of high
ideals. In the lower range, as Uncle Sam and Uncle Tom shake hands
agreeably, a single arrow skewers "Unemployment" and the dead fish
of Semantics, while the St. George of statistics defeats the dragon-
cum-peacock of Inflation. One level up, the alligator of Happiness
bites the tail of a serpent, which represents "the pursuit of," which
in turn bites the alligator's tail in a painful, vicious cycle framed by
Vice and Virtue on one side, Labor and Leisure on the other. At the
apex of this pyramid of power, we find Prosperity in his top hat,
unchained, flanked by busts of Freud and Santa Claus. In the end,
the details are risibly irrelevant. It is a send-up of the pastiche of the
great monuments of an earlier era, a lampoon of their crowded and
mind-numbingly impenetrable allegorical programs. The final non
sequitur: it sits at the edge of a park.

It would be tempting to see Steinberg carrying on Robert Musil's
and Lewis Mumford's discrediting of the monument, drawing a

comical cenotaph for the monument itself. But Steinberg drew farcical monuments with nearly obsessive frequency. If the monument were truly dead, then it would not have been funny; it would not have been a subject at all. It is more intriguing to think of Steinberg working through the monument's unfinished business in a comical reprisal of statuephobia, but only now in the context of a Cold War America that had precious few public modes of expression commensurate to the scale of the issues it faced. Is it possible that Americans needed monuments more than ever? Europeans faced similar issues, also in a climate unfavorable to monuments. A generation before the countermonument would arise in Germany as an attempt in the light of the Holocaust to challenge the heroic premise of monuments, it was already clear that monuments were archaic and inscrutable, if not morally suspect.[1] The monument as a cultural form was moribund, in part because it was, like a dead language, illegible. Yet something kept it in play for Steinberg.

Monuments have been giving moderns fits since the political and economic revolutions of the eighteenth century reinvented them. They sit at the crux of so many of the changeful issues of modernity that their very status is perplexing. They are slow in an age of speed, permanent in an era of obsolescence, useless in a world devoted to profit motive and unrelenting practicality. They lean backward while modernity pitches forward, and they often deal with death amid deep discomfort with it. This leaves aside all of the complexity of their form and placement discussed in this book. In the years since I first began studying the built environment, I have moved from Musil (treating monuments as invisible), to Mumford (seeing them as anathema to modernity), to Steinberg (playfully enjoying their absurdities), and finally to seeing in their conventions of placement and almost limitless range of forms a cultural response to some of the most nettlesome issues of modernity. Upon encountering the thousands of monuments I have seen in person or in images, I have often been reduced to ask: "What is this?!" There is no simple answer. New or old, almost regardless of where they are, no matter how conventional, monuments are oddballs. By way of conclusion, this chapter peels back the layers of strangeness in order to understand the conundrum of their unfinished business, the troubles that led Steinberg to draw his "monument."

Almost immediately, memorials became their own tradition — especially those that leaned on centuries of tradition. In their quest for gravitas, they brokered with tradition itself, seeking ballast to hold them down amid the modern tempest. They became instant heritage, which François Hartog would understand as part of the temporal collapse of presentism.[2] Here, the paradox of a new tradition takes a distinct turn. We know from Hobsbawm and Ranger's insights about invented traditions that the modern world created new cultural forms that appeared to be very old ones in order to negotiate the immense and rapid changes it witnessed.[3] The memorial as a cultural form might be seen as one grand invented tradition. Like so much in nineteenth-century culture, memorials drew from ideas rooted in the deepest recesses of the past. The architectural revivals that washed over the century reflect this habit of mind. Clashing styles turned the nineteenth-century Euro-American city into a historicist circus. The situation troubled architects deeply.[4] The instinct to turn to ancient, medieval, and Renaissance traditions of tombs, public statuary, and monuments is part of the historicism that marks this feverish invention of the past. The modern memorial was part of this mentality, helping it shape the historicist environment. Turning this around, historicism is one of the confounding layers of the monument. This chapter moves through a series of columns or shafts to show how many things this most traditional form of monument has meant over the last two centuries.

The Revolutionary Turn

Early urban monuments embraced eclecticism in the setting of architectural eclecticism. The design for Ker Street, Devonport (1821–24), in England, makes the point clearly. Looming over a Greek Revival town hall, Egyptian Revival school, and a preaching chapel in the

"Oriental" manner — a tossed salad of styles designed by architect John Foulston — is a "commemorative column," similar to the column in the Place Vendôme in Paris (1810), Nelson's Pillar in Dublin (1809), or any number of columnar monuments built in this era (fig. C.2).[5] Devonport's shaft stands on an enormous base that itself sits on a rocky bluff overlooking the town. In the well-known engraving, requisite figures stand at the base as if in some Piranesian ruinscape, but the point is clear: the monument interrupts the self-consciously picturesque Ker Street with a jolt of the heroic sublime, made all the more so by its contrast with the underwhelming spires of the "Hindoo" temple. Its anonymity goes to another point: it is part of the generic furniture of the public urban realm. Heroic and anonymous at once, it is not a monument to a particular person, but rather to Plymouth Dock taking on the new name of Devonport, a monument to the town.[6] It is also a monument to the idea of a monument. Such monuments had been aesthetic elements of urban planning at least since the Renaissance. Pope Sixtus V famously appropriated monuments, including columns and obelisks, for his rebuilding of Rome in the late sixteenth century. But Foulston's column is different. It is not part of the species of monument that Alois Riegl termed "unintentional," an artifact such as the Bastille that is impregnated with meaning because of its history. Nor is it an intentional monument to a particular person, such as the Washington Monument. It is just a magnificent vertical shaft erected to hold down the composition of the town and anchor its ambitions. Like the plague column in Klagenfurt, it is an urban gesture and a social figure, rather than an actual one, deconsecrated on arrival. By the 1820s, such monuments were already obligatory, cliché, a part of urban design before the fact. What is Devonport's column but a blank slate awaiting fate to inscribe it with meaning, a future monument in historicist garb?

Foulston's monument opens onto a future that had popped out of the neck of Louis XVI, like Pegasus from the neck of Medusa (see figure 2.2). Just like this spontaneous birth, the Devonport column began as an ahistoric monument designed shortly after the invention

Figure C.2. The historicist monument and its setting. The statue was never built. Thomas Allom, engraving of Ker Street, Devonport, John Foulston, architect, 1821–24. From the author's collection.

of the historic monument. Let's unpack this admittedly confusing set of ideas. As it turns out, the term "historic monument" dates to the early nineteenth century, almost exactly to the time of Devonport's shaft, which is a physical embodiment of the new term. The French Revolution provided the initial jolt that ushered in a new way of thinking about cultural inheritance.[7] The revolution was a "traumatic rupture in time" that severed societies from their histories, thereby creating the necessary distance for people to look upon the past and its artifacts in a new light.[8] In the words of Françoise Choay, "the awareness of the dawning of a new era . . . created a second layer of mediation and distance with respect to the historic monument, at the same time that it liberated dormant energies in favor of its protection."[9] The radical break in historical time plunged European society into a narrative crisis, which demanded new narratives to fill the breach. Patrimony, understood as an effort to tether cultural inheritance to national sentiment, arose to fill this breach, birthed

Figure C.3. Nelson's Pillar on fashionable Sackville Street, Dublin, Engraving by George Petrie, R. Winkles, H. Fisher, Son and Co., 1829. National Maritime Museum, Greenwich, London.

as an allegory of repair. The historic monument became a narrative device, a way to smooth discontinuities. Foulston's column would not have been possible without this distance and narrative crisis.

The contrast to the Nelson Pillar in Dublin, which is utterly specific and, given their resemblance, could have been Devonport's source, draws out just how generic Foulston's column is (fig. C.3). In Dublin, where a nearly identical square landing sits atop the shaft, the column imposed a massive footprint on its midstreet site.[10] This consumption of space on Sackville Street, Dublin's most fashionable area, was central to its role in the city. While at first blush it resembles the overscaled neoclassical piles that were transforming Dublin in the same decades, the column is different. It thrust a dead man and a war hero into the commercial zone and did so with conspicuous inutility. From the start, the point of this "unmeaning kind of structure" was unclear, save as a loyalist gesture to the crown.[11]

Nelson stood in various states, first with the railing that quarantined it from the everyday, then disencumbered to serve as a seatback. Railings came and went, as did paving schemes.[12] Alongside these changes came others that would alter its urban meaning. In 1870, a marble statue of William Smith O'Brien was placed in the median nearby, followed in 1882 by the squat Daniel O'Connell monument, which alit about a block away. O'Brien led a failed rebellion in 1848. O'Connell, known as "The Liberator," fought for Irish and Catholic rights. They were joined by Sir John Gray and Father Mathew in 1879 and 1893, respectively: Irish ripostes all to the English Nelson. By and by, the street was Gaelicized (fig. C.4).[13] In 1911, a shaft to Charles Stewart Parnell added to the *memento mediana*, raising an Irish nationalist politician in the guise of a beacon nearly into the same rarefied air as Nelson. Five years later, Irish Republicans would try to blow up Nelson during the Easter Uprising, but he stood firm.

In addition to this linear mustering, other urban processes altered the column. When streetcars came to Dublin, tracks veered around it; in fact, it was the terminus for the streetcar system! This made it one of Dublin's most common places to meet. As seen in an

Figure C.4. A row of memorials on the median from O'Connell Bridge looking up Sackville Street, 1890, Dublin. Courtesy of the National Library of Ireland.

engraving from 1884, after the railings had come down, ordinary people – all men – took their leisure or loitered there (fig. c.5). The "notice" pasted on its base has been placed in wry dialogue with the heroic inscription. This is not merely bathos and satire, using the shiftless and bedraggled sitting in boredom beneath the colossal and expensive Nelson for comic relief. It is the nature of the memorial as a modern form. As a public offering, the memorial exists both in some aspirational and political realm and as a place to put your bum. Alas, in 1894, a large iron railing was installed. Gone was the intimate object and seat back. Cars soon followed the streetcars, adding not just their interminable whirl and grind, but also a formidable obstacle. A line of parked cars longer than the shaft took up residence on the former green mall, long before banalized into a median, stretching in a jumble for blocks down O'Connell Street. Urban planning, as opposed to the improvisations that dominate urban change, tried

FOOT OF NELSON'S MONUMENT.

Figure C.5. Monuments are for loitering. Illustration of Nelson's Pillar from Edward Dowden, "Dublin City," *Century Illustrated Monthly Magazine*, December 1884, p. 173.

to have its way as well. Various plans to move or demolish the column were floated in the nineteenth century, to no avail. By the 1920s, in fact, urban planning offered up an argument that amounted to a managerial *damnatio memoriae*, calling it a "hindrance to modern traffic."[14]

James Joyce knew Nelson's formidable incoherence well. In *Ulysses,* Stephen Dedalus tells of two "frisky frumps" who climb to the top of the column of the "one-handled adulterer," where they get "giddy" from the height, proceed to gorge on plums, and spit the stones between the railings. He leaves it to the reader to imagine these "velocitous aeroliths" raining down on the jobbers lolling around the monument below. While this scene, called the "parable of the plums," has come in for much close reading, the crudeness of these women is also a parable about the monument, about its narrative incoherence.[15]

What urban planning could not accomplish, bombs finally did. In

1966, Irish Republicans exploded most of it. Monumentality and its ostentatious placement were its great sins: a giant Englishman stood in the center of Sackville Street (changed to O'Connell Street in 1924, in a verbal act of *damnatio memoriae*). Its remains became a hazard and an eyesore and were subsequently cleared. In 2003, the empty space received the Spire of Dublin, a noncommemorative metal needle flush with the ground and guarded only by metal bollards. People cannot sit comfortably at its base. In fact, a Joycean interlude adds one more layer to the story. In celebration of the millennium of Dublin's founding, in 1988, the Anna Livia Monument (Éamonn O'Doherty, sculptor) was installed at the site. Based on Anna Livia Plurabelle, a character in *Finnegans Wake*, this recumbent female figure lay in the frothing waters of a fountain as an allegorical representation of the river Liffey and as a monument to Dublin's literary heritage. Like Nelson before her, the so-called "Floozie in the Jacuzzi" lapsed into a loiterers' oasis and was removed in 2001. What a curious lineage of monuments, from British war hero to a fictional Irish character to an abstract spire. A fertile literary imagination might still see the velocitous pits pelting poor Plurabelle.

The point of the story for the everyday life of memorials is not about Irish-English politics or the loss of Nelson's memory, but rather the declension in the monument's meaning. Large monuments such as Nelson's are routinely brutalized in moments of upheaval. Indeed, monumentality faces constant threat of parody.[16] The Nelson column, and its site, could fit in every chapter of this book. It was placed in a quintessentially modern spot, almost continuously threatened with displacement or iconoclasm, mustered, used as a site of royalist commemoration, and radically altered by urban processes. In turn, through its size, placement, and form, it served people on multiple scales, providing a meeting place, shade or a place to take the sun, and a focal point for all kinds of activities. Surely its destruction was primarily political, as was its initial impetus, but this only obscures the point that it was replaced by a fictional character and is just as memorable as a place for disgorging plum pits.

Taken together, John Foulston's anonymous column and Dublin's Nelson and its replacements reveal how even in the wake of the French Revolution, monuments were already strange and that their strangeness was a vital and puzzling part of urban life. They did things in cities that no other space or built form could do. Yet this strange utility, this everyday/not-everyday dance they do, is historical, tagged to changes in attitudes toward death, urbanism, and the everyday itself, which is a fluctuating phenomenon in its own right. This strangeness has followed monuments through their meandering history to the present.

"Giant Column"

Other columns drive the story forward. A few years after Nelson's was destroyed in Dublin, the city of Mainz turned to a columnar monument to narrate a particular moment in German memory. Just to line up the facts that describe the Heunensäule (fig. C.6) is to confront a monument with no clear precedent before midcentury, much as John Foulston's column could not have existed before the French Revolution. The city of Mainz erected it in 1975, before memory became a German obsession, before memory studies emerged as a field, and before a clear-eyed sense of debt for World War II and the Holocaust had been widely accepted in Germany. The Heunensäule opens a window onto the obscurity of debt in this moment, if not onto the obscurity of monuments. It stands at the center of one of the most prominent squares of the city, the Domplatz, which is bounded by a range of well-restored early modern buildings, and the cathedral (or *Dom*), a masterpiece of Romanesque architecture. The pedestrian zone hosts a weekly market that swallows up the monument on Saturdays. Café tables and chairs spill out in warmer months.

The name, Heunensäule, from *Hüne* for giant (*Hünen* translates to "megalithic") is the first clue that the column is a descendant of Foulston's anonymous column.[17] The "Giant Column" can be understood as a kind of joke, like Venturi, Scott Brown, and Izenour's "I am a monument" sign jutting out of a nondescript building.[18] The Mainz shaft

Figure C.6. A big, naked shaft whose crown has become its base. Gernot Rumpf, Heunen-säule, 1975, Mainz, Germany. Photograph by the author.

is too small to be monumental in the middle of the capacious Domplatz. This might signal the reticence about monumentality in postwar West Germany, excepting those gestures aimed at the East Bloc.

The real reason for its size, seemingly, is that the column is a leftover from the hundreds quarried for the cathedral a thousand years before; it was erected in commemoration of this millennial milestone.[19] The material, a warm brown sandstone taken from a quarry near Miltenberg, some ninety kilometers away, links up with the cathedral and many of the most prominent historical buildings in Mainz. *Buntsandstein*, as it is called, can be found in a wide swathe of this part of Germany and beyond. Strasbourg's cathedral was built of a pinker variety, as is the Napoleon Monument in Kaiserslautern (see figure P.1). In fact, many of the monuments throughout the towns of this region were built of the same stone. This is all to say that on one level, it is a monument to the stone itself, a column to a column made of a kind of stone that carries historical weight and regional meaning. In this regard, it behaves much like Devonport's column.

The Heunensäule draws some of its meaning from another column in Mainz called the Nagelsäule (literally, "nail column"), erected during World War I in an adjacent square just east of the cathedral, putting them in dialogue (fig. c.7).[20] Another strange monument, this wooden pillar is decorated with hundreds of nails purchased as part of a fundraising drive for the war, along with hand-hammered plaques with the names of prominent donors. The link between the two columns might seem weak, but the Nagelsäule already stretched the typology of the memorial and thus prepared the ground for its later mate. The earlier shaft draws a morbid link between paying for the war and memorializing it via the metaphor of crucifixion, a common, commemorative reference in the period that tapped into "the inaugural absence" of Christ, although to prefigure crucifixion seems like an infelicitous metaphor for a publicity campaign for the war.[21]

That the Nagelsäule is a memorial to the war, at least by default, is beyond doubt, and the catalog of memorial attributes could fill pages. Like so many World War I memorials in Europe, it basks in the

Figure C.7. Anticipatory memorial as fundraiser for World War I. Nagelsäule, erected in 1916, Mainz, Germany, The cathedral is to the left and the Heunensäule is in an adjacent square. Photograph by the author.

aura of the cathedral. The iron cross, that ubiquitous symbol found on German memorials to the Great War, sits on top, and another is nailed into it. A mother with two children, absent the lost father, is carved into the wood (fig. c.8). Like most memorials of its age, it was set apart: lifted atop three steps, girdled by an ornate rail, and surrounded by stone columns topped by statues. This created a dignified setting for a perishable column and saved it from the ravages of the everyday and the natural oblivion of erosion. The Nagelsäule's transformation bears an uncanny likeness to the Heunensäule, which is also a column with vague memorial qualities. Yet as a memorial, it remains slippery, since it is ambiguously commemorative, having come before the devastation of the war, before the losses, and therefore before spiritual debts were incurred. Over time, its memorial quality has become increasingly elusive as it has become a historic monument in its own right, in some measure a monument to itself.

Then there is the fine print, and here, the Nagelsäule shows us something remarkable about the Heunensäule. Most modern columns take their cue from ancient columns such as the one erected to Trajan in Rome and speak either through their shafts or whatever they hold aloft, a statue or symbol. In fact, Mainzers had a local model. The Jupitersäule, an actual Roman column covered with bas reliefs of Roman and Celtic gods with a statue of Jupiter atop, had been unearthed in Mainz in 1905 and reassembled.[22] In the classical tradition, columns such as the Jupitersäule are not just stand-ins for people; they speak to and for them through the scenes that cover their shafts. The Nagelsäule is an extreme version. Its dense pattern of nails and imagery echoes a tradition of speaking columns that dates back to Euripides, if not still further.[23] Its raised base gives this speaking column a rostrum. The Heunensäule, third in a lineage of columns in Mainz, conspicuously subverts this formula. A mute column absent a crown is oddly sunk into an exceptionally chatty base, a base of bronze, no less, with an incredibly complex iconography (fig. c.9). This diminishes the apparent size of the column, rebuffs direct contact with it, and draws attention to a more

Figure C.8. A mother with children and the iron cross fill panels on the Nagelsäule, erected in 1916, Mainz, Germany. Photograph by the author.

Figure C.9. Gernot Rumpf, base of the Heunensäule, with its obscure allegorical detritus and awkward "seats" at the corners, 1975, Mainz, Germany. Photograph by the author.

intimate — nonmonumental — encounter with words, images, and sculpture, which are scaled to force people to lean in if they wish to make sense of the uncanny object.

What does this talking base have to say? On the surface, it is banal. One side tells the history of the pillar, pairing it with the early Christian symbol of the wheel to draw a connection to the cathedral. A second face tells of Miltenberg, where the shaft was found still in situ in the quarry, and of its donation to Mainz. The other two sides, however, begin to speak in tongues. On a third face, we learn that in 1793, the Freiheitsbaum (literally "Freedom Tree") was erected on the Domplatz (figs. c.10 and c.11). Originally Roman in inspiration, freedom trees were appropriated during the American Revolution and then taken up in France in the 1790s. Like its ancestor, the maypole, it was a temporary wooden monument, in France crowned with a liberty cap, around which people gathered to celebrate the revolution and their liberation from the old regime. In the wake of the revolution, a number of free cities bound together to form the Mainz Republic, whose short-lived coinage featured a column with a liberty cap. The liberty trees were understood in their own day explicitly as monuments and served the traditional function of monuments as warnings, in this case, aimed at the old regime, which felt threatened by them.[24] They were, in any case, symbols of disobedience.[25] The Heunensäule recalls this long-vanished pole, making it a column to a column in another way while gesturing to the wooden shaft of the Nagelsäule, which nods self-consciously to the Freiheitsbaum in its material and, unmistakably, in the composition of its flanking columns. The memory of the liberty tree has been carried forward by the Nagelsäule to the Heunensäule.

The rest of the iconography draws the Mainz shaft into a closer fraternity with its revolutionary ancestor. Just beneath an overscaled bronze liberty cap sit two reliefs: Mainz on fire "am 27, Februar 1945" and the conflagration of the Jewish community, undated, but marked with a Jewish star (figs. c.12 and c.13). The lack of date on the latter allows the image to refer to the destruction of the Jewish community

Figure C.10. Gernot Rumpf, bas relief of *Freiheitsbaum*, 1975, Heunensäule, Mainz, Germany. Photograph by the author.

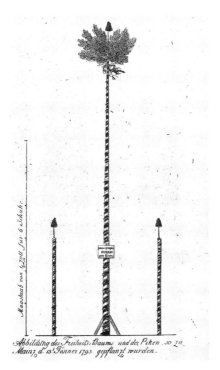

Figure C.11. Image of the *Freiheitsbaum* with its tripartite composition and Phrygian caps, Mainz. Frontispiece to Heinrich August Ottokar Reichardt, ed., *Revolutionsalmanach* (Göttingen: Johann Christian Dieterich, 1794). Public Domain.

339

Figure C.12. The Jewish community burning forever. Gernot Rumpf, Heunensäule, 1975, Mainz, Germany. Photograph by the author.

Figure C.13. Mainz burning in 1945. Gernot Rumpf, Heunensäule, 1975, Mainz, Germany. Photograph by the author.

during the Rhineland massacres of the late eleventh century, its anni-
hilation for being blamed for the plague of 1349, *and* its destruction
during World War II. Whereas Mainz's destruction is part of history,
Jewish disaster is allowed to float free of historical specificity. At the
four corners of the base, a seemingly random heap of royal, religious,
and chivalric symbols round out the ensemble.

It is tempting to see this recounting of Mainz's history on the
column as a simple appropriation of the monumental tradition for
the heritage industry that condenses memory and the historic monument into a presentist mush.[26] And this reading might be right.
But I'm more inclined to see the Heunensäule winking at us darkly.
The absurd empty top, the slightly undersized shaft, the rhetorical subversion of base and shaft, these alert us to a kind of proto-
countermonument, a *Gegendenkmal*, talking out of two sides of its
mouth. The collection of bronze headwear and decoration nods back
to another feature of the liberty trees, which were sometimes surrounded with "the destructive signs of the feudal monarchy."[27] In
fact, the planting of maypoles came after the violent destruction of
an order. Far from concealing that violence, they put it on display,
just like the Heunensäule.[28] In effect, this monument is peeling back
the layers of German memory while coyly plastering over the big one.

In Mainz, the objects and symbols are attributes of an ancien
régime that stretches conspicuously back to Rome and perversely into
the postwar period. The gladiator's helmet — a stylized *murillo* — with
its exaggerated flanges of bronze (the pauldron) recalls Umberto
Boccioni's *Unique Forms of Continuity in Space*, a canonical Futurist
work from 1913 whose striding militant figure presaged World War I
(figs. c.14 and c.15). If this link to Boccioni's piece seems fanciful, the
Italian sculpture was recast ten times in 1972 and disseminated around
the world. The artist of the Heunensäule, Gernot Rumpf, could have
seen it in London, Milan, Otterlo, Cosenza, New York, or several other
cities.[29] The visual echo of the armor can be read as a warning about the
continuities between premodern warfare and the bellicose tragedies
of twentieth-century Germany, if not the dangers of blind futurism.

341

Figure C.14. Gladiator's helmet with snarling fox. Gernot Rumpf, Heunensäule, 1975, Mainz, Germany. Photograph by the author.

Figure C.15. Umberto Boccioni, *Unique Forms of Continuity in Space,* 1913, cast 1950. Courtesy of the Metropolitan Museum of Art.

One more detail unleashes the helmet's full meaning. A fox's snout peaks out, fangs bared, from behind the grille, a simple latch being the only thing that holds him – and by association Germany's repressed viciousness – from leaping into the square (fig. c.14). The cartoonish fox refers plainly to Mainz's mayor, Jockel Fuchs, whose last name means "fox" in German. Fuchs was mayor of the city from 1965 to 1987, when the Heunensäule was being planned and built. This modern mayor hides snarling behind a destructive symbol of the old order, and between Rome and Futurism.[30]

The liberty cap, sometimes called a Phrygian cap, fares no better than the helm (fig. c.16). It keeps watch over the two incendiary moments. Revolutionary freedom watches as the Jews burn and Mainz smolders. Enough has been written about the machinelike efficiency of National Socialism to see this as a coded nod to the complicity of Enlightenment rationality in twentieth-century violence. If these readings seem like a stretch, especially in 1975, Willy Brandt, the chancellor of the German Federal Republic, had kneeled on the steps of the Memorial to the Warsaw Ghetto Uprising in 1970. As Rumpf was designing his monument, guilt and apology were in the air.[31]

The monument itself offers up more evidence. The bronze hats and helms take the place of the symbols that would have crowned the column – one of them, a royal crown, makes the analogy between the capital and the head literal. ("Capital," *Kapital* in German, comes from the Latin *caput*, meaning "head.") It is as if all the possible capitals or heads had fallen and now gather as detritus at the base, a still life of collapsed power. To sit on one of the monument's four "benches," as I observed people doing – to use the monument as a place of repose, as it invites – is to turn your back on these realities, to ignore the very regimes of power that had been the principal monument builders of the past.

"What is this?" we might finally ask of the column. A war memorial? A monument? A countermonument? A historical marker? A piece of instant heritage? A visual and spatial anchor in an otherwise naked public space rather like Klagenfurt's plague column? A bit of tourist furniture? In some measure, it is all of these. This kind

Figure C.16. The liberty cap presides over Mainz burning. Gernot Rumpf, Heunensäule, 1975, Mainz, Germany. Photograph by the author.

of intervention was not possible even a generation before, when, in the aftermath of the Second World War, most of Europe and the United States eschewed monuments. Germany, in particular, came slowly to figure out how to address the war with interventions such as this one. The monument had to be reinvented as a cultural form in relationship to the radically shifting nature of twentieth-century catastrophe, and yet, how similar the Heunensäule is to Foulston's monument to Devonport – and to Steinberg's absurd everything bagel of a monument! They look nothing alike, but they all make the line between sobriety and absurdity wisp thin. Instead of being sites where memory is sedimented, these flirt with being non sequiturs. And yet the Heunensäule is a few layers of plaster away from being a Holocaust memorial.

The Spirit of Los Angeles

A final non sequitur brings this sequence and the everyday life of memorials nearly up to the present. *The Spirit of Los Angeles* (2002) sits in the middle of an outdoor mall in Los Angeles called the Grove. The appearance of allegorical figures ("two graceful angels caught in mid-flight") underscores the pillar's anomalousness.[32] Its closest kin are memorials with angels lifting fallen soldiers to the heavens, or more apropos of the mall, Sherman and "that angel . . . leading the horse into Bergdorf's" (fig. C.17).[33] What would the *Winged Victory of Samothrace*, another obvious forebear, think of *Spirit* if she could peer across the ages? She might yawn while secretly worrying that the Futurist Filippo Marinetti was onto something when he wrote: "A racing car with a hood that glistens with large pipes resembling a serpent with explosive breath . . . a roaring automobile that seems to ride on grapeshot is more beautiful than the Victory of Samothrace."[34] In this odd, time-warped pedestrian zone in America's would-be autopia, such Futurist provocation takes on new meaning. The monument's one-named artist, Delesprie, writes that the "sculpture is Timeless in appearance."[35] The capital "T" cinches the monument as a counterprovocation to Marinetti.

Figure C.17. A pure invention of tradition. Delesprie, *The Spirit of Los Angeles*, 2002, the Grove shopping center, Los Angeles. Photograph by Michael Elowitz.

Strictly speaking neither memorial nor monument (the artist calls it the latter), it operates visually and urbanistically just like many memorials do in everyday life, as eye-catcher, place maker, scale marker, and directional sign while also providing a place to meet. It is like the deconsecrated plague column in Klagenfurt, but without etymon, a generic Kevin Lynch landmark enrobed in vague allusions. Steinberg would chuckle over its appeal to trite ideals: "Faith, Community, Family, and Honesty" are inscribed on its shaft. Foulston would recognize the degeneration of his proud monument to a city into solipsistic banality. Dubliners, well versed in false idols, would know exactly what to do with this paean to false consciousness. And Mainzers might see it as heritage without a past, a pure *Heunensäule*, or a big shaft.

Of course, the Spirit of Los Angeles comes off as non sequitur only if we take it seriously as a monument. It makes more sense as one phrase in the commercial syntax of the mall, if not of greater Los Angeles. It is surrounded by architectural confessions. A mock trolley toodles up and down the lone street, curves around the angels, and heads for a would-be train station with a giant clock and frozen glockenspiel. It never gets there, because the street, with its neat stores, each with its own nostalgic storefront, is interrupted by an artificial pond where a painted bronze boy fishes. Amid all of this jovial fakery, real artifacts set up the potential for the suspension of disbelief. The trolley tracks begin at a defunct gas station, now a preciously preserved folly, where the faux trolley that actually works meets a real historical fragment that does not. A clump of concrete planters hides the bizarre transition. It is one big stage set for consumption, a cross between Disneyland's Main Street and the television town of Mayberry. The train station is a store, the pedestrian area made possible by massive parking garages hidden out of view, and the pond a technique of dispersion, preventing mass gathering in this privately owned public space. Signs warn people to stay out of the green areas surrounding the pond. At the Grove, these shams bury the real grove that once covered these acres in a flurry of nostalgic pangs.

As part of this assemblage of references, the monument goes right where it should, in a pseudo-roundabout that marks a counterfeit intersection. A side street to one side simulates a secondary commercial street in a European town, but its curve hides the fact that it stretches only a few storefronts before it empties into the parking garage tucked behind the pedestrian zone. The Spirit of Los Angeles betrays just how antithetical the Grove is to its surrounding city. After all, the spirit of this city of freeways is not about pedestrians walking toward an idyllic small town center, fishing in a local pond, or civic pride as embodied in monuments, which are scarce in LA. At the Grove, the pretext is not just thin. The Spirit of Los Angeles is a screen memory of sorts, veiling the reality of the site, concealing the layers that had been obliterated to turn an actual grove into a mall. *That* is the real spirit of Los Angeles.

This is not to moralize. More sympathetic readings are obvious. The real and fake are not necessarily ethical categories in architecture. Presuming that historical artifice hoodwinks shoppers is condescending. Here, history is anodyne, an aesthetic aimed at the equally preposterous ahistorical posturing of modernist environments. In this sense, it would be fair to see the Grove as part of the genius loci of Hollywood. This strange memorial in a shopping mall is not an aberration or an outlier, but rather an extreme. It is a fitting way to conclude *The Everyday Life of Memorials*. Malls and shopping areas have taken to erecting bronzes on plazas with plantings and paving that borrow their basic form from memorial traditions, as if to lend commercial areas some of the spirit of a civic space. More widely, cities across Europe and the United States have been adding similar works that straddle – or do they create? – a fuzzy line between commemorative works, public art, and consumption. The idea itself is historical: Klagenfurt's *Mandl* became an urban roommate of Spanheim, Maria Theresa, and the plague column in this sort of commercial milieu beginning in the 1960s. (See Chapter 5.)

This melting of memorials and memorial-like installations has become such a commonplace of the modern cultural and commercial landscape that it is nearly invisible, a convention solidifying under our very noses. The phenomenon is reinforced by the Wiki convention of creating lists of *Kulturdenkmäler*: enumerations of historical buildings, sculptures, fountains, and memorials of all types. Lists have been created even for many small towns across Europe. The logic of this assemblage parallels the way tourist maps and travel guides flatten the historical assets of towns, but the pretense of the Wikis takes on additional meaning. Culture is recast as heritage. The lists are a kind of memory practice, yet they homogenize and assimilate fundamentally dissimilar objects. A trivial sculpture sitting blithely on its square is given equal value to a Holocaust memorial. The result is a virtual cabinet of curiosities. This seems to be one fate of the everyday life of memorials, proof that it has noodled its way into the crowd-sourced memory bank of society's virtual brain.

If the universal solvent of heritage as inventory can make mush of memorials and their cognates in the landscape, events can reconstitute them. Long-ossified Confederate monuments were revived in 2018 to fight new-old battles, only to be removed from the battlefield by activists and in some cases quarantined in museums. In Germany, the former Soviet Union, Argentina, Rwanda, and any place where traumas of the past remain unresolved, memorials come alive to fight proxy wars over unsettled business or where their old bodies can stand in for new grievances. Those that escape destruction or dislocation calm down eventually, grow invisible, fight with traffic, get moved, mustered, displaced, and drawn anew into commemorations and political maelstroms that their original sponsors never could have imagined.

The myopia of the present makes it difficult to divine the future of a memorial. The rawest, most vivid memorials can be buried, lost to time – Ozymandias says as much – even as they can be resurrected by political change or subtler everyday behaviors. It once seemed unthinkable that the Vietnam War Memorial in Washington, DC, would lose its way. When it was unveiled in 1982, emotion about the war and its memory ran high. Here was one memorial that seemed to speak directly. Yet it has been repeatedly glossed. In 1984, a triad of wistful bronze soldiers appeared as a rebuttal to the perceived darkness of Maya Lin's wall, and in 1993, the Vietnam Women's Memorial, a clumpy pietà, was installed nearby. Both additions are glosses done in the margins, but they ink up the original text emphatically. The wall can never be read the same way again. Whatever one may think about these additions, they are commemorative. A small muster of memorials to Vietnam thus took shape within the sprawling memorial emporium of the capital. A major change was proposed in 2001. A plan to build a massive interpretive center into the berm behind the wall aimed to bolster the memorial with a museum and education center as a way of combatting fading knowledge and memory of the war. In one generation, a memory that seemed to live in the gut had exited the head and a new kind of memorial – indeed, a different institution and building type – seemed necessary.

Although the project was dropped in 2018 for lack of funding, the idea itself is telling. It would have subverted the site, turning the wall into a gloss on the inevitable multimedia exhibits of the museum. It is now possible to imagine some future American standing in front of Lin's wall and asking, "What is this?" Except that the memorial would have remained a site for intimate communion between the living and the dead. The teddy bears and cookies, flowers and notes, would continue to be left behind – offerings can be found at much older memorials – and these everyday glosses would continue to be catalogued by the National Park Service in a perpetual fugue of memory and history, life and death, vernacular and official, everyday and not-everyday.

I have been reticent to discuss Washington, DC, because it is an outlier, a place where urban and commemorative infrastructure are so utterly intertwined, planned, and controlled that it leaves less room for memorials to take their rest in the everyday. Yet even in this highly formal necropolis of national memorials and commemorative traffic circles, the same forces are at work constructing and deconstructing the everyday and not-everyday. It is at these extreme sites, at places such as the Tomb of the Unknown Soldier, where the greatest effort to hold back the everyday can be found. As moderns have labored to concretize cultural memory in material form, their work has been quixotic. Memorials are strangely pliable. They are extroverted and then reticent, on the clock and out of time, modern and antimodern, high and low, formal and informal, official and vernacular, sacred and profane. We call them living and dead, but perhaps undead suits many of them best, until it doesn't. With these collisions in mind, this chapter and book has come full circle. The modern world is still in the predicament Steinberg faced in the 1950s: it has precious few public modes of expression commensurate to the scale of the issues it faces. To the well-known troubles of race, class, gender, and sexuality have been added existential quandaries of cancel culture, religious extremism, new pandemics, environmental catastrophe, and technological alienation, the last at the hands of humanity's most potent memory machine, which doubles as its most confounding font of conspiracies. The present has arguably never been less stable. Monuments — hackneyed, absurd, and discredited, but also engrossing, poignant, and resilient — continue to play a vital role in helping people patrol the contested and changeful boundaries of their lives.

Acknowledgments

To my family, friends, colleagues, and students. You have shaped me over these long years, and that in turn has shaped this book. I cannot possibly rank you, so I list you alphabetically, as in a memorial. The better to find one another. Were these pages a shiny granite block, instead of pressed wood pulp, you would see your reflection in it more clearly. You deserve such a thing. It would be broad and deep, its subterranean foundations constructed in layers like the geological strata of the earth, each layer evidence of our time together. And it would stretch into the landscape, erupting here, hugging the grass there, and elsewhere appearing like those erratic boulders the glaciers rolled across the prairies, like us. Everywhere I look, I see you.

Charles Altieri, Jo Ann Barber, Barry Bergdoll, Brandon Block, Michele Bogart, Maryana Breitman, Mark Brilliant, David Brownlee, Julia Bryan-Wilson, Bud Bynack, Elizabeth Byrne, Jon Castro, Francesco Ceccarelli, Ken Conklin, Coffee Conscious, Alexander Craghead, Birgit Däwes, Jacqueline Davidow, Whitney Davis, Fontaine Dearth, Jeroen Dewulf, Edward Diestelkamp, Scott Elder, Michael Elowitz, Jonathan Etkin, Benjamin Forest, Ceil Friedman, Jennifer Anne Gaugler, Stéphane Gerson, Meighan Gale, Ingrid Gessner, Ben Good, Elise Griffin DeMarzo, Carolyn Guile, Marta Gutman, Eva Hagberg, Timothy Hampton, Jacob Hellman, David Hernandes, Leonhard Herrmann, Sophie Hochhäusl, Elizabeth Honig, Peter Howell, Timothy Hudson, Erik Inglis, Kathleen James-Chakraborty, Juliet Johnson, Matico Josephson, Zara Kadkani-Schmitt, Maureen

Killeen, Linda Kinstler, Julia Klineberg, Carol Krinsky, Lauren Kroiz, Thomas Laqueur, Michael Lewis, Sharon Lewis, Sarah Lopez, Waverly Lowell, Paula Lupkin, Rose Lurie, Pieter Maarten, Chris Marino, Jason Miller, Susan Moffat, Kathleen Moran, Ramona Naddaff, Jorge Otero-Pailos, John Pinto, Meghan Reed, Kerstin Roeck, Dave Rosenthal, Valentina Rozas-Krause, Avigail Sachs, Megan Searing, Freek Schmidt, Ben Shanken, Cy Shanken, Edward Shanken, Elias Shanken, Mayor Shanken, Serena Shanken-Skwersky, Diane Shaw, William Skwersky, Susan Solomon, Christine Stevenson, William Stewart, Amanda Su, Alan Tansman, Vika Teicher, Marc Treib, Desirée Valadares, Elie Villareal, Martjin Wallage, Denise Wenig and family, Victoria Young.

Research for this book has been supported by a grant from the Barr Ferree Publication Fund at Princeton University, a President's Research Fellowship in the Humanities, and a Humanities Research Fellowship at the University of California.

Notes

PREFACE

The epigraph is from Robert Musil, "Monuments," trans. Burton Pike, in *Selected Writings*, ed. Burton Pike (New York: Continuum, 1986), p. 320.

1. Some of this was eventually published. See Andrew M. Shanken, "Towards a Cultural Geography of Memorials," in Jill A. Franklin, T. A. Heslop, and Christine Stevenson, eds., *Architecture and Interpretation: Essays for Eric Fernie* (Woodbridge: Boydell and Brewer, 2012).

2. Hayden Lorimer, "Cultural Geography: Worldly Shapes, Differently Arranged," *Progress in Human Geography* 31.1 (2007), p. 96.

3. Ibid., p. 89.

4. Ibid., p. 90.

5. See Nigel Thrift, *Non-Representational Theory: Space, Politics, Affect* (London: Routledge, 2008). Lorimer offered a corrective of this antivisual bias in Hayden Lorimer, "Cultural Geography: The Busyness of Being 'More-Than-Representational,'" *Progress in Human Geography* 29.1 (2005), pp. 83–94.

6. Even some of the most theoretically sophisticated writing by cultural geographers goes out of its way to avoid sustained visual analysis. See Peter Jackson, *Maps of Meaning: An Introduction to Cultural Geography* (London: Routledge, 1992); Edward W. Soja, *Postmetropolis: Critical Studies of Cities and Regions* (Oxford: Blackwell, 1999); Don Mitchell, *Cultural Geography: A Critical Introduction* (Oxford: Blackwell, 2000); Nigel Thift and Ash Amin, *Cities: Reimagining the Urban* (Oxford: Polity, 2002).

7. The moralizing language in architecture can be found as early as the mid-eighteenth century in the writings of Abbé Laugier and later in those of A. W. N. Pugin, William Morris, and more recently in the modern movement.

8. For a ranging account of the sources of this nonrepresentational theory, see Nigel Thrift, *Spatial Formations* (London: Sage, 1996). The works of Raymond Williams, Bruno Latour, Judith Butler, and Gilles Deleuze and Félix Guattari are all central, as is the work of Peggy Phelan in performance studies.

9. Henri Lefebvre, *Critique of Everyday Life*, trans. John Moore, 3 vols. (1947; New York: Verso, 1991), vol. 1, pp. 118–19.

10. I owe Elizabeth Marlowe for connecting memorials to Eliade's idea of hierophany at a conference on cultural heritage at Colgate University in 2011.

11. Mircea Eliade, *The Myth of the Eternal Return*, trans. Willard R. Trask (New York: Pantheon Books, 1954); Erving Goffman, *Behavior in Public Places: Notes on the Social Organization of Gatherings* (New York: Free Press, 1963); Norbert Elias, *The Civilizing Process*, trans. Edmund Jephcott (Oxford: Basil Blackwell, 1978–1982).

12. Thomas W. Laqueur, *The Work of the Dead: A Cultural History of Mortal Remains* (Princeton: Princeton University Press, 2015).

INTRODUCTION: MEMORIALS NO MORE

1. For instance, see George L. Mosse, *Fallen Soldiers: Reshaping the Memory of the World Wars* (New York: Oxford University Press, 1990); Jay Winter, *Sites of Memory, Sites of Mourning: The Great War in European Cultural History* (Cambridge: Cambridge University Press, 1995); James E. Young, *The Texture of Memory: Holocaust Memorials and Meaning* (New Haven: Yale University Press, 1993).

2. See Erika Doss, *Memorial Mania: Public Feeling in America* (Chicago: University of Chicago Press, 2010); Karen Till, "Places of Memory," in John Agnew, Katharyne Mitchell, and Gerard Toal, eds., *A Companion to Political Geography* (London: Blackwell, 2003), pp. 289–301. Dell Upton, *What Can and Can't Be Said: Race, Uplift, and Monument Building in the Contemporary South* (New Haven: Yale University Press, 2015).

3. Michele H. Bogart, *Public Sculpture and the Civic Ideal in New York City, 1890–1930* (Chicago: University of Chicago Press, 1989).

4. Kerwin Lee Klein, "On the Emergence of 'Memory' in Historical Discourse," in "Grounds for Remembering," special issue, *Representations* 69 (Winter 2000), pp. 127–50.

5. Of course, the Sherman statue made more sense in 1903 when it was dedicated, but it would soon become enmeshed in a world of automobiles.

6. Daniel M. Abramson, *Obsolescence: An Architectural History* (Chicago: University of Chicago Press, 2016).

7. By the middle of the present century, the still-hot memory of Vietnam will be as distant as the Franco-Prussian War was to those who fought World War II, and since the middle ground of the past and its deepest recesses blur, one day, it will be as familiar as the Peloponnesian Wars.

8. Robert S. Lopez, "The Crossroads within the Wall," in Oscar Handlin and John Burchard, eds., *The Historian and the City* (Cambridge, MA: MIT Press, 1963), pp. 27–43.

9. Arthur C. Danto, "The Vietnam Veterans Memorial," *Nation*, August 31, 1985, p. 152.

10. Françoise Choay, *The Invention of the Historic Monument*, trans. Lauren M. O'Connell (Cambridge: Cambridge University Press, 2001), p. 11.

11. François Hartog, *Regimes of Historicity: Presentism and Experiences of Time*, trans. Saskia Brown (New York: Columbia University Press, 2015), p. 184. For a similar idea, see Young, *The Texture of Memory*, p. 3.

12. Ibid., p. 3.

13. Ibid.

14. The slippage was scripted into Alois Riegl's pivotal theories on conservation that categorized monuments according to their "commemorative value." Alois Riegl, "The Modern Cult of Monuments: Its Character and Its Origin" (1903), trans. Kurt W. Forster and Diane Ghirardo, *Oppositions* 25 (Fall 1982), pp. 21–51.

15. Sergiusz Michalski, *Public Monuments: Art in Political Bondage 1870–1997* (London: Reaktion Books, 1998), p. 31.

16. Pierre Nora and Lawrence D. Kritzman, eds., *Realms of Memory: The Construction of the French Past*, trans. Arthur Goldhammer, 3 vols. (New York: Columbia University Press, 1996); Paul Ricoeur, *Memory, History, Forgetting*, trans. Kathleen Blamey and David Pellauer (Chicago: University of Chicago Press, 2004); Frances A. Yates, *The Art of Memory* (Chicago: University of Chicago Press, 1966).

17. From pioneering work by Sibyl Moholy-Nagy, J. B. Jackson, Henry Glassie, Paul Groth, Dell Upton, and Margaret Crawford to canonical books such as Bernard Rudofsky's *Architecture without Architects: A Short Introduction to Non-Pedigreed Architecture* (Garden City: Doubleday and Company, Inc., 1964) and Robert Venturi, Denise Scott Brown, and Steven Izenour's *Learning from Las Vegas* (Cambridge, MA: MIT Press, 1972), scholars now understand that every barn, hedgerow, median, and sign is packed with meaning.

18. Norbert Elias, "On the Concept of Everyday Life" (1978), in Johan Goudsblom and Stephen Mennel, eds., *The Norbert Elias Reader: A Biographical Selection* (Malden: Blackwell, 1998), pp. 166–74.

19. Henri Lefebvre, *The Urban Revolution*, trans. Robert Bononno (Minneapolis: University of Minnesota Press, 2003), pp. 21–22.

20. Nora and Kritzman, eds., *Realms of Memory*, pp. 8–9.

21. John E. Bodnar laid out the distinction between official and vernacular memory in *Remaking America: Public Memory, Commemoration, and Patriotism in the Twentieth Century* (Princeton: Princeton University Press, 1992).

22. Hugh Casson, ed., *Monuments* (New York: Taplinger, 1965), p. 10.

23. Joseph Farrell, "The Phenomenology of Memory in Roman Culture," *Classics Journal* 92.4 (April–May 1997), pp. 373–83. Farrell makes the provocative point that the origin of the ancient art of memory was transactional, part of the praise poet's "memory trade," and thus mundane in yet another way (p. 377).

24. Yates, *The Art of Memory*.

25. See Yates's discussion of divine memory and how it has passed through Western thought. Ibid., pp. 19–20, 43, 45, 70, 131.

26. Casson, *Monuments*, pp. 8–9.

27. Ibid., p. 9.

28. I thank Thomas Laqueur for helping me think through these distinctions.

CHAPTER ONE: EVERYDAY MEMORY

1. Pierre Nora, "Between Memory and History," in "Memory and Counter-Memory," special issue, *Representations* 26 (Spring, 1989), pp. 8–9. Andrew M. Shanken, "Planning Memory: Living Memorials in the United States during World War II," *Art Bulletin* 84.1 (March, 2002), pp. 130–47.

2. Nora, "Between Memory and History," p. 8.

3. Ibid., p. 14. Scholars in memory studies routinely follow Nora's opposition between history and memory. Paul Connerton does so gently in *How Societies Remember* (Cambridge: Cambridge University Press, 1989), p. 16.

4. Nora, "Between Memory and History," p. 8.

5. Ibid.

6. Ibid., p. 14.

7. Ibid., p. 7.

8. Ibid., p. 12.

9. Ibid., p. 18.

10. Ibid., p. 23.

11. Ibid.

12. See Kerwin Lee Klein's brilliant discussion: "On the Emergence of Memory in Historical Discourse," in "Grounds for Remembering," special issue, *Representations* 69 (Winter 2000), pp. 127–50. See also Henri Lefebvre's sphinxlike attempts to wrestle with the opposition with regard to monuments in *The Urban Revolution*, trans. Robert Bononno (1970; Minneapolis: University of Minnesota Press, 2003), pp. 22–23.

13. Some of these scholars include Henry Glassie, Dell Upton, Paul Groth, Norbert Elias, Erving Goffman, J. B. Jackson, Peirce Lewis, Margaret Crawford, and others.

14. Rita Fenski observes a similar oppositional character in writing on everyday life. See Rita Fenski, *Doing Time: Feminist Theory and Postmodern Culture* (New York: New York University Press, 2000), pp. 79–80.

15. J. B. Jackson, "The Order of the Landscape: Reason and Religion in Newtonian America," in D. W. Meinig, ed., *The Interpretation of Ordinary Landscapes: Geographical Essays* (New York: Oxford University Press, 1979), p. 155.

16. Norbert Elias, "On the Concept of Everyday Life" (1978), in Johan Goudsblom and Stephen Mennel, eds., *The Norbert Elias Reader: A Biographical Selection* (Malden: Blackwell, 1998), p. 167.

17. The original German text was *Über den Prozess der Zivilisation: Soziogenetische und Psychogenetische Untersuchungen* (Basel: Haus zum Falken, 1939).

18. Elias, "On the Concept of Everyday Life," p. 169.

19. Ibid., p. 171.

20. Henry Glassie, "Vernacular Architecture and Society," *Material Culture* 16.1 (Spring 1984), p. 9.

21. Ibid., p. 10.

22. On the primitive hut, see Joseph Rykwert, *On Adam's Huse in Paradise: The Idea of the Primitive Hut in Architectural History* (Cambridge, MA: MIT Press, 1981); Bernard Rudofsky, *Architecture without Architects: A Short Introduction to Non-Pedigreed Architecture* (Garden City: Doubleday, 1964). Rudofsky notably calls vernacular architecture "non-pedigreed," defining it in the negative and through a series of typical clichés: "immutable," "unimprovable," immune to "fashion cycles," and "eternally valid."

23. Glassie, "Vernacular Architecture and Society," p. 10. This sense of linking the everyday with "authentic experience" and linking modernity, especially capitalism, with alienation from this authenticity is a central theme in volume 1 of Henri Lefebvre's *Critique of Everyday Life*, trans. John Moore, 3 vols. (1947; London: Verso Books, 1991). Also see

Fenski's discussion of this theme in *Doing Time*, p. 79. For the influence of Lefebvre in architectural thought, see Mary McLeod, "Henry Lefebvre's Critique of Everyday Life: An Introduction," in Steven Harris and Deborah Berke, eds., *Architecture of the Everyday* (New York: Princeton Architectural Press, 1997), pp. 9–29.

24. See Casey Nelson Blake, *Beloved Community: The Cultural Criticism of Randolph Bourne, Van Wyck Brooks, Waldo Frank, and Lewis Mumford* (Chapel Hill: University of North Carolina Press, 1990).

25. Glassie, "Vernacular Architecture and Society," p. 11. Gwendolyn Wright notes this inclination to represent the vernacular as "unchanging" and "innocent of history" as being part of what Eric Hobsbawm called the "anxiety of loss in the aftermath of the Industrial Revolution." Gwendolyn Wright, "On Modern Vernaculars and J. B. Jackson," in Chris Wilson and Paul Groth, eds., *Everyday America: Cultural Landscape Studies after J. B. Jackson* (Berkeley: University of California Press, 2003), p. 165.

26. Glassie, "Vernacular Architecture and Society," p. 11.

27. Ibid. This association of the everyday with natural politics and the alienation of modernity is discussed by Alexandra Kogl in "A Hundred Ways of Beginning: The Politics of Everyday Life," *Polity* 41.4 (October 2009), pp. 514–35.

28. See Paul Groth's capsule history of the development of interest in ordinary environments in Paul Groth and Todd W. Bressi, eds., *Understanding Ordinary Environments* (New Haven: Yale University Press, 1997), pp. 1–21.

29. Paul Groth, "Making New Connections in Vernacular Architecture," *Journal of the Society of Architectural Historians* 58.3 (September 1999), p. 444. Dell Upton expresses a similar view in "The Architecture of Everyday Life," *New Literary History* 33.4 (Autumn 2002), pp. 707–23.

30. Upton discusses some of these binaries in "The Architecture of Everyday Life," pp. 708–709. See also Marcel Vellinga, "The End of the Vernacular: Anthropology and the Architecture of the Other," *Etnofoor* 23.1 (2011), pp. 171–92.

31. Dell Upton and John Michael Vlach, eds., introduction to *Common Places: Readings in American Vernacular Architecture* (Athens: University of Georgia Press, 1986), p. xv.

32. Upton, "The Architecture of Everyday Life," p. 707.

33. Harris, "Everyday Architecture," in Harris and Berke, eds., *Architecture of the Everyday*, p. 3. Roark is the fictional hero of Ayn Rand's *The Fountainhead*, an allegorical representation of her extreme ideology of individualism.

34. Raymond Williams, *Keywords: A Vocabulary of Culture and Society*, rev. ed. (New

York: Oxford University Press, 1983), s.v. "Ordinary," pp. 225–26. See also Joe Moran's discussion of similar words in *Reading the Everyday* (London: Routledge, 2005), pp. 12–22.

35. Williams, *Keywords*, p. 226.

36. Ibid., s.v. "Common," p. 71.

37. John R. Stilgoe, *Common Landscape of America, 1580–1845* (New Haven: Yale University Press, 1982), p. x.

38. Michel de Certeau, *The Practice of Everyday Life*, trans. Steven Randall (Berkeley: University of California Press, 1984), p. v. A fanfare is a short musical flourish traditionally used to accompany the entrance of royalty into an occasion. Copeland was inspired by Henry A. Wallace's speech "Century of the Common Man," delivered May 8, 1942, in New York City.

39. Andreas Eckert and Adam Jones, "Historical Writing about Everyday Life," *Journal of African Cultural Studies*, 15.1 (June 2002), p. 8.

40. See Claire Colebrook's analysis in "The Politics and Potential of Everyday Life," *New Literary History* 3.4 (Autumn, 2002), pp. 687–706, especially p. 698.

41. Sergiusz Michalski, *Public Monuments: Art in Political Bondage 1870–1997* (London: Reaktion, 1998), p. 47.

42. See especially Alexandra Kogl's discussion in "A Hundred Ways of Beginning," of the everyday or routine as the opposite of politics (p. 515). For an architect's view of the matter, see Harris, "Everyday Architecture," p. 3. Nora's prodding of historians to act as *lieux de mémoire* resonates with de Certeau's tricksters.

43. For "prepolitical," see Kogel, "A Hundred Ways of Beginning," p. 515. Marcel Vellinga likens the othering of the vernacular to "essentialist stereotypes" such as indigenous, folk, primitive, and tribal, long ago discredited in anthropology. Vellinga, "The End of the Vernacular," p. 172.

44. Hanna Fenichel Pitkin, *The Attack of the Blob: Hannah Arendt's Concept of the Social* (Chicago: University of Chicago Press, 1998), pp. 252, 282. See Kogl's discussion of Pitkin's idea vis-à-vis the everyday in "A Hundred Ways of Beginning," pp. 516–21.

45. Colebrook, "The Politics and Potential of Everyday Life," p. 521.

46. Margaret Crawford, introduction to John Leighton Chase, Margaret Crawford, and John Kaliski, eds., *Everyday Urbanism* (New York: Monacelli Press, 2008), p. 8.

47. Ibid., p. 9.

48. Ibid.

49. Wilbur Zelinsky, "Seeing Beyond the Dominant Culture," in Groth and Bressi,

eds., *Understanding Ordinary Environments*, pp. 157–61; Crawford, introduction, p. 11.

50. Crawford, introduction to *Everyday Urbanism*, p. 11. As an urbanism or resistance rooted in everyday practices, *Everyday Urbanism* goes back to the early-nineteenth-century roots of the vernacular as a people's alternative to the rise of a purportedly alienating and artificial national culture. See Vellinga, "The End of the Vernacular," pp. 176–77.

51. Crawford, introduction to *Everyday Urbanism*, p. 10.

52. Ibid., p. 15. Much of this took its cue from the work of Michel de Certeau and Henri Lefebvre, who aimed their work on the everyday at overcoming the alienation of modern capitalist society.

53. Dell Upton, "The Tradition of Change," *Traditional Dwellings and Settlements* 5.1 (1993), p. 12.

54. Peirce F. Lewis, "Axioms for Reading the Landscape: Some Guides to the American Scene," in D. W. Meinig, ed., *The Interpretation of Ordinary Landscapes: Geographical Essays* (New York: Oxford University Press, 1979), p. 18.

55. The phrase appears in a longer passage in which Adams's patience is tested by a Swiss German who visits him with a vast collection of medals. Adams writes: "Democracy has no forefathers, it looks to no posterity; it is swallowed up in the present, and thinks of nothing but itself. This is the vice of democracy; and it is incurable. Democracy has no monuments; it strikes no medals; it bears the head of no man upon a coin; its very essence is iconoclastic. This is the reason why Congress have never been able to erect a monument to Washington." In Charles Francis Adams, ed., *Memoirs of John Quincy Adams: Comprising Portions of His Diary from 1795–1848*, 12 vols. (Philadelphia: J. B. Lippincott, 1874–77), vol. 3, p. 433.

56. Thomas Carlyle, *Latter-Day Pamphlets* (1851; New York: C. Scribner's Sons, 1901), pp. 335 and 363. As a celebrator of "great men" in history, Carlyle's brooding about monuments is all the more powerful.

57. Philippe Ariès, *Western Attitudes toward Death from the Middle Ages to the Present*, trans. Patricia M. Ranum (Baltimore: Johns Hopkins University Press, 1984), pp. 85, 90.

58. Peter Schjeldahl, "High and Low Relief: Augustus Saint-Gaudens at the Met," *New Yorker*, August 24, 2009, p. 80.

59. Trevor Noah, on *The Daily Distancing Show*, Comedy Central, June 16, 2020, https://www.cc.com/episodes/9b15yw/the-daily-show-with-trevor-noah-june-16-2020-tim-scott-gabrielle-union-season-25-ep-117.

60. Hugh Casson, ed., *Monuments* (New York: Taplinger, 1965), p. 10.

61. James E. Young, *At Memory's Edge: After-Images of the Holocaust in Contemporary Art and Architecture* (New Haven: Yale University Press, 2000), pp. 7–8, 90–119.

62. The creation of the category of "dead white males" not only shifted focus away from living white males, for which they are nothing but a proxy, but also tapped into the death taboo. After all, all living white males eventually become dead ones and, as Philippe Ariès has shown, death has become "shameful and forbidden." The literature that uses the term "dead white males" is vast. A search in any university library catalog will turn up hundreds of examples.

63. Casson, *Monuments*, p. 9.

64. One exception is Reuben M. Rainey, "Hallowed Grounds and Rituals of Remembrance: Union Regimental Monuments at Gettysburg," in Groth and Bressi, eds., *Understanding Ordinary Environments*, pp. 67–80.

65. Richard Walker, "Unseen and Disbelieved: A Political Economist among Cultural Geographers," in Groth and Bressi, eds., *Understanding Ordinary Environments*, p. 167. See also Upton, "The Architecture of Everyday Life." Upton calls for an assimilation of Architecture with a capital "A" with architecture, understood more broadly as the built environment.

66. Crawford, introduction to *Everyday Urbanism*, p. 11.

67. M. M. Bakhtin, "Discourse in the Novel" (1936), trans. Caryl Emerson and Michael Holquist, in Bakhtin, *The Dialogic Imagination: Four Essays* (Austin: University of Texas Press, 1981), p. 276.

68. Crawford, introduction to *Everyday Urbanism*, p. 10. This approach can be found in Anthony D. King, "The Politics of Vision," in Paul Groth, ed., *Vision, Culture, and Landscape: Working Papers from the Berkeley Symposium on Cultural Landscape Interpretation* (Berkeley: University of California, Berkeley, Center for Environmental Design Research, 1990). See also Dell Upton's "The City as Material Culture," in Anna Elizabeth Yentsch and Mary C. Beaudry, eds., *The Art and Mystery of Historical Archaeology: Essays in Honor of James Deetz* (Boca Raton: CRC press, 1992), pp. 51–74. See also Richard Walker's warning about the erosion of "respect for the evidence of material culture," "Unseen and Disbelieved," p. 172.

69. It also shifts attention away from formal analysis, which has been at the center of art and architectural history for generations, and thereby needlessly creates an academic dispute. Bakhtin may have rejected the devaluation of form, as well: "The authentic environment of an utterance, the environment in which it lives and takes shape, is dialogized heteroglossia, anonymous and social as language, but simultaneously concrete, filled with

specific content and accented as an individual utterance." Bakhtin, "Discourse in the Novel," p. 272.

70. Walker, "Unseen and Disbelieved," p. 172. Even the dialectical formulation seems fraught, since it reinforces the very opposition it seeks to resolve.

71. The phrase "denaturalize the everyday" is Richard Walker's, ibid., p. 167.

72. For Rubbiani, see Andrew M. Shanken, "Preservation and Creation: Alfonso Rubbiani and Bologna," *Future Anterior* 7.1 (Summer 2010), pp. 61–81. Portions of the following argument are drawn from this article.

73. He erected other tombs in the same manner in front of San Domenico. For a discussion of "statuemania," see Michalski, *Public Monuments*, especially p. 49.

74. The story is told in Francesco Ceccarelli, "Bologna e la Romagna," in Amerigo Restucci, ed., *Storia dell'architettura italiana: L'Ottocento*, 2 vols. (Milan: Electa, 2005), vol. 1, p. 160.

75. Elias, "On the Concept of Everyday Life," p. 173.

76. Spiro Kostof, *A History of Architecture: Settings and Rituals*, 2nd ed. (New York: Oxford University Press, 1995), p. 127.

77. The metaphor of roof is drawn from Erving Goffman, *Behavior in Public Places: Notes on the Social Organization of Gatherings* (New York: Free Press, 1963), pp. 137, 141, 153.

78. "Monument Given Tar, Feathers," *Lorain Journal*, November 21, 1957, Brady's Bunch of Lorain County Nostalgia, http://danielebrady.blogspot.com/2016/05/lagranges-civil -war-monument-part-2.html. This is not an isolated phenomenon. More recently, a monument to Jefferson Davis was tarred and feathered in Arizona. "Arizona Civil War Monument Tarred and Feathered," *Arizona Daily Independent*, August 18, 2017, https:// arizonadailyindependent.com/2017/08/18/arizona-civil-war-monument-tarred-and -feathered.

79. Richard Ford, "Planning Laws Leave War Memorials at Risk, Says London Assembly," *The Times*, July 6, 2009, https://www.thetimes.co.uk/edition/news/planning-laws -leave-war-memorials-at-risk-says-london-assembly-39f3ox88c26.

80. I owe this sense of memory studies being substantially funneled through Holocaust studies to Valentina Rozas-Krause. See also Debarati Sanyal, *Memory and Complicity: Migrations of Holocaust Remembrance* (New York: Fordham University Press, 2015).

81. Duchamp's *L.H.O.O.Q.* of 1919.

82. It is unclear when exactly the second rail appeared. The first line of defense appeared by the first half of the eighteenth century, as seen in Giuseppe Zocchi's or

Bernardo Bellotto's paintings of the Piazza della Signoria. A single iron railing is also visible in photographs taken in the late nineteenth century.

83. Gavin Stamp, "Bring Back the Railings," in *Anti-Ugly: Excursions in English Architecture and Design* (London: Aurum Press, 2013), pp. 233–37.

84. Ibid., p. 234.

85. Ibid.

86. Ibid., p. 235.

87. On June 16, 2020, an armed militiaman shot a man who was part of a crowd taking down a monument to the Spanish conquistador Juan de Oñate. Matt Zapotosky, "Former City Council Candidate Arrested after Man Is Shot at New Mexico Protest with Militia Group," *Washington Post*, June 16, 2020, https://www.washingtonpost.com/nation/2020/06/16/albuquerque-militia-shooting-protest.

88. Erica Doss, *Memorial Mania: Public Feeling in America* (Chicago: University of Chicago Press, 2010).

89. The trash can and mural are linked to the Veterans Resource Program, which operated out of the building behind the trashcan but now appears to be defunct.

90. An example brings this point home. In the 1990s, ceremonial guards were removed from Lenin's Mausoleum and later posted in front of the Tomb of the Unknown Soldier in Moscow. This vividly shows the sites that the Russian government believes need to be elevated and protected.

91. Andrew Charlesworth, "Contesting Places of Memory: The Case of Auschwitz," *Environment and Planning D: Society and Space* 12 (1994), pp. 579–93.

92. Sergiusz Michalski considers the statue of Don Juan of Austria in Messina, Italy, erected in 1572, to be the first statue explicitly placed in public space. Michalski, *Public Monuments*, p. 8. Of course, there are earlier statues that were erected in quasi-public spaces, such as Donatello's equestrian of Gattamelata, erected in 1453 in Padua.

93. I thank my Berkeley colleague Elizabeth Honig for this observation.

94. Eric Hobsbawm and Terence Ranger, eds., *The Invention of Tradition* (Cambridge: Cambridge University Press, 1983).

95. Eric Hobsbawm, *The Age of Revolution 1789–1848* (1962; London: Sphere Books, 1991), pp. 13–16.

96. For the changing shape of time, see Stephen J. Gould, *Time's Arrow, Time's Cycle: Myth and Metaphor in the Discovery of Geological Time* (Cambridge, MA: Harvard University Press, 1987). For acceleration, see Reinhart Koselleck, *The Practice of Conceptual History:*

Timing History, Spacing Concepts, trans. Todd Samuel Presner, et al. (Stanford: Stanford University Press, 2002).

97. Andrew M. Shanken, "Keeping Time with the Good War," *American Studies Journal* 59 (Spring 2015), http://www.asjournal.org/59-2015/keeping-time-with-the-good-war.

CHAPTER TWO: LABILE MEMORY

1. Stephen Rombouts, "Art as Propaganda in Eighteenth-Century France: The Paradox of Edme Bouchardon's Louis XV," *Eighteenth-Century Studies* 27.2 (Winter 1993–94), p. 256.

2. Andrew McClellan, "The Life and Death of a Royal Monument: Bouchardon's 'Louis XV'," *Oxford Art Journal* 23.2 (2000), p. 7.

3. Robert Musil, "Monuments," trans. Burton Pike, in *Selected Writings*, ed. Burton Pike (New York: Continuum, 1986), p. 320.

4. Richard Sennett, *Flesh and Stone: The Body and the City in Western Civilization* (New York: W. W. Norton, 1994), p. 303. The statue originally was encircled with a large railing. It is possible that this had been destroyed and melted down along with the statue.

5. By happenstance, an Egyptian obelisk from Luxor was erected there in 1836, importing remote history and colonialism to cool off the overheated space and redirect its associations to the distant French possession.

6. This is an obvious foretaste of what has happened to many Confederate monuments in recent years. There was also an important distinction to be made between spontaneous acts of destruction, understood as vandalism, and the systematic iconoclasm guiding the emerging laws of the state. Dominique Poulot writes about the rise of vandalism as a cultural idea invented to make this distinction. See Dominique Poulot, "Revolutionary 'Vandalism' and the Birth of the Museum: The Effects of a Representation of Modern Cultural Terror," in Susan Pearce, ed., *Art in Museums* (London: Athlone, 1995), pp. 192–214.

7. McClellan, "The Life and Death of a Royal Monument," p. 5.

8. Karl Jaspers, *The Question of German Guilt*, trans. E. B. Ashton (1947; New York: Fordham University Press, 2000), p. 49.

9. Thomas W. Laqueur, *The Work of the Dead: A Cultural History of Mortal Remains* (Princeton: Princeton University Press, 2015), p. 62.

10. Sennett, *Flesh and Stone*, pp. 299–303.

11. Ibid., p. 305.

12. Ibid., p. 306. Note that the Bastille was one of the first buildings to be labeled a historic monument, tellingly while it was "earmarked for demolition." See François Hartog,

Regimes of Historicity: Presentism and Experiences of Time, trans. Saskia Brown (New York: Columbia University Press), p. 161.

13. The American army would do the same thing to a statue of Saddam Hussein some two hundred years later. See the front page of the *San Francisco Chronicle*, March 19, 2006.

14. Françoise Choay, *The Invention of the Historic Monument*, trans. Lauren M. O'Connell (Cambridge: Cambridge University Press, 2001), pp. 12 and 89. In fact, the title of Choay's original French version, *Allégorie du patrimonie*, makes the point best. The vast change in translation betrays just how awkwardly the rhetoric of patrimony, and thus the entire argument, translates to an Anglo-American audience.

15. For the talismanic power of the king and the crisis of representation in the wake of the revolution, see Lynn Hunt, *Politics, Culture, and Class in the French Revolution* (Berkeley: University of California Press, 1984), especially chapter 3. See also Hartog, who writes: "after all, how could one possibly venture to think beyond an absolute monarch." Hartog, *Regimes of Historicity*, p. 107.

16. Hartog, *Regimes of Historicity*, p. 107.

17. Sennett, *Flesh and Stone*, p. 308.

18. Paul Connerton makes this point when he writes: "To construct a barrier between the new beginning and the old tyranny is to recollect the old tyranny." Paul Connerton, *How Societies Remember* (Cambridge; New York: Cambridge University Press, 1989), p. 10.

19. Quoted in Hunt, *Politics, Culture, and Class in the French Revolution*, p. 91.

20. Sennett, *Flesh and Stone*, p. 308.

21. See Sergiusz Michalski, *Public Monuments: Art in Political Bondage 1870–1997* (London: Reaktion Books, 1998), p. 31.

22. McClellan suggests the contrast but does not see *The Death of Marat* as a monument manqué, "The Life and Death of a Royal Monument," p. 6.

23. George L. Mosse claims that war monuments in public places and in civilian cemeteries "became routine after the wars of the Revolution and Napoleon." See George L. Mosse, *Fallen Soldiers: Reshaping the Memory of the World War* (New York: Oxford University Press, 1990), p. 46.

24. I use the phrase "secular everyday" to distinguish the disenchanted everyday of modernity from the highly spiritual everyday life of the premodern world discussed by Arthur E. Imhof, *Lost Worlds: How Our European Ancestors Coped with Everyday Life and Why Life Is So Hard Today*, trans. Thomas Robisheaux (Charlottesville: University of Virginia Press, 1996).

25. Lewis Mumford coined the term "neotechnic" to designate a new phase of civilization in which the machine would be made the servant of mankind, freeing people for higher pursuits than labor. See Lewis Mumford, "The Neotechnic Phase," in *Technics and Civilization* (New York: Harcourt, Brace, 1934), pp. 107–42.

26. Monuments to individuals had been erected since the fifteenth century as "individual tokens of respect," but not as public monuments. Michalski, *Public Monuments*, p. 8.

27. Ibid., pp. 44–49.

28. Ibid., p. 9.

29. Ibid., pp. 34, 39. For a colorful Victorian discrediting of the phenomenon, see Thomas Carlyle, "Hudson's Statue," in *Latter-Day Pamphlets* (1851; New York: C. Scribner's Son, 1901).

30. The maze on the back is surely meant to liken Sanmicheli to Dedalus, the mythic Minoan architect who designed the labyrinth, and the broken Ionic column capital that peaks out behind his robes is another hint that this is an architect. But having previously seen few monuments to architects, I overlooked these clues.

31. Eric Hobsbawm and Terence Ranger, eds., *The Invention of Tradition* (Cambridge: Cambridge University Press, 1983).

32. Thanks to writer Ceil Friedman for identifying the monument.

33. Giulio Camuzzoni, *Discorso per l'inaugurazione del monument a Michele Sanmicheli* (Verona: Tipografia Premiata de Gaetano Franchini, 1874), p. vii.

34. Ibid.

35. Choay dates the self-conscious use of "historic monument" to the first appearance of the term in French in the 1830s. The English usage predates this by at least a generation, but is relatively rare until the 1830s. Choay, *The Invention of the Historic Monument*, pp. 14–15. Hartog, *Regimes of Historicity*, chapter 3.

36. Hartog, *Regimes of Historicity*, p. 107.

37. Maria D'Anniballe Williams, "Urban Space in Fascist Verona: Contested Grounds for Mass Spectacle, Tourism, and the Architectural Past," PhD diss., University of Pittsburgh (2010), p. 45. Similar shifts were part of an international medieval and Gothic revival. Far from the painstaking work of preservation today, restoration was a highly inventive process. See Alfonso Rubbiani's work in Bologna as an important example: Andrew M. Shanken, "Preservation and Creation: Alfonso Rubbiani and Bologna," *Future Anterior* 7.1 (Summer 2010), pp. 61–81.

38. Williams, "Urban Space in Fascist Verona," p. 46. Some of this work was conducted by Camillo Boito, a key figure in early preservation in Italy. This medievalism was common across much of Italy.

39. A very similar process is explored in the Estonian film *Friendship* (2006), about teenagers at the Monument to the Liberators of Tallinn.

40. Mircea Eliade, *Sacred and Profane: The Nature of Religion*, trans. Willard R. Trask (New York: Harcourt, Brace, 1959), p. 26.

41. Erving Goffman, *Behavior in Public Places: Notes on the Social Organization of Gatherings* (New York: Free Press, 1963), p. 25.

42. Ibid., p. 74.

43. Ibid., p. 38.

44. Ibid., p. 25.

45. In 2018, a homeless Romanian was found dead on a park bench in the piazza. Vagrants, many of them migrants from Africa and Eastern Europe, are routinely cleared out of the piazza. See "Verona, degrade nel centro storico: Continua la lotta per render più sicura la zona," *Veronasera*, June 22, 2015, https://www.veronasera.it/cronaca/verona-degrado-centro-storico-lotta-per-sicurezza-zona-22-giugno-2015.html; "Daspo urbano a Verona," *Veronasera*, July 12, 2018, https://www.veronasera.it/cronaca/daspo-urbano-54-allontanate-due-settimane-12-luglio-2018.html; "Senzatetto al freddo in città, Sperotto lancia l'appello al sindaco: 'È ora d'intervenire,'" *Veronasera*, January 26, 2018, https://www.veronasera.it/cronaca/morto-freddo-smentita-alberto-sperotto-appello-sindaco-senza-tetto-26-gennaio-2018-.html.

46. "Rome," *San Francisco Chronicle*, July 31, 1961, quoted in Goffman, *Behavior in Public Places*, p. 167, n. 3.

47. Ibid.

48. London confronts similar issues. See Stephen Heathorn, "The Civil Servant and Public Remembrance: Sir Lionel Earle and the Shaping of London's Commemorative Landscape, 1918–1933, *Twentieth Century British History* 19.3 (January 1, 2008), p. 275.

49. Youth unemployment in Italy is a significant social problem, with recent figures as high as 40 percent for those without high school degrees. So acute is the problem that in 2016, the Italian government created a "culture bonus," a grant of 500 euros for eighteen-year-olds to spend on "culturally enriching pursuits" such as museums, concerts, theaters, and books. Nearly six hundred thousand teenagers qualified at a cost of 290 million euros. Nick Squires, "Italian Teenagers to Receive €500 'Cultural Bonus' from

Government" *Telegraph*, August 23, 2016, http://www.telegraph.co.uk/news/2016/08/23/italian-teenagers-to-receive-500-cultural-bonus-from-government.

50. At least since the 1954 Plan of Verona, the Piazza Pradaval has been part of a heritage conservation plan to direct growth, traffic, and unwanted businesses away from the historic center in order to leverage the historic assets of the town. Sergio Stumpo, "The Sustainability of Urban Heritage Preservation: The Case of Verona, Italia," Discussion Paper no. IDB-DP-1 28, Inter-American Development Bank, 2010, https://publications.iadb.org/publications/english/document/The-Sustainability-of-Urban-Heritage-Preservation-The-Case-of-Verona-Italia.pdf.

51. In recent years, Verona has cleaned the statue, installed surveillance cameras and bright lighting in the piazza, added a café kiosk to invite commercial life, and flushed out the homeless and drug dealers. They have removed Sanmicheli's countercultural cloak. "Statue of Sanmicheli Ready to See the Light of Day Again," read one newspaper article. See Chiara Pasotti, "Videosorveglianza per piazza Pradaval," *Veronasera*, July 2, 2009, https://www.veronasera.it/cronaca/videosorveglianza-per-piazza-pradaval.html.

52. See in particular Hartog, *Regimes of Historicity*, chapter 5.

53. "Unattractive Back," *Architectural Forum* 82 (January 1945), p. 38.

54. This idea about the transmogrification of water comes from Maria Kaika, "Interrogating the Geographies of the Familiar: Domesticating Nature and Constructing the Autonomy of the Modern Home," *International Journal of Urban and Regional Research* 28 (March 2004), pp. 265–86.

55. Ibid., p. 266.

56. See Andrew M. Shanken, "Planning Memory: The Rise of Living Memorials in the United States during World War II," *Art Bulletin* 84 (March 2002), pp. 130–47.

57. In order to demonstrate the inappropriateness of these everyday practices, Israeli artist Shahak Shapira created a set of montages that superimpose people doing various noncommemorative things at the Berlin memorial over actual Holocaust scenes.

58. Grindr Remembers is a website set up to catalog the profile photographs taken at the Berlin memorial. See http://grindr-remembers.blogspot.com.

59. Charles Baudelaire, *The Painter of Modern Life, and Other Essays*, trans. Jonathan Mayne (London: Phaidon, 1964), p. 13. See the work of Nonument, which documents twentieth-century monuments whose meanings have changed, https://nonument.org.

60. Lewis Mumford, "The Death of the Monument," in J. L Martin, Ben Nicholson, and Naum Gabo, eds., *Circle: International Survey of Constructive Art* (London: Faber and Faber, 1937), p. 263.

61. Françoise Choay extends Mumford's dim view: "The symbolic monument, erected *ex nihilo* for commemorative purpose, has practically no currency in our developed society." Choay, *Invention of the Historic Monument*, p. 12. Of course, the monument as a cultural form seemed moribund when she was writing in 1992.

62. For an Italian example, see D. Medina Lasansky, "Urban Editing, Historic Preservation, and Political Rhetoric: The Fascist Redesign of San Gimignano," *Journal of the Society of Architectural Historians* 63.3 (September 2004), pp. 320–53; Hobsbawm and Ranger, eds., *The Invention of Tradition*; Jeffrey Herf, *Reactionary Modernism: Technology, Culture, and Politics in Weimar and the Third Reich* (Cambridge: Cambridge University Press, 1984).

63. For an exploration of this relationship between time and space, see the introduction to Reinhart Koselleck, *Sediments of Time: On Possible Histories*, ed. and trans. Stefan-Ludwig Hoffmann and Sean Franzel (Stanford: Stanford University Press, 2018).

64. Thomas W. Laqueur, *The Work of the Dead: A Cultural History of Mortal Remains* (Princeton: Princeton University Press, 2015), p. 67.

CHAPTER THREE: PLACING MEMORY

1. Arthur E. Imhof, *Lost Worlds: How Our European Ancestors Coped with Everyday Life and Why Life Is So Hard Today* (Charlottesville: University of Virginia Press, 1996), p. 165. The following account is informed by Imhof's book.

2. Thomas W. Laqueur, *The Work of the Dead: A Cultural History of Mortal Remains* (Princeton: Princeton University Press, 2015), p. 184.

3. Ibid.

4. Imhof makes this point repeatedly.

5. Laqueur, *The Work of the Dead*, p. 186.

6. Ibid., p. 67.

7. Robert Rosenblum, *Transformations in Late Eighteenth-Century Art* (Princeton: Princeton University Press, 1967), p. 69.

8. Caroline Winterer demonstrates how closely linked Enlightenment thought in British America and later in the early United States was to French thinkers. Caroline Winterer, *American Enlightenments: Pursuing Happiness in the Age of Reason* (New Haven: Yale University Press, 2016), especially the introduction and chapter 1.

9. Quoted in Winterer, *American Enlightenments*, p. 64.

10. A shared nomenclature speaks to the overlapping project of the study of nature and culture. The word "specimen," used to describe rocks and shells that were instrumental

and controversial in overturning a biblical sense of time, was also used to describe elements and entire styles of architecture, which were used to periodize cultural epochs. Specimens of, say, early Norman arches could be as politically charged as a shell found on a mountaintop that challenged the biblical flood. Likewise, the word "nondescript," used in natural history for a specimen that had not yet been named or described, came to be used for architectural elements of a previously unknown class. Every new monument entered this dense thicket of associations between architecture and time; every stylistic decision was potentially laden with political, nationalistic, and racial meaning.

11. Ellen Zetzel Lambert, *Placing Sorrow: A Study of the Pastoral Elegy Convention from Theocritus to Milton* (Chapel Hill: University of North Carolina Press, 1976).

12. In fact, Old Saint Johns had fallen into disuse after the War of 1812, when the "churchyard was used by the public as a grazing ground for cattle, horses and hogs." This aligns with Philippe Ariès's account (see below) of the medieval burial ground. Lyon G. Tyler, *History of Hampton* (Hampton: The Board of Supervisors of Elizabeth City County, 1922), p. 47. Tyler writes of a "religious awakening" that began in the 1820s, which corresponds to the Second Great Awakening, when the church was restored. The tumultuous history of the church, along with its destruction and the burning of the town, has left relatively little documentation about this important church.

13. Tyler, *History of Hampton*, pp. 52–54. Also, Marion L. Starkey, *The First Plantation* (Hampton: Housing Printing and Publishing House, 1936), p. 82.

14. Starkey, *The First Plantation*, pp. 82–83. In fact, Black residents had returned to the town and used what chimneys remained standing to improvise shelter for themselves. These were so well built that the Union evicted the residents in order to house troops. Robert Francis Engs, *Freedom's First Generation: Black Hampton, Virginia, 1861–1890* (Philadelphia: University of Pennsylvania Press, 1979), p. 34.

15. Many Confederate memorials in this period were erected at courthouses, as well, placing racial claims on legal grounds.

16. Stanley French, "The Cemetery as Cultural Institution: The Establishment of Mount Auburn and the 'Rural Cemetery' Movement," *American Quarterly* 26.1 (March, 1974), pp. 42, 46–47.

17. Dell Upton, *What Can and Can't Be Said: Race, Uplift, and Monument Building in the Contemporary South* (New Haven: Yale University Press, 2015), p. 27.

18. Philippe Ariès, *The Hour of Our Death*, trans. Helen Weaver (New York: Knopf, 1981), p. 62.

19. Ibid.

20. Ibid., p. 63.

21. Ibid., pp. 63–64.

22. Ibid., p. 64.

23. E. Champeaux, *Les cimetiéres et le marchés du vieux Dijon* (Dijon: J. Mourry, 1906), p. 6, cited in Ariès, p. 64.

24. Ariès, *The Hour of Our Death*, pp. 68–69.

25. Ibid., p. 66.

26. Ibid., pp. 64–66.

27. Ibid., p. 67.

28. Ibid.

29. Ibid., pp. 64–65.

30. Laqueur demonstrates that these hygienic arguments were largely invented, rather than being based on medical evidence. See especially Laqueur, *The Work of the Dead*, pp. 211–38.

31. Ariès, *The Hour of Our Death*, pp. 475–96.

32. Neolithic people often buried their dead under the floors of their houses and oriented them in ways that suggest the harmonization of domesticity, death, and cosmic concerns.

33. Anthony Vidler, *Claude-Nicholas Ledoux: Architecture and Social Reform at the End of the Ancien Régime* (Cambridge, MA: MIT Press, 1990).

34. Ariès, *The Hour of Our Death*, pp. 502–503.

35. Ibid, p. 494.

36. Ibid., p. 531.

37. George L. Mosse, *Fallen Soldiers: Reshaping the Memory of the World Wars* (New York: Oxford University Press, 1990), p. 46. War memorials have continued to be erected in Père-Lachaise throughout the twentieth century.

38. Spiro Kostof, *America by Design* (New York: Oxford University Press, 1987), p. 219.

39. Ibid., pp. 428–29.

40. Sergiusz Michalski, *Public Monuments: Art in Political Bondage 1870–1997* (London: Reaktion Books, 1998), p. 34.

41. Ariès, *The Hour of Our Death*, p. 547. Mosse, *Fallen Soldiers*, p. 44. Mosse notes that military cemeteries were established in 1862 in the United States, but that European nations would not systematize military cemeteries until after World War I. Mosse, *Fallen Soldiers*, p. 45.

42. Ariès, *The Hour of Our Death*, p. 549.

43. William Godwin, *Essay on Sepulchres* (London: Printed for W. Miller, 1809), pp. 44–45.

44. Ibid., pp. 98–99.

45. Ibid., p. 100.

46. Ibid., p. 107.

47. Ibid., pp. 96, 99.

48. Ariès, *The Hour of Our Death*, p. 549.

49. Ibid.

50. Drew Gilpin Faust, *This Republic of Suffering: Death and the American Civil War* (New York: Alfred A. Knopf, 2008), p. 6.

51. Ibid.

52. Ibid.

53. Ibid., p. 9.

54. Ibid., pp. 6–9.

55. French, "The Cemetery as Cultural Institution," pp. 52, 56. Ariès, *The Hour of Our Death*, pp. 503 and 517. So linked are parks and cemeteries that in the late nineteenth century, *Park and Cemetery* was launched as a journal. In fact, it eventually became *Park and Cemetery and Landscape Gardening*, revealing just how interconnected these fields were.

56. Ariès, *The Hour of Our Death*, p. 533.

57. French, "The Cemetery as Cultural Institution," p. 37.

58. Bowditch was originally buried in Trinity Church in Boston but was later moved into a stone sarcophagus in Mount Auburn Cemetery that is distinct from his statue.

59. Alene Tchekmedyian, Veronica Rocha, and Irfan Khan, "Hollywood Forever Cemetery Removes Confederate Monument After Calls from Activists and Threats of Vandalism," *Los Angeles Times*, August 16, 2017, https://www.latimes.com/local/lanow/la-me-ln-hollywood-forever-monument-20170815-story.html.

60. Jessica Mitford, *The American Way of Death* (New York: Simon and Schuster, 1963).

61. Ariès, *The Hour of Our Death*, p. 553.

62. James Stevens Curl, "The Architecture and Planning of the Nineteenth-Century Cemetery," *Garden History* 3.3 (Summer 1975), p. 13.

63. Filippo Tommaso Marinetti, "The Founding and Manifesto of Futurism," in Lawrence Rainey, Christine Poggi, and Laura Wittman, eds., *Futurism: An Anthology* (New Haven: Yale University Press, 2009), p. 49; *Le Figaro*, February 20, 1909, p. 1.

64. Geoffrey Gorer, "The Pornography of Death," *Encounter*, October 1955, pp. 49–52.

65. This memorial, which became the focus of civil unrest, was moved to the cemetery of Estonian Defense Forces. Julia Bryan-Wilson, "Monument Monumentum," in Mihnea Mircan, ed., *Undone / Hans van Houwelingen* (Heijningen: Jap Sam Books, 2001), p. 87. Two statues of Confederate soldiers in Lexington, Kentucky were moved from the courthouse square to a cemetery. See Stu Johnson, "Confederate Statues In Lexington Moved To Cemetery," *WKMS*, https://www.wkms.org/post/confederate-statues-lexington-moved-cemetery#stream/0. See also Dell Upton's discussion of the Nathan Bedford Forrest monument in Selma, Alabama, in Upton, *What Can and Can't Be Said*, p. 49. The Monument to the Liberators of Tallinn tells a similar story.

66. Thanks go to Louisa Hoffman, an archivist at the Oberlin College Archives.

67. Thomas Bender, "The 'Rural' Cemetery Movement: Urban Travail and the Appeal of Nature," *New England Quarterly* 47.2 (June 1974), p. 207.

68. George F. Chadwick, *The Park and the Town: Public Landscape in the 19th and 20th Centuries* (London: The Architectural Press, 1966), p. 182.

69. Andrew Jackson Downing, *A Treatise on the Theory and Practice of Landscape Gardening* (1841; New York: A. O. Moore, 1859), p. 561.

70. David Schuyler, *The New Urban Landscape: The Redefinition of City Form in Nineteenth-Century America* (Baltimore: Johns Hopkins University Press, 1986), p. 101. Statuemania is a recurring theme in Michalski, *Public Monuments*, especially pp. 17, 29, 31, 34, 44, 49–54.

71. For example, see Charles H. W. Smith, *Landscape Gardening, or Parks and Pleasure Grounds* (New York: C. M. Saxton, 1853); Clarence Cook, *A Description of the New York Central Park* (New York: F. J. Huntington, 1869).

72. Schuyler, *The New Urban Landscape*, pp. 64–67.

73. Ibid., p. 59.

74. Kostof, *America by Design*, p. 211.

75. Ibid.

76. Ibid., p. 214. See also Edward T. Price, "The Central Courthouse Square in the American County Seat," in Dell Upton and John Michael Vlach, eds., *Common Places: Readings in American Vernacular Architecture* (Athens: University of Georgia Press, 1986), pp. 124–45.

77. Kostof, *America by Design*, p. 214.

78. Ibid.

79. Ibid., p. 216. In this way, they are of a piece with the world's fairs that came of

age in the same moment. Paul Rydell, *All the World's a Fair: Visions of Empire at American International Expositions, 1876–1916* (Chicago: University of Chicago Press, 1984), pp. 2–3.

80. Rydell, *All the World's a Fair*, p. 2.

81. Kostof, *America by Design*, p. 222. Schuyler, *The New Urban Landscape*, p. 93.

82. Degas's idea is mentioned in Michalski, *Public Monuments*, p. 45, but the source is not cited.

83. Galen Cranz, *The Politics of Park Design: A History of Urban Parks in America* (Cambridge, MA: MIT Press, 1982), pp. 55–56.

84. Kostof, *America by Design*, p. 226.

85. Ibid.

86. Atypically, the memorial was dedicated only in 1941, but the stock doughboy statue comes from a cast copyrighted in 1920.

87. François Hartog, *Regimes of Historicity: Presentism and Experiences of Time*, trans. Saskia Brown (New York: Columbia University Press), p. 149. Hartog links heritage to a series of cultural preconditions, including traditions of collecting and conservation, alongside modern attitudes about "a past that the present cannot or does not want to relinquish" (p. 152).

88. See Jack Pearce, "Every Woman Memorial, Women's Park, Warren, Ohio," https://www.flickr.com/photos/jwpearce/9546238929.

89. Michèle McHugh Griffin, "As a Woman I Have No Country," *Peace Review* 10.2 (1998), pp. 255–59.

90. In Winchester, England, a plan to place a Jane Austen memorial on the cathedral grounds could set up a similar counterpoint with the King's Royal Rifle Corps War Memorial. Austen would appear eerily like "every woman," framed by bronzed foliage.

91. Kostof, *America by Design*, p. 236.

92. Schuyler, *The New Urban Landscape*, pp. 96–97. By this time, the French had changed their approach and looked to England. Having grown "tired and frightened by Haussmann's changes of the Parisian street system," they placed new monuments "in gardens and public parks seemingly at random." Michalski, *Public Monuments*, p. 29.

93. Schuyler, *The New Urban Landscape*, p. 186. See J. B. Jackson's lively account of the proponents of statues in Central Park in *American Space: The Centennial Years, 1865–1876* (New York: Norton, 1972), especially p. 211.

94. For debates in New York City about placement, see Michele H. Bogart, *Public Sculpture and the Civic Ideal in New York City, 1890–1930* (Chicago: University of Chicago Press,

1989), pp. 18–19, 201–202, 185–86. For the "City Beautiful" and statuary, see pp. 55–60, 69–70.

95. "New Statues in New York," *Garden and Forest*, August 15, 1894, p. 322.

96. Mariana Griswold Van Rensselaer, *Art Out-of-Doors: Hints on Good Taste in Gardening* (1893; New York: Charles Scribner's Sons, 1925), p. 206.

97. The same attitude has continued to this day under the aegis of cultural resources management. See "Public Monuments and Outdoor Sculpture," special issue, *Cultural Resources Management* 18.1 (1995). Kirk Savage notes: "In the nineteenth century monuments were expected to double as high art and popular expression. They were usually thought of as architectural landmarks." Kirk Savage, *Standing Soldiers, Kneeling Slaves: Race, War, and Monument in Nineteenth-Century America* (Princeton: Princeton University Press, 1997), p. 66.

98. Van Rensselaer, *Art Out-of-Doors*, p. 213. This attitude continued to dominate Anglo-American thinking on the subject through much of the twentieth century. The British architect Hugh Casson wrote: "Then we see many a beautiful prospect ruined with some frumpish, lumpish memorial to a person outstandingly unmemorable." Hugh Casson, ed., *Monuments* (New York: Taplinger, 1965), p. 10.

99. Van Rensselaer, *Art Out-of-Doors*, p. 213.

100. Ibid.

101. Ibid., p. 215.

102. Ibid., p. 221.

103. Henry Vincent Hubbard and Theodora Kimball, *An Introduction to the Study of Landscape Design* (1917; New York: Macmillan, 1924), p. 211.

104. George Burnap, *Parks: Their Design, Equipment, and Use* (Philadelphia: J. B. Lippincott, 1916), p. 178.

105. Chadwick, *The Park and the Town*, p. 184.

106. Reginald Blomfield and F. Inigo Thomas, *The Formal Garden in England* (London: Macmillan, 1892), p. 214.

107. Burnap, *Parks*, p. 177.

108. Ibid., pp. 174–78.

109. Ibid., p. 172.

110. Frederick Law Olmsted, Jr., "Parks as Memorials," *American Magazine of Art*, September 1919, pp. 415–19. For a meditation on the rise of names on memorials, see Thomas W. Laqueur, "Memory and Naming in the Great War," in John R. Gillis, ed., *Commemorations: The Politics of National Identity* (Princeton: Princeton University Press), pp. 150–67.

111. On cemeteries as memorial parks, see J. B. Jackson, "Vanishing Epitaph," *Landscape*

17–18 (Winter 1967–68), p. 25.

112. Stephen Jay Gould, *Time's Arrow, Time's Cycle: Myth and Metaphor in the Discovery of Geological Time* (Cambridge, MA: Harvard University Press, 1987); Andrew M. Shanken, "Keeping Time with the Good War," *American Studies Journal* 59 (Spring 2015). The latter is an online journal, http://www.asjournal.org/59-2015/keeping-time-with-the-good-war.

113. Schuyler, *The New Urban Landscape*, p. 93.

114. Valentina Rozas-Krause, "Memorials and the Cult of Apology," PhD diss., University of California, Berkeley, 2020, p. 53.

115. Mircea Eliade, *Cosmos and History: The Myth of the Eternal Return*, trans. Willard R. Trask (New York: Harper and Brothers, 1959), pp. 46, 48, 95.

116. I thank Amanda Su for drawing my attention to the example in Taiwan.

117. For instance, see Dolores Hayden, *The Power of Place: Urban Landscapes as Public History* (Cambridge, MA: MIT Press, 1995), pp. 46–48, and Edward S. Casey, *Remembering: A Phenomenological Study* (Bloomington: Indiana University Press, 1987), pp. 186–87.

118. Lambert, *Placing Sorrow*, p. xiv.

119. Karl Marx and Friedrich Engels, *The Communist Manifesto*, ed. Samuel H. Beer (New York: Appleton-Century-Crofts, 1955), p. 13.

CHAPTER FOUR: MISPLACING MEMORY

The epigraph is from Hugh Casson, ed., *Monuments* (New York: Taplinger, 1965), p. 10.

1. For instance, see Maya Bell, "Holocaust Memorial Stirs Anger," *Orlando Sentinel*, January 28, 1990, https://www.orlandosentinel.com/news/os-xpm-1990-01-28-9001263238-story.html.

2. Information about the memorial comes from Holocaust Memorial Miami Beach website, https://holocaustmemorialmiamibeach.org/about/history.

3. Mariana Griswold Van Rensselaer, *Art Out-of-Doors: Hints on Good Taste in Gardening* (1893; New York: Charles Scribner's Sons, 1925), pp. 213–14.

4. George Burnap, *Parks: Their Design, Equipment, and Use* (Philadelphia: J. B. Lippincott, 1916), p. 92. See also L. H. Weir, ed., *Parks: A Manual of Municipal and County Parks . . .*, 2 vols. (New York: A. S. Barnes, 1928), vol. 1, pp. 171–72.

5. Michele H. Bogart, *Public Sculpture and the Civic Ideal in New York City, 1890–1930* (Chicago: University of Chicago Press, 1989), pp. 66–68.

6. For every formally placed monument, Paris has an abundance of more informally situated ones, such as Ernest Guilbert's Monument to Etienne Dolet, which sits on an

irregular patch of pavement on Place Maubert at the convergence of multiple streets. For the role of elegy in creating settings for death, see Ellen Zetzel Lambert, *Placing Sorrow: A Study of the Pastoral Elegy Convention from Theocritus to Milton* (Chapel Hill: University of North Carolina Press, 1976).

7. For an analysis of the memorials in Whitehall, see Quentin Stevens and Shanti Sumartojo, "Memorial Planning in London," *Journal of Urban Design* 20.5 (August 2015), pp. 623–25.

8. So effective is this site that the Women of World II Memorial joined it in the median.

9. Double-decker buses came into use only after World War II in London, but double-decker trams had been in existence since the late nineteenth century, the first ones being horse-drawn.

10. The placement of the Royal Fusiliers Memorial followed earlier precedents. The earliest model in London is the equestrian statue of Charles I, which found its place at Charing Cross in the late seventeenth century. It replaced a medieval Eleanor Cross. A more contemporary example is the equestrian statue of Prince Albert unveiled in 1874 in nearby Holborn Circus — really a convergence of many roads. After more recent reorientation of the roads, Albert now sits in the median like the Royal Fusilier. As originally sited, Albert raised his hat courteously to other horsemen, carriages, and strollers at the Circus, which Charles Dickens, Jr., the novelist's son, described as "the finest piece of street architecture in the City." Charles Dickens, Jr., *Dickens's Dictionary of London: An Unconventional Handbook* (1888; Moretonhampstead: Old House Books, 1993), s.v. "Holborn." If nothing else, Albert entered a fashionable and exceedingly modern urban setting, one soon choked with traffic. The Royal Fusiliers just entered the traffic.

11. Tracy Wilkinson, "A New Battle: Latino Veterans Fight to Protect East L.A. Memorial," *Los Angeles Times,* April 19, 1990, https://www.latimes.com/archives/la-xpm-1990-04-19-me-2198-story.html. Vertical Files, Chicago Resource Center, Los Angeles County Library, Los Angeles. The Department of Public Works sandblasts graffiti.

12. See the various Boyle Heights Community plans from the Los Angeles Department of City Planning in 1974, 1978, 1980, 1985, and 1998. These can be found at the map collections at the University of California, Los Angeles, and the Los Angeles Public Library.

13. See Barrio Planners Incorporated, *Nuestro Ambiente East Los Angeles Visual Survey and Analysis* (1973). University of California, Berkeley, library.

14. "City Says Boyle Heights Traffic Roundabout Is Moving in Right Direction," *Eastsider,* January 16, 2014, https://www.theeastsiderla.com/real_estate/

architecture_and_urban_design/city-says-boyle-heights-traffic-roundabout-is-moving-in-the-right-direction/article_e4e06782-b65f-5753-a972-3db83b748403.html. In a series of emails and calls to the Los Angeles Department of Planning, I couldn't find a single planner who knew the site or memorial. While the planners were curious and helpful, it became clear that Cinco Puntos is not on their radar.

15. Since archival sources for this area are scarce, it is unclear when these commemorative strategies began or how they have evolved. The Chicano Resource Center has clippings files going back decades but almost nothing on the origins and development of the site. The area is so institutionally fragile that the local Veterans of Foreign Wars and American Legion posts, though active, have no contact information.

16. See figure 9.4 in Bogart, *Public Sculpture and the Civic Ideal in New York City*, p. 190. Sergei Eisenstein must have seen similar street dramas in Riga and St. Petersburg.

17. Olmsted and Vaux, map of Central Park, 1870. The map was prepared for the Thirteenth Annual Report of the Board of Commissioners of Central Park.

18. Bogart, *Public Sculpture and the Civic Ideal in New York City*, p. 61.

19. *Oxford English Dictionary* online, s.v. "Circle."

20. The best account is still John Bodnar, *Remaking America: Public Memory, Commemoration, and Patriotism in the Twentieth Century* (Princeton: Princeton University Press, 1993), pp. 78–93.

21. James Philip Fadely, "The Veteran and the Memorial: George J. Gangsdale and the Soldiers and Sailors Monument," *Traces of Indiana and Midwestern History* 18.1 (Winter 2006), pp. 33–35.

22. Bodnar, *Remaking America*, p. 81.

23. Mauricio Tenorio Trillo, "1910 Mexico City: Space and Nation in the City of the Centenario," *Journal of Latin American* Studies 28.1 (February 1996), p. 86. Dozens of other commemorative statues punctuate the Paseo de la Reforma.

24. See Françoise Choay's analysis of the rise of the monument as a shift in mentality in *The Invention of the Historic Monument*, trans. Lauren M. O'Connell (New York: Cambridge University Press, 2001).

25. Robert Rosenblum, *Transformations in Late Eighteenth-Century Art* (Princeton: Princeton University Press, 1967), pp. 50–51.

26. Ibid., pp. 50–51.

27. Ibid., p. 56.

28. In a similar vein, François Hartog writes: "The topics of *historia magistra* had

allowed the past to connect with the future through the exemplary model to be imitated: in looking back at famous men, I could also find them in front or ahead of me." François Hartog, *Regimes of Historicity: Presentism and Experiences of Time*, trans. Saskia Brown (New York: Columbia University Press, 2015), p. 105.

29. Rosenblum, *Transformations in Late Eighteenth-Century Art*, pp. 50–51.

30. Rosalind Krauss, "Sculpture in the Expanded Field," *October* 8 (Spring 1979), p. 33.

31. Rosenblum, *Transformations in Late Eighteenth-Century Art*, p. 72.

32. Ibid., p. 75. John Onians, "Greek Temple and Greek Brain," in George Dodds and Robert Tavernor. eds., *Body and Building: Essays on the Changing Relation of Body and Architecture* (Cambridge, MA: MIT Press, 2002), p. 54.

33. See Choay, *The Invention of the Historic Monument*, pp. 63–80.

34. The memorial as *exemplum virtutis* could take many forms. In places where the Gothic was central to national identity, the Gothic Revival expanded the vocabulary to spires or medieval ciboria. The Martyrs Memorial (George Gilbert Scott, 1843), which sits at a crossroads in Oxford, is but one of many examples that appeared in American and British towns in the mid to late nineteenth century. The memorial commemorates three Protestants who were burned at the stake for their beliefs. Real medieval monuments, such as the Eleanor Crosses erected by Edward I after the death of his wife, may have served as models. The Prussian National Monument for the Wars of Liberation in Kreuzberg, Berlin (1826) and the now destroyed Civil War Memorial in Oberlin, Ohio (1871), are two other examples.

35. Michel de Certeau held a bleaker view: "Called *Everyman* (a name that betrays the absence of a name), this anti-hero is thus also *Nobody, Nemo*." Michel de Certeau, *The Practice of Everyday Life*, trans. Steven F. Rendall (Berkeley: University of California Press, 1984), p. 2.

36. The phenomenon is widely noted, but too easily dismissed as a symptom of the period of nation building and the invention of tradition in Europe. The "'great man' metonymically represented the nation." Karen E. Till, "Places of Memory," in John Agnew, Katharyne Mitchel, and Gerard Toal, eds., *Companion to Political Geography* (Malden: Blackwell, 2003), pp. 292–94.

37. Part of the invention of tradition, these figures joined the barbarian Arminius, who defeated Roman legions in the Teutoburg Forest, among other figures lost in the murky past of Europe.

38. Casson, ed., *Monuments*, p. 23.

39. A parallel can be found in other post-Soviet lands, such as Serbia, where in 1989,

Slobodan Milosevic rededicated Gazimestan (literally "hero place"), a medievalized monument to the Battle of Kosovo of 1389, that was built in 1953 to the design of Aleksandar Deroko. Each year, the monument is draped with a neo-Byzantine icon of Prince Lazar, the hero of the battle, who stands with a decapitated head of the vanquished Turkish sultan tucked under his arm. The annual commemoration lines up with St. Vitus Day, an important day in the Serbian Orthodox calendar, Vidov Day, when a Bosnian Serb assassinated Archduke Ferdinand.

CHAPTER FIVE: DISPLACING MEMORY

An earlier version of this essay was published as "Meet Me at the Plague Column: Monuments and Conservation Planning," *Future Anterior* 14.1 (Summer 2017), pp. 126–41.

1. For Klagenfurt's cultural history, see Siegfried Hartwanger, *Klagenfurt, Stadt: Ihre Kunstwerke, historischen Lebens- und Siedlungsformen* (Salzburg: St. Peter, 1980), and Dieter Jandl, *A Brief History of Klagenfurt* (Klagenfurt: Heyn, 2000).

2. More recently, the city followed the capitulation of European cities to automobile tourism and dug a parking garage under the Renaissance Neuer Platz that abuts the Altstadt. This move thrust elevators and stairwells into the Neuer Platz, disrupting sight lines and pedestrian paths and bringing travel directly into the square.

3. Arthur E. Imhof, *Lost Worlds: How Our European Ancestors Coped with Everyday Life and Why Life Is So Hard Today* (Charlottesville: University of Virginia Press, 1996), pp. 4–6.

4. Ibid., p. 7.

5. At the time of writing, the Covid-19 pandemic threatens to challenge this assertion about plague. Time will tell if it is a blip in history or marks a sea change in the human relationship to disease.

6. As an aside, commemorative place names (toponyms) have also been "displaced." The Neuer Platz was formerly called Adolf Hitler-Platz (from 1938 until the end of the war), and before that, Franz-Joseph-Platz and Dollfußplatz, after Engelbert Dollfuß, the chancellor of Austria in the early 1930s.

7. Originally, an angel was awkwardly perched on her eminence, which trumpeted the perpetual arrival of the empress of the Hapsburg Empire. In a dizzying catalog of changes, she now sits on the base of a seventeenth-century monument to her grandfather, Leopold I, who was melted down for his metal. Maria Theresa met the same fate as her grandfather, but she was rebuilt in 1870, liberated from her angel, and mounted on a different base.

8. For a discussion of the reconstruction of Nuremberg after the war, see Nancy Moses

Finch, *Fakes, Forgeries, and Frauds* (Lanham: Rowman and Littlefield, 2020), especially pp. 85–108.

9. To be sure, fanciful statues such as the *Mandl* have a long history. The most obvious precedents for him are the *Mannekin Pis* in Brussels (originally 1619) and the *Gooseman* of Nuremberg (mid-sixteenth century), a fountain statue of a man holding a goose under each arm while water gushes out of their mouths into the basin. Like the *Mandl*, the *Gooseman* is understood as a drunk.

10. Related issues can be found in D. Medina Lasansky and Brian McLaren, eds., *Architecture and Tourism* (Oxford: Berg, 2004).

11. G. J. Ashworth, "From History to Heritage: From Heritage to Identity: In Search of Concepts and Models," in Gregory Ashworth and Peter Larkham, eds., *Building a New Heritage: Tourism, Culture, and Identity in the New Europe* (London: Routledge, 1994), pp. 13–30.

12. Spiro Kostof, *The City Shaped: Urban Patterns and Meanings through History* (London: Thames and Hudson, 1991), p. 82.

13. G. J. Ashworth and J. E. Tunbridge, *The Tourist-Historic City* (London: Belhaven, 1990), p. 102.

14. Ibid. See also Brian Graham, G. J. Ashworth, and J. E. Tunbridge, *A Geography of Heritage: Power, Culture and Economy* (New York: Routledge, 2000).

15. For the general context, see the essays in Ashworth and Larkham, eds., *Building a New Heritage*. Also, see Kostof, *The City Shaped*, p. 82.

16. Ashworth and Tunbridge, *The Tourist-Historic City*, pp. 10–14.

17. Ibid., p. 13.

18. Françoise Choay, *The Invention of the Historic Monument*, trans. Lauren M. O'Connell (Cambridge: Cambridge University Press, 2001), especially pp. 117–37.

19. Ashworth and Tunbridge, *The Tourist-Historic City*, p. 14.

20. Le Corbusier, *The City of Tomorrow and Its Planning*, trans. Frederick Etchells (London: J. Rodker, 1929).

21. Ashworth and Tunbridge, *The Tourist-Historic City*, p. 17. See also Zbigniew Zuziak, *Managing Historic Cities* (Krakow: International Cultural Centre, 1993), and Zuziak, *Managing Tourism in Historic Cities* (Krakow: International Cultural Centre, 1992).

22. Camillo Sitte, *Der Städtebau nach seinen künstlerischen Grundsätzen* (Vienna: G. Prachner, 1965). The same year, Christiane Crasemann Collins and George R. Collins published their English translation, *City Planning According to Artistic Principles* (London: Phaidon, 1965). I thank Marta Gutman for suggesting the connection to Sitte.

23. Kostof, *The City Shaped*, pp. 82–83.

24. Sitte, *City Planning According to Artistic Principles*, pp. 156–57.

25. Ibid., p. 162.

26. Gordon Cullen, *The Concise Townscape* (London, Architectural Press, 1971), p. 17.

27. Kevin Lynch, *The Image of the City* (Cambridge, MA: MIT Press, 1960).

28. Ibid., p. 102.

29. Ibid.

30. For the resonance of the Holocaust in Austria, see chapter 4 in James E. Young, *The Texture of Memory: Holocaust Memorials and Meaning* (New Haven: Yale University Press, 1993), pp. 91–112.

31. The idea that monuments are allegorical is drawn from Choay, *The Invention of the Historic Monument*.

32. Joseph Hudnut, "The Monument Does Not Remember," *Atlantic Monthly*, September 1945, p. 57.

33. Manuel Castells, *The Informational City: Information, Technology, Economic Restructuring and the Urban-Regional Process* (Oxford: Blackwell, 1989).

34. Ibid., p. 348.

35. Ibid.

36. Ibid., p. 349.

37. Jean Baudrillard, *Simulacra and Simulation*, trans. Shiela Faria Glaser (Ann Arbor: University of Michigan Press, 1994), especially pp. 164–84.

38. For a nineteenth-century example, see Andrew M. Shanken, "Preservation and Creation: Alfonso Rubbiani and Bologna," *Future Anterior* 7.1 (Summer 2010), pp. 61–81. For the Italian fascist example, see D. Medina Lasansky, "Urban Editing, Historic Preservation, and Political Rhetoric: The Fascist Redesign of San Gimignano," *Journal of the Society of Architectural Historians* 63.3 (September 2004), pp. 320–53.

39. Castells, *The Informational City*, p. 349.

40. As I write this, I'm under a stay-at-home order in Berkeley, California due to the Covid-19 pandemic. Time will tell whether this pandemic becomes as indistinct as the one that swept through Klagenfurt long ago or if it will settle into history in some more substantial way. Either way, as this most recent world-historical disease spread through Austria, people in Vienna turned to their famous plague column, lighting candles and leaving messages. They transformed this long-dormant column, now a fixture of tourism, into an active memorial again.

CHAPTER SIX: MUSTERING MEMORY

1. Walter Benjamin, "On the Concept of History," in Howard Eiland and Michael W. Jennings, eds., *Walter Benjamin: Selected Writings, Volume 4, 1938–1940* (Cambridge, MA: Belknap Press of Harvard University Press, 2003), p. 392.

2. Ibid.

3. George Hersey, *The Lost Meaning of Classical Architecture: Speculations on Ornament from Vitruvius to Venturi* (Cambridge, MA: MIT Press, 1992), p. 9.

4. See George L. Mosse, *Fallen Soldiers: Reshaping the Memory of the World Wars* (New York: Oxford University Press, 1990).

5. Reinhart Koselleck, *Sediment of Time: On Possible Histories*, ed. and trans. Sean Franzel and Stefan-Ludwig Hoffmann (Stanford: Stanford University Press, 2018), p. 4.

6. I've borrowed this phrase from David Brownlee, who used "making space for time" in a talk on nineteenth-century architecture at the University of Pennsylvania in 2000.

7. Dorothy Stroud, "Hyde Park Corner," *Architectural Review* 106 (December 1949), p. 397.

8. Ibid.

9. Steven Brindle, "The Wellington Arch and the Western Entrance to London," *Georgian Group Journal* 11 (2001), pp. 47–51.

10. Ibid., p. 59.

11. Ibid., p. 61.

12. Ibid., p. 64.

13. Ibid., pp. 65–66.

14. Ibid., p. 47.

15. See, for instance, "Hyde Park Corner: Proposed Alterations," 1882, Work 32/416, National Archives, Kew. Hereafter "Kew."

16. This had been in discussion for over a decade. See "Plan of Hyde Park Corner," ca. 1872, Work 32/138, Kew.

17. Brindle, "The Wellington Arch and the Western Entrance to London," p. 80.

18. Ibid., p. 47.

19. Ibid., p. 80.

20. These are apparent in maps from the 1882. See, for instance, "Mr. Mitford's Proposed Improvements," January 10, 1882, Work 32/416, Kew.

21. Stephen Heathorn, "The Civil Servant and Public Remembrance: Sir Lionel Earle and the Shaping of London's Commemorative Landscape, 1918–1933," *Twentieth Century British History* 19.3 (January 1, 2008), pp. 267–68.

22. Lionel Earle to Sir Henry Sclater, August 11, 1920, Pro Works/20/151, Kew. For the larger context of Earl's work, see Heathorn, "The Civil Servant and Public Remembrance."

23. Lionel Earle to Sir Henry Sclater, July 17, 1920, Pro Works/20/151, Kew.

24. The Committee on Sites for Monuments in the London Area, Meeting Notes, undated, Prof Works/20/151, Kew.

25. The Committee on Sites for Monuments in the London Area, Meeting Notes, June 28, 1921, Pro Works/20/151, Kew.

26. Such mundane issues as traffic often played an outsized role in the placement of memorials. Similar issues surrounded the World War I memorial in Cambridge, England. See Jay Winter, *Sites of Memory, Sites of Mourning: The Great War in European Cultural History* (Cambridge: Cambridge University Press, 1995), p. 86.

27. LGB (?) to Lionel Earle, March 20, 1924, Pro Works/20/151, Kew.

28. The complexities of memorial planning in London are discussed in Quentin Stevens and Shanti Sumartojo, "Memorial Planning in London," *Journal of Urban Design* 20.5 (August 2015), pp. 615–35.

29. Sir Lionel Earle rejected the use of royal parks out of hand, using much the same logic that Olmsted and Van Rensselaer had used a generation earlier in the American context. See Heathorn, "The Civil Servant and Public Remembrance," pp. 269–70.

30. "Machine Gun Corps Memorial Unveiled," May 10, 1925, Pro Works 20/146, Kew.

31. Sir Henry Slater to Lionel Earle, July 3, 1920, Pro Works/20/151, Kew.

32. Stroud, "Hyde Park Corner," p. 397.

33. "Re-Planning Hyde Park Corner: A Scheme by Sir Edwin Lutyens, R.A., and Sir Charles Bressey," *Architect and Building News*, May 1937, pp. 146–47.

34. *Truth*, May 5, 1937, which can be found in Work 16/1095, Kew.

35. Ministry of Works, January 23, 1958, Works/20/221, Kew. A similar story can be told in Paris. See Sergiusz Michalski, *Public Monuments: Art in Political Bondage 1870–1997* (London: Reaktion Books, 1998), p. 167.

36. On the obsession with memory, see Paul Fussell, *The Great War and Modern Memory* (Oxford: Oxford University Press, 1975), and Stephen Heathorn, "The Mnemonic Turn in the Cultural Historiography of Britain's Great War," *Historical Journal* 48.4 (2005), pp. 1103–24.

37. The literature on this is too vast to cite, but Heathorn provides historiographical

commentary on it in "The Mnemonic Turn in the Cultural Historiography of Britain's Great War," pp. 1103–10.

38. Paul Fussell, *Wartime: Understanding and Behavior in the Second World War* (New York: Oxford University Press, 1989), p. 132.

39. "Royal Artillery Memorial," *Builder*, June, 1949, pp. 711–12.

40. In fact, the rebuilding of the churches of Christopher Wren was seen as a form of memorialization, one that echoed the rebuilding of London after the Great Fire of 1666.

41. Various other memorials to World War II have found their place nearby. The Chindit Forces Memorial (David Price, architect, 1990) was dedicated to the soldiers recruited from Burma, Hong Kong, India, Nepal, West Africa, and elsewhere who fought in Burma during World War II. The Canadian Memorial (Pierre Granche, sculptor, 1994) at Queen's Gardens at the east end of Green Park was dedicated to the Canadians who served in both world wars. The RAF Bomber Command Memorial was installed in Green Park in 2012. The Monument to the Women of World War II (John W. Mills, 2005) was placed in the median on Whitehall about three hundred feet north of the Cenotaph. A bit farther afield, the Gurkha Regiments Memorial was erected in Whitehall.

42. Stevens and Sumartojo, "Memorial Planning in London," p. 619.

43. Roger H. Bowdler and Steven P. Brindle, *Wellington Arch, Marble Arch and Six Great War Memorials* (London: English Heritage, 2015).

44. Stevens and Sumartojo show how proximity has been used as an argument in the placement of memorials in London, "Memorial Planning in London," pp. 619, 622.

45. Mosse, *Fallen Soldiers*, pp. 15–36.

46. Jay Winter draws this connection in *Sites of Memory, Sites of Mourning*, p. 223.

47. See Dell Upton, *What Can and Can't Be Said: Race, Uplift, and Monument Building in the Contemporary South* (New Haven: Yale University Press, 2015).

48. Philip Johnson, "War Memorials: What Aesthetic Price Glory?," *Art News*, September 1945, p. 9.

49. For the Skansen, see Michael Conan, "The Fiddler's Indecorous Nostalgia," in Terence Young and Robert Riley, eds., *Theme Park Landscapes: Antecedents and Variations* (Washington, DC: Dumbarton Oaks Research Library and Collection, 2002), pp. 91–117.

50. For the *centro storico*, see Filippo De Pieri, "Un paese di centri storici: Urbanistica e identità locali negli anni Cinquanta e Sessanta," *Rassenga di architettura e urbanistica* 46.136 (2002), pp. 92–100.

CHAPTER SEVEN: ASSEMBLING MEMORY

1. Henri Lefebvre, *Critique of Everyday Life*, trans. John Moore, 3 vols. (1947; New York: Verso, 1991), vol. 1, pp. 118–19.

2. Ibid., p. 119.

3. It is all part of an attempt to stimulate tourism in a town whose population has been in steady decline since World War II and that depends on tourism, particularly hiking.

4. James E. Young, "The Counter-Monument: Memory against Itself in Germany Today," *Critical Inquiry* 18.2 (Winter 1992), pp. 269–70.

5. For references to the metaphorical roof, see Erving Goffman, *Behavior in Public Places: Notes on the Social Organization of Gatherings* (New York: Free Press, 1963), pp. 102, 141, 153, 155–56.

6. See James E. Young, "Austria's Ambivalent Memory," in Young, *The Texture of Memory: Holocaust Memorials and Meaning* (New Haven: Yale University Press, 1993), pp. 91–112.

7. George L. Mosse, *Fallen Soldiers: Reshaping the Memory of the World Wars* (New York: Oxford University Press, 1990), p. 160. For martial rhetoric in the United States between the wars, see William E. Leuchtenburg, "The New Deal and the Analogue of War," in Leuchtenburg, *The FDR Years: On Roosevelt and His Legacy* (New York: Columbia University Press, 1995), pp. 35–75. In France, the connection between the two wars is particularly poignant: see Pierre Miquel, *Les Poilus: La France sacrifiée* (Paris: Plon, 2000), p. 428. Miquel goes so far as to conflate the wars as "la guerre de trente ans."

8. Antoine Prost, "Monuments to the Dead," in Pierre Nora and Lawrence D. Kritzman, eds., *Realms of Memory: The Construction of the French Past*, trans. Arthur Goldhammer, 3 vols. (New York: Columbia University Press, 1996), vol. 2, p. 308. Prost creates a taxonomy of different World War I memorials in France.

9. See John Bodnar, "Pierre Nora, National Memory, and Democracy: A Review," *Journal of American History* 87.3 (December 2000), p. 956.

10. See Mosse, *Fallen Soldiers*, pp. 160–81, especially the case of the Nazi memorial to the assassins of Walther Rathenau, p. 169.

11. I thank Leonhard Herrmann of the University of Leipzig for pointing this out.

12. Mosse details Christian motifs in *Fallen Soldiers*. The resurrection theme can be found on pp. 72–79, 105, 110. Also see Jay Winter, *Sites of Memory, Sites of Mourning: The Great War in European Cultural History* (Cambridge: Cambridge University Press, 1995), p. 85.

13. "War Memorials Advisory Council," *Journal of the Royal Society of Arts* 95.4736 (January 31, 1947), p. 156. Edwin Lutyens expressed a similar idea. See Mosse, *Fallen Soldiers*, p. 221.

14. Remembrance Day in the Commonwealth became formalized in 1919. In the United States Memorial Day began after the Civil War as Decoration Day and was increasingly formalized after World War I. Veterans Day originally marked the service of veterans of World War I, becoming a holiday after the Korean War.

15. The habit has jumped from war memorials to monuments of other kinds. In Bowling Green, Virginia, a small obelisk marking African-American history was designed with one side blank in anticipation of adding content later. See Dell Upton, *What Can and Can't Be Said: Race, Uplift, and Monument Building in the Contemporary South* (New Haven: Yale University Press, 2015), p. 67.

16. These issues were broached in the context of reconsidering commemoration of World War II in *American Studies Journal* 59 (2015). Remarkably, it came out of a session at the American Studies Association run by two German scholars, Birgit Däwes and Ingrid Gessne, who also edited the issue. Susan Neiman explicitly calls for an American form of *Vergangenheitsbewältigung* in her *Learning from the Germans: Confronting Race and the Memory of Evil* (London: Allen Lane, 2019).

17. This account of the memorial is drawn from Geoffrey Blodgett's excellent history, *Oberlin Architecture, College and Town: A Guide to Its Social History* (Kent: Kent State University Press, 1985), pp. 207–208.

18. Richard P. Harmond and Thomas J. Curran, *A History of Memorial Day: Unity, Discord and the Pursuit of Happiness* (New York: Peter Lang, 2002).

19. I thank Professor Erik Inglis of Oberlin for photographs and more recent information on the memorial.

20. Penny Balkin Bach, *Public Art in Philadelphia* (Philadelphia: Temple University Press, 1992), pp. 125 and 226. See also Association for Public Art, "All Wars Memorial to Colored Soldiers and Sailors (1934)," https://www.associationforpublicart.org/artwork/all-wars-memorial-to-colored-soldiers-and-sailors.

21. "McAllen TX War Memorial Park," *War Memorial HQ*, http://www.warmemorialhq.org/items/show/318. This is a National Endowment for the Humanities sponsored website on the history of memorials.

22. "WWI Walls Complete at McAllen's Veterans War Memorial of Texas," *The Monitor*, April 10, 2016, https://mcallenmonitor.newspaperarchive.com/mcallen-monitor/2015-05-10/page-37/.

23. The Barry Goldwater Memorial in Paradise Valley, Arizona, is also car dependent for similar reasons. It sits at an intersection of upscale subdivisions and resorts, where the

corners are set back and landscaped. This is land with no income potential, but useful as a visual barrier and signage.

24. This account draws on Benjamin Forest and Juliet Johnson, "Unraveling the Threads of History: Soviet-Era Monuments and Post-Soviet National Identity in Moscow," *Annals of the Association of American Geographers* 92.3 (September 2002), pp. 524–47.

25. See Valerie Sperling, "Making the Public Patriotic: Militarism and Anti-Militarism in Russia," in Marlène Laruelle, ed., *Russian Nationalism and the National Reassertion of Russia* (London: Routledge, 2009), especially p. 245.

26. Victoria Haydenko interprets Defenders of the Fatherland Day in the Ukraine quite differently. She writes that it has been transformed into "Day of the Mother-land's Defense," a change in gender that makes sense of its doubling as Men's Day. "In this case," she writes, "military service for men is a proof of their masculinity, while for women it symbolizes their safety and protection." Victoria Haydenko, "The For-mation of Gender Differences among the Young during Post-Communist Transition in Ukraine," in Lisa N. Gurley, Claudia Leeb, and Anna Aloisia Moser, eds., *Feminists Contest Politics and Philosophy* (Brussels: P.I.E.-Peter Lang, 2005), pp. 219–71, especially p. 245.

27. Benjamin Forest and Juliet Johnson, "Unraveling the Threads of History: Soviet-Era Monuments and Post-Soviet National Identity in Moscow," a talk delivered at the Annals of the Association of American Geographers, 2001, pp. 2 and 23–24. The talk can be found at: http://www.dartmouth.edu/~crn/crn_papers/Forest-Johnson.pdf.

CHAPTER EIGHT: WHAT WE DO AT MEMORIALS

1. On the Tomb of the Unknown Soldier, see Robert Poole, Patricia Blassie, Bill Thomas, Chris Calhoon, and Vince Gonzales, "The Known Unknown," episode 344, March 5, 2019, in *99% Invisible*, produced by Joe Rosenberg, podcast, 46:36, https://99percentinvisible.org/episode/the-known-unknown/. Thanks to Desiree Valadares for this reference.

2. Carole Blair, V. William Balthrop, and Neil Michel, "The Arguments of the Tombs of the Unknown Soldiers: Relationality and National Legitimation," *Argumentation* 25.4 (2011), pp. 449–68.

3. Tellingly, the very name of the memorial has never been formally designated.

4. At the British Tomb of the Unknown Soldier, different wards hold the everyday at bay. It sits in the nave of Westminster Abbey, a kind of English pantheon that is already a highly controlled space (which now requires a pricey admission ticket) where photographs

are forbidden, barring tourists from falling into conventions of behavior that would challenge the high intentions of the tomb.

5. The history of how people have intervened by guarding monuments or interposed
living bodies to protect markers of dead ones is a subject unto itself. The practice goes back
to maypoles in the eighteenth century. See Mona Ozouf, *Festivals and the French Revolution*,
trans. Alan Sheridan (Cambridge, MA: Harvard University Press, 1988), p. 241.

6. Erving Goffman, *Behavior in Public Places: Notes on the Social Organization of Gatherings* (New York: The Free Press, 1963), p. 25.

7. The idea of a socially circumscribed roof is drawn from Goffman, who writes about
carnival: "During these costumed street celebrations, a roof and its rights is by social
definition spread above the streets, bringing persons into contact — a contact facilitated
by their being out of role." Ibid., p. 137.

8. "Recreation Department," *Greenbelt News Review*, August 9, 1962, p. 6, and "Swimming Starts on Memorial Day," *Greenbelt Cooperator*, May 25, 1945, p. 3. "Pool, Tennis Courts
Jammed as Old Sol 'Turns on the Heat,'" *Greenbelt Cooperator*, June 12, 1942, p. 3.

9. James M. McPherson, "When Memorial Day Was No Picnic," *The New York Times*,
May 25, 1996, https://www.nytimes.com/2008/05/25/opinion/25opclassic.html. The contrast with the experience of Armistice Day in France is instructive. For the structure of
French commemorations, see Antoine Prost, "Monuments to the Dead," in Pierre Nora
and Lawrence D. Kritzman, eds., *Realms of Memory: The Construction of the French Past*,
trans. Arthur Goldhammer, 3 vols. (New York: Columbia University Press, 1996), vol. 2,
pp. 307–32.

10. McPherson, "When Memorial Day Was No Picnic."

11. Stephen Kern, *The Culture of Time and Space 1880–1918* (London: Weidenfeld and
Nicolson, 1983), p. 111.

12. McPherson, "When Memorial Day Was No Picnic."

13. The weekend emerged as a demand of the working classes in late nineteenth-cen-
tury England, was concretized on both sides of the Atlantic at the turn of the century, and
in the United States became established as a norm only after the passage of the Fair Labor
Standards Act of 1938. It became a standard of industrial capitalism in the postwar decades.
For a short digest of the idea of the weekend, see Witold Rybczynski, "Waiting for the
Weekend," *The Atlantic*, August 1991, pp. 25–52.

14. Sigmund Freud, "Remembering, Repeating and Working Through," in *The Standard Edition of the Complete Psychological Works of Sigmund Freud*, trans. James Strachey,

24 vols. (London: Hogarth Press, 1953–), vol. 12, p. 151. Paul Connerton turns to this essay, as well, in *How Societies Remember* (Cambridge: Cambridge University Press, 1989), p. 26. While Freud's centrality to memory studies means he could be useful in almost any part of this book, the repetition in this image and more generally in commemoration makes his work especially suited to understanding the image.

15. Freud, "Remembering, Repeating and Working Through," p. 154.

16. In 1968, the U.S. Congress officially changed Memorial Day from May 30 to the final Monday in May.

17. Evidence from advertisements in newspapers demonstrates that the 1960s were a transitional moment when Memorial Day occasioned both sales and days of closure. See the advertisement for Remines-Smith Ford, *Radford News Journal*, May 26, 1960, https:// newspaperarchive.com/radford-news-journal-may-26-1960-p-7. Compare this with the advertisement for Polk Bros. appliances, which makes clear that it is closed on Memorial Day, *Chicago Tribune*, May 29, 1960, p. 11, https://www.newspapers.com/clip/20414615/ memorial_day_sale_1960.

18. Ad for A. C. McIntyre and Co., *The Ogenburg Journal*, May 25, 1870, reproduced in David Brooks, "Upstate News You Can't Use: Decorate This!," *Exploring Upstate*, May 23, 2019, https://exploringupstate.com/upstate-news-you-cant-use-decorate-this.

19. For the meaning of children at French Armistice Day events, see Prost, "Monuments to the Dead," p. 325.

20. Goffman, *Behavior in Public Places*, p. 38.

21. Ibid., pp. 32–34.

22. Ibid., p. 39.

23. This is hardly an ahistorical idea. By the time that the sweaty veteran sat on the grass in Greenbelt in 1942, a Victorian ritual had been woven into recreation, norms of behavior in public had relaxed, and the setting had changed. In other words, what people owed the commemoration had been undergoing constant change since the inception of the special day in the 1860s.

24. An in-depth study of such programs would be a welcome addition to the literature.

25. These comments on the program lean on Goffman, *Behavior in Public Places*, p. 51.

26. Asaf Darr and Trevor Pinch, "Performing Sales: Material Scripts and the Social Organization of Obligation," *Organization Studies* 34.11 (2013), p. 1607.

27. Of course, a separate book could be written on the subject. The comments here are intended to conceptualize, rather than historicize or give a detailed account of the topic.

28. Darr and Pinch, "Performing Sales," p. 1607. Much of my thinking on this analogy comes from a lecture Pinch gave, "The Sound of Economic Change," talk given at The Society for the Humanities Annual Faculty Invitational Lecture (Berkeley, California, February 15, 2012).

29. Darr and Pinch, "Performing Sales," pp. 1608–10.

CHAPTER NINE: WHAT MEMORIALS DO AT MEMORIALS

1. Thomas W. Laqueur, *The Work of the Dead: A Cultural History of Mortal Remains* (Princeton: Princeton University Press, 2015), p. 67.

2. For a study of gesture in monuments, see Ted Hyunhak Yoon, ed., *Decoding Dictatorial Statues* (Eindhoven: Onomatopee, 2019).

3. Dell Upton, *What Can and Can't Be Said: Race, Uplift, and Monument Building in the Contemporary South* (New Haven: Yale University Press, 2015), p. 21.

4. On Epicurus and death, see Laqueur, *The Work of the Dead*, p. 21.

5. See, for instance, Paul J. Kosmin, *Time and Its Adversaries in the Seleucid Empire* (Cambridge, MA: Belknap Press of Harvard University Press, 2018), and G. W. Bowersock's excellent review in the *The New York Review of Books* 66.17, November 7, 2019, pp. 29–31.

6. Laqueur, *The Work of the Dead*, pp. 5–10.

7. Rosalind Krauss, "Sculpture in the Expanded Field," *October* (Spring 1979), p. 13.

8. Erika Doss, *Memorial Mania: Public Feeling in America* (Chicago: University of Chicago Press, 2010); Quentin Stevens and Karen A. Franck, *Memorials as Spaces of Engagement: Design, Use and Meaning* (New York: Routledge, 2016).

9. Martijn Wallage, "A Life Abiding in the Same: The Statue as Image of the Eternal Soul," in Yoon, ed., *Decoding Dictatorial Statues*, p. 118.

10. Ibid.

11. The metaphor comes from Reinhart Koselleck, *Sediments of Time: On Possible Histories*, ed. and trans. Sean Franzel and Stefan-Ludwig Hoffmann (Stanford: Stanford University Press, 2018).

12. In fact, the "old dean" turns out to be the Albrecht Daniel Thaer Monument (1859), at the corner of the Schillerstraße and the Universitätsstraße. Albrecht Daniel Thaer (1752–1828) is known as the founder of agronomy but was not a dean. I thank Martijn Wallage for identifying him for me.

13. See "Alfred the Great's Memorial," *San Francisco Chronicle*, September 22, 1901, p. 6. In San Francisco, the building trades successfully established the eight-hour working day in 1900.

14. Walter Benjamin, "Awakening," in *The Arcades Project*, ed. Rolf Tiedemann, trans. Howard Eiland and Kevin McLaughlin (Cambridge, MA: Belknap Press of Harvard University Press, 1999), p. 462.

15. See François Hartog's discussion of Benjamin and Arendt in *Regimes of Historicity: Presentism and Experiences of Time*, trans. Saskia Brown (New York: Columbia University Press, 2015), p. 129.

16. Sergiusz Michalski, *Public Monuments: Art in Political Bondage 1870–1997* (London: Reaktion, 1998), p. 108.

17. Verlyn Klinkenborg, "What Were Dinosaurs For?," *The New York Review of Books* 66.20, December 19, 2019, p. 38, https://www.nybooks.com/articles/2019/12/19/what-were-dinosaurs-for.

18. Robert Musil, "Monuments," trans. Burton Pike, in *Selected Writings*, ed. Pike (New York: Continuum, 1986), p. 320.

19. Reinhart Koselleck discusses this idea in various places in his writings. See *The Practice of Conceptual History: Timing History, Spacing Concepts*, trans. Todd Samuel Pressner (Stanford: Stanford University Press, 2002), p. 104. See also Koselleck, *Sediments of Time*, p. xiv.

20. Francesca Rigotti, "Metaphors of Time," *ETC: A Review of General Semantics* 43.2 (Summer 1986), p. 158.

21. Susan Sontag, *On Photography* (New York: Farrar, Straus and Giroux, 1977), p. 15.

22. Mircea Eliade, *Cosmos and History: The Myth of the Eternal Return*, trans. Willard R. Trask (New York: Harper and Brothers, 1954), p. xi.

23. Ibid., p. 151.

24. This phrasing reworks the words of Lionel Blue, a British rabbi: "Jews are just like everyone else, only more so." While widely quoted, the exact source is unclear.

25. Eliade, *Cosmos and History*, p. 153.

26. The point is made by Stefan-Ludwig Hoffmann, in Koselleck, *Sediments of Time*, p. 5.

27. The projections were the work of artist Dustin Klein.

28. Mona Ozouf, *Festivals and the French Revolution*, trans. Alan Sheridan (Cambridge, MA: Harvard University Press, 1988), p. 133.

29. Hartog, *Regimes of Historicity*, p. 11.

30. Laqueur, *The Work of the Dead*, p. 49.

31. Jules Michelet, quoted in Hartog, *Regimes of Historicity*, p. 177. Will white nationalists feel the same when they visit the museums where sleep Confederate Monuments to Robert E. Lee, Jefferson Davis, and Stonewall Jackson?

32. This discussion was stimulated by Hartog's thoughts on changes in historicity after the revolution in *Regimes of Historicity*, p. 107.

33. Hartog, *Regimes of Historicity*, p. 107. Filippo Tommaso Marinetti, "The Founding and Manifesto of Futurism," in Lawrence Rainey, Christine Poggi, and Laura Wittman, eds., *Futurism: An Anthology* (New Haven: Yale University Press, 2009), p. 49; *Le Figaro*, February 20, 1909, p. 1.

34. A few references give a sense of the usage: Rebecca Kraybill. "Who's That Dead White Guy on a Horse? Jessica Unger Answers," *Knowledge Commons DC*, October 20, 2016, http://knowledgecommonsdc.org/blog/dead-white-guy-horse-jessica-unger-answers; Javier Pes, "Meet Hew Locke, the Artist Who Dresses Up 'Patriotic' Statues to Reveal Their Whitewashed Histories," *ArtNet News*, October 11, 2018, https://news.artnet.com/exhibitions/hew-locke-1369636; Mark White, "Statues of Limitations: Why the Present Shouldn't Attack the Past," *Maclean's*, April 25, 2018, https://www.macleans.ca/opinion/statues-of-limitations-why-the-present-shouldnt-attack-the-past.

35. Hartog, *Regimes of Historicity*, p. 110. Monuments are so labile that this judgment is easily reversed. In 2020, when a wave of iconoclasm swept over the United States in the wake of the killing of George Floyd, defenders of Confederate monuments claimed that history was being swept away. In this view, history is precious and, troublingly, monuments are synonymous with history.

36. See Laqueur's discussion in *The Work of the Dead*, p. 38.

37. I thank Ramona Naddaff for helping me draw out the rhetorical issues of the word "dead."

38. Elizabeth P. McGowan, "Tomb Marker and Turning Post: Funerary Columns in the Archaic Period," *American Journal of Archaeology* 99.4 (October 1995), pp. 615–32.

39. It shows up in a poignant visual obituary in *Colophon* 1.1 (1935).

40. Mona Ozouf, "Célébrer, savoir et fêter," in Maurice Agulhon, et al., *1789: La commemoration* (Paris: Gallimard, 1999), p. 322.

41. Bruno Latour, "Where Are the Missing Masses?: The Sociology of a Few Mundane Artifacts," in Weibe E. Bijker and John Law, eds., *Shaping Technology / Building Society: Studies in Sociotechnical Change* (Cambridge, MA: MIT Press, 1992), p. 154.

42. Ibid., p. 159.

43. I thank the literary scholar Charles Altieri for pointing me in this direction. Little is known about how ancient Greeks performed elegies or the sorts of settings in which they were performed. Gregory Nagy, "Ancient Greek Elegy," in Karen Weisman, ed., *The*

Oxford Handbook of the Elegy (Oxford: Oxford University Press, 2010), pp. 13–45, also available online from the Harvard Center for Hellenic Studies, https://chs.harvard.edu/CHS/article/display/3989.

44. Laqueur, *The Work of the Dead*, pp. 215–38.

45. Kirk Savage, "The War Memorial as Elegy," in Weisman, ed., *The Oxford Handbook of the Elegy*, p. 637.

46. Of course, not all elegies operate like the elegy to Yeats. Auden himself wrote the more prosaic "In Memory of Sigmund Freud," also in 1939, which skirts the issues discussed in this chapter.

47. While "disappearing" something is awkward in English, it is standard usage in Spanish. The "disappeared" (*desaparecidos*) from Chile and Argentina's dictatorship is one way that their death is forestalled. They are not called "dead," and the memorials to them refuse their finality. They are held in this state of limbo as a way to compel the state to action, to force reparations. This suggests a continuum of states of "almost dead," from barely living to barely dead, and this squares with Laqueur's history of how dead bodies have been treated. Arthur Imhof writes of early modern Christians who watched for the faintest signs of life, sometimes inventing or imagining them in unbaptized babies so that they might baptize them before they succumbed.

48. Laqueur, *The Work of the Dead*, p. 62.

49. Auden had a dim view of actual monuments, as can be seen in two other poems from this period, "The Unknown Citizen" and "Here War Is Simple." In the former, he proposes an inscription for a fictional monument to a pitiful anonymous man who has died after living a completely conventional life.

50. Sligo, the county where Yeats was born, erected only one, on the fiftieth anniversary of his death in 1989, by sculptor Ronan Gillespie. Henry Moore sculpted an abstract Yeats for Dublin in 1967.

51. Kirk Savage, "The War Memorial as Elegy," p. 639.

52. Ellen Zetzel Lambert, *Placing Sorrow: A Study of the Pastoral Elegy Convention from Theocritus to Milton* (Chapel Hill: University of North Carolina Press, 1976), p. xiii.

53. Karen Weisman, introduction to *The Oxford Handbook of the Elegy*, ed. Karen Weisman (Oxford: Oxford University Press 2010), p. 6.

54. Ibid., p. 7.

55. It is true that people continued to install war memorials in and around churches, but these were usually intimate, aimed at the parish and its community.

56. Lambert, *Placing Sorrow*, p. xv.

57. Many ancient elegies also make reference to cities, which Auden's poem seems to emulate.

58. In Oberlin's now-destroyed memorial, names of the dead take the place of the sculpted bodies.

59. Some possible precedents only reinforce its oddity: the plague column in Košice, Slovakia, with its putti ascending heavenward, or the strange Monumento del Fréjus in Turin, Italy, where fallen titans struggle on a pile of boulders topped by Genius.

CONCLUSION: WHAT IS THIS?

1. On countermonuments, see James E. Young, *At Memory's Edge: After-Images of the Holocaust in Contemporary Art and Architecture* (New Haven: Yale University Press, 2000). See also Quentin Stevens, Karen A. Franck, and Ruth Fazakerley, "Counter-Monuments, the Anti-Monumental and the Dialogic," *The Journal of Architecture* 17.6 (2012), pp. 951–72.

2. François Hartog, *Regimes of Historicity: Presentism and Experiences of Time*, trans. Saskia Brown (New York: Columbia University Press, 2015).

3. Eric Hobsbawm and Terence Ranger, eds., *The Invention of Tradition* (Cambridge: Cambridge University Press, 1983).

4. Heinrich Hübsch, *In What Style Shall We Build?: The German Debate on Architectural Style*, trans. Wolfgang Hermann (Santa Monica: Getty Center for the History of Art and the Humanities, 1992).

5. Thanks to Kathleen James-Chakraborty for pointing me to Nelson's Monument in Dublin. An earlier precedent for this genre of monument is Christopher Wren and Robert Hooke's Monument to the Great Fire of London, 1671–77.

6. Frank Jenkins, "John Foulston and His Public Buildings in Plymouth, Stonehouse, and Devonport," *Journal of the Society of Architectural Historians* 27.2 (May 1968), pp. 124–35. Henry E. Carrington, *The Plymouth and Devonport Guide* (London: Longman, 1828). According to this early source, a statue of George IV was to grace the top, but this revealingly never came to fruition.

7. Françoise Choay notes that the first use in French appears in the 1830s. Françoise Choay, *The Invention of the Historic Monument*, trans. Lauren M. O'Connell (Cambridge: Cambridge University Press, 2001), pp. 14–15. The first English usage is a generation earlier.

8. Ibid., pp. 89–90.

9. Ibid., p. 90.

10. The obvious source for this motif is Trajan's Column in Rome.

11. "Nelson's Pillar," *Dublin Penny Journal*, June 20, 1835, p. 401.

12. An engraving from 1848 shows a temporary wooden fence was erected.

13. The point is strengthened by the fact that at the same time, Dubliners rejected statues to British luminaries. Donald Fallon, *The Pillar: The Life and Afterlife of the Nelson Pillar* (Stillorgan: New Island Books, 2014), pp. 49–50.

14. "Nelson to Leave Sackville Street," *The Manchester Guardian*, March 26, 1926, p. 9.

15. See Irene Orgel Briskin, "Some New Light on 'The Parable of the Plums'," *James Joyce Quarterly* 3.4 (Summer 1966), pp. 236–51.

16. Monumentality has been parodied at least since Lucian took the piss out of King Mausolus for the pompous inutility of his tomb, the Mausoleum of Halicarnassus, the eponym for the mausoleum. See Thomas W. Laqueur, *The Work of the Dead: A Cultural History of Mortal Remains* (Princeton: Princeton University Press, 2015), pp. 38–39.

17. The name seems to be invented for this monument, but it resonates with Hünengrab and Grosssteingrag, terms used for megalithic graves.

18. Robert Venturi, Denise Scott Brown, and Steven Izenour, *Learning from Las Vegas* (Cambridge, MA: MIT Press, 1972), p. 156.

19. Other Heunensäulen were erected in Nuremburg in 1972, mounted on a stone base typical of a column in the courtyard of the German National Museum, and in Munich, where the column sits without a base at the Archäologische Staatssammlung. It was taken to Munich in 1880 but was moved to the archaeological museum in 1975, the same year Mainz's column was erected.

20. Many Nagelsäulen were erected across Germany and Austria during the war.

21. Hartog, *Regimes of Historicity*, p. 189.

22. Beginning in 1963, it stood in the State Museum in Mainz. Later, a replica of the column was placed on Ernst Ludwig Platz.

23. In Euripides's *Iphigenia Taurica*, Iphigenia has a dream in which a lone column is left standing after her house collapses. It sprouts golden hair and takes on a human voice, after which she consecrates it with water and states that the "male children are the pillars of the houses." See Caroline P. Trieschnigg, "Iphigenia's Dream in Euripides' 'Iphigenia Taurica'," *Classical Quarterly* 58.2 (2008), p. 461. Of course, Egyptian columns were often inscribed with words that detailed the great events of the lives of the pharaohs. Many of Sandow Birk's imaginary monuments exaggerate the talking column. See his "Proposal

for a Monument to Capital Punishment," 2018, among others, at Sandow Birk, Imaginary Monuments, https://sandowbirk.com/imaginary-monuments.

24. Mona Ozouf, *Festivals and the French Revolution*, trans. Alan Sheridan (Cambridge, MA: Harvard University press, 1988), p. 240.

25. Ibid., p. 234.

26. See Hartog, *Regimes of Historicity*, chapter 5.

27. Ozouf, *Festivals and the French Revolution*, p. 241.

28. Ibid., p. 243

29. Maria Elena Versari, "Recasting the Past: On the Posthumous Fortune of Futurist Sculpture," *Sculpture Journal* 23.3 (2014), pp. 349–68.

30. Conversations with two colleagues suggest other possible readings. Jeroen Dewulf called attention to the resonance of the sly fox as a common usage in German, and Valentina Rozas-Krause noted the likeness between fox and wolf, the latter a persistent symbol of Nazism (and neo-Nazism). Reinforcing this reading, the hook that is clasped to the helm's comb could be a *wolfsangel*, a heraldic symbol of a wolf trap taken up by German fascists. In this reading, Fuchs is trapped in the helm of Roman Mainz, or more broadly in the city's history, and is snarling to free himself.

31. See Valentina J. Rozas-Krause, "Memorials and the Cult of Apology," PhD diss., University of California, Berkeley, 2020, pp. 34–43. Ozouf's excellent work on the symbols of the French Revolution, including liberty trees, had begun to be published in the 1970s. It is possible that the artist had seen some of this research.

32. Delesprie, Spirit of Los Angeles, http://www.delesprie.com/portfolio/spirit-of-los-angeles.

33. There are precedents in malls and department stores, one of the best known being the Eagle in John Wannamaker's Department Store in Philadelphia.

34. Filipo Tommaso Marinetti, "The Founding and Manifesto of Futurism," in Lawrence Rainey, Christine Poggi, and Laura Wittman, eds., *Futurism: An Anthology* (New Haven: Yale University Press, 2009), p. 51.

35. Delesprie, Spirit of Los Angeles, http://www.delesprie.com/portfolio/spirit-of-los-angeles.

Works Cited

Abramson, Daniel M. *Obsolescence: An Architectural History*. Chicago: University of Chicago Press, 2016.

Adams, Charles Francis, ed. *Memoirs of John Quincy Adams: Comprising Portions of His Diary from 1795–1848*. 12 vols. Philadelphia: J. B. Lippincott, 1876.

"Alfred the Great's Memorial." *San Francisco Chronicle*, September 22, 1901.

Ariès, Philippe. *The Hour of Our Death*. Trans. Helen Weaver. New York: Knopf, 1981.

———. *Western Attitudes toward Death from the Middle Ages to the Present*. Trans. Patricia M. Ranum. Baltimore: Johns Hopkins University Press, 1984.

"Arizona Civil War Monument Tarred and Feathered." *Arizona Daily Independent*, August 18, 2017, https://arizonadailyindependent.com.

Ashworth, G. J. "From History to Heritage: From Heritage to Identity: In Search of Concepts and Models." In Gregory Ashworth and Peter Larkham, eds., *Building a New Heritage: Tourism, Culture, and Identity in the New Europe*. London: Routledge, 1994, pp. 13–30.

———, and J. E. Tunbridge. *The Tourist-Historic City*. London: Belhaven, 1990.

"All Wars Memorial to Colored Soldiers and Sailors (1934)," *Association for Public Art*. https://www.associationforpublicart.org/artwork/all-wars-memorial -to-colored-soldiers-and-sailors.

Bakhtin, M. M. "Discourse in the Novel" (1936). Trans. Caryl Emerson and Micahel Holquist. In M. M. Bakhtin, *The Dialogic Imagination: Four Essays*. Austin: University of Texas Press, 1981.

Balkin Bach, Penny. *Public Art in Philadelphia*. Philadelphia: Temple University Press, 1992.

Barrio Planners Incorporated, *Nuestro Ambiente East Los Angeles Visual Survey and Analysis*. 1973.

Baudelaire, Charles. *The Painter of Modern Life, and Other Essays*. Trans. Jonathan Mayne. London: Phaidon, 1964.

Baudrillard, Jean. *Simulacra and Simulation*. Trans. Shiela Faria Glaser. Ann Arbor: University of Michigan Press, 1994.

Bell, Maya. "Holocaust Memorial Stirs Anger." *Orlando Sentinel*, January 28, 1990, https://www.orlandosentinel.com/news/os-xpm-1990-01-28-9001263238-story.html.

Bender, Thomas. "The 'Rural' Cemetery Movement: Urban Travail and the Appeal of Nature." *New England Quarterly* 47.2 (June 1974), pp. 196–211.

Benjamin, Walter. "Awakening." In *The Arcades Project*, ed. Rolf Tiedemann, trans. Howard Eiland and Kevin McLaughlin. Cambridge, MA: Belknap Press of Harvard University Press, 1999.

———. "On the Concept of History." In Howard Eiland and Michael W. Jennings, eds., *Walter Benjamin: Selected Writings, Volume 4, 1938–1940*. Cambridge, MA: Belknap Press of Harvard University Press, 2003, pp. 389–400.

Birk, Sandow. "Imaginary Monuments," *Sandow Birk*, https://sandowbirk.com/imaginary-monuments.

Blair, Carole, V., William Balthrop, and Neil Michel. "The Arguments of the Tombs of the Unknown Soldiers: Relationality and National Legitimation." *Argumentation* 25.4 (2011), pp. 449–68.

Blake, Casey Nelson. *Beloved Community: The Cultural Criticism of Randolph Bourne, Van Wyck Brooks, Waldo Frank, and Lewis Mumford*. Chapel Hill, University of North Carolina Press, 1990.

Blodgett, Geoffrey. *Oberlin Architecture, College and Town: A Guide to Its Social History*. Kent: Kent State University Press, 1985.

Blomfield, Reginald, and F. Inigo Thomas, *The Formal Garden in England*. London: Macmillan, 1892.

Bodnar, John. "Pierre Nora, National Memory, and Democracy: A Review." *Journal of American History* 87.3 (December 2000), pp, 951–63.

———. *Remaking America: Public Memory, Commemoration, and Patriotism in the Twentieth Century*. Princeton: Princeton University Press, 1992.

Bogart, Michelle H. *Public Sculpture and the Civic Ideal in New York City, 1890–1930*. Chicago: University of Chicago Press, 1989.

Bowersock, G. W. "The Invention of Time." *The New York Review of Books*, November 7, 2019, pp. 29–31.

Brindle, Steven. "The Wellington Arch and the Western Entrance to London." *Georgian Group Journal* 11 (2001), pp. 47–51.

Bowdler, Roger H., and Steven P. Brindle. *Wellington Arch, Marble Arch and Six Great War Memorials.* London: English Heritage, 2015.

Briskin, Irene Orgel. "Some New Light on 'The Parable of the Plums'." *James Joyce Quarterly* 3.4 (Summer 1966), pp. 236–51.

Brooks, David. "Upstate News You Can't Use: Decorate This!" *Exploring Upstate*, May 23, 2019, https://exploringupstate.com/upstate-news-you-cant-use-decorate -this.

Bryan-Wilson, Julia. "Monument Monumentum." In Mihnea Mircan, ed., *Undone / Hans van Houwelingen.* Heijningen: Jap Sam Books, 2001, pp. 81–90.

Burnap, George. *Parks: Their Design, Equipment, and Use.* Philadelphia: J. B. Lippincott, 1916.

Camuzzoni, Giulio. *Discorso per l' inaugurazione del monument a Michele Sanmicheli.* Verona: Tipografia Premiata de Gaetano Franchini, 1874.

Carlyle, Thomas. *Latter-Day Pamphlets.* 1851; New York: C. Scribner's Sons, 1901.

Carrington, Henry E. *The Plymouth and Devonport Guide.* London: Longman, 1828.

Casey, Edward S. *Remembering: A Phenomenological Study.* Bloomington: Indiana University Press, 1987.

Casson, Hugh, ed. *Monuments.* New York: Taplinger, 1965.

Castells, Manuel. *The Informational City: Information, Technology, Economic Restructuring and the Urban-Regional Process.* Oxford: Blackwell, 1989.

Ceccarelli, Francesco. "Bologna e la Romagna." In Amerigo Restucci, ed., *Storia dell'architettura italiana: L'Ottocento.* 2 vols. Milan: Electa, 2005, vol. 1, pp. 142–65.

Chadwick, George F. *The Park and the Town: Public Landscape in the 19th and 20th Centuries.* London: The Architectural Press, 1966.

Champeaux, E. *Les Cimetiéres et le Marchés du vieux Dijon.* Dijon: J. Mourry, 1906.

Charlesworth, Andrew. "Contesting Places of Memory: The Case of Auschwitz." *Environment and Planning D: Society and Space* 12 (1994), pp. 579–93.

Chicago Tribune, May 29, 1960, p. 11, https://www.newspapers.com/clip/20414615/ memorial_day_sale_1960.

Choay, Françoise. *The Invention of the Historic Monument.* Trans. Lauren M. O'Connell. Cambridge: Cambridge University Press, 2001.

"City Says Boyle Heights Traffic Roundabout Is Moving in Right Direction." *Eastsider*, January 16, 2014, https://www.theeastsiderla.com/real_estate/architecture

_and_urban_design/city-says-boyle-heights-traffic-roundabout-is-moving-in-the
-right-direction/article_e4e06782-b65f-5753-a972-3db83b748403.html.

Colebrook, Claire. "The Politics and Potential of Everyday Life." *New Literary History* 3.4 (Autumn 2002), pp. 687–706.

Collins, Christiane Crasemann and George R. Collins. *City Planning According to Artistic Principles.* London: Phaidon, 1965.

Conan, Michael. "The Fiddler's Indecorous Nostalgia." In Terence Young and Robert Riley, eds., *Theme Park Landscapes: Antecedents and Variations.* Washington, DC: Dumbarton Oaks Research Library and Collection, 2002, pp. 91–117.

Connerton, Paul. *How Societies Remember.* Cambridge: Cambridge University Press, 1989.

Cook, Clarence. *A Description of the New York Central Park.* New York: F. J. Huntington, 1869.

Cranz, Galen. *The Politics of Park Design: A History of Urban Parks in America.* Cambridge, MA: MIT Press, 1982.

Crawford, Margaret. Introduction to John Leighton Chase, Margaret Crawford, and John Kaliski, eds., *Everyday Urbanism.* New York: Monacelli Press, 2008, pp. 6–12.

Cullen, Gordon. *The Concise Townscape.* London, Architectural Press, 1971.

Curl, James Stevens. "The Architecture and Planning of the Nineteenth-Century Cemetery." *Garden History* 3.3 (Summer, 1975), pp. 13–41.

Danto, Arthur C. "The Vietnam Veterans Memorial." *The Nation*, August 31, 1985, pp. 152–55.

Darr, Asaf, and Trevor Pinch. "Performing Sales: Material Scripts and the Social Organization of Obligation." *Organization Studies* 34.11 (2013), pp. 1601–621.

"Daspo urbano a Verona." *Veronasera*, July 12, 2018, https://www.veronasera.it/cronaca/daspo-urbano-54-allontanate-due-settimane-12-luglio-2018.html.

De Certeau, Michel. *The Practice of Everyday Life.* Trans. Steven Randall. Berkeley: University of California Press, 1984.

De Pieri, Filippo. "Un paese di centri storici: urbanistica e identità locali negli anni Cinquanta e Sessanta." *Rassenga di architettura e urbanistica* 46.136 (2002), pp. 92–100.

Dickens, Jr., Charles. *Dickens's Dictionary of London: An Unconventional Handbook.* 1888; Moretonhampstead: Old House Books, 1993.

Doss, Erica. *Memorial Mania: Public Feeling in America.* Chicago: University of Chicago Press, 2010.

Downing, Andrew Jackson. *A Treatise on the Theory and Practice of Landscape Gardening.* 1841; New York: A. O. Moore, 1859.

Eckert, Andreas, and Adam Jones, "Historical Writing about Everyday Life." *Journal of African Cultural Studies* 15.1 (June 2002), pp. 5–16.

Eliade, Mircea. *Cosmos and History: The Myth of the Eternal Return.* Trans. Willard R. Trask. New York: Harper and Brothers, 1959.

———. *The Myth of the Eternal Return.* Trans. Willard R. Trask. New York: Pantheon, 1954.

———. *Sacred and Profane: The Nature of Religion.* Trans. Willard R. Trask. New York: Harcourt, Brace, 1959.

Elias, Norbert. *The Civilizing Process.* Trans. Edmund Jephcott. Oxford: Basil Blackwell, 1978–1982.

———. "On the Concept of Everyday Life." In *The Norbert Elias Reader: A Biographical Selection*, ed. Johan Goudsblom and Stephen Mennel. Malden: Blackwell, 1998, pp. 166–74.

———. *Über den Prozess der Zivilisation: Soziogenetische und Psychogenetische Untersuchungen.* Basel: Haus zum Falken, 1939.

Engs, Robert Francis. *Freedom's First Generation: Black Hampton, Virginia, 1861–1890.* Philadelphia: University of Pennsylvania Press, 1979.

Fadely, James Philip. "The Veteran and the Memorial: George J. Gangsdale and the Soldiers and Sailors Monument." *Traces of Indiana and Midwestern History* 18.1 (Winter 2006), pp. 33–35.

Fallon, Donald. *The Pillar: The Life and Afterlife of the Nelson Pillar.* Stillorgan: New Island Books, 2014.

Farrell, Joseph. "The Phenomenology of Memory in Roman Culture." *Classics Journal* 92.4 (April–May 1997), pp. 373–83.

Faust, Drew Gilpin. *This Republic of Suffering: Death and the American Civil War.* New York: Alfred A. Knopf, 2008.

Fenski, Rita. *Doing Time: Feminist Theory and Postmodern Culture.* New York: New York University Press, 2000.

Finch, Nancy Moses. *Fakes, Forgeries, and Frauds.* Lanham: Rowman and Littlefield, 2020.

Ford, Richard. "Planning Laws Leave War Memorials at Risk, Says London Assembly." *The Times*, July 6, 2009, https://www.thetimes.co.uk/edition/news/planning-laws-leave-war-memorials-at-risk-says-london-assembly-39f30x88c26.

Forest, Benjamin, and Juliet Johnson. "Unraveling the Threads of History: Soviet-Era Monuments and Post-Soviet National Identity in Moscow." *Annals of the Association of American Geographers* 92.3 (September 2002), pp. 524–47.

———. "Unraveling the Threads of History: Soviet-Era Monuments and Post-Soviet National Identity in Moscow." Talk delivered at the Annals of the Association of American Geographers, 2001, http://www.dartmouth.edu/~crn/crn_papers/Forest-Johnson.pdf.

French, Stanley. "The Cemetery as Cultural Institution: The Establishment of Mount Auburn and the 'Rural Cemetery' Movement." *American Quarterly* 26.1 (March 1974), pp. 37–59.

Freud, Sigmund. "Remembering, Repeating and Working Through." In *The Standard Edition of the Complete Psychological Works of Sigmund Freud*. Trans. James Strachey, 24 vols. London: Hogarth Press, 1953–. Vol. 12, pp. 145–56.

Fussell, Paul. *The Great War and Modern Memory.* Oxford: Oxford University Press, 1975.

———. *Wartime: Understanding and Behavior in the Second World War.* New York: Oxford University Press, 1989.

Glassie, Henry. "Vernacular Architecture and Society." *Material Culture* 16.1 (Spring 1984), pp. 4–24.

Godwin, William. *Essay on Sepulchres.* London: Printed for W. Miller, 1809.

Goffman, Erving. *Behavior in Public Places: Notes on the Social Organization of Gatherings.* New York: Free Press, 1963.

Gorer, Geoffrey. "The Pornography of Death." *Encounter*, October 1955, pp. 49–52.

Gould, Stephen J. *Time's Arrow, Time's Cycle: Myth and Metaphor in the Discovery of Geological Time.* Cambridge, MA: Harvard University Press, 1987.

Graham, Brian, G. J. Ashworth, and J. E. Tunbridge. *A Geography of Heritage: Power, Culture and Economy* (New York: Routledge, 2000).

Griffin, Michèle McHugh. "As a Woman I Have No Country." *Peace Review* 10.2 (1998), pp. 255–59.

Groth, Paul. "Frameworks for Cultural Landscape Study." In Paul Groth and Todd W. Bressi, eds., *Understanding Ordinary Environments.* New Haven: Yale University Press, 1997, pp. 1–21.

———. "Making New Connections in Vernacular Architecture." *Journal of the Society of Architectural Historians* 58.3 (September 1999), pp. 444–51.

Harmond, Richard P., and Thomas J. Curran. *A History of Memorial Day: Unity, Discord and the Pursuit of Happiness.* New York: Peter Lang, 2002.

Harris, Steven. "Everyday Architecture." In Steven Harris and Deborah Berke, eds., *Architecture of the Everyday.* New York: Princeton Architectural Press, 1997, pp. 1–8.

Hartog, François. *Regimes of Historicity: Presentism and Experiences of Time*. Trans. Saskia Brown. New York: Columbia University Press, 2015.

Hartwanger, Siegfried. *Klagenfurt, Stadt: Ihre Kunstwerke, historischen Lebens- und Siedlungsformen*. Salzburg: St. Peter, 1980.

Hayden, Dolores. *The Power of Place: Urban Landscapes as Public History*. Cambridge, MA and London: MIT Press, 1995.

Haydenko, Victoria. "The Formation of Gender Differences among the Young during Post-Communist Transition in Ukraine." In Lisa N. Gurley, Claudia Leeb, and Anna Aloisia Moser, eds., *Feminists Contest Politics and Philosophy*. Brussels: P.I.E.-Peter Lang, 2005, pp. 219–71.

Heathorn, Stephen. "The Civil Servant and Public Remembrance: Sir Lionel Earle and the Shaping of London's Commemorative Landscape, 1918–1933." *Twentieth Century British History* 19.3 (January 1, 2008), pp. 259–87.

———. "The Mnemonic Turn in the Cultural Historiography of Britain's Great War." *Historical Journal* 48.4 (2005), pp. 1103–24.

Herf, Jeffrey. *Reactionary Modernism: Technology, Culture, and Politics in Weimar and the Third Reich*. Cambridge: Cambridge University Press, 1984.

Hersey, George. *The Lost Meaning of Classical Architecture: Speculations on Ornament from Vitruvius to Venturi*. Cambridge, MA: MIT Press, 1992.

Hobsbawm, Eric. *The Age of Revolution 1789–1848*. 1962; London: Sphere Books, 1991.

———, and Terence Ranger, eds. *The Invention of Tradition*. Cambridge: Cambridge University Press, 1983.

Hubbard, Henry Vincent, and Theodora Kimball. *An Introduction to the Study of Landscape Design*. 1917; New York: Macmillan, 1924.

Hübsch, Heinrich. *In What Style Shall We Build?: The German Debate on Architectural Style*. Trans. Wolfgang Hermann. Santa Monica: Getty Center for the History of Art and the Humanities, 1992.

Hudnut, Joseph. "The Monument Does Not Remember." *Atlantic Monthly*, September 1945, pp. 55–59.

Hunt, Lynn. *Politics, Culture, and Class in the French Revolution*. Berkeley: University of California Press, 1984.

Imhof, Arthur E. *Lost Worlds: How Our European Ancestors Coped with Everyday Life and Why Life Is So Hard Today*. Trans. Thomas Robisheaux. Charlottesville: University of Virginia Press, 1996.

Jackson, J. B. *American Space: The Centennial Years, 1865–1876*. New York: Norton, 1972.

———. "The Order of the Landscape: Reason and Religion in Newtonian America." In D. W. Meinig, ed., *The Interpretation of Ordinary Landscapes: Geographical Essays*. New York: Oxford University Press, 1979, pp. 153–63.

———. "Vanishing Epitaph," *Landscape* 17–18 (Winter 1967–68), pp. 22–26.

Jackson, Peter. *Maps of Meaning: An Introduction to Cultural Geography*. London: Routledge, 1992.

Jandl, Dieter. *A Brief History of Klagenfurt*. Klagenfurt: Heyn, 2000.

Jaspers, Karl. *The Question of German Guilt*. Trans. E. B. Ashton. 1947; New York: Fordham University Press, 2000.

Jenkins, Frank. "John Foulston and His Public Buildings in Plymouth, Stonehouse, and Devonport." *Journal of the Society of Architectural Historians* 27.2 (May 1968), pp. 124–35.

Johnson, Philip. "War Memorials: What Aesthetic Price Glory?" *Art News*, September 1945, pp. 8–10, 24–25.

Kaika, Maria. "Interrogating the Geographies of the Familiar: Domesticating Nature and Constructing the Autonomy of the Modern Home." *International Journal of Urban and Regional Research* 28 (March 2004), pp. 265–86.

Kern, Stephen. *The Culture of Time and Space 1880–1918*. London: Weidenfeld and Nicolson, 1983.

King, Anthony D. "The Politics of Vision." In Paul Groth, ed., *Vision, Culture, and Landscape: Working Papers from the Berkeley Symposium on Cultural Landscape Interpretation*. Berkeley: University of California, Berkeley, Center for Environmental Design Research, 1990, pp. 134–44.

Klein, Kerwin Lee. "On the Emergence of 'Memory' in Historical Discourse." In "Grounds for Remembering," special issue, *Representations* 69 (2000), pp. 127–50.

Klinkenborg, Verlyn. "What Were Dinosaurs For?" *New York Review of Books*, December 19, 2019, https://www.nybooks.com/articles/2019/12/19/what-were-dinosaurs-for/.

Kogl, Alexandra. "A Hundred Ways of Beginning: The Politics of Everyday Life." *Polity* 41.4 (October 2009), pp. 514–35.

Koselleck, Reinhart. *The Practice of Conceptual History: Timing History, Spacing Concepts*. Trans. Todd Samuel Presner, Kerstin Behnke, and Jobst Welge. Stanford: Stanford University Press, 2002.

———. *Sediments of Time: On Possible Histories*, ed. and trans. Stefan-Ludwig Hoffmann and Sean Franzel. Stanford: Stanford University Press, 2018.

Kosmin, Paul J. *Time and Its Adversaries in the Seleucid Empire*. Cambridge, MA: Belknap Press of Harvard University Press, 2018.

Kostof, Spiro. *America by Design*. New York: Oxford University Press, 1987.

———. *The City Shaped: Urban Patterns and Meanings through History*. London: Thames and Hudson, 1991.

———. *A History of Architecture: Settings and Rituals*. 2nd ed. New York: Oxford University Press, 1995.

Krauss, Rosalind. "Sculpture in the Expanded Field." *October* 8 (Spring 1979), pp. 30–44.

Kraybill, Rebecca. "Who's That Dead White Guy on a Horse? Jessica Unger Answers." *Knowledge Commons DC*, October 20, 2016, http://knowledgecommonsdc.org/blog/dead-white-guy-horse-jessica-unger-answers.

Lambert, Ellen Zetzel. *Placing Sorrow: A Study of the Pastoral Elegy Convention from Theocritus to Milton*. Chapel Hill: University of North Carolina Press, 1976.

Laqueur, Thomas W. "Memory and Naming in the Great War." In John R. Gillis, ed., *Commemorations: The Politics of National Identity*. Princeton: Princeton University Press, pp. 150–67.

———. *The Work of the Dead: A Cultural History of Mortal Remains*. Princeton: Princeton University Press, 2015.

Lasansky, D. Medina. "Urban Editing, Historic Preservation, and Political Rhetoric: The Fascist Redesign of San Gimignano." *Journal of the Society of Architectural Historians* 63.3 (September 2004), pp. 320–53.

———, and Brian McLaren, eds. *Architecture and Tourism*. Oxford: Berg, 2004.

Latour, Bruno. "Where Are the Missing Masses?: The Sociology of a Few Mundane Artifacts." In Weibe E. Bijker and John Law, eds., *Shaping Technology / Building Society: Studies in Sociotechnical Change*. Cambridge, MA: MIT Press, 1992, pp. 151–80.

Le Corbusier. *The City of Tomorrow and Its Planning*. Trans. Frederick Etchells. London: J. Rodker, 1929.

Lefebvre, Henri. *Critique of Everyday Life*. Trans. John Moore. 3 vols. 1947; New York: Verso, 1991.

———. *The Urban Revolution*. Trans. Robert Bononno. 1970; Minneapolis: University of Minnesota Press, 2003.

Leuchtenburg, William E. *The FDR Years: On Roosevelt and His Legacy*. New York: Columbia University Press, 1995.

Lewis, Peirce F. "Axioms for Reading the Landscape: Some Guides to the American

Scene." In D. W. Meinig, ed., *The Interpretation of Ordinary Landscapes: Geographical Essays*. New York: Oxford University Press, 1979, pp. 11–32.

Lopez, Robert S. "The Crossroads within the Wall." In Oscar Handlin and John Burchard, eds., *The Historian and the City*. Cambridge, MA: MIT Press, 1963, pp. 27–43.

Lorimer, Hayden. "Cultural Geography: The Busyness of Being 'More-Than-Representational'." *Progress in Human Geography* 29.1 (2005), pp. 83–94.

———. "Cultural Geography: Worldly Shapes, Differently Arranged." *Progress in Human Geography* 31.1 (2007), pp. 89–100.

Lynch, Kevin. *The Image of the City*. Cambridge, MA: MIT Press, 1960.

"McAllen TX War Memorial Park." War Memorial HQ, http://www.warmemorialhq. org/items/show/318. Marinetti, Filippo Tommaso. "The Founding and Manifesto of Futurism." In Lawrence Rainey, Christine Poggi, and Laura Wittman, eds., *Futurism: An Anthology*. New Haven: Yale University Press, 2009, pp. 49–53. *Le Figaro*, February 20, 1909, p. 1.

Marx, Karl, and Friedrich Engels. *The Communist Manifesto*, ed. Samuel H. Beer. New York: Appleton-Century-Crofts, 1955.

McClellan, Andrew. "The Life and Death of a Royal Monument: Bouchardon's *Louis XV*," *Oxford Art Journal* 23.2 (2000), pp. 1–27.

McGowan, Elizabeth P. "Tomb Marker and Turning Post: Funerary Columns in the Archaic Period." *American Journal of Archaeology* 99.4 (October 1995), pp. 615–32.

McLeod, Mary. "Henry Lefebvre's Critique of Everyday Life: An Introduction." In Steven Harris and Deborah Berke, eds., *Architecture of the Everyday*. New York: Princeton Architectural Press, 1997, pp. 9–29.

McPherson, James M. "When Memorial Day Was No Picnic." *The New York Times*, May 25, 1996, p. 11, https://www.nytimes.com/2008/05/25/opinion/25opclassic.html.

Michalski, Sergiusz. *Public Monuments: Art in Political Bondage 1870–1997*. London: Reaktion Books, 1998.

Miquel, Pierre. *Les Poilus: La France sacrifiée*. Paris: Plon, 2000.

Mitchell, Don. *Cultural Geography: A Critical Introduction*. Oxford: Blackwell, 2000.

Mitford, Jessica. *The American Way of Death*. New York: Simon and Schuster, 1963.

"Monument Given Tar, Feathers." *Lorain Journal*, November 21, 1957, Brady's Bunch of Lorain County Nostalgia, http://danielebrady.blogspot.com/2016/05/lagranges-civil-war -monument-part-2.html.

Moran, Joe. *Reading the Everyday*. London: Routledge, 2005.

Mosse, George L. *Fallen Soldiers: Reshaping the Memory of the World Wars*. New York: Oxford University Press, 1990.

Mumford, Lewis. "The Death of the Monument." In J. L Martin, Ben Nicholson, and Naum Gabo, eds., *Circle: International Survey of Constructive Art*. London: Faber and Faber, 1937, pp. 263-70.

———. *Technics and Civilization*. New York: Harcourt, Brace, 1934.

Musil, Robert. "Monuments." Trans. Burton Pike. In *Selected Writings*, ed. Burton Pike. New York: Continuum, 1986, p. 320.

Nagy, Gregory. "Ancient Greek Elegy." In Karen Weisman, ed., *The Oxford Handbook of the Elegy*. Oxford: Oxford University Press, 2010, pp. 13-45. Also available online from the Harvard Center for Hellenic Studies, https://chs.harvard.edu/CHS/article/display/3989.

National Archives, Kew.

Neiman, Susan. *Learning from the Germans: Confronting Race and the Memory of Evil*. London: Allen Lane, 2019.

"Nelson to Leave Sackville Street." *The Manchester Guardian*, March 26, 1926, p. 9.

"Nelson's Pillar." *Dublin Penny Journal*, June 20, 1835, p. 401.

"New Statues in New York." *Garden and Forest*, August 15, 1894, pp. 321-22.

Noah, Trevor. *The Daily Distancing Show*, Comedy Central, June 16, 2020, https://www.cc.com/episodes/9b15yw/the-daily-show-with-trevor-noah-june-16-2020-tim-scott-gabrielle-union-season-25-ep-117.

Nora, Pierre. "Between Memory and History." In "Memory and Counter-Memory," special issue, *Representations*, 26 (Spring 1989), pp. 7-24.

———, and Lawrence D. Kritzman, eds. *Realms of Memory: The Construction of the French Past*. Trans. Arthur Goldhammer. 3 vols. New York: Columbia University Press, 1996.

Pitkin, Hanna Fenichel. *The Attack of the Blob: Hannah Arendt's Concept of the Social*. Chicago: University of Chicago Press, 1998.

Olmsted, Jr., Frederick Law. "Parks as Memorials." *American Magazine of Art*, September 1919, pp. 415-19.

Onians, John. "Greek Temple and Greek Brain." In George Dodds and Robert Tavernor, eds., *Body and Building: Essays on the Changing Relation of Body and Architecture*. Cambridge, MA: MIT Press, 2002, pp. 44-65.

Ozouf, Mona. "Célébrer, savoir et fêter." In Maurice Agulhon, Jean-Denis Bredin, and Guy Chaussinand-Nogaret. *1789: La commémoration*. Paris: Gallimard, 1999, pp. 318–56.

———. *Festivals and the French Revolution*. Trans. Alan Sheridan. Cambridge, MA: Harvard University Press, 1988.

Pasotti, Chiara. "Videosorveglianza per piazza Pradaval." *Veronasera*, July 2, 2009, https://www.veronasera.it/cronaca/videosorveglianza-per-piazza-pradaval.html.

Pes, Javier. "Meet Hew Locke, the Artist Who Dresses Up 'Patriotic' Statues to Reveal Their Whitewashed Histories." *ArtNet News*, October 11, 2018, https://news.artnet.com/exhibitions/hew-locke-1369636.

"Pool, Tennis Courts Jammed as Old Sol 'Turns on the Heat'." *Greenbelt Cooperator*, June 12, 1942, p. 3.

Poole, Robert, Patricia Blassie, Bill Thomas, Chris Calhoon, and Vince Gonzales. "The Known Unknown," episode 344, March 5, 2019. In *99% Invisible*, produced by Joe Rosenberg. Podcast, 46:36, https://99percentinvisible.org/episode/the-known-unknown/.

Poulot, Dominique. "Revolutionary 'Vandalism' and the Birth of the Museum: The Effects of a Representation of Modern Cultural Terror." In Susan Pearce, ed., *Art in Museums*. London: Athlone, 1995, pp. 192–214.

Price, Edward T. "The Central Courthouse Square in the American County Seat." In Dell Upton and John Michael Vlach, eds., *Common Places: Readings in American Vernacular Architecture*. Athens: University of Georgia Press, 1986, pp. 124–45.

Prost, Antoine. "Monuments to the Dead." In Pierre Nora and Lawrence D. Kritzman, eds., *Realms of Memory: The Construction of the French Past*. Trans. Arthur Goldhammer. 3 vols. New York: Columbia University Press, 1996, vol. 2, pp. 307–32.

"Public Monuments and Outdoor Sculpture." Special issue, *Cultural Resources Management* 18.1 (1995).

Radford News Journal, May 26, 1960, https://newspaperarchive.com/radford-news-journal-may-26-1960-p-7.

Rainey, Reuben M. "Hallowed Grounds and Rituals of Remembrance: Union Regimental Monuments at Gettysburg." In Paul Groth and Todd W. Bressi, eds., *Understanding Ordinary Environments*. New Haven: Yale University Press, 1997, pp. 67–80.

"Recreation Department." *Greenbelt News Review*, August 9, 1962, p. 6.

"Re-Planning Hyde Park Corner: A Scheme by Sir Edwin Lutyens, R.A., and Sir Charles Bressey." *Architect and Building News*, May 1937, pp. 146–47.

Ricoeur, Paul. *Memory, History, Forgetting.* Trans. Kathleen Blamey and David Pellauer. Chicago: University of Chicago Press, 2004.

Riegl, Alois. "The Modern Cult of Monuments: Its Character and Its Origin" (1903). Trans. Kurt W. Forster and Diane Ghirardo. *Oppositions* 25 (Fall 1982), pp. 21–51.

Rigotti, Francesca. "Metaphors of Time." *ETC: A Review of General Semantics* 43.2 (Summer 1986), pp. 157–68.

Rombouts, Stephen. "Art as Propaganda in Eighteenth-Century France: The Paradox of Edme Bouchardon's Louis XV." *Eighteenth-Century Studies* 27.2 (Winter 1993–94), pp. 255–82.

Rosenblum, Robert. *Transformations in Late Eighteenth-Century Art.* Princeton: Princeton University Press, 1967.

"Royal Artillery Memorial." *Builder*, June 1949, pp. 711–12.

Rozas-Krause, Valentina. "Memorials and the Cult of Apology." PhD diss., University of California, Berkeley, 2020.

Rudofsky, Bernard. *Architecture without Architects: A Short Introduction to Non-Pedigreed Architecture.* Garden City: Doubleday, 1964.

Rybczynski, Witold. "Waiting for the Weekend." *The Atlantic*, August 1991, pp. 25–52.

Rydell, Paul. *All the World's a Fair: Visions of Empire at American International Expositions, 1876–1916.* Chicago: University of Chicago Press, 1984.

Rykwert, Joseph. *On Adam's House in Paradise: The Idea of the Primitive Hut in Architectural History.* Cambridge, MA: MIT Press, 1981.

Sanyal, Debarati. *Memory and Complicity: Migrations of Holocaust Remembrance.* New York: Fordham University Press, 2015.

Savage, Kirk. *Standing Soldiers, Kneeling Slaves: Race, War, and Monument in Nineteenth-Century America.* Princeton: Princeton University Press, 1997.

———. "The War Memorial as Elegy." In Karen Weisman, ed., *The Oxford Handbook of the Elegy.* Oxford: Oxford University Press 2010, pp. 637–56.

Schjeldahl, Peter. "High and Low Relief: Augustus Saint-Gaudens at the Met." *The New Yorker*, August 24, 2009.

Schuyler, David. *The New Urban Landscape: The Redefinition of City Form in Nineteenth-Century America.* Baltimore: Johns Hopkins University Press, 1986.

Sennett, Richard. *Flesh and Stone: The Body and the City in Western Civilization.* New York: W. W. Norton, 1994.

"Senzatetto al freddo in città, Sperotto lancia l'appello al sindaco: 'È ora d'intervenire.'"

Veronasera, January 26, 2018, https://www.veronasera.it/cronaca/morto-freddo-smentita-alberto-sperotto-appello-sindaco-senzatetto-26-gennaio-2018-.html www. veronasera.it.

Shanken, Andrew M. "Keeping Time with the Good War." *American Studies Journal* 59 (Spring 2015), http://www.asjournal.org/59-2015/keeping-time-with-the-good-war.

———. "Meet Me at the Plague Column: Monuments and Conservation Planning." *Future Anterior* 14.1 (Summer 2017), pp. 126–41.

———. "Planning Memory: Living Memorials in the United States during World War II." *Art Bulletin* 84.1 (March, 2002), pp. 130–47.

———. "Preservation and Creation: Alfonso Rubbiani and Bologna." *Future Anterior* 7.1 (Summer 2010), pp. 61–81.

———. "Towards a Cultural Geography of Memorials." In Jill A. Franklin, T. A. Heslop, and Christine Stevenson, eds., *Architecture and Interpretation: Essays for Eric Fernie*. Woodbridge: Boydell and Brewer, 2012, pp. 357–80.

Sitte, Camillo. *City Planning According to Artistic Principles*. Trans. Christiane Crasemann Collins and George R. Collins, London: Phaidon, 1965.

———. *Der Städtebau nach seinen künstlerischen Grundsätzen*. Vienna: G. Prachner, 1965.

Smith, Charles H. W. *Landscape Gardening, or Parks and Pleasure Grounds*. New York: C. M. Saxton, 1853.

Soja, Edward W. *Postmetropolis: Critical Studies of Cities and Regions*. Oxford: Blackwell, 1999.

Sontag, Susan. *On Photography*. New York: Farrar, Straus and Giroux, 1977.

Sperling, Valerie. "Making the Public Patriotic: Militarism and Anti-Militarism in Russia." In Marlène Laruelle, ed., *Russian Nationalism and the National Reassertion of Russia*. London: Routledge, 2009, pp. 218–71.

Squires, Nick. "Italian Teenagers to Receive €500 'Cultural Bonus' from Government." *Telegraph*, August 23, 2016, http://www.telegraph.co.uk/news/2016/08/23/italian-teenagers-to-receive-500-cultural-bonus-from-government.

Stamp, Gavin. *Anti-Ugly: Excursions in English Architecture and Design*. London: Aurum Press, 2013.

Starkey, Marion L. *The First Plantation*. Hampton: Housing Printing and Publishing House, 1936.

Stevens, Quentin, Karen A. Franck, and Ruth Fazakerley. "Counter-Monuments, the Anti-Monumental and the Dialogic." *The Journal of Architecture* 17.6 (2012), pp. 951–72.

———, and Shanti Sumartojo. "Memorial Planning in London." *Journal of Urban Design* 20.5 (August 2015), pp. 615–35.

———, and Karen A. Franck. *Memorials as Spaces of Engagement: Design, Use and Meaning.* New York: Routledge, 2016.

Stilgoe, John R. *Common Landscape of America, 1580–1845.* New Haven: Yale University Press, 1982.

Stroud, Dorothy. "Hyde Park Corner." *Architectural Review* 106 (December 1949), pp. 379–97.

Stumpo, Sergio. "The Sustainability of Urban Heritage Preservation: The Case of Verona, Italia." Discussion Paper no. IDB-DP-1 28, Inter-American Development Bank, 2010, https://publications.iadb.org/publications/english/document/The-Sustainability-of-Urban-Heritage-Preservation-The-Case-of-Verona-Italia.pdf.

"Swimming Starts on Memorial Day." *Greenbelt Cooperator*, May 25, 1945, p. 3.

Tchekmedyian, Alene, Veronica Rocha, and Irfan Khan. "Hollywood Forever Cemetery Removes Confederate Monument after Calls from Activists and Threats of Vandalism." *Los Angeles Times*, August 16, 2017, https://www.latimes.com/local/lanow/la-me-ln-hollywood-forever-monument-20170815-story.html.

Thrift, Nigel. *Non-Representational Theory: Space, Politics, Affect.* London: Routledge, 2008.

———. *Spatial Formations.* London: Sage Publications, 1996.

———, and Ash Amin. *Cities: Reimagining the Urban.* Oxford: Polity, 2002.

Till, Karen E. "Places of Memory." In John Agnew, Katharyne Mitchell, and Gerard Toal, eds., *A Companion to Political Geography.* London: Blackwell, 2003, pp. 289–301.

Trieschnigg, Caroline P. "Iphigenia's Dream in Euripides' 'Iphigenia Taurica'," *Classical Quarterly* 58.2 (2008), pp. 461–78.

Trillo, Mauricio Tenorio. "1910 Mexico City: Space and Nation in the City of the Centenario." *Journal of Latin American Studies* 28.1 (February 1996), pp. 75–104.

Tyler, Lyon G. *History of Hampton.* Hampton: The Board of Supervisors of Elizabeth City County, 1922.

"Unattractive Back." *Architectural Forum* 82 (January 1945), p. 38.

Upton, Dell. "The Architecture of Everyday Life." *New Literary History* 33.4 (Autumn, 2002), pp. 707–23.

———. "The City as Material Culture." In Anna Elizabeth Yentsch and Mary C. Beaudry, eds., *The Art and Mystery of Historical Archaeology: Essays in Honor of James Deetz.* Boca Raton: CRC press, 1992, pp. 51–74.

———. "The Tradition of Change." *Traditional Dwellings and Settlements* 5.1 (1993), pp. 9–15.

———. *What Can and Can't Be Said: Race, Uplift, and Monument Building in the Contemporary South*. New Haven: Yale University Press, 2015.

———, and John Michael Vlach, eds. *Common Places: Readings in American Vernacular Architecture*. Athens: University of Georgia Press, 1986.

Van Rensselaer, Mariana Griswold. *Art Out-of-Doors: Hints on Good Taste in Gardening*. 1893; New York: Charles Scribner's Sons, 1925.

Vellinga, Marcel. "The End of the Vernacular: Anthropology and the Architecture of the Other." *Etnofoor* 23.1 (2011), pp. 171–92.

Venturi, Robert, Denise Scott Brown, and Steven Izenour. *Learning from Las Vegas*. Cambridge, MA: MIT Press, 1972.

"Verona, degrado nel centro storico: continua la lotta per render più sicura la zona." *Veronasera*, June 22, 2015, https://www.veronasera.it/cronaca/verona-degrado -centro-storico-lotta-per-sicurezza-zona-22-giugno-2015.html.

Versari, Maria Elena. "Recasting the Past: On the Posthumous Fortune of Futurist Sculpture." *Sculpture Journal* 23.3 (2014), pp. 349–68.

Vidler, Anthony. *Claude-Nicholas Ledoux: Architecture and Social Reform at the End of the Ancien Régime*. Cambridge, MA: MIT Press, 1990.

Walker, Richard. "Unseen and Disbelieved: A Political Economist among Cultural Geographers." In Paul Groth and Todd W. Bressi, eds., *Understanding Ordinary Environment*. New Haven: Yale University Press, 1997, pp. 162–73.

Wallage, Martijn. "A Life Abiding in the Same: The Statue as Image of the Eternal Soul." In Ted Hyunhak Yoon, ed., *Decoding Dictatorial Statues*. Eindhoven: Onomatopee, 2019, pp. 116–23.

"War Memorials Advisory Council." *Journal of the Royal Society of Arts* 95.4736 (January 31, 1947), pp. 155–59.

Weir, L. H., ed. *Parks: A Manual of Municipal and County Parks*. 2 vols. New York: A. S. Barnes, 1928.

Weisman, Karen. Introduction to *The Oxford Handbook of the Elegy*, ed. Karen Weisman. Oxford: Oxford University Press 2010, pp. 1–10.

White, Mark. "Statues of Limitations: Why the Present Shouldn't Attack the Past." *Maclean's*, April 25, 2018, https://www.macleans.ca/opinion/statues-of-limitations -why-the-present-shouldnt-attack-the-past.

Wilkinson, Tracy. "A New Battle: Latino Veterans Fight to Protect East L.A. Memorial."

Los Angeles Times, April 19, 1990, https://www.latimes.com/archives/la-xpm-1990-04
-19-me-2198-story.html.

Williams, Raymond. *Keywords: A Vocabulary of Culture and Society*. Rev. ed. New York:
Oxford University Press, 1983.

Winter, Jay. *Sites of Memory, Sites of Mourning: The Great War in European Cultural History*.
Cambridge: Cambridge University Press, 1995.

Winterer, Caroline. *American Enlightenments: Pursuing Happiness in the Age of Reason*. New
Haven: Yale University Press, 2016.

Wright, Gwendolyn. "On Modern Vernaculars and J. B. Jackson." In Chris Wilson and Paul
Groth, eds., *Everyday America: Cultural Landscape Studies after J. B. Jackson*. Berkeley:
University of California Press, 2003, pp. 163–77.

"WWI Walls Complete at McAllen's Veterans War Memorial of Texas." *The Monitor*, April
10, 2016, mcallenmonitor.newspaperarchive.com.

Yates, Frances A. *The Art of Memory*. Chicago: University of Chicago Press, 1966.

Yoon, Ted Hyunhak, ed. *Decoding Dictatorial Statues*. Eindhoven: Onomatopee, 2019.

Young, James E. "The Counter-Monument: Memory against Itself in Germany Today."
Critical Inquiry 18.2 (Winter 1992), pp. 267–96.

———. *At Memory's Edge: After-Images of the Holocaust in Contemporary Art and Architecture*.
New Haven: Yale University Press, 2000.

———. *The Texture of Memory: Holocaust Memorials and Meaning*. New Haven: Yale University
Press, 1993.

Zapotosky, Matt. "Former City Council Candidate Arrested after Man Is Shot at New
Mexico Protest with Militia Group." *Washington Post*, June 16, 2020, https://www.
washingtonpost.com/nation/2020/06/16/albuquerque-militia-shooting-protest.

Zelinsky, Wilbur. "Seeing Beyond the Dominant Culture." In Paul Groth and Todd W.
Bressi, eds., *Understanding Ordinary Environments*. New Haven: Yale University Press,
1997, pp. 157–61.

Zuziak, Zbigniew. *Managing Historic Cities*. Krakow: International Cultural Centre, 1993.

———. *Managing Tourism in Historic Cities*. Krakow: International Cultural Centre, 1992.

Index

Hengge, Joseph, mural at Berchtesgaden, 240–42, *241, III.*

Hercules (Klagenfurt), *180,* 181.

Heritage conservation, 184–88. *See also* Preservation and conservation.

Heroes, 74, 82, 88, 111, 167–68, 222, 230, 290, 306, 308; Greco-Roman, 167, 181. *See also* Great-man memorials.

"Heteroglossia" (Bakhtin), 52–53, 56, 363 n.69.

Heunensäule (Rumpf, Mainz), 331–33, *332, 334,* 344–46, 348, 398 n.17; base, *337;* bas relief of *Freiheitsbaum, 339;* gladiator's helmet, 341–44, *342;* Jewish community burning forever, 338–41, *340;* liberty cap, 338, 344, *345;* and the Nagelsäule, 333–38.

Hierophany (Eliade), 12, 93, 190, 229, 285.

Historical pivots, 15, 208, 219, 295–96, 298.

Historic cores, *176,* 187, 198–99, 231.

Historicism, 104, 298, 323.

Historic monuments, 83, 87, 92, 189, 324–27, 335, 341, 366 n.12; use of term, 325, 368 n.35, 397 n.7. *See also* Heritage conservation.

History, 92, 395 n.35; Nora on, 37–40, 41, 180.

Hitler, Adolf, 240, *241, III.*

Hobsbawm, Eric, 75, 323, 360 n.25.

Hoffbauer, Theodor, engraving of Saints Innocents Cemetery (Paris), *117.*

Holidays of commemoration, 18; Defenders of the Fatherland Day (Soviet), 256, 390 n.26; Holocaust and Heroism Remembrance Day, 312; Veterans Day, 159–60, 389 n.14. *See also* Decoration Day; Memorial Day; Remembrance Day.

Hollywood Forever Cemetery (Los Angeles), Confederate Memorial, 126–28, *127.*

Holocaust, 294, 313, 322. *See also* Holocaust memorials.

Holocaust and Heroism Remembrance Day, 312.

Holocaust Memorial (Treister, Miami Beach), 20–22, *21,* 151–53, *152,* 313–19, *315, 317;* Arm from view platform, *318;* Zyklon B cannisters, 314, *315.*

Holocaust Memorial boulder (Seifert and Lovejoy, Hyde Park), 29, *30.*

Holocaust memorials, 29, *30,* 63, 196, 346; kitsch, 319; placement of, 151–52; *Stolpersteine,* 70, *71. See also* Holocaust Memorial

(Miami Beach); Memorial to the Murdered Jews of Europe; Museum of Martyrdom.

Holocaust Museum (Libeskind, Berlin), 316.

Hooke, Robert, 397 n.5.

Hubbard, Henry Vincent, *An Introduction to the Study of Landscape Design,* 141.

Hudnut, Joseph, 196.

Hughes, Robert Ball, Nathaniel Bowditch statue, 125–26, *126.*

Hunt, Richard Morris, 139, 140.

Hussein, Saddam, 367 n.13.

Hyde Park (London), 210; railings, 68. *See also* Hyde Park Corner; Hyde Park memorials.

Hyde Park Corner (London), 132, 205, *206,* 208–209; Lutyens's plan for, 217–18; as memorial site, 214; pedestrian underpass, *221;* road system and traffic, 212–18, *215, 218;* as "saturation zone," 222; tourism, 207–208, 222–23, *224–25;* war memorials and plaques, 219–20. *See also* Hyde Park memorials.

Hyde Park memorials, 29, 205; Australian War Memorial to World War II (Tonkin Zulaikha Greer/Laurence), 220, *221;* David statue, 207, 218, 219, *221;* Holocaust Memorial boulder, 29, *30;* Machine Guns Corps Memorial (Wood), 207, 208, 214–18, *215, 216;* as "muster," 207–209, 220–22, *221,* 230, 283; New Zealand War Memorial (Smith/Dibble), *221;* Norwegian War Memorial, 29, *30;* photography of, 207–208; screen and arch, 210, *215;* on their islands, 215. *See also* Royal Artillery Memorial; Wellington memorials.

ICONOCLASM, 14–15, 22, 51, 70; and abstraction, 196; versus appropriation, 62; and Black Lives Matter, 14, 50, 296, 395 n.35; circles and, 164; and "dead white males," 301; dislocation of memorials as, 193, 229; distinguished from vandalism, 366 n.6; in Eastern Europe, 19; French Revolution, 15, 77–80, 86–87; rhetorical, 100; and statuephobia, 88. *See also* Confederate monuments: destruction and removal.

Ideal City of Chaux (Ledoux), 120.

Illava, Karl Morningstar, 107th United States Infantry Memorial (Central Park), 142–43, *142.*

Zone Books series design by Bruce Mau

Image placement and production by Julie Fry

Typesetting by Meighan Gale

Printed and bound by Maple Press